BUILDING IDEAS

MJP Architects

essays and speculations
by Richard MacCormac

with contributions by

Richard Burdett

Richard Cork

Peter Davey

Francis Duffy

Robert Harbison

Bryan Lawson

Richard Murphy

Margaret Richardson

Richard Sennett

Colin Stansfield Smith

texts by

Nicola Jackson

edited by

Ian Latham

BUILDING IDEAS

MJP Architects

essays and speculations
by Richard MacCormac

Acknowledgements

MJP believe that the execution of our work is enriched by collaboration with others. Throughout the history of the practice we have had the opportunity to work with very talented engineers, designers, manufacturers and artists. We thrive by working with enlightened clients who drive us to design buildings that we all enjoy, and we have a number of repeat clients who help further advance our ideas.

Many of these collaborators are referenced in the six chapters, and a number are listed in the Buildings and Projects section at the back.

The creation of this book has also been developed in a truly collaborative way, and we would like to thank in particular Nico Jackson, working alongside Richard MacCormac, for her skilful and diplomatic writing, and Ian Latham for his steady hand and patience throughout the development of this book. We are indebted to Richard Robinson and Stephen Morey for coordinating and managing the process. We would also like to thank Peter Kent for his research skills and dedication to accuracy, Sue Barnes for her trawl through the archives, and the guest writers for their personal and insightful contributions.

Finally we would like to thank all staff, past and present, who have worked on our projects over the years, including those that have helped in the creation of this book.

MJP Architects

Edited and designed by Ian Latham

First published by Right Angle Publishing
161 Rosebery Avenue, London EC1R 4QX

British Library Cataloguing in Publication Data
A catalogue record for this book is available from the British Library

ISBN 0 9532848 6 7
ISBN-13: 978-0-9532848-6-3

Perspectives on MJP: four views

RICHARD MURPHY

In a brilliant turn of phrase President John F Kennedy, conferring honorary American citizenship on Winston Churchill in 1963, described how in the dark days of 1940 Churchill had 'mobilised the English language and sent it into battle'. Without wishing to stretch the analogy too far, the 1980s were pretty dark too. British architecture was under attack from the twin forces of imported transatlantic postmodernism and home-grown Prince Charles fogeyism and only high tech seemed to be the answer. At that time I found myself as a very junior lecturer at Edinburgh University and, by luck, Richard MacCormac had been appointed as our visiting professor – I chauffeured to and from the airport in my yellow Ciröen 2CV.

Collecting MacCormac, I simply had to utter the words 'And what are you up to at the moment?' and then just sit back, listen and enjoy the ride. Why? Because he would describe the state of the evolution of a current particular project in language that was truly intoxicating. Light was 'incandescent' as it filtered through a particular species of tree; buildings 'engaged' with walls; landscape was 'embraced' by a window; Soanian tricks of light 'vibrated' onto wall planes; college student kitchens became 'social heart-beats' of residences, shops and office became 'places of local and remote exchange' – just a few of the many phrases that stick in my mind. Such a rich use of the English language (and, I discovered later when working at Heneage Street, also the funniest of raconteurs) seems to me almost a prerequisite to the reality that his architecture is some of the richest in the UK. And it is no accident that in recently compiling a list of Cambridge buildings to visit for a potential college donor, sceptical about modern architecture, it was MJP's work that stood out above that of everyone else.

Richard MacCormac is also the most complete architect I know. He can turn his hand to any type of building, size or location. He can discuss in totally refreshing terms ideas of urban design, materials, construction, geometry, space planning, social patterns and history. He can make connections between buildings across the centuries (Wright's prairie houses and Hardwick Hall for example) that would floor any historian. He can connect his own works to those of the past, such as the reference to Schinkel's stage design for the Magic Flute in his collaboration with the artist Alex Beleschenko at the brilliant Southwark tube station. His continuing ability to control detailing and invent the crafting of the building has been remarkable, particularly as the practice has grown in size – and how can I forget spending a month trying in vain to develop a sliding, folding, disappearing corner window for Fitzwilliam College under his tutelage? As a writer, his essay on the evolution of the office as a type, published in the Architectural Review, remains for me the definitive history. Similar excursions into discussions about hierarchy in suburbia have been unequalled. And on and on. The breadth of this much overdue book and the range of its contributors tell the same story.

In the tradition of architectural family trees there are a number of notable practices that have emerged from MJP – Shillam & Smith, Patel Taylor, Horden Cherry Lee, Wright & Wright, to name a few. Our own modest work in Edinburgh owes a massive debt to the time I spent at Heneage Street, not to mention our 2CV dialogues. Richard has remained a friend, a mentor and an inspiration and, to borrow a quote from Ted Cullinan (talking of Denys Lasdun), 'he is my architectural dad', and I'm very honoured to be asked to make this small contribution offered on behalf of all the Heneage Street kids.

COLIN STANSFIELD SMITH

To study in a city like Cambridge is one thing but to be taught architecture there is something else. The all-absorbing awareness of architecture within this medieval environment is inescapable. One breathes the dialectic, the rhetoric, the passion and the controversy that goes not only with precious buildings but with collegiate enclosure, artefacts, sculpture and sublime gardens. This earthly paradise of beautiful river settings, of King's College Chapel and the backs is filled with architectural ghosts – Wren, Gibbs, Wilkins and even Hawksmoor – haunted by dreams of projects imagined but not realised and all in a 'gothic' aura.

MacCormac's architectural baptism was in this place. He absorbed its history, its memories, its pretentions and aspirations but also its contradictions. He had the good fortune to have mentors and sponsors like Leslie

Martin, Sandy Wilson and Colin Rowe. Here was a world of alternative modernism with its obligation to the 'social contract' – the Scandinavian influences of Aalto, Asplund and Scharoun with their pragmatism, sensitivity and innovation associated with buildings that welcome and invite within a prescribed context. His early career was about a philosophical challenge to a tired International Style and mean socialist programmes in the public sector. He demonstrated how it was possible to integrate precious heritage with a setting of well-crafted building full of originality and optimism. No contemporary modern architect has embraced and celebrated heritage and historical continuity so cleverly and richly. Not for him the big iconic gesture but the sane, well-balanced stability of a 'Practical Art'. He inherited the sensitivity of the English Free School and Arts and Crafts tradition and gave an intellectual rebirth to the aspirations of Ruskin and Morris.

MJP's portfolio of work in Cambridge is impressive with Burrell's Field in its romantic natural setting and the exquisite Fitzwilliam Chapel with its metaphors of boats and arks, quite outstanding. The professional acclaim for these projects has been inspirational for so many students.

However the work in Oxford has a conviction and self-confidence that is seminal. MacCormac developed a relationship and trust with the academics in St John's College that has led to a sequence of projects all of which express his developing talents and evolving philosophy. The recent Senior Common Room is delightful. Rigorously modern, almost high tech with its uncompromising glazing, its elegant sophistication has given much pleasure to its users. Nothing has been spared and one admires the financial commitment to a timeless investment. We await with anticipation the completion of the Kendrew Quadrangle at St John's.

Returning to Worcester College in Oxford after 30 years is an uplifting experience. Here is a project finished in the late 1970s that has improved with time. Set in an inspiring context of playing fields and water garden with its Lloyd Wrightian qualities, it characterises the best of what we called Modern Architecture, using traditional materials with originality and innovation. It stimulates our interest and acclaim with its elegant overhanging eaves, interesting geometry and fenestration.

MJP's portfolio of work has been a seminal reference for most of its contemporaries for both its range and quality. At the same time Richard MacCormac's writing has revealed analytical thought and scholarship that has engaged a wider philosophical debate when we were beginning to understand the importance of urban culture.

It is perhaps not surprising that MacCormac's career should have had parallels with Colin St John Wilson's frustrating years building the British Library. In his essay on the nineteenth century Law Courts project in the Strand, Wilson describes an archetypal tragi-comedy that seems to be the norm when the English Establishment finds itself committed to building a corporate monument. That we have been denied any design evidence of MJP's BBC Broadcasting House project is so disappointing and it is difficult to understand how such creativity could be so abandoned.

It is reassuring that MJP has survived this ordeal and with such exceptional experience now has the capacity to accept future challenges.

RICHARD BURDETT

Despite his love of nineteenth century fishing smacks, Richard MacCormac is a quintessential urbanist. Literally and phenomenally (*pace* Colin Rowe) his personality and his work reveal the complexity of the urban dimension. It doesn't take long for him to make reference to a city or an urban episode. The social life of Venetian squares, the composed order of eighteenth century Bath, the elegance of Edinburgh New Town or the organic messiness of London crop up in conversation and permeate his designs.

From the informal meeting spaces outside the offices of the sadly-missed BBC project in Portland Place to the canonical masterplan for the redevelopment of Spitalfields Market – cheek by jowl with the voracious City of London – MacCormac uses the city as a source of inspiration. But it is not the cleansed and sanitised image of Burnham's City Beautiful, Haussmann's Paris or Le Corbusier's Ville Radieuse that inspires him. It is muscular and visceral engagement with the multi-layered complexity of everyday city living that drives his search for urban form. The sounds, smells and activities of the everyday city, the 'transactions' between people and buildings, inform his analysis and his designs.

As a zealous urban enthusiast, MacCormac moves, talks and thinks fast. His stories of the low-life in multicultural Brick Lane in East London – brought to life by convincing impersonations of local mobsters, landlords and gangsters – give texture and meaning to one's understanding of the urban culture that has shaped the social life of the rapidly gentrifying territory that he has inhabited with his partner Jocasta Innes for more than three decades. It's hard to keep up with him on the short walk from his home and office in Heneage Street just off Brick Lane to the backstreets and alleyways of Spitalfields in search of a favourite restaurant or bar. En route, he makes passing references to the urban practices of early Huguenot and Jewish immigrants and contemporary Bangladeshis; he points out the stonemason's craftsmanship of Hawksmoor's brooding Christ Church; and he muses inaudibly along the congested pavements about how density is the prerequisite of urban life.

And it is the search for density – of people, experience, narratives and materials – that has defined his work for several decades. MacCormac's plan for Spitalfields, for example, was the first of his generation to propose recreating the intensity of street life with new buildings that maintained the scale and pattern of interaction between the public and the private. As an inadvertent reference to the writings of the great post-war urbanist Jane Jacobs and her stoic defence of the social potential of the New York urban block, MacCormac described his masterplan in sociological rather than architectural terms. His observation that a sense of urbanity derives from 'local transactions' that occur at street level (rather than the 'foreign transactions' of corporations and companies) chimes with Jacobs belief that community is enhanced by designs which promote informal interaction and the security afforded by 'eyes on the street'.

In his urban work MacCormac recognises that building types such as mono-cultural office blocks can 'kill the street' unless they are mediated by architectural form which activates their edges and gives life to the section. In this he endorses what urbanist Richard Sennett has so accurately described, in 'The Fall of Public Man' and subsequent writings, as a failure of modernism to create environments which sustain many levels of complexity, that are resilient and adaptable to social change, that recognise the importance of time and the need for cities to accommodate rather than reinforce difference. Many of MJP's masterplans reject the utopian perfection of the Modernist Movement and its revisions – from Le Corbusier to the Smithsons – in favour of a less structured, more open and humane urbanism.

Perhaps it is no surprise to discover that MacCormac's deeply social reading of cities was triggered by the pioneering work of Peter Wilmott and Michael Young who co-authored Family and Kinship in East London. MacCormac collaborated with the authors of this canonical study which identified the profound links between social solidarities of working class families and their spatial environments. One can see this urban thread run through a number of the practice's masterplans: from the gridded arrangement for West Cambridge or the successful public spaces of the London School of Economics, the retrofitting of the Ballymun housing schemes in Dublin to the more recent attempt to reconcile the needs for increased density with the English love of suburban lifestyles.

And indeed – despite his neo-European inquisitiveness and neo-American openness – MacCormac is a profoundly English urban architect. He belongs to a lineage that finds its roots in an eighteenth century English architecture that celebrated the picturesque and embraced the pragmatic, so aptly described by John Summerson as a 'happy coincidence of intent and circumstance' – an eloquent summary of MacCormac's urban oeuvre.

FRANCIS DUFFY

The design of offices confronts architects with two principal strategic choices. The first and more obvious is whether to expend more design energy and imagination on the exterior or the interior. The second and more subtle choice is whether office design should be seized upon primarily as the opportunity to create an artefact – crafted, self contained and complete in itself – or whether office design should be regarded as a client-focused process – transformational in business terms and open-ended in creating new opportunities. Both choices are interrelated and obviously depend on whether the client is a developer, whose motivation is likely to be driven by the imperative to let the building as quickly as possible, or by a user client whose business interests are more likely to be particular, complex and thus more challenging to the architectural imagination.

As a workplace strategist I am inclined to rate more highly office buildings whose interiors have been shaped by a strong interior concept which can be exploited by an ambitious and imaginative user client for long-term, transformative business purposes. Herman Hertzberger's Centraal Beheer, Richard Rogers' Corporation of Lloyds building and Niels Torp's SAS headquarters in Stockholm are three obvious examples. Not even the magnificent exterior of Mies van der Rohe's Seagram building can compensate for the relative insignificance of its interior office spaces.

MJP's portfolio of office buildings is not huge but cumulatively it demonstrates a very high order of design skill at several scales. Building One in Warwick Court, Paternoster Square, a developer-led project, is very successful both urbanistically – it fits like a glove into its august environment – and, unusually for a speculative office building, also succeeds in being innovative internally – given its clever and ambitious top-lit, stepped atrium. Two other MJP office buildings, 10 Crown Place in Broadgate and the unbuilt 77-95 Victoria Street, are also confidently robust in their elevational treatment, suggesting a new commercial vernacular at least as strong as Victorian precedents. The completed exterior of the first phase of the BBC's reconstruction of Broadcasting House, which compositionally unites the refurbished 1930s building and Nash's All Soul's Church, is extremely skilful in creating a new public place at the BBC's threshold while complementing Nash's sleight of hand in both completing the long view north from Regent Street and leading the eye around the corner into Portland Place.

Tantalisingly, since the quality of its design played a significant part in winning planning permission for the redevelopment of the whole of the Broadcasting House site, MJP had already demonstrated the architectural skills to create a great user-driven office building with a catalytic interior on a highly sensitive urban site. The BBC had almost achieved a similarly audacious feat on an adjacent location twenty years earlier when, following a limited competition, they chose a brilliantly original proposal by Norman Foster for a new

production centre on the site of the Langham Hotel. Late in the day, however, the corporation decided to abandon this ambitious project, which would have been Foster's best London building to date, thus establishing a most unfortunate precedent. In 2006 the BBC, having outsourced its procurement processes and preferring a simpler, safer and more economical solution, decided to abandon MJP's proposals for rebuilding Broadcasting House as a whole. Two invaluable internal features were lost for ever: a multi-level internal street that could have acted as the BBC's locus for serendipitous internal, inter-departmental interaction and an amazing look-no-hands column-free newsroom, the largest in the world, which would have been the heart of both the building and of the BBC's national and international mission.

A business school case study should be written about the conditions under which great architectural imagination can be successfully aligned with strong organisational purpose. High expectations on the part of the BBC as a cultural client, an abundance of imagination and talent in MJP, good intentions all round combined with the corporation's selection of a delivery process incompatible with all three set the scene for a second major disappointment. The best that can be said about this double catastrophe is that hard lessons about office design may eventually be derived from both. One such lesson stands out: architectural talent, however great, on its own is never enough. What is equally necessary for clients such as the BBC, especially given the corporation's still huge cultural responsibility, is to devise equivalently unconventional procurement processes such as those that other complex and ever-changing clients, such as Centraal Beheer, the Corporation of Lloyds and SAS, have used so confidently and successfully in order to derive maximum business advantage from architectural imagination.

Geometry, pattern and typology

Geometry, pattern and typology

Bryan Lawson

The work of MJP is driven by shared interests and values that are subjected to rigorous testing and refinement.

Frank Lloyd Wright's mother, who took a leading role in her son's development and education, warned him against introspection. She believed the creative process of a great architect is so fragile that it might easily evaporate under the spotlight of self examination. Clearly Richard MacCormac does not suffer from the inhibitions of one of his heroes.[1] He chose to celebrate his presidency of the RIBA with an exhibition on The Art of the Process, a project on which I collaborated.[2] We invited a whole series of his most interesting contemporaries to submit materials but it was MacCormac's own insights that in the end made the most penetrating contribution. He regards the design process as a journey and strongly believes that design thinking should be seen as a form of thought in its own right. These ideas underpin the work of the MJP practice.

The MJP partnership model consciously exploits the individual strengths of the partners. Just as Richard MacCormac became president of the RIBA the practice was expanding significantly as the result of two larger than normal jobs: Cable & Wireless headquarters and Southwark underground station on London's Jubilee Line extension. MacCormac saw his role as one of generating and stirring up ideas, whereas 'Peter Jamieson takes a kind of technical/contractual role in the practice and… David Prichard is very much a job runner'. Thus at any one time Jamieson could be on site sorting out technical issues while Prichard was leading the design team back in the office on one of the larger jobs and MacCormac floats, dipping into projects at times that he judges to be critical.[3]

Identifying these moments is clearly an art form in its own right. MacCormac talks of his interventions as using 'shock tactics'. He feels he can come into a project and shake things up not so much by being critical but saying 'what if we do this kind of thing'. He can often recognise a moment when he needs to 'create a crisis by recognising that something is not right'. But he realises too that to turn this intervention into something useful he must collaborate. 'I seize on somebody in the team who understands what the crisis is, and you have to find this person who sees what it is otherwise it's hopeless.' Interestingly MacCormac thinks he makes different kinds of interventions when MJP has experience of the building typology. He describes their work on such familiar territory as a 'kind of vernacular, in the sense that it is a common language… one of process rather than the product which is certainly not uniform'.

The MJP approach obviously depends on the development of this shared common language. Conversations with different people in the practice are littered with similar but often exotic words such as 'belvedere', acting as short-hands for sophisticated and complex sets of ideas.

A discussion with MacCormac tends to deal with basic design concepts and ideas. He has a particular skill at being able to uncover principles that were buried in the design thinking but were not yet fully explicit. MacCormac is characteristically unpossessive about these ideas recognising that the process is a team effort; something that the critics often seem to miss by focussing on the end product. He can thus describe in detail the process of arriving at the main formal ideas behind the Cable & Wireless scheme with its 'great wall' of residential accommodation and the 'oculus' courtyard that connects it to the main educational and administrative spaces sitting under the wave-form roofs. But he often cannot recall the origin of each of these key ideas.

Geometry has always been fundamental to the thinking at MJP, and we can trace the history here. Richard MacCormac and Peter Jamieson both studied in Cambridge where they were heavily influenced by Leslie Martin and Lionel March who were researching the relationship of geometry to the built environment. Clearly the young MacCormac was inspired by their ideas and at the same time developed 'an almost obsessive interest' in the Prairie Houses of Frank Lloyd Wright, which he studied at first hand on a travelling scholarship. Although MacCormac is voraciously eclectic in his influences – and references to Wright, Kahn and Soane are frequent – it is this basic grounding in the application of geometry to solve problems of circulation, structure and light that underpins the thinking. 'We look for a clear geometric analogy for the content of the problem. All our schemes have a geometric basis, whether it is the pinwheel arrangement of Westoning, the courtyard system of Coffee Hall flats and Robinson College, the specific tartan grid of the Blackheath houses or the circle based geometry of Hyde Park Gate.'

With these shared concepts, and often the use of narrative too, the members of an MJP team can carry an idea through to the detail in a consistent manner. The exquisite chapel at Fitzwilliam College, in which the upper-floor worship space became a vessel floating against a harbour wall, is a particularly effective example where the consistency and thoroughness of the detail is such that it suggests the work of a single hand rather than a team.

So MJP is a practice shares a common set of values concerning detail, scale, geometry and light, and these are harnessed to produce a consistently humane and accessible form of architecture. Rather than reinventing itself every few years the practice focuses on building a substantial opus that demonstrates its values while refining the approach with continuous reflection.

1 How Architects Design: Design Delegation, Philip Dowson and Richard MacCormac (Architects' Journal 192, 1990).
2 Bryan Lawson, in The Art of the Process: Architectural Design in Practice (RIBA, 1993).
3 Design in Mind, Bryan Lawson (Butterworth 1994).

Bryan Lawson is an architect and a psychologist. He has practised in both the public and private sectors, been both Head of School and Dean of Architecture at Sheffield University, and held visiting professorships in Australia, Singapore and Malaysia. His research has been mainly into the nature of the design process and the psychology of places. His book How Designers Think (1997) was first published in 1980 and his book on The Language of Space in 2001. His most recent book, with Kees Dorst, on Design Expertise was published in 2009. His work on outstanding designers, Design in Mind (1994), included a study of Richard MacCormac. He has published widely in journals and other books and lectured at numerous universities and conferences around the world.

1 Geometry, pattern and typology

An architect's office speaks volumes about the history of a practice, its design priorities and the message it projects to clients and contemporaries. Number 9 Heneage Street, off Brick Lane in London's Spitalfields district, encapsulates the spirit of MacCormac Jamieson Prichard. This modern yet sympathetic conversion of a brewery warehouse houses a network of open-plan rooms that are conducive to team work and reflect a convivial, non-hierarchical atmosphere.

One of the fundamental motivations in MJP's work has been 'to reconcile the pragmatism and the language of making, which are the legacy of both the Arts and Crafts tradition and the Modern Movement, with independently expressive ideas which are specific to client and place and which draw on a wide range of historical precedent'.[1] Broadly speaking, the work of the practice can be identified by its preoccupations with particular themes rather than by a recognisable signature. Ideas about space, form and technology can be traced from one project to another even though they may bear little resemblance to one another. Having established the essential parameters of its typological repertoire early on, the practice has allowed itself the freedom to experiment and constantly to surprise and delight clients and critics alike.

'Design can be described as a process of invention but it is better described as a process of discovery, like a journey to an unknown destination. All creative activity is of this kind.'[2]

MJP staff in 1981 (above) and 2004 (left) at the Heneage Street office in Spitalfields.

Right
Tesco, Ludlow: 1.
Wellcome Wing, Science Museum: 2, 15.
Cable & Wireless College: 4, 7, 16, 30.
Garden Quadrangle, St Johns: 3, 12, 18, 19, 20, 21, 25, 26.
Southwark Station, Jubilee Line Extension: 6, 8, 9, 10, 24, 28.
Blue Boar Court, Trinity College: 11, 13.
BBC Broadcasting House: 5, 14, 17, 27, 29.
Balliol College: 22.
Burrell's Field: 23.

The context of British architecture in the early years of the practice: Richard Seifert's Centre Point (1967), an emblem of the 1960s property boom; system-built public sector housing at Southwark's Aylesbury Estate (1970); James Stirling's Staatsgalerie, Stuttgart (1983); Norman Foster's Sainsbury Centre for the Visual Arts, University of East Anglia (1977); Edward Cullinan's Highgrove housing in Hillingdon (1977).

In the beginning

In the June 1958 issue of Architectural Design magazine James Stirling wrote of work by young architects in Britain, built 'against a very considerable opposition from the public and their elders… the young architect's lot is not a happy one.'[3]. Two decades later, in 1977, AD published another editorial selection of recent British architecture. Much of what Stirling had railed against – from the luck required when setting up a practice, to the disappointing results of competitions and the problem of bureaucratic client bodies, remained apt. The decades of expansion and public funding were fading fast, with the number of architects working in the public sector dwindling by the day.

The profession was suffering from an image problem, partly due to some of the office developments that had been spawned by the property boom of the late 1960s and early 1970s, of which London's Centre Point was a conspicuous emblem, not least because it had lain empty for some years after it was built. In the public sector a Faustian pact was formed between local authorities, central government and big system builders to rationalise construction into prefabricated highrise buildings. It was against this backdrop that young, aspirational architects with a social conscience, such as Richard MacCormac and Peter Jamieson, began to flourish. There was an interest in examining the notion of suburban development in the belief that it could suggest a better way of designing domestic environments. There was also more of a concern for the context in which they were building, both in terms of site and landscape, and the historical continuum.

The architects published in AD's 1977 selection included MacCormac and Jamieson as well as Foster Associates, James Stirling & Partner, Douglas Stephen & Partners, Edward Jones and Edward Cullinan Architects. Each practice was demonstrating in individual ways their responses to the first machine age. Foster Associates had already had two triumphant successes with the Willis Faber building in Ipswich and the Sainsbury Centre at the University of East Anglia; Stirling, with partner Michael Wilford, had just begun work on the complex forms and undulating walls of the Staatsgalerie in Stuttgart. In contrast, Edward Cullinan and MacCormac Jamieson, wrote David Wild in his introduction, attempted 'a fusion of rational and romantic elements by putting a human face to social grids. The current attempt to discover a language of architecture, starting from the refined vocabulary of purism indicated in the early work of Douglas Stephen & Partners and Ed Jones and Mike Gold, is followed by the search for a more populist, vernacular vocabulary by Martin Richardson and MacCormac and Jamieson…'[4] which provided a basis for more aesthetically thoughtful private housing.

Richard MacCormac and Peter Jamieson's formal architectural

education began on the degree course at Cambridge in the early 1960s, and continued with the diploma course of the Bartlett School of Architecture at the University of London, where they met David Prichard. MacCormac and Jamieson's years at Cambridge – where they were influenced by architects and teachers Leslie Martin, Colin St John Wilson, Colin Rowe and Lionel March, (director of the Centre of Land Use and Built Form, subsequently renamed The Martin Centre) – informed the subsequent direction of the practice they were to set up. The research led by Martin and March generated an approach to design based on the general characteristics of building form. Their 'speculations' lay on the boundary between setting the agenda of the project, and the abstract ideas about pattern, geometry and typology, and the pragmatics of fulfilling the brief. MacCormac became engaged by what he called 'the translation of complex and essentially formless functional requirements, into an architectural language of spatial, physical and geometric relationships'.

Richard MacCormac's work with the London Borough of Merton before founding the practice, in which a typological repertoire is created out of three basic elements (pavilions, terraces, and courts) launched what had been a largely academic enquiry into the arena of design practice. As early as 1977 the pivotal role of geometry and pattern language in MacCormac and Jamieson's designs was explicit.[5] 'We look for a clear geometric analogy for the content of the problem. All our schemes have a geometric basis, whether it is the pinwheel arrangement of Westoning, the courtyard system of Coffee Hall flats and Robinson College or the specific tartan grid of the Blackheath houses.'[6]

The geometric basis for the design of an MJP building, although inherent from the start, is not always given formal articulation in initial discussions and presentations to clients. Today the practice often approaches competitions by presenting the jury with a diagram. The conceptual drawing crystallises what the architect perceives is the client's aspiration for its organisation, rather than providing it with a fully resolved solution. In the case of the BBC's Broadcasting House on Portland Place, the competition scheme expressed, and in a way reconciled, the ideological shift in the corporation's aspirations from being a collection of quite independent business centres which were physically disparate, and competitive, into One BBC, without erasing the directorates' individual identities.

'We recognised that the original Broadcasting House building had to remain part of the total redevelopment with an open end to the north which could be linked into an east-west spine that would run across the site. I suddenly realised that this relationship could set the pattern for the whole scheme and that all the new production buildings could be plugged into the spine end on. It

Pavilion – Terrace – Court
Leslie Martin and Lionel March's identification of these three fundamental typologies set out a way of thinking about building form which has generated much of the practice's work and influenced the approach to issues of density, social organisation and construction.

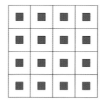 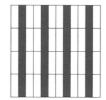 

The geometry of early projects
Right The courtyard scale of the Milton Keynes flats at Coffee Hall reconciled density, outlook and flexible wide-frontage flats.
Far right The 'pinwheel' arrangement of the Westoning houses for special needs children clustered groups of individual rooms for staff and children around a central social space. Adjacent clusters relate together to enclose external play areas and gardens.
Below The 'tartan' grid of the Blackheath houses produced a complex pattern of indoor and outdoor rooms within a simple structural discipline of brick piers and timber beams.
Bottom 'One BBC' concept diagram for Broadcasting House (2006).

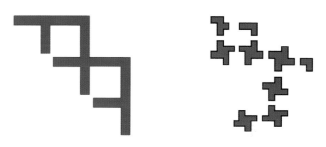

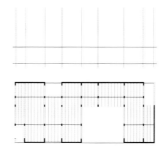 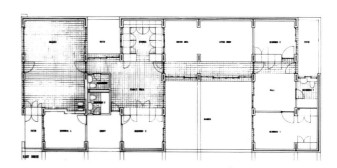

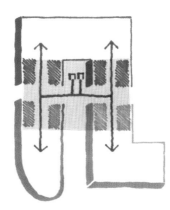

was a very simple organisational concept which addressed the desire of the Director General to create One BBC, while recognising that within this bigger envelope there remains the tribal individuality of all the directorates. The beauty of the diagram was the way in which it both provided a sense of the whole which can be experienced as you see north and south into the production areas, and at the same time provide thresholds into each production floor which would allow identity.'

The exploration of patterns and geometry using physical models is for MJP a psychological tactic, as well as a design method, that allows the architects to distil the complexity of what they're tackling. This way of approaching the design process is both aesthetic and pragmatic. It involves a way of thinking that is operational; it is about the process, not only about the outcome. This procedure inverts the pedagogic homily that form follows

Aesthetic motivation
Frank Lloyd Wright's Robie House (top, 1910) and Fallingwater (middle, 1936). Wright's houses are recapitulations of formal themes. Fallingwater is a dramatic reworking of the Robie House with the master bedroom projecting cross-axially over the longitudinal living room. The composition of the Manor Road Law Library, Oxford (bottom, 1959-64), by Leslie Martin and Colin St John Wilson, reiterates the theme of central volumes emerging out of peripheral spaces.

function. 'You can't think function into form, but you can think form into function. That is what precipitated the concept in the case of the BBC, for example. Thinking in an abstract way about what used to be called the "problem" and the "solution" can generate a repertoire of possible geometric relationships. At some stage in a reiterative process a potentiality is discovered that fulfils the key aspirations of the brief.'

This repertoire of geometric relationships is manifest in different variations and combinations throughout the portfolio; from the early social housing schemes through to the many education projects at Oxford and Cambridge universities and more recent built work as diverse as Cable and Wireless, the Wellcome Wing of the London Science Museum and Southwark underground station for the Jubilee Line. Of course, there are historical precedents for this approach. This rearrangement of a set of formal and geometric ideas can also be seen in Frank Lloyd Wright's architecture, which has been a particular source of inspiration for Richard MacCormac. Wright's domestic architecture, he believes, describes 'a sense that the whole conception of a house is one idea, one model; a short piece of music or sonata which, like Mozart, he simply rearranges over and over again. For example, Fallingwater is actually surprisingly close to the Robie house, built some twenty years earlier.'

Interestingly, it is the aesthetic motive that can generate a pragmatic outcome. This compositional approach which employs explicit geometric arrangements (and which might be called a 'pattern language'[6]) is driven by an aesthetic motive that delivers the organisational arrangements that meet the requirements of the brief. When Leslie Martin died in 2000, Richard MacCormac wrote in the Architectural Research Quarterly about the Oxford Law Library – a scheme which, he said, demonstrated a highly pragmatic employment of architectural language that arose from an aesthetic distinction between large central volumes and peripheral spaces, resulting in a compositional tour de force in which the reading rooms emerge dramatically out of the complex of smaller rooms.

'Martin shared with Aalto the sense of analogy between architecture and landscape… We see this in the reading rooms in the Manor Road Libraries at Oxford as raised daylit plateaux around which other territories are clustered. The form… is immediately intelligible because of the sequence of entrance, top-lit reading room, book stacks and perimeter carrels. Here the idea of the generic organizing principle applicable to the different scale of each of the three libraries is very persuasive and, in fact, proved highly influential.'

Much of the work of the practice is driven by this process of thought that usually addresses necessity. Interestingly, in the lakeside building commissioned by the Sainsbury family for Worcester College, Oxford, the motivation was more subjective than pragmatic. The sense of the building growing out of the landscape is reminiscent of the stacking of the Manor Road libraries and the Aaltoesque analogy with landscape. Completed in 1983, the Sainsbury Building is a staging post along the evolutionary road of the practice, from architects accustomed to being accountable predominantly to primary practical issues, to architects with a distinctive and conceptual flexibility.

Above The Sainsbury Building at Worcester College, Oxford (1980-83) is essentially a cruciform arranged on a diagonal axis with a series of room clusters that are stacked in a stepped sequence away from the lake.

Below The linear sequence of the Cable & Wireless College is simple and flexible.

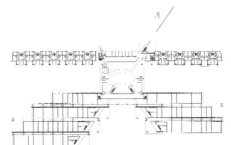

Top Family housing at Pollards Hill (1967-71).

Above There was a common assumption in the 1960s that tower blocks, such as Basil Spence's Queen Elizabeth Square, Glasgow (1965), were necessary to achieve dense redevelopment. However, the Pollards Hill project demonstrated that, laid horizontally, equivalent densities (about 120 person/acre) could be achieved. Every family house has a garden and a parking space or garage on plot. Reconfigured into courts, the density is sustained, but the distance between buildings increased with benefits for privacy and sense of space. Perimeter development is achieved by allocating public open space to the centre of the site.

Courtyard and perimeter site plans
Top Pollards Hill.
Middle Eastfields, Mitcham, as built (1969).
Bottom Unbuilt study for Eastfields, which included adjacent land as part of the development, extending the perimeter around playing fields – high density in a park setting.

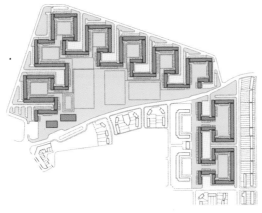

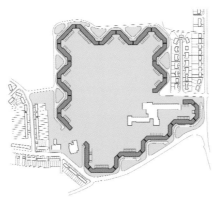

Courts, Perimeters and Linearity

Much of MacCormac and Jamieson's early work involved the partial or complete realisation of the largely abstract theoretical studies of Leslie Martin and Lionel March. These studies had arisen from a fundamental need to question the direction of planning and design in public housing in the 1960s, which had moved towards high-rise developments. March had established that it was not necessary to build high in order to achieve high density. His mathematical analysis of courts, streets and pavilion forms demonstrated the plot ratio advantages of courts at a theoretical level, without reference to a particular building type. MacCormac and Jamieson's housing work pursued this courtyard idea, testing its theoretical virtues against the particular content of housing.

Before establishing the practice, Richard MacCormac worked for the London Borough of Merton with Peter Bell, David Lea and Nick Alexander on two low-rise housing schemes. Out of the theoretical propositions of Martin and March emerged two ground breaking high density housing schemes, Pollard's Hill and Eastfields, which achieved the same density as the towers and access gallery flats being built in other London boroughs. These 'represented a change from a revolutionary to evolutionary view of housing design'.[7] At Pollard's Hill three-storey houses with integral garages and small private gardens were built with a density of 288 people per hectare (116/acre) on a 33-acre housing site arranged as a perimeter around 7 acres of common land. One of the virtues of perimeter development, the elusive 'added value', is that manipulating the land uses to connect deep rectangular areas into linear strips of housing around open space achieves a sense of spaciousness and prospect for the housing that's usually only achieved with lower density developments. This was not achieved at Eastfields, but unbuilt studies showed how unconstricted this high density housing site could have been if housing had been arranged around the land of the adjacent secondary school.

The scheme by MacCormac and Jamieson for Duffryn, a community of 957 houses and flats for Newport Borough Council (1974-78), continued to explore the geometry of the court, and, in particular, the difficulties in translating the theoretical courtyard studies into buildable housing incorporating road access and on-plot parking. The intersections in a continuous courtyard grid

Above/right At the Duffryn housing, Newport, South Wales (1974-78), the perimeter is extended around recreational land to widen house frontages and create larger back gardens.

Below left Great Linford 12, France Furlong, Milton Keynes (1975-78) – car courts take parking off the street, and maximise space for back gardens in a two-layer terrace layout. The original proposal (inset plan) consisted of continuous terraces of housing.

Below right Oakwood housing, Warrington (1977-78) – a pattern of car courts and small recreational spaces set around a park.

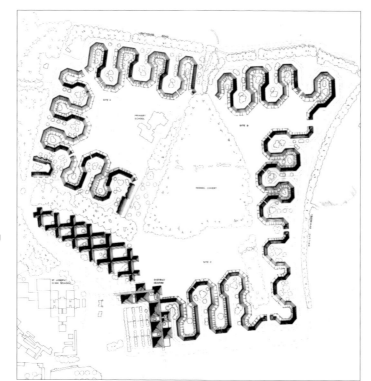

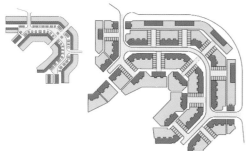

result in closed spaces and make no provision for vehicular access. In The Architect (March 1975, Theory into Practice) Richard MacCormac wrote that it was Leslie Martin's contribution to the 1968 RIBA Cambridge conference on education that had had the most direct influence on the masterplan for Duffryn. At that conference Martin proposed that the density of housing in terrace form could be maximised if housing land was arranged around another land use, such as a school, instead of being considered in isolation. The value of this approach had already been investigated in the Merton schemes. At Duffryn the same principles applied, although at the more modest density of 185 people per hectare. The layout of Duffryn evolved from the earlier schemes, in this case using 45 degree angles to 'allow the housing to snake its way around the parkland at the centre of the site taking up the irregular shape in a way that a right angle could not'. The fronts of the houses address the road in vehicle courts, and the backs overlook large private gardens and communal garden courts.

The initial design of France Furlong, Great Linford, Milton Keynes (1975-78) with 83 houses for Milton Keynes Development Corporation was also a linear perimeter development which maximised frontage. In the final scheme pairs of houses were moved back from the street line at regular intervals along the curved linear form. Cars could be parked in the resulting shared courts beside the houses rather than in front. The area for back gardens was maximised and streets were defined by pavements rather than small front gardens. This two-layered terrace layout was developed by David Prichard in his entry for the Bracknell Housing Competition in 1972, and for successive Milton Keynes housing schemes.

The design of Oakwood, (350 flats and houses for the Warrington New Town Corporation, 1976), followed the France Furlong scheme and continued the architects' interest in perimeter development. Whereas at Pollards Hill and Duffryn, for example, the depth of the perimeter band is more or less constant, at Oakwood the wedge-shaped boundary to the park varies the length of each cul-de-sac. Four-storey pavilions of flats for small families and older people are sited along the distributor road, separated from the larger but lower family houses to the south by an access road. This gives the former group interesting foreground views of pedestrian and vehicle activity and a glimpse southwards to the park, whilst locating young families around communal gardens and close access to the park. The road pattern is 'subtly worked out to foil, with cunning and sleight of hand, the road access/parking beast, which has here been tamed and harnessed and even made to perform tricks.'[8]

The Huddersfield Building Society competition reflected MacCormac's interest in a cult book of the 1960s, Community and

Privacy by Serge Chermayeff and Christopher Alexander, about modern middle class family housing. The linear house, likened by MacCormac to a railway carriage, developed the idea of adaptability and the relationship of groups of rooms to one another. It could work in a number of different configurations with various semi-permanent subdivisions (see also chapter three). A scheme for eight flexible private houses at Woughton Green, Milton Keynes (1973) was an attempt to realise the principles behind the Huddersfield competition. Two groups of four houses clustered around a courtyard. Entrance courts to each house buffered the prefabricated timber frame construction from the shared cul-de-sac, and each house was given a large L-shaped garden.

Roughly contemporary with Duffryn is another courtyard scheme, Chapter House, Coffee Hall (1974-77), with 89 flats for rent for single people in Milton Keynes – what would now be called keyworkers' homes. This reverts to a geometry that relates more closely to March's theoretical studies. Here, unlike the family housing, there was not the same need for on-plot parking since the whole development was actively managed by a warden. The parking was moved away from the buildings to the perimeter, within the precinct wall. Early studies suggested that accommodation could take the form of either a three storey L-shaped block or a small-scale grid of single storey courts. The two-storey arrangement was chosen because it proved the most economic solution and best exploited the views to the south-west of the site. The courtyard geometry generated linearity which provided an unusual degree of adaptability and, as a consequence, wide-fronted flat plans were possible, resulting in a novel reassessment of single-person accommodation. This was a precursor to investigations in student accommodation, and relates directly to the Robinson College, Cambridge competition (also 1974).

Chapter House flats at Coffee Hall, Milton Keynes (1974-77)
Spacious courts are surrounded by two-storey buildings with exceptionally wide-frontage single-person flats. The preliminary schemes (above) included one-, two- and three-storey options. The plan of the built scheme (below) comprises five L-shaped buildings with ground-level primary and secondary footpaths and landscaped open space. The ground- and first-floor room plans show the wide frontage of the flats.

Linear court houses and adaptability
Huddersfield Building Society competition (1972, top); proposed court houses at Woughton Green, Milton Keynes. Key: living room (green), bedrooms (blue), circulation (orange), bathroom (light blue), kitchen/diner (yellow), playroom (pink), childrens' bedroom (red), covered parking (grey).

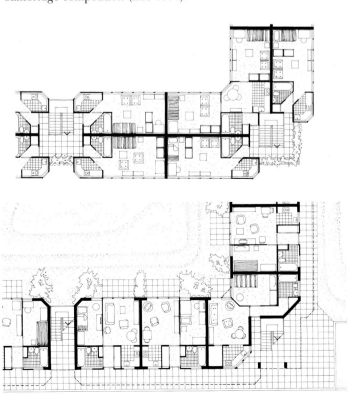

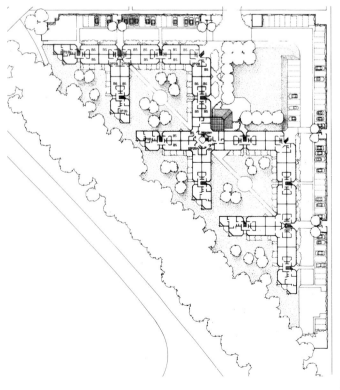

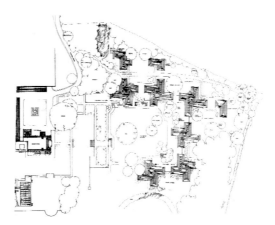

Ground floor room plans

Top Westoning Manor (1972-75), a home for children with special needs, comprises houses as combined freestanding pavilions which together define enclosed courts.

Middle Robinson College competition, Cambridge (1974), site and house plan. The rigorous geometry developed from the Coffee Hall flats and Westoning houses to provide exceptionally adaptable wide-frontage student rooms overlooking courts in buildings which reach out into the wooded landscape.

Below Frank Lloyd Wright's unbuilt McCormick House (1907-8) can be interpreted as a combination of cruciforms and courts.

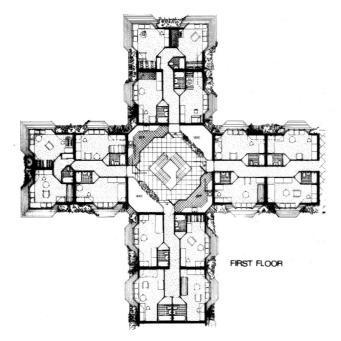

FIRST FLOOR

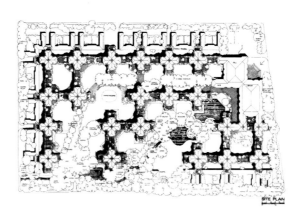

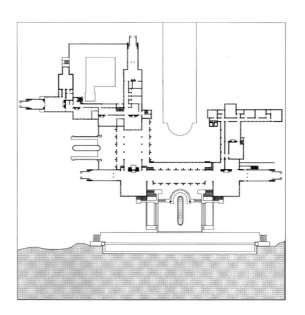

Courts and Pavilions

Although Lionel March's preoccupation was with the geometric efficiency of courtyards he was also interested in the characteristics of linear and pavilion forms and in cruciforms which might be seen as the intersections of courts. Both March and MacCormac have had a special interest in Frank Lloyd Wright's unbuilt McCormick House, and its court/cruciform combination. A generative early scheme which reflects this interest was a project for a community of ten houses for children with special needs at MacIntyre School, Westoning Manor, Bedfordshire (1972-75). Here, the series of cruciforms, out of which the 'pinwheels' are formed, make up courts.

'We found (just as Wright had) that as soon as [pavilions] threw out their arms, they embraced space and made places, and so became both buildings and backgrounds – truly part of the landscape.'[9]

This provides one of the key links between the early housing and the Oxbridge student accommodation projects. Westoning and Chapter House directly influenced the Robinson College competition, with the implicit idea that the intersections of courtyards can become pavilions. In turn, the first Worcester College Sainsbury Building was developed from one cruciform of the Robinson scheme. Robinson College was, in a sense, the most exhaustive exploration of court/pavilion characteristics in relation to an ecologically diverse existing landscape.

In 1979, five years after the Robinson College competition, MJP won a competition for the Faculty of Arts at Bristol University. The university was obliged to accommodate the 13 arts departments in a row of listed buildings – each an Italianate 'pavilion'. The proposal connected these departmental pavilions to linear faculty buildings, creating a series of L-shapes which enclose a series of courtyards formed from the back of the pavilions and the two sides of the 'L'. The need for a moveable boundary between the territories of departments, with permanent staff offices, and the time shared faculty, was recognised. The continuity of form allows a department to increase in size by encroaching into the time shared faculty spaces.

The second scheme at Great Linford, Cottesford Crescent, for 13 private houses for Greenwood Homes (1980), was unlike almost all the housing schemes that preceded it but was motivated, like Woughton Green, by the desire to find a geometric composition for clusters of large luxurious private houses. At Cottesford Crescent four pavilions enclose a shared gravelled car court and face outwards with large private gardens, an arrangement partly inspired by settlement patterns of farm buildings.

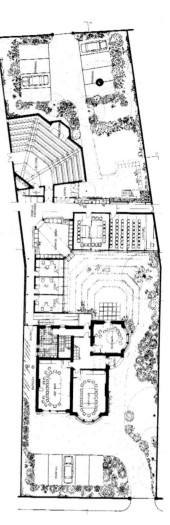

Above Cottesford Crescent (1981-84), a later housing scheme in Milton Keynes, combines clusters of pavilions, arranged around shared gravelled car courts that face outwards into large private gardens.

Right/below Bristol University Faculty of Arts (1979-86), plan and site plan. The existing Victorian houses are combined into continuous courtyard forms and are thereby made highly adaptable.

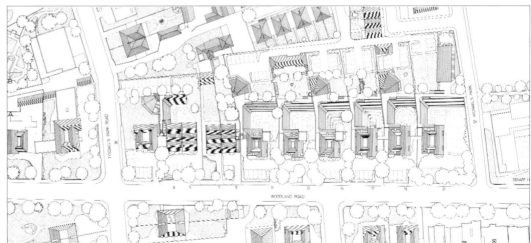

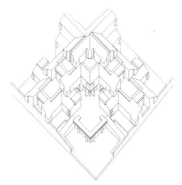

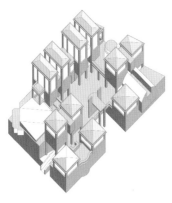

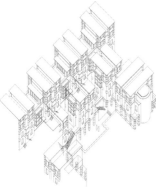

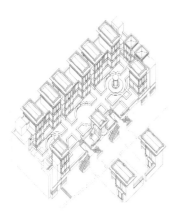

Courts, Pavilions and Plinths

Plinths consolidate the sense of place, and define boundaries without enclosure. In MJP's work the first Sainsbury building for Worcester College, Oxford, is the first to emerge out of the plinth which defines its peninsular like projection into the lake and acknowledges the escarpment of the site by projecting the upper level as a plinth-like common room. Inherent in the idea of the plinth is a psychological distinction between upper and lower worlds which works itself out in the university residential projects.

The second unbuilt proposal for Worcester, consisted of a court on a plinth around which emerged a series of pavilions. The Bowra building for Wadham College (1989) develops these themes. In this case, these small residential towers stand on top of public rooms and are linked to the existing library terrace, which becomes a narrow lane linking each staircase. Here, the geometry of pavilions, both freestanding and linked, creates an unexpectedly high density of nearly 300 students per acre. The arrangement is similar in the Garden Quadrangle for St John's College. The public rooms form a lower ground level and explore the psychology of a top-lit underworld. Above these a landscaped terrace forms a complementary upper world for undergraduate rooms arranged in towers. Similarly, Jowett Walk, student accommodation for Balliol College, Oxford, consists of a series of pavilions linked together by the common space on the ground floor. Perhaps paradoxically, this Balliol scheme can be read as a very dense court scheme with courts alternating with pavilions.

The two student residential schemes for Trinity College Cambridge employ the idea of the plinth for very different reasons. Blue Boar Court, which redeveloped the site of the old Blue Boar Hotel, raised student accommodation on a plinth which extended the existing raised level over commercial space, shops and service yards, adding to the existing pattern of courts leading to college staircases. In contrast, Burrells Field, although it has no lower level accommodation, is like the first Worcester College building setting its pavilions at the levelled edge of the escarpment of the Cambridge floodplain.

Linked pavilions on raised plinths
Top to bottom: The Sainsbury Building, Worcester College, Oxford (1980-83), is a development of the cruciform employed in the Robinson College project (1974), but here it floats on the plinth. The second Worcester College proposal (1986); Bowra Building at Wadham College, Oxford (1989-92); and the Garden Quadrangle at St John's College, Oxford (1990-93).

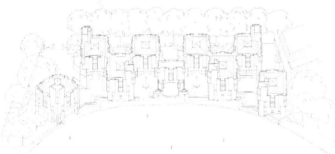

Above left Balliol College, Oxford (1994-2004), in which larger pavilions with seven rooms per floor alternate to enclose small open-sided courts, forming a very dense group of student rooms above shared spaces.
Above Burrell's Field, Trinity College, Cambridge (1989-95), is made up of a series of pavilions into which existing buildings are incorporated on a level escarpment which defines the edge of the Cambridge flood plain.
Below Blue Boar Court, Trinity College, Cambridge (1986-90), is raised on a plinth above commercial accommodation in the centre of Cambridge.

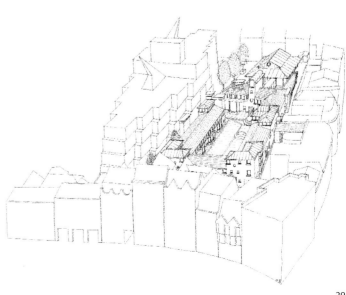

Linearity

In the courtyard and perimeter schemes, linearity is maximised to create residential frontage with prospect and privacy. Functions other than residential, such as work places, can be organised linearly to achieve high plot ratios and internal flexibility. The Cable and Wireless training college in Coventry is perhaps the most obviously expressed linear arrangement built in a dense single storey for flexibility, natural light and ventilation. Three recent projects are based on the typology of linear office plates alternating with top lit atria; Warwick Court at Paternoster Square, the unbuilt scheme for the Home Office in Marsham Street, and the scheme for the redevelopment of Broadcasting House.

With these projects linear forms, courts, cruciforms (the intersections of courts), and pavilions, latent in the grid of courts, reveal themselves to a greater or lesser extent. Ideas which started as abstract and quantitative gradually become expressive, psychologically interesting and related to landscape.

**Cable & Wireless Training College,
Warwickshire (1990-93)**
The college is sited so as to create a plinth and the sense of an escarpment which helps define the territory of the place.

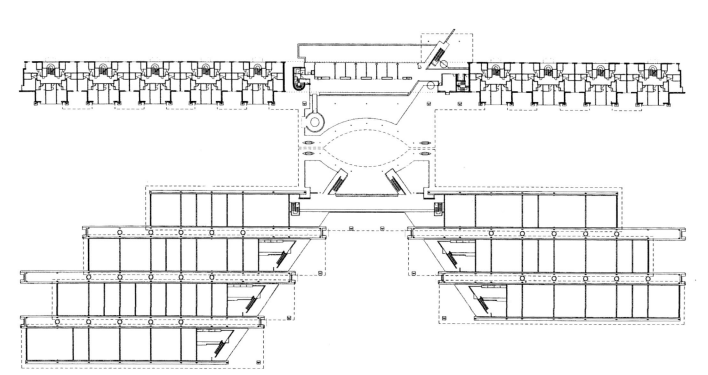

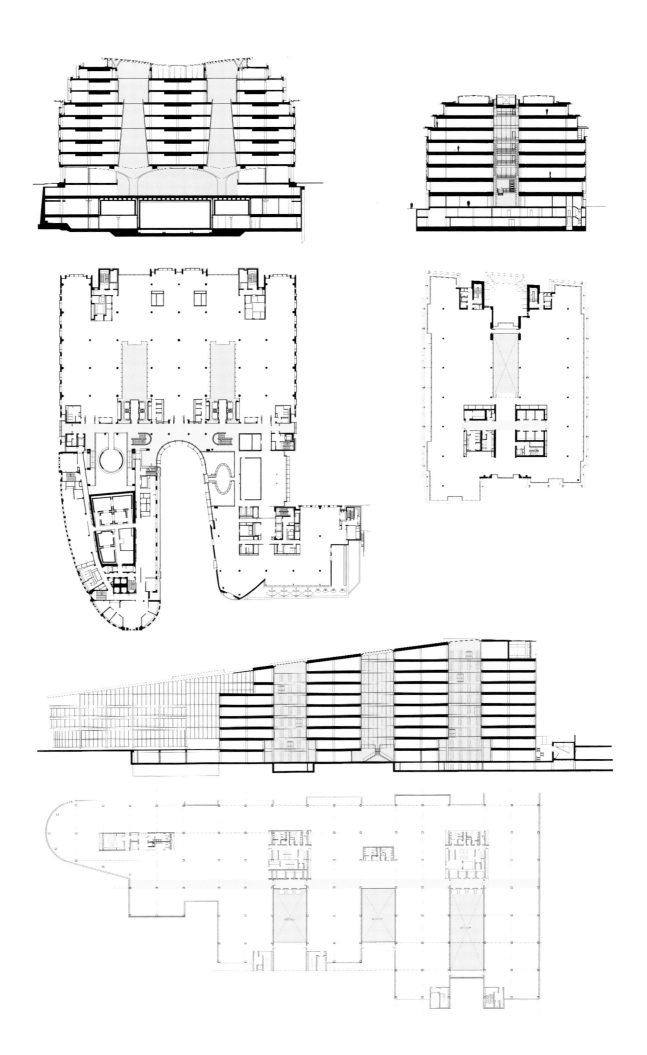

Right BBC Broadcasting House (2000-06); Warwick Court at Paternoster Square (1996-03). **Below** Marsham Street proposal, London (1999). In each of these projects, linear office floor plates alternate with glazed atria which are intersected by circulation routes and shared spaces.

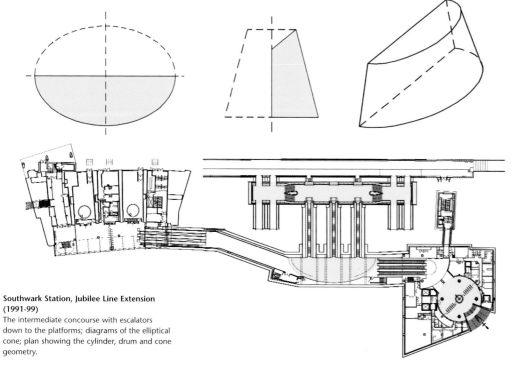

Southwark Station, Jubilee Line Extension (1991-99)
The intermediate concourse with escalators down to the platforms; diagrams of the elliptical cone; plan showing the cylinder, drum and cone geometry.

Advanced geometries

More recently MJP's projects have made use of the advances in computer aided design and have consequently been able to explore more complex geometries where appropriate.

Richard MacCormac believes that 'there is a high probability, in my opinion, that the orthogonal will be sustained, partly because there's a predictability about aggregating orthogonal spaces together which is fundamental to space planning.' Of course, it is also important to point out that the majority of building types discussed in this chapter, and still designed by the practice, are as managing director Jeremy Estop notes, 'the smaller buildings that you actually have to live or work in'. Such buildings are necessarily subdivided, and therefore do not present the same opportunities for freeform internal volumes and circulation systems as the very large public buildings, which are generally built on significant sites, and designed with the new geometric freedoms offered by advanced technologies.

Consequently, it is on MJP's larger public commissions that you begin to witness the stretching of geometrical boundaries. 'Where we've abandoned the orthogonal in the BBC is in the circulation', explains MacCormac. 'Where a building is principally to do with the movement of people, in for example an underground station [such as MJP's Southwark Jubilee Line station], a ferry terminal, or an airport, there may be strong cases for using other geometries. Similarly, in large volume buildings, like concert halls, museums and galleries, the aggregation of small, cellular spaces is not prevalent, [and the use of more conventional geometries therefore less relevant]. What is also important to recognise is that the question of the orthogonal is a question of a building's plan, not its section. You can see this in our design for the roofs at Cable and Wireless, in the unprecedented section of the interior of the Wellcome Wing, and in the unrealised competition design for West Bromwich Bus Station.'

In the design of high-profile office buildings, MJP's orthogonal approach has, says MacCormac, enabled the practice to 'get a quantitative handle on issues. For example, in the case of the BBC and its precursors at Paternoster and Marsham Street [unbuilt], our approach enabled us to optimise relationships between longitudinal floorplates and atria, to achieve very high plot ratios, but also to achieve unexpected sectional effects.' At the BBC, this can be seen in the two very different scales of the regular nine metre square grid of the production floors and in relation to the huge 40 metre transfer structure over the newsroom in which two structural patterns are reconciled.

1 Richard MacCormac, Five Buildings exhibition catalogue.
2 ibid.
3 Architectural Design, June 1958, quoted in Architectural Design 9-10, 1977, p592.
4 Architectural Design, 9-10 1977, p592.
5 Christopher Alexander, A Pattern Language (Oxford University Press 1977).
6 Architectural Design, 9-10 1977, p691.
7 Architectural Design, 9-10 1977.
8 Louis Hellman, Routes in Cheshire, Architectural Review October 1985.
9 Richard MacCormac, Explicitness to Ambiguity, Architectural Design 3, 1976, p143.

BBC Broadcasting House, London (2000-06)
Newsroom and diagram showing geometry of the transfer structure which takes the loads of the floors above onto four massive columns to create the open-plan space – the great unifying concept of the BBC project.

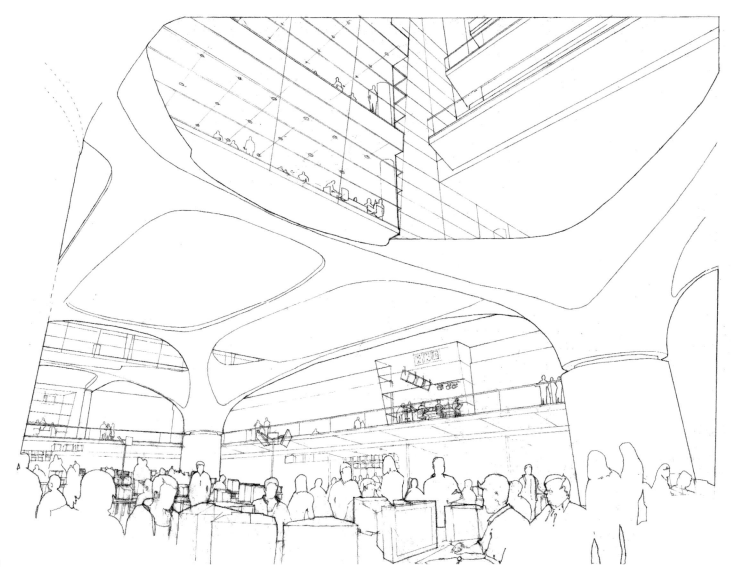

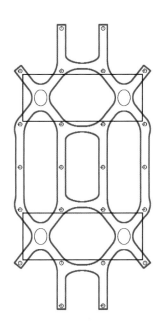

West Bromwich bus station (1995, below)
Sheltering canopies form a catenary structure, with steel cables suspended between tall A-frame entrance and exit portals. The elliptical plan is split along the proposed station's axis.

Wellcome Wing, Science Museum, London (1996-2000, below right)
The section derives from the rake of the suspended Imax cinema. The angled 45 degree void is immediately apparent to the visitor and enables the building to be understood as a whole.

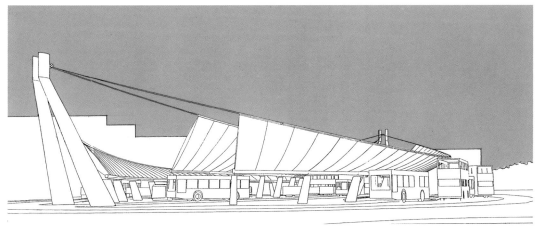

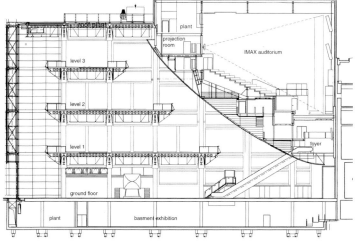

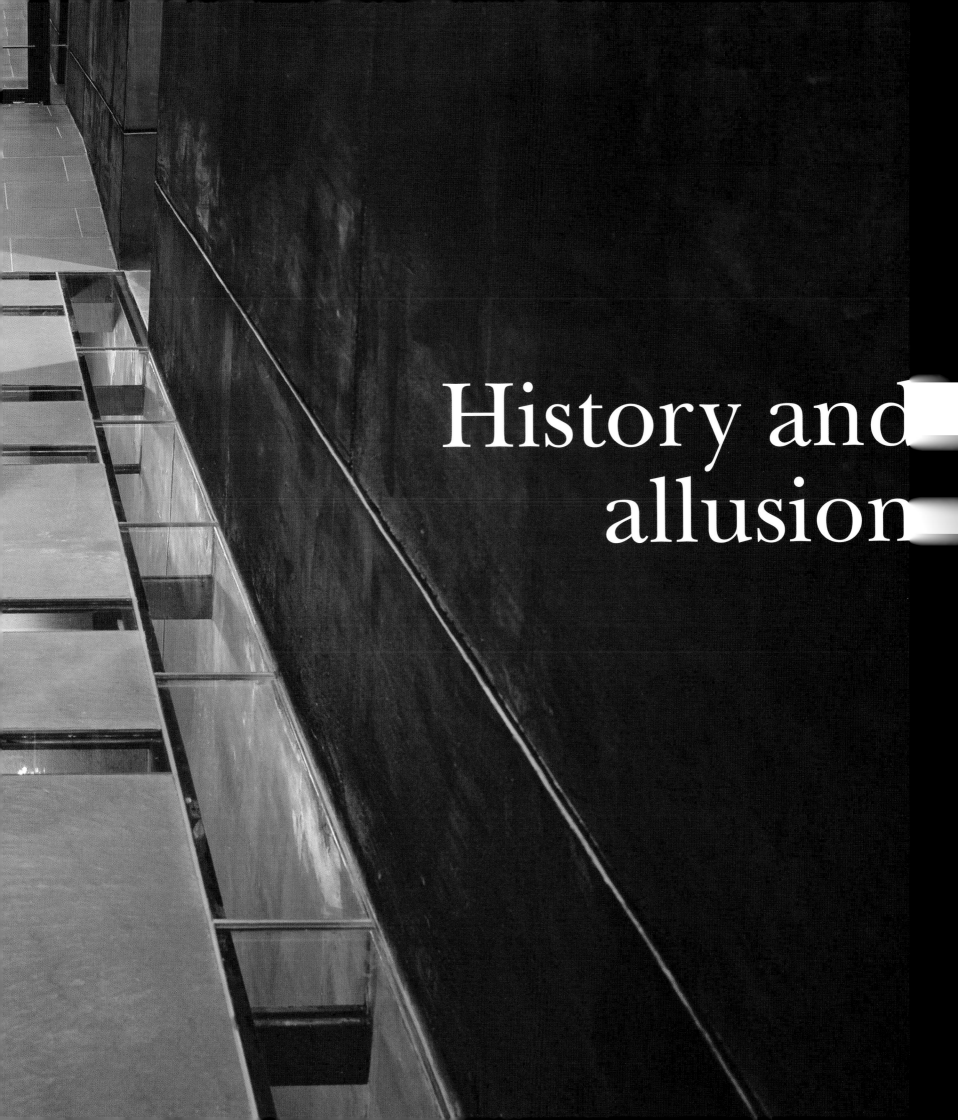

History and allusion

History and allusion

Robert Harbison
MJP's fusion of precedent and meaning with the modern project is exemplified in the Ruskin Library.

The Ruskin Library greets you like a single letter in an alphabet of symbols. It sits at the end of a raised causeway, raised far enough above its sea of grass that you are no more likely to walk on the lawn than you are to jump off a vaporetto into the Venetian lagoon. Your walk towards the building is a magical progress or a period of reflection during which you are bound to speculate on what you are walking toward. You know it is a library, which is something like a city, a conglomerate made of lots of small units and encompassing impossible variety. At this distance this library looks simpler than that, like a large bivalve which has parted to suggest entry.

Writing about this building, Richard MacCormac has said that the beauty of metaphors is their indefiniteness, not just one thing but many. But as he points out, buildings cannot be fundamentally indefinite, as poems can. Trying to match the waywardness of Ruskin's paragraphs in architecture is well nigh unthinkable. Yet buildings can suggest more than one thing at a time, and at this moment this one does, by seeming to contradict some of the simplest facts about its own situation. You feel you are about to enter a complete and separate world, set off from the rest of life like art or Ruskin's own life devoted to Italy and Biblical narrative and forbidding mountain peaks. This separate world takes the shape of a fish or a ship or an island.

I don't mean that you are necessarily conscious of these possibilities in the two minutes it takes to reach the building. Still, the library's form is inscrutable and its situation is unusual, a combination that encourages speculation. The exterior is relatively featureless, no openings of any kind in its long curved flanks, just green and white banding reminiscent of the coloured marble on the facades of the old Tuscan churches Ruskin liked best. But step inside the doors, and you are beset by a riot of rich materials and textures.

Riots of the senses were the effect Ruskin the Puritan most hankered after and became adept at conjuring up in the presence of art. Here the effect begins with red plaster which looks more like velvet or waterstained marble, marked off in panels like the walls of St Mark's. Underfoot is another watery effect, a paving alternating between silvery stone and glimpses through glass of spaces far beneath. A small building within the building rises up precipitously in front of us like one of those devotional shrines in architectural form. Right in the middle of its facade is a ghostly image of a Byzantine portal etched on glass. Now you can only guess what it is and how it was produced. Later you find out that it is an enlargement onto glass of a Ruskin daguerreotype showing his favourite way into St Mark's.

For me the idea of Ruskin is conjured up at every turn in this building. Before my visit I had heard enough about the Ruskin treasures the building contains that the day threatened to turn into a pilgrimage. Such a strong connection between architecture and literary content might give a modernist pause. It turns out that the Ruskin scholar who first had the idea of this library has left Lancaster. The collection of Ruskinian material – diaries, letters, drawings, books, memorabilia – could leave too, because it outgrew these quarters perhaps, but we don't need to pursue such scenarios. Just to think of

36

the building without the Ruskin connection might tell us something about it.

Now the exterior speaks of Tuscan Gothic and the vestibule of Venetian canals. But suppose these associations no longer fit? Important buildings often outlive their original purposes and must adapt to unforeseen new ones to survive. One could imagine the Ruskin Library as the headquarters of a small humanities institute that had nothing to do with Ruskin or Venice or the nineteenth century. The red walls would still be rich, the transparent floor unsettling, the huge daguerreotype mysterious.

Is it a perverse or a necessary effort to separate the features of a building from its associations? Perhaps it is a purely modern compulsion, and earlier ages would not have understood unease because a work of architecture fits its purpose so well that it seems fixed in place by it. One thinks of Mies van der Rohe's pavilion in Barcelona, that arch-Modernist work, which lies at the furthest remove from this kind of marriage between the substance of a building and its subject. Mies creates pure functionless space that does not tolerate permanent inhabitants. Yet I think these two buildings might overlap more than you'd expect, in aestheticising their materials until the walls themselves resemble works of art.

This is one of the most intensely symbolic interiors I know, a haunt of strangeness, more like Soane's house than any Miesian interior in its attitude to meaning. Soane's is a home which could drive one mad, and the Ruskin Library produces no such effect. To test this environment of rich oddity for livability, one would want to spend a day in the little reading room, which matches the double-height vestibule at the other end, but is appropriately less rich.

In this space I experienced a Miesian abhorrence of clutter – extra desks have been inserted because the intended overseer's post did not work, and cupboards that the Ruskin School in Oxford grew tired of have been slotted in between. I felt, as on a boat, that this curved sliver of space should be arranged just-so, without loose and extra insertions. The collision between the space and the furniture reminds us how hard the mixture of the symbolic and the everyday is to bring off, and helps us appreciate the ways in which the Ruskin Library fuses modernist forms and construction with intricate symbolism. I like to think it is a building Ruskin would see the beauty of.

Robert Harbison is professor of architectural history and theory at London Metropolitan University. He studied at Amherst College and Cornell University, and his research interests range widely across cultural history and include gardens, architecture and the other arts, overlaps between different cultures, and the Baroque. He has taught at the Architectural Association, Cornell University and Washington University, St Louis and his publications include Eccentric Spaces (1977), Deliberate Regression (1980), The Built, the Unbuilt and the Unbuildable, in Pursuit of Architectural Meaning (1991), The Shell Guide to English Parish Churches (1992), Reflections on Baroque (2000) and Travels in the History of Architecture (2009).

2 History and allusion

For MJP architecture is inextricably linked to memory and history, and Richard MacCormac set out his views on this in the catalogue of the Five Buildings exhibition in 1995. 'In our work we have set out to challenge the dichotomy between the self-referential, pragmatic and technological architecture of late British "modernism" and the kind of classicism and post-modernism which treats history passively as an inventory of styles. We believe that the vitality of the past depends upon active interpretation and that in engaging with history the architect not only amplifies our sense of the present but affects our understanding and feeling about the past, our connection with it.' [1]

Contrary to widely held beliefs, an interest in history was an important part of twentieth century architecture. Many of the great modernists, not least Le Corbusier, Alvar Aalto and Mies van der Rohe, were inevitably trained in the classical tradition and for most it remained a subtle part of their work. As Colin Rowe speculated in Mathematics of the Ideal Villa in 1947, a geometric comparison of the plans of the villas of both Palladio and Le Corbusier reveals a shared conceptual territory. Mies van der Rohe's early neoclassical work alluded to Schinkel and, as Richard MacCormac noted in a lecture coinciding with the Mies exhibition at London's Whitechapel Gallery in 2003, the Barcelona Pavilion, though appearing to break with the past, in fact shares the same overall arrangement as Schinkel's Charlottenhof palace in Sanssouci.

MJP's engagement with history has often been noted. Dan Cruickshank, writing in the Architects' Journal in 1993, cited the Bowra building at Wadham College Oxford as a project where history was an inspiration, rather than an opportunity for pastiche, and suggested a way of 'synthesising various aspects to form a new contemporary architecture. If you do no more than take and copy a model from the past, then your design will always be judged by its model and will always be found wanting by comparison.' [2]

Learning from university buildings

Bristol Faculty of Arts (1979-88) was MJP's first education project and also the first to engage in a dialogue with an existing historical environment. The project is located within a street of detached villas, mainly nineteenth-century merchants' houses, and MJP looked particularly at the distinctive grain formed by the red sandstone walls of their back gardens. In the resulting design the garden walls serve several purposes: to give identity to the individual academic departments, and to provide containment for each phase of construction, giving each phase a sense of completion. Each single-storey L-shaped component contains both departmental and faculty space, with flexible boundaries between them. The strategy was to devise a relationship between the new

Below Richard MacCormac has observed that Schinkel's Sanssouci/Charlottenhof palace in Potsdam and Mies van der Rohe's Barcelona Pavilion share the same general arrangement, with the main building addressing the long axis of a terrace on a raised plinth which is enclosed, on one side, by a pergola and a wall. This asymmetry creates a cross axis which in Sanssouci opens a prospect to the park and in Barcelona gives the pavilion a commanding position at the edge of the exhibition ground.

Bristol Faculty of Arts (1979-86)
This project (bottom left and right) involved the refurbishment of a row of Italianate houses and linking them with new low L-shaped blocks to form intimate south-facing courts to the rear of each house.

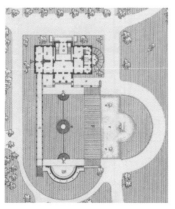
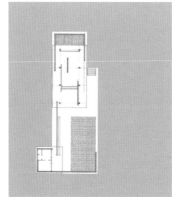
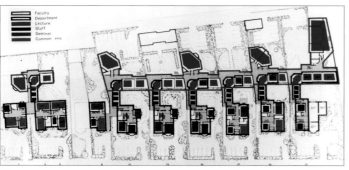

Sainsbury Building, Worcester College,
Oxford (1980-83)

The original eighteenth century buildings at Worcester College were designed by Nicholas Hawksmoor with George Clarke. The eighteenth century loggia under the library forms a threshold to the quad and the landscape beyond. The Sainsbury Building (1980-83) creates a threshold with similar relationship to the lake. This is viewed from a raised terrace on the diagonal axis which itself recalls the original intention of raising the level of the eighteenth century quad.

and old that would enable the scheme to be phased and flexible, without obliterating the overall structural organisation of the site. Porches, conservatories, porters' desks and staircases connect the old and new structures. Victorian conservatories were an appropriate precedent for the attached extension which provides a unifying space in which ramps and steps reconcile the changes in levels. New construction materials – masonry, timber and glass – contrast with those of the existing houses and walls.

The projects MJP has undertaken for Oxford and Cambridge colleges have often involved sites that are rich in historical memory, both social and architectural, and these aspects have often provided a basis for the designs. But there has also been an opportunity to reflect and reinterpret the work and ideas of other architects, not least John Soane, Frank Lloyd Wright and Alvar Aalto. Hugh Pearman, reviewing the Sainsbury Building for Worcester College in Oxford, noted how MJP 'layers and intersects the volumes, providing them with wide, oversailing pitched roofs à la Frank Lloyd Wright, and throwing in a dash of subtle classicism by forming the upper rooms into broken pediments. At Wadham [College], the site is much tighter… and the effect is, appropriately enough, of a crowded Elizabethan alley system, though nobody would mistake this architecture for that of an earlier era. The towers and bays may recall such houses as Hardwick, but the

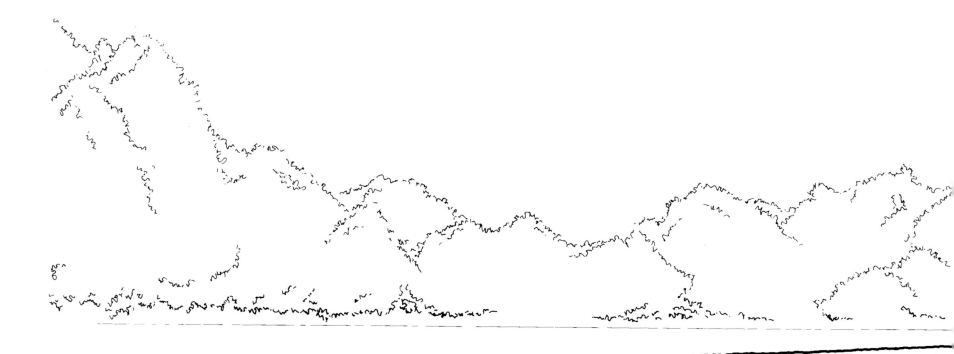

influence of Wright is still there to be found in the flat projecting tower roofs.'[3]

The design of the Sainsbury Building is both influenced by and contributes to an understanding of the original college buildings. The project creates a threshold between the outer world (the city of Oxford) and the inner landscape (the college garden). This reflects the composition of the early eighteenth century buildings designed by Nicholas Hawksmoor and George Clarke – both the original and the new counterpart have an entrance court and loggia with views to the landscape beyond. MJP translated the formal eighteenth century plan into a contemporary sequence on the diagonal, at the same time forming an end piece to the serpentine lake in the picturesque tradition. This process of historical evaluation informs the design of new buildings while simultaneously recharging the significance of the old, a notion that immediately appealed to Worcester's provost, historian Asa Briggs.

MJP's broad interests have led some projects to draw not only on architectural precedent but landscape, ecology and, in the case of Robinson College in Cambridge, literary allusions. In the 1974 competition for the new college, Richard MacCormac considered the plan of the proposed buildings from two related perspectives. The first was the notion that a formal system (a grid of 30 metre square courtyards) might be eroded by a natural system (the

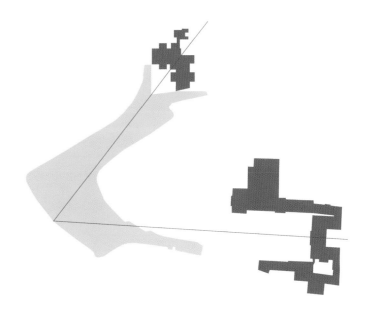

MJP's Sainsbury Building became an end-piece to Worcester College's lake. The plan and section show the sightlines across lake towards the new building and views out to the landscape beyond.

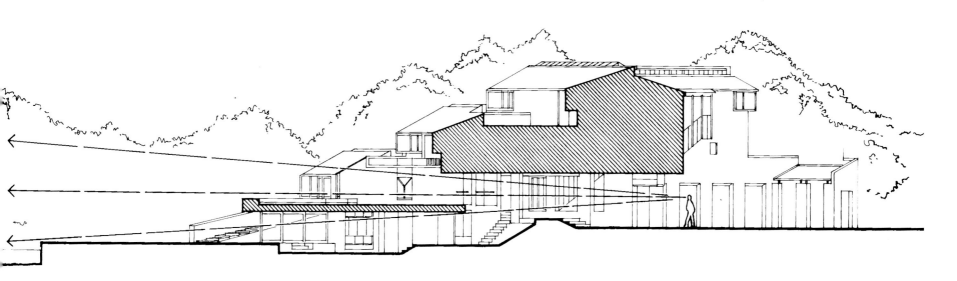

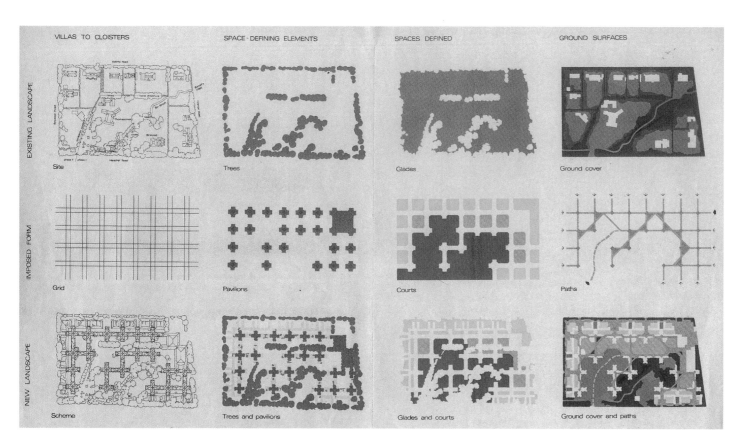

VILLAS TO CLOISTERS	SPACE-DEFINING ELEMENTS	SPACES DEFINED	GROUND SURFACES

EXISTING LANDSCAPE

Site — Trees — Glades — Ground cover

IMPOSED FORM

Grid — Pavilions — Courts — Paths

NEW LANDSCAPE

Scheme — Trees and pavilions — Glades and courts — Ground cover and paths

Above The grid of student accommodation for MJP's 1974 competiton entry for Robinson College, Cambridge, recalls Tenniel's chessboard across the landscape.

Left John Tenniel's illustration from Lewis Carrol's Alice through the Looking Glass (1872); Frank Lloyd Wright's McCormick House (1907-08) both encloses and reaches out into the landscape.

ecology of Bin Brook and the trees that covered half the site). The approach was inspired by MacCormac's recent visit to a ruined Cistercian abbey in France. 'The abbey was blown up in the French Revolution and a forest grew into the rigour of the Cistercian plan, so you get something rather like the John Tenniel illustration of the chess board in Alice through the Looking Glass.' In addition, underlying the mathematical system of grids is the allusion to the monastic courtyard that lies within traditional Cambridge colleges. Like Frank Lloyd Wright's houses the Robinson project both encloses and reaches out into the surrounding landscape. Likewise the subsequent Sainsbury Building at Worcester College in Oxford which, in this sense, represents a fragment of the unbuilt Robinson scheme.

In a number of the Oxbridge schemes, not least the Bowra building at Wadham College (1992) and the Garden Quadrangle at St John's College (1993), MJP found that it could increase density by combining pavilions with towers (see chapter one). The approach also reflects an interest in Robert Smythson's Hardwick Hall in Derbyshire (1590-97), which was completed just a decade before the original Wadham College, and John Vanbrugh's Castle Howard (1699-1712). As Vanbrugh found, towers can contribute something that courtyards alone lack, creating visual relationships that extend from the foreground to the background. The most

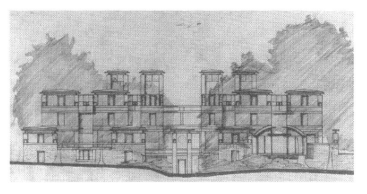

Towers
Top MJP's second scheme for Worcester College, Oxford (1986).
Middle Bowra Building, Wadham College, Oxford (1989-92).
Bottom Model of Garden Quadrangle, St John's College, Oxford (1990-93).

complex investigation of this approach was for a second, unbuilt project for Worcester College, but the most Vanbrughian of all is the Garden Quadrangle at St John's. Here the Fellows' pavilions in the foreground are attached to a seventeenth century wall at the edge of the college garden, while towers housing undergraduate rooms lend complexity of the silhouette. At lower ground level the auditorium and dining room form an underworld beneath the landscaped terrace of the upper world, an idea provoked by historic images of cavernous top-lit spaces.

The theme of a lower plinth that draws disparate elements of a built composition together recurs in a number of MJP's Oxbridge residential projects. Based on classical precedent, the device was employed by Alvar Aalto at Säynätsalo village hall and civic centre (1949-59) where a plinth is formed from a natural escarpment, amplifying the building's presence like an acropolis. The site of the first (realised) Worcester College building has a fall in level of about two-thirds of one storey, as at Säynätsalo. This suggested the idea of raising the building on a mound that emerges out of the slope, with the common room overlooking the lake like an inhabited underworld. In the unrealised Worcester project this idea extended to include a secret passage or cryptoporticus leading the Fellows from the garden up into their governing body room.

At Worcester the sectional idea involved raising a plinth out of an

Above Robert Smythson's Hardwick Hall; Alvar Aalto's Säynätsalo Town Hall provided a precedent for the creation of a 'raised place' at the heart of the Worcester College Sainsbury Building scheme.

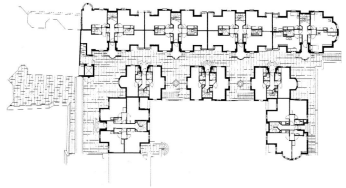

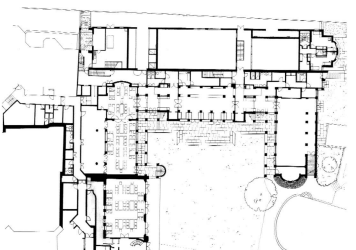

Bowra Building, Wadham College, Oxford (1989-92, right)
Longitudinal public space at ground level with a series of linked or detached pavilions and prospect towers above. Ground floor and deck-level plans (left).

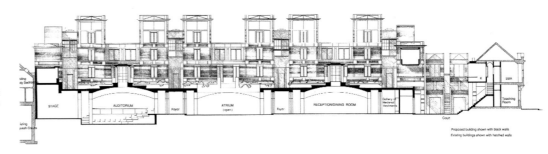

Underworlds and top-lit spaces
Left John Soane's Bank of England Consols Transfer Office (1798-1799), painting by Joseph Michael Gandy (left).
Middle Francois Chauveau's 1652 engraving of the Prologue of Pierre Corneille's opera 'Andromede' with set design by Giacomo Torelli (left middle).
Middle lower Alexander Pope's Grotto at his villa in Twickenham, painting by William Kent (left below).

Garden Quadrangle, St John's Oxford (1990-93)
Section, ground floor and terrace-level plans; the 'underworld' at St Johns (right).

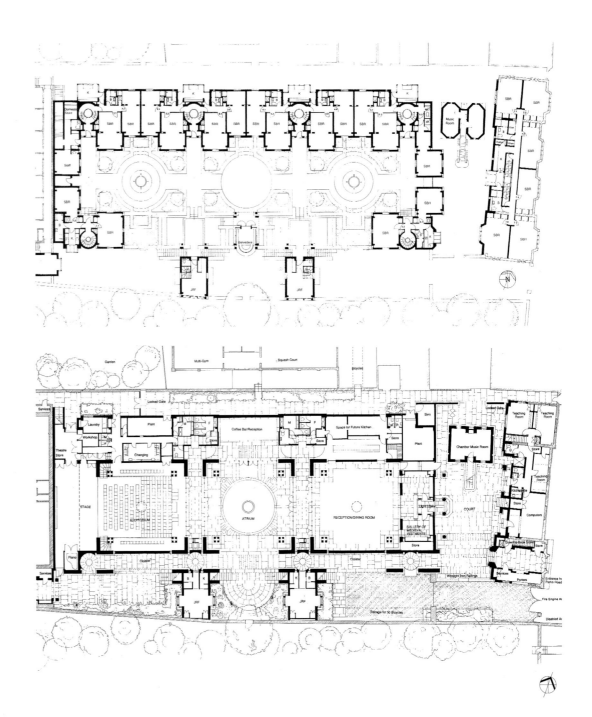

Above John Vanbrugh's sketch of an imagined cemetery at Surat, India, from 'Mr Van-Brugg's Proposals about Building ye New Churches'.

Top Burrell's Field reflects a pastoral image evoked in Gwen Raverat's Period Piece: A Cambridge Childhood (1952).
Middle Schinkel's Schloss Charlottenhof villa (1826) suggested picturesque relationships between formal and informal landscape buildings, plinths and water.
Bottom Frank Lloyd Wright's Ocotillo Desert Camp (1927) creates a palisade from which towers break out.

escarpment and this was also employed at Burrell's Field for Trinity College in Cambridge (1995). 'We recognised that there was a hint of an ancient natural escarpment marking the edge of the Cam floodplain right across the site', says MacCormac. 'This was later authenticated by archaeologists, who also found evidence of an iron age encampment along the escarpment of the Burrell's Field site.' The scheme also refers to Frank Lloyd Wright's temporary studio, the Ocotillo desert camp in Arizona (1927), where habitable spaces emerge from a continuous palisade rather like towers on a castle wall.

At Burrell's Field a series of pavilions emerges out of the continuous wall that defines the edge of the escarpment and encloses the perimeter of the site. The pavilions overlook the principal external circulation routes, which also helps enhance security at the site. Some 80 student rooms are contained in clusters of two- and three-storey brick towers, while interlocking glazed lead-clad steel cubes introduce a 45-degree geometry in response to the triangular site. The towers, linked by lower buildings, frame views down and across the pedestrian routes. From the bridge over Bin Brook the impression is of a walled town rising from the flood plain, which remains a meadow rich with native flora. Two existing Edwardian villas are integrated within the site, their gardens reinvented with topiary and formal planting. As Peter Buchanan observed, 'built in a buff brick used elsewhere in Cambridge, the geometry of the stubby towers reflects MacCormac's studies of Frank Lloyd Wright, although the linking garden walls and pergolas were inspired by a Schinkel etching. The vocabulary is new to Cambridge, yet the complex looks as if it has always been there.' [4]

Burrell's Field, Trinity College, Cambridge, (1989-95)
The site plan shows the two existing hostels (Adrian and Butler Houses), designed by David Roberts, which responded to the diagonal geometry of the site and set the scene for the pathways that form the armature of MJP's project (see also overleaf).

Peter Hull's perspective drawings show the path from the Fellow's Garden crossing the Bin Brook on a slender bridge; the causeway entrance; and the path, parallel to the Bin Brook which binds the scheme together.

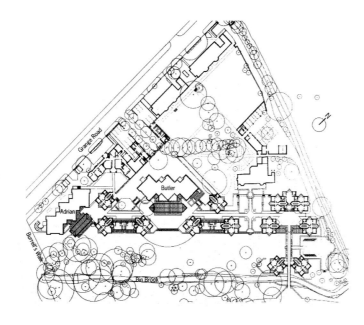

The Ruskin Library, Lancaster University (1992-97)
The building is conceived as a keep connected to the university by a causeway. Richard MacCormac's preliminary sketch (above right), made on the train returning from Lancaster, explores the building's isolated presence.

Right Floor plans – the building as an eye. 'The worst of me is that the desire of my eyes is so much to me! Ever so much more than the desire of the mind' (John Ruskin, 1875).

Left The thirteenth century Gothic Cathédrale Ste-Cécile of Albi – the choir as a building within a building.
Furniture by Gothic-revivalist William Burges (1827-1881) – the ambiguous furniture/building idea influenced the idea of the archive.
The organ at the chapel of King's College, Cambridge – a presence that affects the perception of the interior.
Richard Serra's Weight and Measure installation, Tate Gallery (1992) – displacing the visitor.

Previous pages Burrell's Field, Cambridge, and the Ruskin Library.

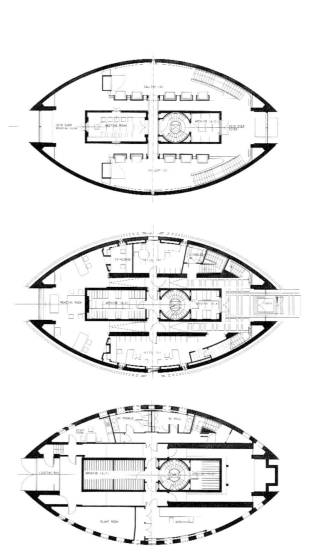

Interpreting Ruskin

It is not easy for an architect to act on the precepts of Ruskin's 1849 essay The Lamp of Memory, according to Richard MacCormac. 'He writes that buildings are touched by what has happened to them, so the older the building or landscape the more profound it is as a record of human actions and experiences.' Ruskin saw gothic architecture as a repository of an evolving cultural tradition, 'a kind of palimpsest'.

The Ruskin library at the University of Lancaster (1997) alludes to the gothic tradition in a metaphorical, almost subliminal, way. For MacCormac 'the technique is surrealist, layering up a series of allusions that are not necessarily connected, rather like a dream.' In this respect conversations with Michael Wheeler, director of the Ruskin programme, were crucial to the genesis of the design.

Historical allusions are many. 'The building, as a symbol of Venice, is separated from the university by a causeway that crosses a dry moat, representing the lagoon. This causeway enters the building and the metaphor of island and lagoon is replicated with the archive itself emerging through an underlit transparent glass and slate floor to convey the perilous maritime condition of the city and to allude to Ruskin's dream of looking into its waters, and seeing the horses of St Mark's being harnessed.' [5]

The library can also be read as a gothic church, with a narthex, choir and sanctuary represented by the entrance, archive and reading room. The archive is a treasure chest that, like a William Burges cabinet, can be read as either a large piece of furniture or a small building. The archive is uninhabited apart from a meeting room for the trustees which faces west to Morecambe Bay. 'It is like an ark because it's a container for Ruskin's "sacred" texts… project architect Oliver Smith came up with the idea that it was the "corpus" of Ruskin's work, so it represented a sort of tomb as well.' At the same time Richard MacCormac had been impressed by sculptor Richard Serra's installation Weight and Measure at the Tate Gallery in which two forged steel blocks displaced viewers from the centre of the Duveen Gallery. At the Ruskin Library, the archive seems to symbolise Ruskin himself – occupying the centre of the space and impossible to miss, you have to walk round him.

Some critics expected MJP's architectural response to this commission to be more overtly gothic, but neither MacCormac nor Wheeler believed this approach would work. After all, Ruskin had objected to the employment of Venetian gothic for pub porches in Dulwich; this was an architectural vocabulary that could not be applied uniformly. 'The sixth chapter of Ruskin's Seven Lamps of Architecture is the Lamp of Memory, in which he says "we cannot remember" without architecture. The chapter resonates with analogous words – monument, memory, history, historical, story – all of which emphasise the idea of recall, and invites us to find the means of recall without losing the authenticity of the architecture of the present. And this, in turn, stimulates the realisation that architecture, like literature and landscape, is part of our collective memory, which we must incorporate into our present experience.' [6]

In the event there is a welcoming familiarity in the ecclesiastical sequence of the arrangement. The highly wrought centrepiece, with its beautiful glossy Venetian plaster and carefully crafted character, carries a particular reference to the arts and crafts movement and its origins in Ruskin's medievalism.

John Ruskin, watercolour of the Baptistry in Florence (1870), which he described as being 'one large piece of engraving: white substance, cut into, and filled with black and dark green' (Ruskin, Arata Pentelici, 1890). The striations inspired the green polished precast concrete bands of MJP's Ruskin Library.

Left Interior view of the Ruskin Library looking along the top-lit glass and slate floored path towards the reading room. The transparent floor, set over the basement, evokes the depths of a Venetian canal and the reflective polished black and red plaster suggests a sinister calle.

Top View from within the Ruskin Library through Alexander Beleschenko's amplified image of John Ruskin's daguerreotype that depicts the north-west porch of St Marks Cathedral in Venice. The image has the Proustian intent of trying to capture the barely retrievable past.

Above Venice provides a similarly brooding setting for director Nicolas Roeg's 1973 film Don't Look Now, starring Donald Sutherland.

Reading the landscape

At the heart of many MJP projects is the interaction of formal architectural ideas with the landscape. With the Sainsbury Building at Worcester College the lakeside setting was informed by Romantic eigteenth century landscapes such as Stourhead in Wiltshire. The building terminates the vista at the end of the lake but rather than abruptly stopping at the terrace, the lake divides in two, with a tumbling fall on one side and the other side terminating in reeds.

The idea of buildings and landscape – or buildings as landscape – was a key generator in the design of the Cable & Wireless training college (1993), the most significant of the three projects MJP has undertaken for the company. The college is located outside Coventry on a four hectare site overlooking the Warwickshire green belt. Like Palladio's villas, many of which were working farms, the college is both workplace and emblem, opening out to address the landscape to the south with outstretched wings. Yet, in the English country house tradition, the entrance approach is oblique so as to preserve the central open space as a parterre. The asymmetry of the arrangement, says David Prichard, 'tickles the brain', and forms an essential component of the scheme.

Another influence on the design was Colin Rowe and Robert Slutzky's essay Transparency: Literal and Phenomenal (1963). 'Rowe had the notion that you can set up a virtual field in which the architectural events are a manifestation of an invisible structure', says MacCormac. 'He cited Le Corbusier's League of Nations competition scheme, in which an implied lateral field is entered obliquely. At Cable & Wireless the virtual field – the phenomenal transparency – is set up by a series of layers with wave-breaking roofs, which are also penetrated obliquely.' The wave shape of the roof plays a role in the passive environmental control of the building and provides north lights over the teaching spaces,

Cable & Wireless Training College, Coventry (1990-93)
Left Jørn Utzon's sketch of a Chinese temple roof floating over its masonry platform; Colin Rowe's analysis of Le Corbusier's 1927 League of Nations project (published in 1963); Palladio's Villa Badoer (1556) plan compared with the Cable & Wireless footprint.

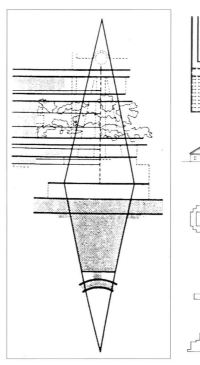

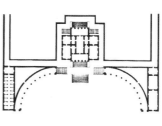

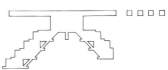

as well as reflecting the company's significant interests in China and Japan. The roof form was influenced by Jørn Utzon's drawings of Chinese temple roofs and raised plateaux, like great cumulus clouds, and it drew on the oriental notion (also sensed in Frank Lloyd Wright) of a roof floating above a plinth.

The concept evolved further after Richard MacCormac saw an exhibition of jade burial coats from the Hang dynasty in Singapore. 'They had little tablets of jade joined together at the corners by gold thread that could respond to the three dimensional nature of the body, and that suddenly made me think of jade blue faience tiles for the Cable & Wireless roofs.' The gold wire was translated into stainless steel yacht rigging and the heavy faience tiles, set above the roof insulation to help reduce thermal shock, hold down the whole roof without penetrating the roof membrane.

The idea of interpreting buildings in terms of landscape is not confined to the exterior. John Britton, writing in 1828, described the interiors of John Soane's houses at Lincoln's Inn Fields as being like a condensed eighteenth century landscape with a series of anticipated episodes.[7] Likewise MJP's Ruskin Library can be read as an internal landscape that cannot be fully comprehended immediately upon entering. By blocking the view, the archive gives the visitor a sense of anticipation of an unseen destination, the reading room. A more complex example is Southwark underground station, where the subterranean concourses form a controlled sequence, as in a picturesque landscape, with a series of interim destinations in which to re-orientate yourself before setting off again. Mark Hines, then a director at MJP, described the approach as 'very disciplined about the way you manipulate not only the landscape around a building but people's experiences and their views through a building, so you can think about the interior as a kind of eighteenth century landscape'.

Cable & Wireless Training College, Coventry (1990-93)
'This Zen monastery – with its rows of graceful wave roofs clad in big blue-green tiles strung on wires like pieces of jade; with its oval administration centre, its semicircular waterfall, its rivulets and lake; and with its separate, very collegiate row of bedroom staircase blocks – is a composition that gets nearly everything right. It does so with assurance, handling its palette of materials – stone, steel, glass, timber, ceramic – with deftness and skill.' (Hugh Pearman, The Sunday Times, 15 May 1994). Left: The turquoise ceramic roof tiles; jade burial coat at the Hang Dynasty exhibition in Singapore.

Southwark Station, Jubilee Line Extension, London (1991-99)
Left Alexander Beleschenko's glass cyclorama for the intermediate level of Southwark Jubilee Line station.

Above Schinkel's cyclorama for the Queen of the Night in Mozart's Magic Flute (1815); the station is conceived as an intelligible sequence of constrasting spaces which form an underground landscape.

Fitzwilliam College Chapel
Above Christ in a ship, a Jungian interpretation of ship symbolism, from The Great Mother: an Analysis of the Archetype, Erich Neumann (1955); Vasa, Stockholm; Viking Burial Ship.
Right Fitzwilliam Chapel – staircases separate the 'floating' vessel from the outer walls.
Below Breakfast room at John Soane's 13 Lincoln's Inn Fields; the Fitzwilliam Chapel interior translates a circle in a square into a square in a circle.

The chapel at Fitzwilliam College in Cambridge (1991), which contributes to Denys Lasdun's original and incomplete 1960s masterplan, was envisaged as a translation of John Soane's breakfast room at number 13 Lincoln's Inn Fields. 'The chapel is the most radical reinterpretation of the breakfast room. At the upper level the central space is cubic rather than circular and the outer defining walls circular rather than square. Daylight falls between, hardening the silhouette of the concrete posts, which defines the central space, and softening and gently pushing outwards the rendered outer arcs. At the lower level the disengagement of walls and ceiling is achieved by the convex underside of the vessel.' [8] The congregational space is designed as an independent structure, separated from the outer envelope by staircases, like a vessel afloat in the building, and recalling the conserved hulls of the Vasa in Stockholm and viking burial ships in Oslo.

Complex internal topography is also a characteristic of the Fitzwilliam College residential building, which was designed before the chapel. This stems in part from a re-evaluation of the relationship between kitchens and stairways and making their relative locations different throughout the building.

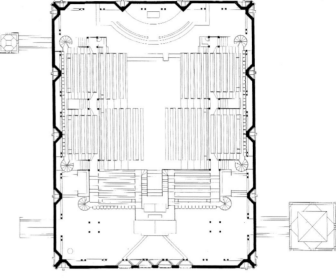

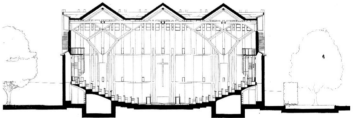

Tonbridge School Chapel (1988)
Peter Hull's drawing depicts the latern-like quality of the chapel at night. Gothic qualities were sought in the vaulting of the roof, the clerestorey and the light shafts in the external walls.

While the Fitzwilliam College chapel was under construction, MJP won the competition for the design of a new chapel at Tonbridge School in Kent (1989), organised after its existing Edwardian chapel was severely damaged by fire. Unfortunately the scheme remained unbuilt but the model shows how the idea of 'building within a building' is fulfilled by a congregational 'vessel' that is separate from the outer envelope. The project also explored ways in which light could be reflected through the interior spaces, while the elaborate structure of ribbed vaults recall the nineteenth century interpretation of gothic architecture as a forest. Perimeter high-level windows suffuse the space with light, highlighting the interior 'vessel' in silhouette.

Coventry Phoenix
Initiative – Priory Place

63

Historic urban contexts

Among a number of major urban projects in which the existing historic context has been a key component, MJP has been responsible for masterplans at Ballymun in Dublin, West Cambridge, the Durham Millennium Project and the Phoenix Initiative in Coventry.

MJP's masterplan for Coventry is arguably the most important economic and physical regeneration initiative in the city since its reconstruction after the second world war. The scheme extends and elaborates Coventry's role as a place of international reconciliation, while also making reference to the city's clock-making past and its role in car manufacturing. Central to the design is a new route through the city, linking Basil Spence's cathedral to the eleventh century priory, the Coventry Transport Museum and ultimately, the new Garden of International Friendship. The scheme also addresses issues of historical memory through the work of local and international artists who collaborated with MJP and landscape architect Rummey Design Associates on public art works throughout the project.

Durham's cathedral dominates the city even more than Coventry cathedral, soaring alongside the Norman castle from a ridge above the River Wear and commanding the wooded valley below. MJP's Durham Millennium City Project, consisting of a theatre, a library and offices grouped around the new Millennium Square, extends the spine of buildings along the narrow outcrop that defines the boundary of the old city. The project is as much about what David Prichard describes as 'urban mending' as it is about providing new civic buildings. The Gala theatre is designed to act as a beacon, with a flash of red denoting the auditorium that can been seen from the railway viaduct. The library and offices, although less dramatic, define the entry into Millennium Place and heal the scar

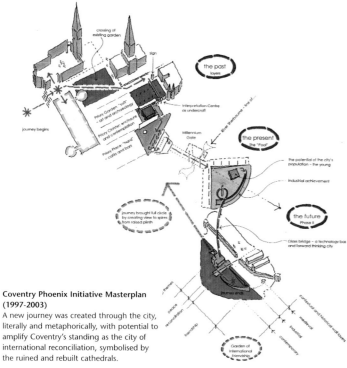

Coventry Phoenix Initiative Masterplan (1997-2003)
A new journey was created through the city, literally and metaphorically, with potential to amplify Coventry's standing as the city of international reconciliation, symbolised by the ruined and rebuilt cathedrals.

left by the ring road that cuts into the existing Claypath frontages. The elevated terrace on which these buildings sit has views down to the River Wear and the proposed Riverside Park. Prichard was influenced by the Royal Festival Hall's 'egg in a box' composition for the volumetric expression of the hall.

In tune with the work of many of their contemporaries, a number of MJP's urban schemes demonstrate a response to the detrimental effects modernist architecture has had on the fabric of the UK's cities. 'MacCormac's Manifesto', published in the Architects' Journal in June 1983, offered a reappraisal of the traditional grain of London's East End and the housing scheme at Vining Street in Brixton (1986) was the first of several projects for the Metropolitan Housing Trust that realised elements of the manifesto.[9] The essay had suggested that urban fabric could be stitched together like a rug, with housing used to protect the public space and also to create common spaces for which residents feel some sense of ownership. In Vining Street the high-density low-rise low-cost housing incorporated off-road car parking to connect and sustain the street frontages, helping mend a piece of the fragmented city.

In Ludlow, the architects faced a different challenge. The site was a former cattle market on the edge of the historic town centre, close to the railway station, where Tesco wanted to build a supermarket – arguably the most drastic intervention in this famous market town since the nineteenth century station. The pre-history of the site as a cattle market helped define the project. A wall was built to enclose the site and car park, and to bind it into the town centre. The scheme can be read as a 'book end' to the continuous fabric of Corve Street which leads down the hill from the town centre. Beyond, the urban density starts to break down with large walled gardens, trees, freestanding houses and fragments

Durham Millennium City Project (1996-2001)
The project included a new square surrounded by a civic hall, library and visitor centre, all located close to the historic centre of the city.

Left Vining Street housing, Brixton (1986-90).

Below Tesco supermarket, Ludlow (1997-2000).

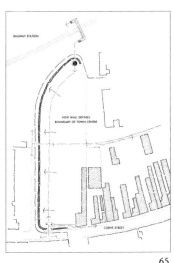

BBC Broadcasting House, London (2000-09)
Richard MacCormac's initial sketch (below)
explores the relationship between convexity
and concavity and the relationship with the
spire of All Souls. The convex extension shown
in Peter Hull's drawing (above) echoes the
front of Broadcasting House at a smaller scale
and, whereas the front of Broadcasting House
relates to Regent Street, the new extension
faces the spire of All Souls as a kind of
supplicant.

Right The complementary relationship
between massive convexity and delicate
concavity. The glass cone and spire of light are
equivalent to the radio mast of Broadcasting
House.

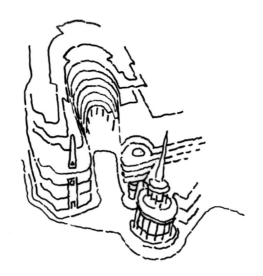

of terrace. The supermarket is set back from the street so that the
cafe, kitchen and staff room combine to form the last 'house' in
the historic core of the town. Although inevitably bulkier than the
housing the project seems nonetheless in keeping with the
incongruities of scale characteristic of Corve Street.

The redevelopment of the BBC's Broadcasting House at the
north end of Regent Street is the ultimate testimony of MJP's ability
to design exciting, contemporary buildings while simultaneously
demonstrating a deep appreciation and celebration of the historic
context. The grade-two listed headquarters building and John
Nash's grade-one listed All Souls church informed the principal
concept. The convex ship-like existing building is complemented
by a concave extension, scooped out between its prow and the new
counterpart. The resulting space not only provides a new outdoor
arena for public events, but provides a new setting for All Souls.

So are Richard MacCormac's thoughts of 1995 which opened the
chapter still relevant to the way MJP considers its work in the early
twenty-first century? Certainly the practice still sets a course distinct
from those who pursue technology as an end and those who seek
solace in established styles. Now however MJP finds itself in the
company of architects such as Richard Murphy, Tony Fretton,
Caruso St John and Sergison Bates, who together represent a
faction of British architecture characterised by concern for aspects
such as memory, conviviality and the everyday.

In the first decade of the twenty-first century, says MacCormac,
MJP has become more specifically interested in 'the reciprocal
relationship with a new building's neighbours, than in "context".
There should be an exchange between a new building and its
surroundings that is more than mere imitation; the newcomer has
an obligation that is akin to a kind of "citizenship".' Today, it seems
that 'reciprocal' is a more accurate and meaningful word to
describe MJP's approach to history, than 'contextual'. In the
convex-concave relationship between Broadcasting House and
MJP's new development this notion of reciprocity is perfectly
illustrated; the concave space carved out between the two is the
negative expression of Broadcasting House's stone prow, with the
new building on the Egton House site refering to and respecting
the form of the prow, without directly imitating it.

1 Richard MacCormac, The Presence of the Past, Five Buildings catalogue (1995).
2 Dan Cruickshank, Why plundering the past is not always the answer, Architects'
Journal (20 January 1993).
3 Hugh Pearman, Romantic with a Design Blue, Sunday Times (12 July 1992).
4 Peter Buchanan, Cambridge Expands, Architecture (Sept 1996).
5 Richard MacCormac, Architecture, Memory and Metaphor, The Architecture of
Information catalogue, British Pavilion, Venice Biennale (1996).
6 ibid
7 John Britton, The Union of Architecture, Sculpture and Painting (1827).
8 as 1
9 The other schemes were at Strathleven Road, Mauleverer Road, Sandmere Road and
Kildoran Road in Brixton, Selby Road in Tottenham, and Cubitt Terrace in Clapham.

Conviviality

Conviviality

Richard Sennett
What vital ingredients are needed to produce sociable architecture?

The work of Richard MacCormac and MJP makes good on the promise of a sociable architecture – an architecture which invites people to interact, an architecture which enables them to study, work, shop, and dwell amicably. Most architects practicing today promise to achieve this result, few make good on it. I've been long intrigued by how and why MJP has succeeded; its buildings stimulate sociability in subtle ways.

MacCormac attracted the notice of urbanists outside Britain early on in his career by his use of materials; his is a very sensuous architecture, mixing wood, steel, glass and stone, friendly to colour as well as to light. In the 1980s, when his work began to be known, it seemed to argue against an ethos of austerity in which a building's form counts for more than its materiality. In the making of urban architecture, in particular, formalism has a deadening social consequence: austerity subordinates the massed inhabitants of a building to becoming mere spectators; the awe inspired by pure form is passive. In the heyday of austere formalism, architects did not produce architecture which invited a more active, engaged response – yet here was a British architect producing buildings of an almost Mediterranean warmth.

So much was immediately obvious: MJP produced, and continues to produce, a very tactile architecture, buildings people feel they can touch. The subtlety of the work lies in the formal consequences of tactile architecture.

In the history of modern architecture, MacCormac's forms may seem closest in spirit to someone in northern Europe, Alvar Aalto. As with Aalto, throughout his career MacCormac has sought to make buildings which, no matter how large in scale, are shorn of monumentality, even in so large a structure as the giant BBC project in central London. Aalto's way of combatting monumentality lies principally in the use of light, light which fragments solid form. MacCormac's way of minimising the monumental uses the solids of a building in unexpected ways.

As he writes in this book, he wants to harness 'chance encounters' in buildings through placing walls, orienting corridors, cutting entrances and windows in ways which are not severely functional. He envisions the circulation systems which result as 'social thoroughfares'; the odd solids break up and subvert merely mechanical flow. Sometimes and prosaically described as the 'water-cooler principle', this sensitivity to spaces for unprogrammed encounter gives life both to individual structures and to MJP's masterplans for urban streets.

One subtle strength of this work, then, is the marriage of the tactile to the informal. A particularly strong bond between the two appears in the Cable & Wireless College at Coventry where, unexpectedly, the dining hall becomes a hub for all the other activities of the college; the noise of dining, and of hanging out here between meals, is acoustically separated but visually integrated to the rest of the college's life. The design of the dining hall itself fragments long, linear tables with round pods and bits of gallery above the diners; strong, contrasting colours tie the top and the bottom of the tall dining hall together. The materials, like the students, talk and argue; it's a good place to hang out.

MacCormac refers to this marriage of tactile and informal architecture as 'convivial', a word which suggests the pleasures of intimacy. I think this word does him a disservice; I'd add the word 'public', since it invites sociability as well among strangers.

One of MJP's most impressive urban schemes is David Prichard's revamp of part of Milton Keynes, a British new town that has only partly worked. Though efficiently designed in its original planning, the town has suffered from a weak social glue among its parts. Prichard sought to glue houses together through such simple devices as pergolas, and to use a mix of materials to relieve the stripped-down feel of much low-cost housing. Urbanistically, uses are layered over each other outside the house; there are unexpected meeting points, abetting informality; though small in size, the housing feels complex in scale. Above all, this is a scheme which invites strangers in.

MJP's urbanism in London, as in Shadwell Basin in the Docklands and the Vining Street project in Brixton, issues just the same invitation. At a time when the gated community has become the model for local residential development, MJP have made an important declaration about the politics of urban architecture: this is that the formal barriers between inside and outside have to be reduced. It's not a new declaration; Jane Jacobs argued a half century for permeable edges between within and without. MJP have found ways to build that permeability.

The public architecture practiced by MJP is essentially theatrical in character. That is, it treats both solid buildings and the open spaces around them as stages. The analogy is not mine; it's often been observed about the firm's work that it emphasises visual drama – but theirs is theatre of a quite special sort.

Drama has long defined both architectural practice and urban design. All theatre sharpens the senses; the question is how it does so. The Ringstrasse in Vienna exemplifies one kind of architectural drama, its buildings writing large the grandeur of a regime already politically and economically in decline; the theatre, university and government palace were literally larger than life. The realm of formalist austerity in which Richard MacCormac began his practice tended to the Ringstrasse idea of architectural drama, even if the modern buildings looked nothing like their imperial predecessors. Modern 'starchitecture' also tends to the Ringstrasse version of visual drama; it may at times produce great art, but is socially perverse, in the sense that the inhabitants are forced to remain spectators.

Quite another version of theatricality was formulated by Sebastiono Serlio in the Renaissance; for him, the built fabric of the city functions like a stage set for social action. This scene-setting is not neutral: it has to encourage the human players to interact; grandeur and monumentality, architecture larger than life, will inhibit them from doing so. For Serlio, the scenography of urban life has to suggest, above all, how the inhabitants of a city could actually live, as actors rather than spectators. It's this tradition into which the projects in this book fit.

As I've come to know more closely the work of MJP, it's reminded me of the scenography of the Merce Cunningham dance group, with whom I worked as a young man. That dance theatre emphasised scenography as, in Cunningham's words, 'a light enclosure', something realised in stone, glass and steel in the permeable walls of this architecture which focus attention on human entrances and exits rather than on the wall-solid in itself; the informal character of human encounters in these buildings shares something with Cunningham dancers improvising on stage; or again, the tactile, touchable feel of the buildings seems more akin to the bodily arousal of modern dance than of classical ballet.

Whatever these particular reactions are worth, I think it's generally right to say that the projects in this volume show how the dramatic work of arousal can be achieved visually strictly in terms of framing and scene-setting. 'Light enclosure' is their method – the method of all social architecture, whether convivial among intimates or public among strangers.

Richard Sennett was born in Chicago in 1943 and grew up in the Cabrini Green Housing Project, one of the first racially-mixed public housing projects in the United States. A promising musical career was curtailed in 1963 by a hand injury. He studied at the University of Chicago and at Harvard University, moving to New York where, in the 1970s, he founded, with Susan Sontag and Joseph Brodsky, The New York Institute for the Humanities at New York University. In the mid-1990s Sennett began to divide his time between New York University and the London School of Economics. His publications include The Uses of Disorder (1970), The Fall of Public Man (1977), The Conscience of the Eye, (1990), Flesh and Stone (1992) and The Craftsman (2008).

3 Conviviality

Edwin Lutyens' Homewood (1900), Knebworth, was built for his mother-in-law, the Countess of Lytton. The theme of a classical pavilion wrapped in a farmhouse is explored in Cottesford Crescent in Milton Keynes.

Collins' dictionary defines convivial as 'sociable, jovial or festive, from the Latin convivium – a living together'. The creation of convivial environments is something that instinctively concerns MJP, both in the way they design buildings, and the way in which they practise architecture; members of the office certainly seem to have an appetite for parties and need little excuse to share a pint at the neighbouring Pride of Spitalfields pub. Encouraging social interaction – whether by chance encounter or more formal meeting – is central to the development of almost all of their projects, from housing and education schemes, to offices, museums and masterplans.

Spitalfields is at the junction of two very different types of city. To the west lies the City of London with its large office blocks overlaid on the intricate medieval street pattern. To the north and east is the East End, with its vibrant street life, markets, and multi-use buildings, not all of them small-scale (think of Spitalfields Market and Truman's Brewery), but almost all are low-rise. On the doorstep are the myriad small curry houses lining either side of Brick Lane, and a short walk to the west is the vast Skidmore, Owings & Merrill and Arup Associates-designed Broadgate development alongside Liverpool Street Station. You can wander among the bric-a-brac stalls in the covered market, newly extended by Foster & Partners, past the houses and studios of leading contemporary artists such as Tracey Emin, Jake and Dinos Chapman and Gilbert and George, or rub shoulders with City traders in a nearby pub or wine bar. It is a cosmopolitan environment perfectly suited to the personality of the practice.

Community and privacy

As a student at Cambridge, Richard MacCormac had been drawn to the seminal book by Serge Chermayeff and Christopher Alexander, *Community and Privacy: Toward a New Architecture of Humanism* (1963). The authors likened houses to towns, with shared spaces and private refuges, a notion that seemed to be embodied in Frank Lloyd Wright's Wingspread, a family house in which the independent parent, children, guest and staff wings come together in a central forum. Spurred on by the investigations of architects such as Aldo van Eyck, who referred to rooms within houses as 'bunches of places', and Louis Kahn, who talked of 'societies of rooms', MacCormac became preoccupied by the characteristics that are common to cities, workplaces and housing, irrespective of scale.

These ideas were developed in the small-scale housing projects that formed the focus of much of MJP's early work. The architects experimented with the design of homes that could be reconfigured so as to accommodate the different stages of family life. MacCormac's winning scheme for the Huddersfield Building Society competition in 1972, much influenced by Chermayeff and Alexander, was just such a house. The single-storey house could be inhabited as a single home in its entirety, it could be used in two halves, with distinct adult and children territories, or it could be reconfigured to accommodate a granny flat. The linearity of the house, with separate points of access along its length, was likened to a railway carriage.

This organisational idea came to fruition in two houses in Blackheath, designed by MacCormac with Peter Bell. The

Plan and model of grouped court houses at Woughton Green in Milton Keynes (1973).

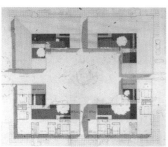

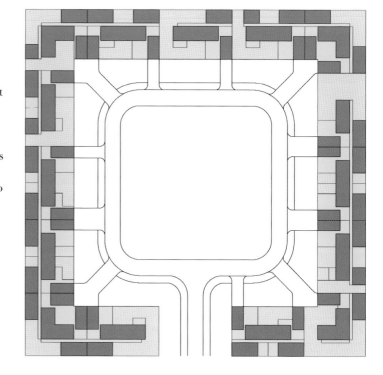

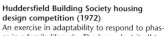

Huddersfield Building Society housing design competition (1972)
An exercise in adaptability to respond to phases in a family lifecycle. The house lent itself to modular timber-frame prefabrication.

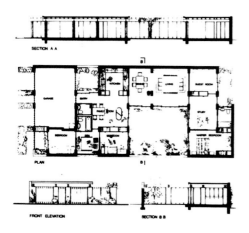

Blackheath houses (1972-74)
Like the Woughton Green project (1973, opposite) the Blackheath scheme developed ideas about family territories with kitchens forming the pivot between adults and children or formal and informal living areas.

Cottesford Crescent, Milton Keynes (1981-84)
The kitchen is centrally located and relates to the surrounding range of formal and informal spaces.

Organisation

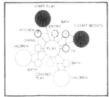
Pinwheels

Typology

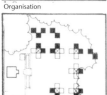
Cruciform

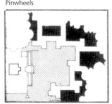
Spaces

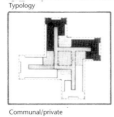
Communal/private

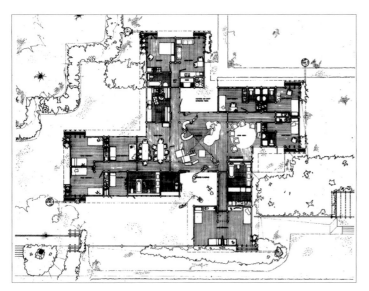

MacIntyre School, Westoning Manor, Bedfordshire (1972-75)
In this housing project for children with special needs, the staff and childrens' wings come together around a central living area which is distinguished by its greater volume. Like a game of dominoes the wings of the house combine to suggest distinct outdoor spaces.
Top: Interior of children's bedroom.
Middle: Diagrams showing 'pinwheel' plans.

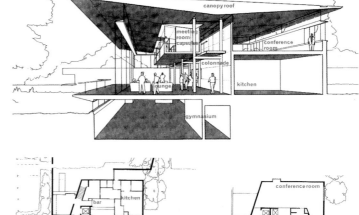

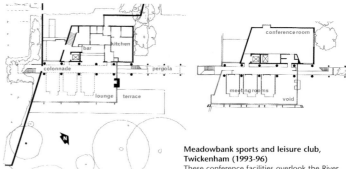

Meadowbank sports and leisure club, Twickenham (1993-96)
These conference facilities overlook the River Thames; the breakout spaces dramatically suspended from the colonnade open into the double-height conference area.

Blackheath houses were followed by a project for grouped court houses in Woughton Green, Milton Keynes which, although never built, led to a related scheme in Milton Keynes at Cottesford Crescent, Great Linford, which was completed in 1980. 'They were sparked off by a house that Edwin Lutyens designed for his mother-in-law, a little classical pavilion around which was wrapped a farmhouse. It had an extraordinary duality. One face was formal and the other was domestic and rural', says MacCormac. This duality was exploited in the Great Linford scheme, which appeared like a classical cube, clad in white panels marked by timber cover strips, and wrapped by a single-storey brick house containing the garage, kitchen, utility areas and a playroom.

The Huddersfield and Blackheath schemes shared relationships that were adaptable to evolving family arrangements. A group of ten timber houses designed for children with special needs at the MacIntyre School, Westoning Manor, in Bedfordshire, demonstrated a different formal response to the provision of privacy, this time within a communal environment. The cruciform shape of the individual houses created a series of 'pinwheels' which combined together to form courts.

At Meadowbank, a club and conference building designed for Cable & Wireless for a site overlooking the River Thames at Twickenham, the building's conference functions generated a relationship between the large central space and the breakout rooms. The design was inherently adaptable and, when the client sold the building its fate was the reverse of Frank Lloyd Wright's Wingspread. Wright's pinwheel plan lent itself to conversion into a conference centre with associated residential and breakout space, while MJP's Meadowbank club was readily adapted into an unusually spacious private residence.

In 2003 Richard MacCormac was invited by the architectural writer Charles Jencks to join a list of well-known architects who were designing Maggie's Centres around the UK – holistic cancer support and care facilities built in memory of Jencks' late wife Maggie Keswick. MJP's project, associated with but independent from Cheltenham Royal Hospital, is informed by the need to provide a convivial atmosphere for patients to socialise both with each other and with their families, as well as providing private, contemplative spaces. The scheme, which extends an existing lodge, is house-like rather than institutional, and creates territories that are both shared and private. A major social space, which incorporates the kitchen and dining area, occupies the centre of the plan. An inglenook is amplified into a little 'house' for quiet conversation, beyond which is another more secluded living space. Outside these core areas two private refuges overlook the garden and the river Chelt, recalling Frank Lloyd Wright's houses that create contrasts between prospect and refuge. Here, the refuges have good prospects too.

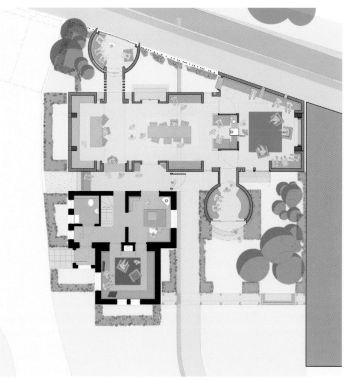

Maggie's Centre, Cheltenham (2003-)
The living areas are contained and subdivided by smaller enclosures to create a sociable environment which supports group and private conversation.

**Pollards Hill (above) and Eastfields (below),
London Borough of Merton (1967-70)**
The Merton housing schemes comprise three
storeys with private gardens opening onto safe
shared spaces for children. The schemes
achieved the same densities as the towers and
slab blocks being built at the time in other
London boroughs.

Houses and neighbourhoods

The political and social upheavals of the 1960s, during which
Richard MacCormac and Peter Jamieson were students at
Cambridge, clearly played a part in influencing their subsequent
early housing work. MacCormac admits to participating in 'a bit of
a rebellion at Cambridge, because we thought that sociology was
really important and tried to insist that it was part of the
curriculum. So I went to work for Peter Wilmott at the Institute of
Community Studies, Michael Young's initiative, in Bethnal Green.'
Wilmott and Young's 1957 study Family and Kinship in East
London had been of particular interest to MacCormac. He was
attracted to the institute's investigations into the links between
social and physical organisation, something he explored in a social
survey in Stevenage New Town in 1963-64, which made him 'alert
to people's prejudices and the way in which they use spaces'.

When MacCormac came to work for the London Borough of
Merton he continued to investigate and write about problems and
solutions in social housing. By then he was certain in his conviction
that high-rise was not the solution for family accommodation. Like
a number of south London boroughs, Merton was committed to
using industrialised building systems which resulted in subsequently
notorious developments such as Angell Town in Lambeth.
MacCormac's quest – along with Peter Bell, David Lea and Nicholas

Duffryn, Newport (1974-78, right)
The most extensive application of perimeter development around school and recreational land, with low-rise housing (957 units) on a park and woodland site in South Wales.

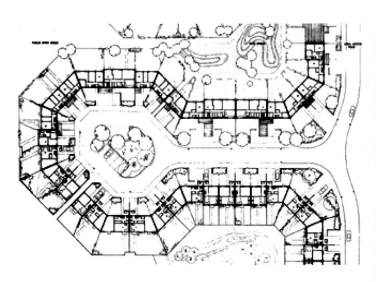

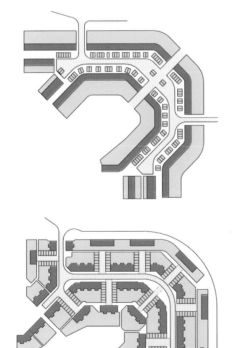

France Furlong, Great Linford, Milton Keynes (1975-78)
The overall layout follows the site contours in a series of faceted curves, but the terraces are broken up, with alternating units being pushed out from the road. This allows spaces for parking courts and allowed MJP to introduce a system of pathways behind back gardens, providing an explorable children's world. The plans show the initial proposed layout, with continuous curving blocks, and the final layout.

Alexander – was to find ways of giving every family a house with a
parking space, a small garden and access to a shared space that
would be safe for children. 'I'm not sure we ever got that
completely right', says MacCormac, 'but we had broken the then
conventional wisdom of high-rise.'

The MJP project that relates most directly to the early work at
Pollards Hill and Eastfields (for Merton Borough, 1967-70) is a
scheme for 957 houses and flats in Duffryn, Newport (1974-8), for
which they were the masterplan architects. The aim was to design
groups of wide-fronted houses with as much accommodation as
possible related to the large private back gardens. The geometry
was relatively simple, and it developed to great advantage in the
subsequent scheme at Great Linford, France Furlong, the first of
several housing projects in Milton Keynes by MJP, where the single
terrace-type of Duffryn was broken and layered into shorter groups
of houses to create a pattern of enclosed spaces connected by lanes.
The design of 350 flats and houses for the Warrington New Town
Corporation at Oakwood (1977) followed the France Furlong
scheme and continued the architects' growing interest in perimeter
development as a model for suburban housing.

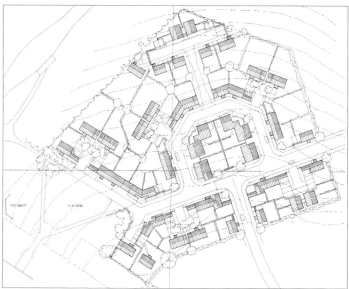

Great Holm, Milton Keynes (1982-84)
Affordable family housing with 50 dwellings, mostly three-bedroom houses, and some two-bedroom bungalows and one-bedroom 'starter' homes.

Shenley Church End, Milton Keynes (1987-90)
Housing scheme for 50 dwellings.

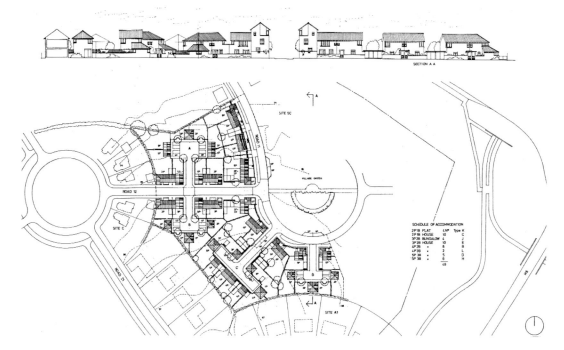

SECTION A.A

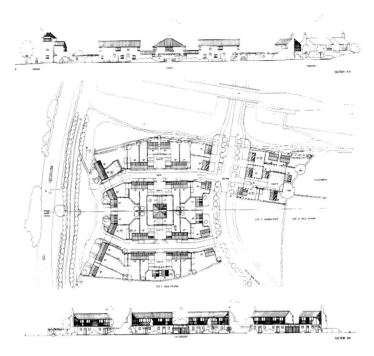

The later projects in Milton Keynes, mostly led by David Prichard, sustained the typological idea of maximising density by maximising linearity, but with the more complex and fragmented layers initiated by the France Furlong project. By breaking down the scale and moving from generalities to more specific solutions, the results became increasingly interesting. A particular concern for Prichard was the character of the spaces between the houses. 'We had a deep commitment to the sense of arrival and the quality of the common space. Details such as pergolas and rails from which to hang plants were inevitably extra to the brief, but they could be added without significant extra cost.'

These low-cost housing schemes were built to design-and-build contracts and turned around very quickly, with some starting on site as little as 15 weeks after the initial commission. Prichard developed a method of setting up a schedule of drawings from a site plan, and many of the details were repeated across the schemes. 'It was a question of how to allocate the budget and ration resources, and how to invest intellectual effort in the right places at the right time.'

In parallel with these projects the practice undertook studies into the relationships between housing and land-use and these were developed in the concept for a new rural settlement planned in Cambridgeshire by Stanhope called Great Common Farm. The central observation was that new settlements such as Milton Keynes were taking up too much land and were unnecessarily dispersed. By some measures, the gross density in Milton Keynes was as low as five dwellings per hectare, against an average of around 25-40 per hectare within its estates. It seemed that the extravagant road network and extensive areas of landscape and buffer zones between developments were creating this disparity. Not only did this seem wasteful of land, but it also resulted in excessive expenditure on infrastructure, particularly roads, in linking the separate and socially discontinuous developments.

There was also the key social issue of security. In densely populated urban areas, houses tend to overlook the streets but many newly planned environments, such as Milton Keynes, with networks of roads and footpaths and isolated estates, have proved far from secure. The architects concluded that it might be possible to leave out part of the conventional road system. Richard MacCormac published a hypothetical study in the Architectural Review called

Willen Park, Milton Keynes (1983-85)
This 48-house scheme is located adjacent to the Grand Union Canal. Houses immediately next to the canal have living rooms with balconies on the first floor. All houses front village-like streets with discreet car parking in courts. The design reflects traditional canal-side buildings, with simple brick elevations with black-stained boarding and painted balconies.

Bradwell Common, Milton Keynes (1985)
Scheme for 26 homes.

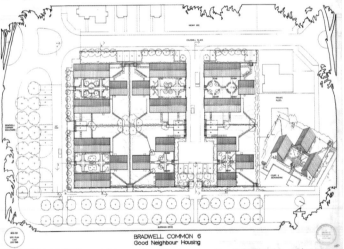

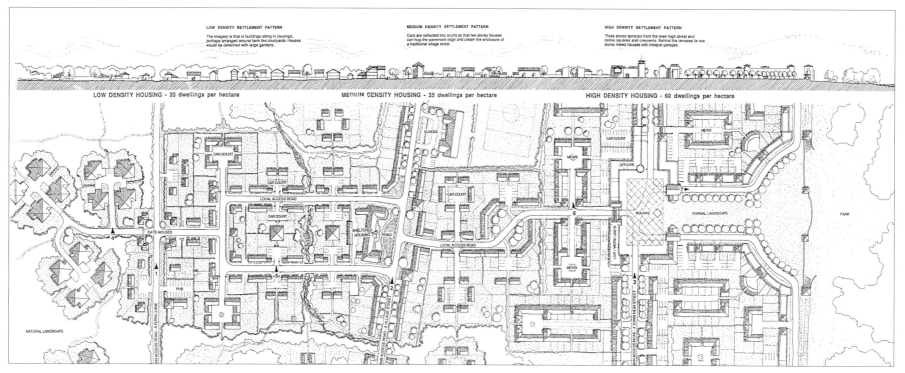

LOW DENSITY SETTLEMENT PATTERN

The imagery is that of buildings sitting in clearings, perhaps arranged around farm like courtyards. Houses would be detached with large gardens.

MEDIUM DENSITY SETTLEMENT PATTERN

Cars are collected into courts so that two storey houses can hug the pavement ridge and create the enclosure of a traditional village street.

HIGH DENSITY SETTLEMENT PATTERN

Three storey terraces front the town high street and define squares and crescents. Behind the terraces lie two storey mews houses with integral garages.

LOW DENSITY HOUSING - 20 dwellings per hectare

MEDIUM DENSITY HOUSING - 35 dwellings per hectare

HIGH DENSITY HOUSING - 60 dwellings per hectare

Great Common Farm, Cambridgeshire (1990-91)
A privately-funded new town was planned by Stanhope who approached MJP to design a single prototype grid square. But rather than design an isolated square, MJP proposed a character study of how a theoretical section of the town, from rural edge low density, through suburban middle density, to market town higher density, would look and feel. The study demonstrated how the road hierarchy fundamentally determines the character of the places.

Left High density – mews houses with integral garages.
Middle Medium density – semi-detached houses around car courts.
Bottom Low density – detached houses with lounge gardens.

Suburban Syntax (1985), which suggested that 'you might keep the primary fast road system but omit the local distributor system to create high streets straight off the primary system. The densely populated high streets would be sufficient to sustain public transport and residents would be able to get in and out of the city quickly. It would be a cellular network of perimeter developments around public space allocated to functions such as parks and allotments or playing fields, all recognisable kinds of common space. The idea was to be much more deliberate and economical about how land was used. Today we would call this sustainable development.'

MJP's commitment to residential development led to a major project at Ballymun, north of Dublin. The challenge was to prepare a masterplan for the regeneration of a run-down 1960s estate made famous by author Roddy Doyle as a place of roaming horses and drug addiction. MJP's proposal focused on the creation of a rejuvenated town for 30,000 people with its own main street and, crucially, a new open space and road hierarchy to bring distinctive identities to the five constituent neighbourhoods. Here, the roads are used not as boundaries but rather, explains David Prichard, as tools for place-making. The dual carriageway that had previously divided the estate has been narrowed and traffic tamed and, with the addition of new civic facilities, has become the new heart of Ballymun.

Coultry Park Terrace, one of the first completed projects, takes its cues from the buildings of central Dublin. Long curved terraces overlook the new Coultry Park, reflecting the eighteenth century Dublin squares, with prominent staircases and a rhythm of rendered fronts on a continuous background of brickwork. The close behind the three-storey terraces houses two-storey cottages, also drawing on precedents in Dublin.

David Prichard recalls 'driving around the site in the pouring rain and feeling increasingly desperate, with the huge swathes of featureless space and no sense of place'. The immediate problems centred on the failing fabric of a 15-storey tower and eight-storey slab blocks and the council's letting policy which concentrated young single-parent families in this isolated location. The estate lacked both security and any kind of convivial social space. At the outset Prichard organised a series of public consultations with the aim of ensuring that the stakeholders had a sense of ownership in the redevelopment. To the amazement of all concerned 2,000 people turned up to the open planning day, and more than 5,000 visited the public exhibition of the masterplan.

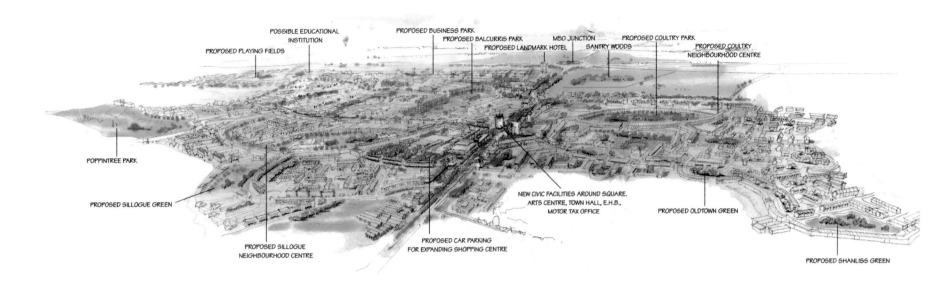

PROPOSED PLAYING FIELDS
POSSIBLE EDUCATIONAL INSTITUTION
PROPOSED BUSINESS PARK
PROPOSED BALCURRIS PARK
PROPOSED LANDMARK HOTEL
M50 JUNCTION
SANTRY WOODS
PROPOSED COULTRY PARK
PROPOSED COULTRY NEIGHBOURHOOD CENTRE
POPPINTREE PARK
PROPOSED SILLOGUE GREEN
PROPOSED SILLOGUE NEIGHBOURHOOD CENTRE
PROPOSED CAR PARKING FOR EXPANDING SHOPPING CENTRE
NEW CIVIC FACILITIES AROUND SQUARE. ARTS CENTRE, TOWN HALL, E.H.B., MOTOR TAX OFFICE
PROPOSED OLDTOWN GREEN
PROPOSED SHANLISS GREEN

Ballymun Masterplan, Dublin (1998)
Site plan and diagrams illustrating Ballymun's regeneration with roads and open spaces given new identities.

Approach to Ballymun from the M50 motorway – the tree-lined fast road gives the first impression, and traffic slows as it approaches the Main Street with traffic light controlled crossings.

Ballymun Road as a Main Street with 4-5 storey buildings with tree-lined colonnades fronting shops, showrooms and offices.

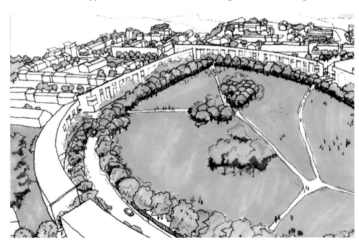

The new park in Coultry gives the village a specific identity and a social focus.

Village Green in Shanagan – the destination and focus for this community.

Sustainable Suburbia
Housing Density Study (2007–)
The circular diagrams represent 5000 dwellings within a 600 metre radius (about 10 minutes' walk), ie 100 hectares at 50 dwellings per hectare. The square diagrams show how a generic cluster of 26 houses can be varied to provide different configurations of suburban space. The perspective view shows patterns of open space and local intensifications of density.

MJP's considerable experience in researching and constructing housing over three decades has been brought together in an evolving study called Sustainable Suburbia which, in some respects, anticipated the government planning policy statement PPS3. 'The aim', explains MacCormac, 'is to demonstrate how to reconcile the suburban objectives of family houses, with front doors onto the street, private garden, parking and so on, with the communal – which is usually associated with higher urban densities. The objective is a maximum of ten-minutes walk to shops, schools, employment and transport networks to reduce car dependence. Around 5,000 homes at a density of at least 50 per hectare can achieve this.' This ongoing study has attracted interest from central and local government as well as volume housebuilders and MJP is

currently developing a density primer to aid in masterplanning.

The development of the project for a rural settlement at Great Common Farm in Cambridgeshire, which initiated a denser suburban layout with a hierarchy of different house types, suggested the organisational structure for a contrasting urban scheme at Lavender Dock (1983). The client body, the London Docklands Development Corporation, was something of a welcome anomoly in an era when local authorities were being stripped of their power. MJP persuaded the corporation that the river frontage would be be appropriate for eight-storey buildings which, in the years before Canary Wharf emerged, was considered tall. MJP's idea derived from the Warrington project (in which four-storey apartment buildings faced a major distributor road), and the

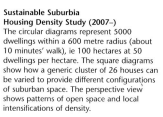

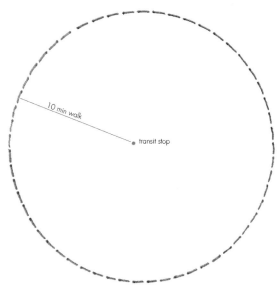

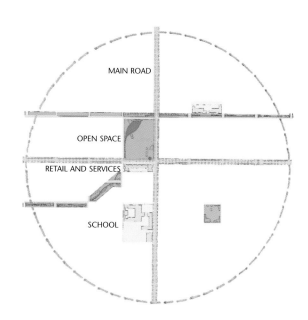

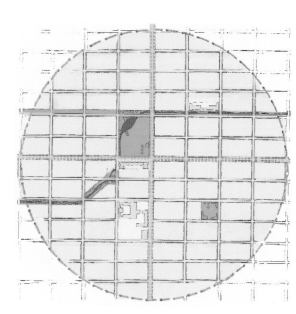

Lavender Dock East, London Docklands (1983)
MJP was commissioned in 1982 by the LDDC
to produce a guideline study for 230 units.

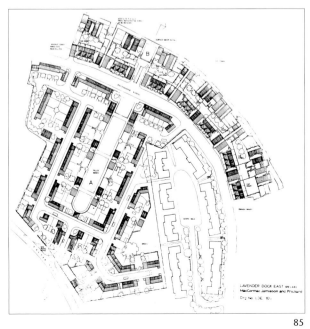

**Shadwell Basin, London Docklands
(1982-87)**
Homes are designed with masonry pavilions to
house the smaller rooms, while the larger
living rooms have lightweight glass and metal
screens incorporating balconies that overlook
the basin.

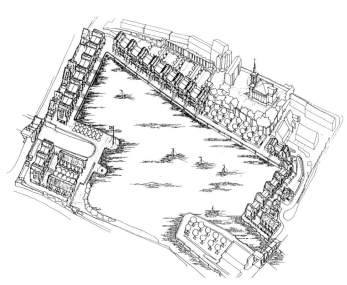

composition evolved as a landscape of different house-types and densities to build up a topography of low density in the hinterland to the high density of dramatic tall buildings along the river. 'The composition was an array of "peaks" on the river bend, with a twin split peak heralding the axis of the new basin to bring the value of the river views deeper into the site', says MacCormac.

At Shadwell Basin, across the river from Lavender Dock, MJP built 217 houses and flats set behind the remains of high nineteenth century dockyard security walls, with a range of building types that referenced the local warehouses and dockmasters' houses. The imagery was influenced too by Jesse Hartley's celebrated Albert Dock in Liverpool (1845), with its bold colonnade and arches facing onto the publicly accessible quayside. A comparatively high density was achieved by arranging the flats with service rooms, kitchens and bathrooms in the middle of the plan, and living space and bedrooms front and back.

The attention generated by Shadwell Basin led developer Stuart Lipton and the London Regeneration Consortium to commission MJP in 1990 to undertake a study for the social housing provision within the initial Kings Cross railway lands regeneration project. Working within Foster & Partners' masterplan, another firm of architects had been struggling with the very high densities, and had responded with tall buildings needing lifts, access galleries and underground car parking. MJP identified a political dimension to the problem in Islington council's demand for a quantum of housing too great for the area of site that the developer was prepared to concede. MJP took the view that the residential capacity of the site should be determined by the density they could achieve with no cars underground, no lifts and no access galleries.

With a mix of five-storey flats and narrow-frontage terraced housing for families, however, MJP attained densities of 600 people to the hectare. Shared stairs were exposed at the front of the flats to encourage self-policing and deter vandals, while private staircases, giving access to the top maisonettes, limited the requirement for shared access. 'The limit to density was car parking. Along with back gardens and roads it saturated the ground level. In that sense, the scheme's land use was 100 per cent efficient. The cars could all be parked in small courtyards, overlooked by the residents so that they too would be relatively safe from vandalism', says MacCormac. This innovative unrealised solution for Kings Cross became the basis of the scheme built at Vining Street in Brixton.

Kings Cross housing study for London Regeneration Consortium (1990, left)
For security, shared access stairs are visible, while internal stairs are private.

Vining Street, Brixton (1990, below)
An inner-city housing scheme with a mix of one- and two-person flats, four-person shared short stay accommodation with warden supervision, and four shop units. The shared stairs give access to first-floor flats and internal private stairs to second and third floor maisonettes. Residents like to sit on the front steps talking and playing music.

In 2004, MJP won a competition for the British Embassy Compound in Bangkok comprising six houses and eighteen flats with recreational and staff facilities. In striking contrast to the bustle and crowded character of the city, the compound is designed as a green oasis with the landscape and ambassador's residence revealed through a sequence of views and spaces in the picturesque manner associated with English country houses. The staff accommodation is arranged along the west side of the compound in a mix of flats and houses. All the living spaces face the gardens and have private terraces and hanging gardens.

British Embassy, Bangkok (2005-09) Staff residences; interior of house.
Site plan of the embassy compound: 1 swimming pool, 2 clubhouse, 3 staff accomodation, 4 deputy ambassador's residence, 5 ambassador's residence, 6 consulate, 7 chancery, 8 Gurkhas' mess, 9 gatehouse, 10 workshop, 11 Gurkhas' accommodation, 12 pergola.

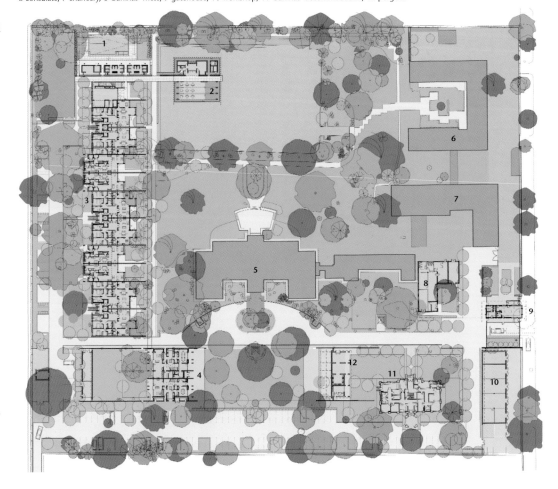

Single person and student accommodation

Coffee Hall, a housing association project completed in 1974 in Milton Keynes, relates both to the Westoning Manor houses and the Robinson College competition of the same year. The key idea was to provide a series of courtyards with routes which intersected at a social focus in the middle. 'A trick, which was to become important in our student residential schemes, was to generate enough frontage by using a courtyard grid, to spin out the area of very small flats into wide frontages with lots of window and uninterrupted back walls – the reverse, for example, of Le Corbusier's Marseille Unité d'Habitation flats.'

In terms of conviviality, a critical observation was made about staircases in Oxbridge colleges, initiated by research by David Roberts, one of MacCormac's former teachers at Cambridge. Roberts had concluded that both staircases and kitchens would become more sociable if they overlooked each other. 'We saw these college buildings as having a convivial core and then the circulation branching off to the individual rooms as private destinations.' The sequence of college schemes, all of which have different permutations of circulation-kitchen relationships, runs through Robinson College, the Sainsbury Building at Worcester College, Fitzwilliam College, Queen Mary Phase 1, Wadham College Bowra Building, St John's Garden Quadrangle, the Wychfield Buildings at Trinity Hall, Cambridge (in which two staircases wind around a double-height living space), Myddelton Street and the Jowett Buildings at Balliol College.

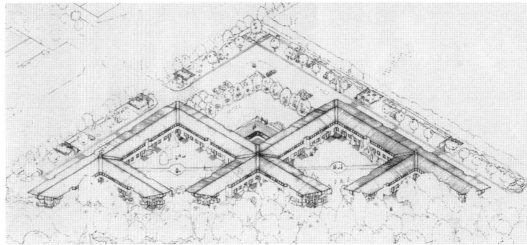

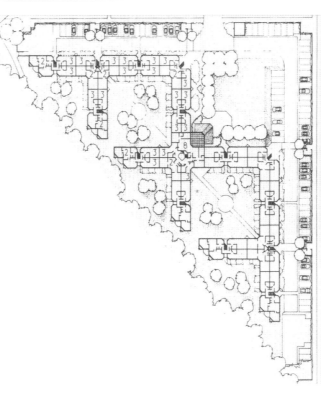

Chapter House, Coffee Hall, Milton Keynes (1974-77)
Some 89 flats for short term rent by single people. The ground floor flats are conventional, with separate bedrooms, and the first-floor bedsitting rooms for younger residents are single aspect with very wide frontages. At the entrance and hub of the scheme there is the common room with bar and laundry and a managers flat.

Robinson College, Cambridge (1974)
Kitchens and voids alternate across a central staircase in this competition proposal. The comparative plans and axonometrics illustrate the relationships between staircases (blue) and kitchens (yellow).

Worcester College, Oxford (1980-83)
Kitchen interior, axonometric, plans and model; the kitchen/dining room space is on axis with the staircase.

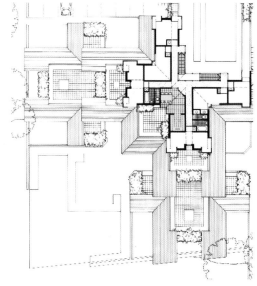

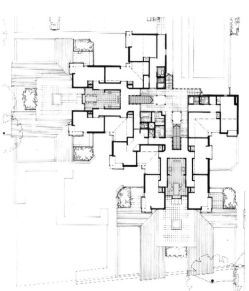

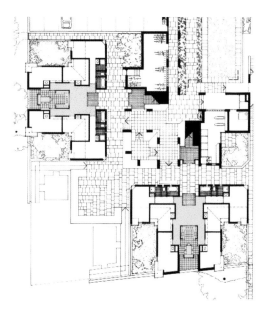

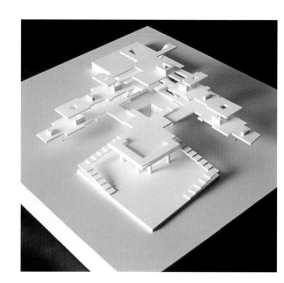

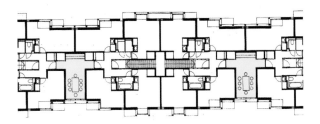

New Court, Fitzwilliam College, Cambridge (1983-86)
Entrance with first-floor kitchen above; from here the staircase splits into two separate flights leading to two further kitchens.

Wychfield, Trinity Hall, Cambridge (1990-93)
Floor plans and interior of kitchen; the kitchens and staircases are arranged around and overlook a double-height living room.

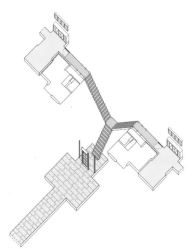

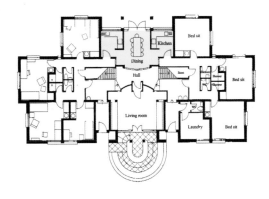

Wadham College, Oxford (1989-92)
First-floor plan and view looking down the street with chapel at end; the first-floor kitchens cantilever out over the street. Wadham, St Johns and Balliol share a similar axial relationship between the staircase and kitchen.

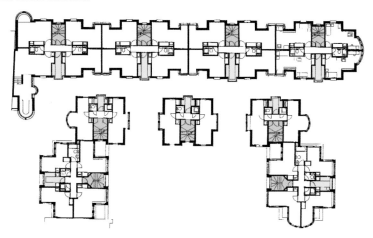

St John's College, Oxford (1990-93)
Terrace-level plan showing kitchens facing outwards and view of first-floor kitchen hung between towers overlooking the terrace.

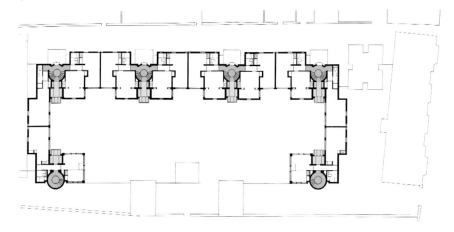

Balliol College, Oxford (1994-2004)
First-floor plan and view of kitchen oriel windows overlooking street.

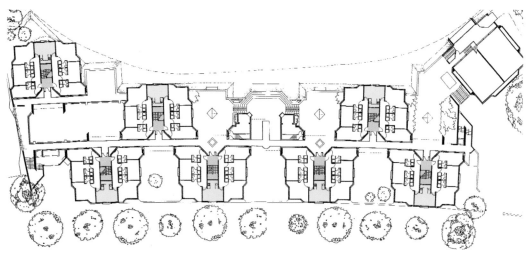

Friendship House, Belvedere Place, Southwark (2001-03)
Right: The spiral form of the building rises to form a marker to the road, while the zinc-tiled wall presents a protective elevation to the railway. Glazed kitchen-dining rooms overlook the entrance.
Below left: The common room forms a social focus within the tight courtyard.
Below right: Common room and main route into the scheme running from the entrance through the courtyard to the rear garden.

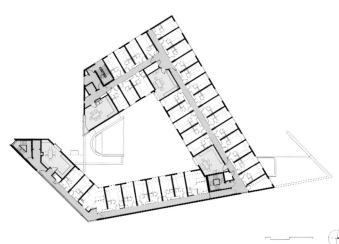

For MJP 'conviviality' is still the word used to describe the social aspect of contemporary architecture. 'For me, conviviality in architecture means something really quite simple – it's finding ways of bringing people together', says director Duncan McKinnon. It involves focusing on those places within buildings that are sometimes overlooked qualitatively, such as circulation spaces, which have social potential. By creating internal and external views and considering issues of light and enabling people to be aware of one another, the treatment of staircases and corridors becomes as critical to the success as the design of the primary spaces.

The London Hostels Association's brief for Friendship House on Belvedere Place in south-east London was different to the practice's other student housing projects as it provides affordable housing for working people as well as student residences. The site was restricted by its location next to a railway viaduct, so the 179 bed-sits were arranged in a tight spiral around a central courtyard with a pool and fountain which reflect light and mask the noise of the nearby railway and roads.

MJP has a long history of working with St John's College, Oxford, the latest aspect of which was the design of new accommodation in Kendrew Quadrangle, a traditional form which was specifically requested by the client. It houses more accommodation than MJP's earlier Garden Quadrangle and is of a comparable scale to some of the college's original quads. The scheme continues the theme of associating the kitchen/dining rooms with the staircases but, to provide efficient disabled access, corridors were required. The kitchens are designed to provide legibility and identity while common facilities – the cafe, library and teaching rooms – are located on the ground floor, with an arts centre to the west of the main quadrangle.

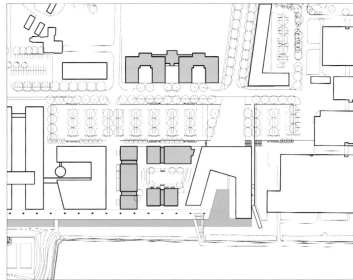

West Cambridge, North and South Residences (2001-04)
Above: Site plan showing the two residences; North (left) and South (right) Residences. The project provides flats for staff and students and a nursery. Four-storey wings are connected by lower accommodation with the nursery at the centre to create three south-facing garden courts which form a focus for the residents and enliven the public realm. The three buildings of the South Residences are developed to an urban density as they sit next to large academic buildings.

Kendrew Quadrangle, St John's College, Oxford (2005-10, left top and bottom)

Social space in the university context

The John Watkins Plaza, which opened in 2003, was an unanticipated development within a wider environmental improvement scheme for the London School of Economics. The brief required a small building to house a cafe on the plaza outside the library. However, MJP convinced the client that what was needed was not a freestanding building but a 'sheltered edge' to the plaza which would provide both a cafe and an external meeting place. Located outside the Lionel Robbins Building and on the roof of the single storey library archive, the plaza quickly established itself and remains a well-used space. The concept of sheltered meeting places defined by canopied structures took a further step in MJP's scheme for London's Victoria Embankment.

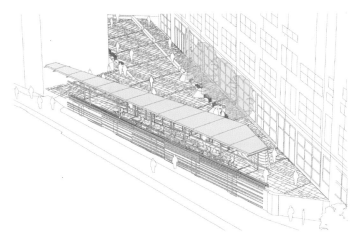

John Watkins Plaza, London School of Economics (1997-2003)
A meeting space of hard and soft landscaping, with a small cafe acting as the social focus. A canopy provides shelter along one edge and defines the space. Its stainless steel 'roof' is a strong feature when viewed from above. Working with artist Bruce Allen, blue LED strips were set in the paving which, with uplighters to the new trees, extend the life of the plaza well into the evening.

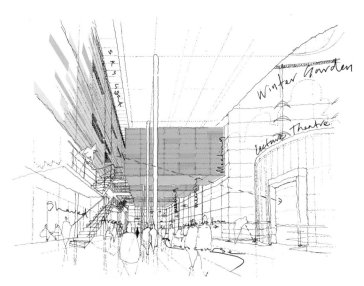

East Forum, West Cambridge (2001)
The East Forum provided a focus for West Cambridge at the point where the main cycle route to the city centre entered the site. With an innovative mix of social facilities, science incubators and offices for entrepreneurs, the building was designed to promote discussion and knowledge transfer. It included a lively double-height street and a winter garden.

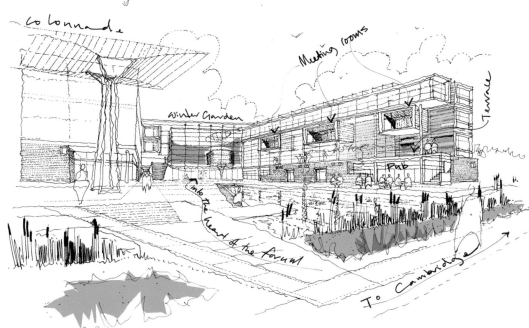

Convivial workplace

Before taking root in Spitalfields, MJP was one of the first tenants to occupy the pioneering shared workspace housed in a converted warehouse at 5 Dryden Street in London's Covent Garden. Set up by architect David Rock, who established his practice there, tenants included artists, magazine publishers, dance company administrators, industrial designers and builders. The idea, new to London, was to share flexible space, facilities and administrative staff, and while there were some cross-collaborations, there was always a sense of community. MJP resolved to establish a similar initiative when it moved to 9 Heneage Street in 1980, forming Spitalfields Workspace, a company distinct from the practice, which still owns the building. Serviced workspaces were made available to small businesses that, like Dryden Street, came from a range of arts and building disciplines. In practical terms the arrangement helped pay off the bank loan for the purchase of the building and ensured that there would be space into which the practice could expand. The foyer provided a venue for exhibitions of artists' work for five years until MJP grew to occupy most of the space.

Also derived from Dryden Street, the Niccol Centre in Cirencester, Gloucestershire (1983), was created from a brewery warehouse about the same size as 9 Heneage Street. The brief was for a community building which would provide recreational and learning opportunities for people who were unemployed or retired. The project had a community theatre at its core and galleries with green rooms around the periphery, which could also be used as workspaces; in addition there were studios, offices for small businesses, a bar and a cafe. A similar unbuilt project on St John Street in Clerkenwell was to incorporate retail units at ground level with workshops in the basement and serviced offices above.

MJP's Spitalfields office in 1982 (left) and 2004 (below).

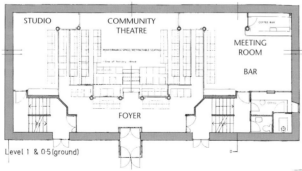

Level 1 & 0·5 (ground)

Niccol Centre, a community centre in Cirencester, Gloucestershire (1984)
A small project derived from ideas at 5 Dryden Street, Covent Garden (1971), was created from a brewery warehouse, about the same size as 9 Heneage Street. The brief was for a building for the unemployed and retired in which both recreation and learning could be embraced. It had a community theatre at its core and galleries and green rooms around the periphery, which could also be workspaces and studios, as well as offices for small businesses, a bar and a cafe. This idea was developed further in an unbuilt scheme for a development in St John's Street, Clerkenwell (below).

St John Street, London (1984, right)
Basement workshops, ground floor retail and offices above.

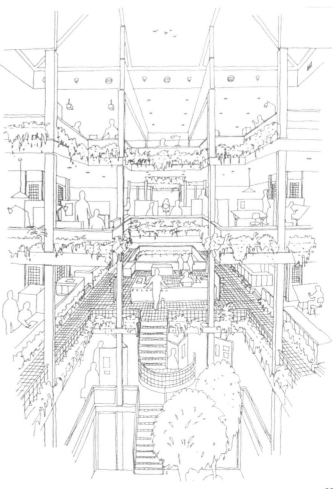

The Hampshire County Council offices in Havant provided a stepping stone between MJP's relatively small early office buildings and the larger city offices of the late 1990s. Here, much against convention at the time, the administrative core for each department occupied a central location within a double-height hall, around which were clustered two floors of cellular offices.

More radical in terms of workplace design, however, is the Cable and Wireless College, near Coventry, which combines teaching, research and residential space. Here, long diagonal routes intersect at an oval oculus, the social heart of the building where a double-height refectory faces onto a garden. The main staff meeting points are located at the ends of the teaching wings and overlook the circulation routes. As in the Faculty of Arts in Bristol, the Informatics Teaching Laboratory at Queen Mary & Westfield College and the BBC's Broadcasting House, the carefully considered arrangement of social and circulation space means that the occupants can both see and be seen with the intention of enhancing the likelihood of chance encounters and social and intellectual exchange.

At Cable & Wireless the individual learning and residential components of the scheme are clearly delineated. The layered parallel bands of naturally-ventilated learning spaces form a welcoming V-shaped entrance court to the south of the site. On the north side the row of residences, with hotel-style rooms arranged on collegiate staircases, is linked to the learning facilities by the oculus, with further recreational and social space, including a swimming pool, housed in a separate pavilion to the east.

Hampshire County Council offices, Havant (1984-89, above, left)
A space designed to increase the possibilities of chance encounters and social exchange.

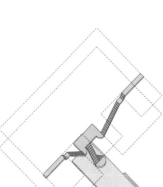

Queen Mary Informatics Teaching Laboratory (1987-89, above, left)

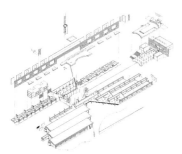

Cable & Wireless Technical College, Warwickshire (1990-93, right, left)
Dining takes place at the focus of the circulation systems which serve the teaching, residential and social components at the college.
Opposite: View from the oculus at the centre of the college towards the swimming pool.

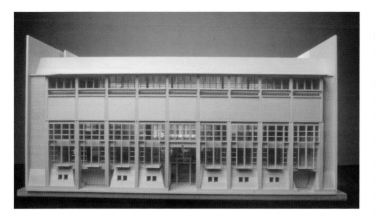

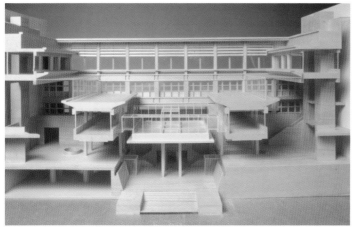

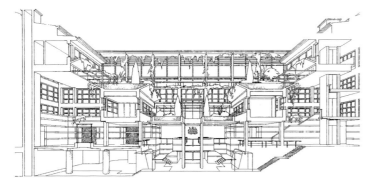

British Embassy, Berlin (1994-95)
This competition design was intended to give the embassy a quintessentially British identity, while engaging with the architectural traditions of Berlin. The site lies immediately west of the medieval city and is part of an urban block bounded on three sides by other developments and constrained by the strict city planning policy that dictated the building line and cornice levels. Floor heights required by the brief produced a facade of imposing scale and presence. The massing responded to the large volume of the site, its need to look inwards and to the historic form of the city block in this part of Berlin. Above a plinth of publicly accessible spaces two parallel ranges of secure offices were arranged at the front and back of the site. Between them a series of bridges spanned a central courtyard. The court was a climate moderator and conserved energy.
Top: Elevation to street.
Middle, bottom: Long sections.

MJP's competition entry for the new British Embassy in Berlin was generated in part by the city's prescriptive planning policy, which defined the cornice level and height of three party walls. The principal elevation was an exercise in classical composition, deriving also from security requirements: stringent guidelines required a secure base, while a glazed band ran along at first-floor level; above, secure spaces were safeguarded from radio interference by a protective frieze, over which hovered a cornice with a loggia-like set-back. Recognising the need for new embassies to accommodate commercial as well as diplomatic functions, the plinth was given over to publicly accessible space, above which two parallel ranges of secure offices were arranged at the front and back of the site. The dramatic interior rose from the entrance in both directions as a cascade of space with top lighting. A stepped roof garden conformed to another planning regulation and climbing plants helped shade the cafe which ran all along the back of the site.

The design of the corporate workplace has shifted away from the idea that productivity is maximised by the greatest production area towards the notion that an organisation's creativity is enhanced by environments that provide settings conducive to staff interaction. In The Changing Workplace, Frank Duffy anticipated the new vocabulary of breakout spaces, table-tennis tables and bean bags. A number of MJP projects are planned so as to promote chance encounters through the systems of circulation and by opening up vertical combinations of space. In the practice's proposal for Marsham Street, circulation running across the edge of the atrium at every floor links the floor plates, overlooks the cafe and connects the breakout spaces and coffee points. At Warwick Court at Paternoster Square an internal 'street' connects the two entrances on Paternoster Square and Warwick Lane while a stepped atrium unifies the whole building.

At Broadcasting House the east-west circulation across the centre of the site was interpreted as an interstitial zone of social activity lying between the five production buildings. From this MJP developed an internal landscape with a rich and varied series of 'settings'; the convivial spaces, for example, are signalled by complex and interlocking double-height spaces that are quite distinct from the wide, relatively low-ceilinged production areas. These spaces would be traversed daily by staff emerging from lifts or visiting tea and coffee points. Stairs with landings large enough for impromptu meetings visibly link the floors (which fire escape stairs do not) and enhance the possibilities of social and intellectual exchange. These spaces would also create an intermediary between the general scale of the interior and the scale of Regent Street. In this sense the double-height spaces and staircases behind the concave facade function as porticos similar in intent as Schinkel's Altes Museum in Berlin, where inside-outside spaces dramatically engage with views across the city.

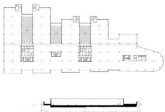

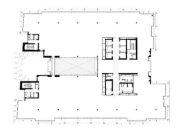

Marsham Street, London (1999), plan showing 'thoroughfare' in yellow; Warwick Court at Paternoster Square, London (1996-2003), section and plan.

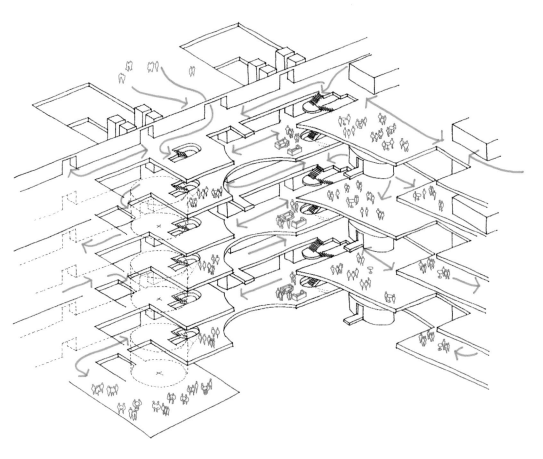

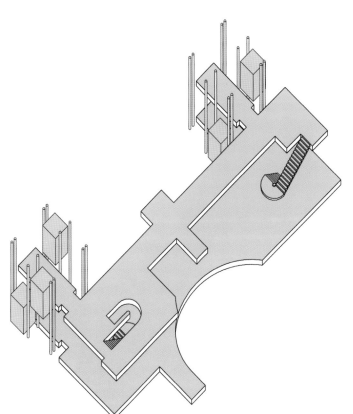

BBC Broadcasting House, London (2000-06)
Diagrams showing interlocking double-height social and circulation spaces, plus sequence of images showing breakout spaces.

Urban projects

MJP's exploration of the city as a diverse environment that can bring people together began around 1979 when they were asked by the Italian broadcaster RAI to develop ideas about cities of the future for a television programme. A decision was made to concentrate on Spitalfields, and in particular the market; this was strangely prescient, given the practice's subsequent decision to move the office from Covent Garden. The programme was made in Venice where MJP and a group of students undertook analyses of the city, and this uncovered some unexpected ideas that were to stay with them. Observations were made about how people used places and how they were animated by people, rather than simply how they appear – how and why do people congregate in specific places, and what keeps them there? The group's observation of the permeability of public and private spaces in Venice led to ideas in the Spitalfields study about compatible arrangements between non-permeable buildings, such as offices, and permeable local facilities. In this, MJP's first Spitalfields study, the mix of retail and business facilities at ground level represented the notion that local life could slide in underneath the world of corporate capitalism. 'We called it the lasagne project', says MacCormac. 'The mixed development was the sauce, and the lasagne itself represented the capitalist layers above it. It entranced the Italian television crews who had never suspected that we'd produce the real dish for the cameras!'

This vision of mixed development was pursued in the real world with the Spitalfields Development Group through the late 1980s and early 1990s in two masterplans. The first, with Fitzroy Robinson, was granted planning permission in 1987, but never realised. MJP resigned from the second masterplan in 1992 when the executive architects and the client's motivations changed and the social and urban agendas set by MJP looked to be lost for good.

Lasagne Project, Venice (1979)
Lasagne acted as a metaphor for reconciling the global transactions of corporate capitalism with the local transactions of restaurants, shops and bars characteristic of the area. Plan analysis showing Venice sensory observation; people, noise, smell.

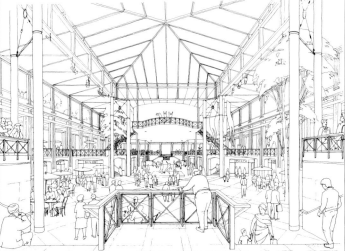

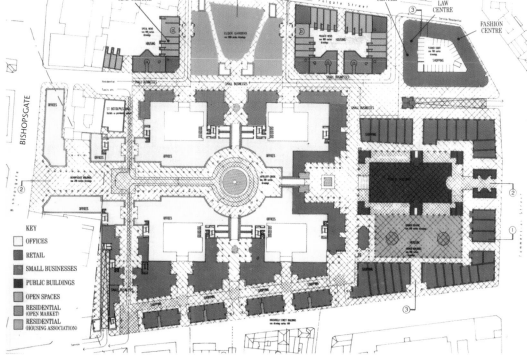

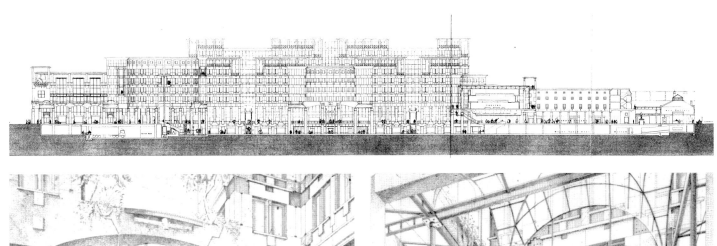

Spitalfields masterplan (1987, left)
Ground floor offices form the core around a major axis from Bishopsgate. The scale breaks down to meet the existing scale and character to the north and south; residential and small businesses to the north, retailing and residential to the south. The existing market buildings are retained to the east. Alleys and glazed arcades penetrate the scheme and link it into the pattern of surrounding streets.

Subsequent Spitalfields masterplans (right)
Whereas in the 1987 proposal the emphasis was to create a highly prestigious office address off Bishopsgate in the centre of the site in the form of a circus and to surround this with substantially retail functions – in subsequent studies the centre of the site became a retail galleria with offices on the periphery entered through courts from north and south sides of the site. As in 1987 the consented scheme, small scale retailing was arranged interstitially. The scheme later developed by Hammersons and designed by Foster & Partners, with a separate housing development to the north, adopts a broadly similar strategy.

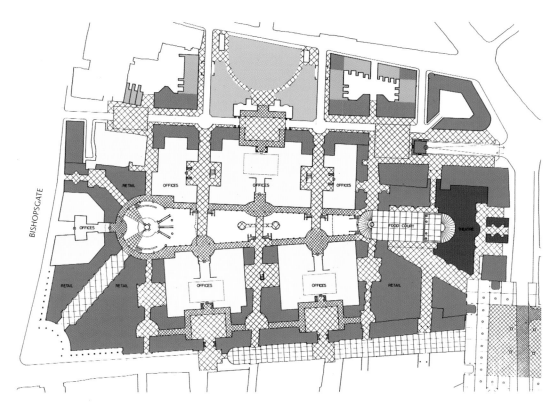

The social aspiration had at its core the seed of MacCormac's later 'dominoes theory', which was set out in his essays Understanding Transactions and Anatomy of London. Here distinctions were made between 'foreign' transactions (that is, global functions that take place in offices) and 'local' transactions that serve pedestrians and thus the locality.[1]

MacCormac proposed that in order to reconcile variety and consistency in urban planning, scales and functions across a street should be congruous. By drawing sections through the traditional urban form of parts of the West End of London MacCormac demonstrated this to be so, concluding that when the scales and functions of one street are different to those of the next street it follows that the block is asymmetrical. Matching the scale and character of the areas to the north and the south of the Spitalfields proposals exemplified these principles.

The 1989 redevelopment plan of Millharbour for the London Docklands Development Corporation followed the precepts of the Spitalfields plan. The high density centre marks the core business area. Shops at ground level animate both sides of the principal streets. Small businesses and residences fringe the development and relate to existing housing.

This would have been the first district in London's Docklands to embody a 'sustainable' policy based on draft Building Research Establishment guidelines on energy efficiency and the specification of components. The plans, in which individual buildings formed part of an overall idea of making public spaces represented a marked contrast to the government's prevailing laissez-faire policy.

MJP reanimated a lost part of Coventry by opening up a previously derelict area of the city centre and making connections between the commercial quarter, cultural quarter and the residential hinterland to the north. The three hectare project includes 84 flats, 3,000 square metres of retail, two public squares, a visitor centre, plus cafes and bars. The Transport Museum was also refocused to create an improved civic space and tourist destination.

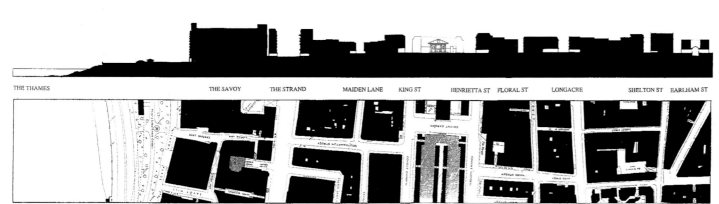

THE THAMES   THE SAVOY   THE STRAND   MAIDEN LANE   KING ST   HENRIETTA ST   FLORAL ST   LONGACRE   SHELTON ST   EARLHAM ST

Richard MacCormac's 'dominoes theory'
Dominoes section through London's West End. Dominoes have different values at each end, but connect when they are the same. This analogy relates to buildings being symmetrical across streets but asymmetrical across blocks.
1 The Savoy – the palazzo on the river.
2 The Savoy subsumed within The Strand.
3 Stepping down to the scale of Maiden Lane.
4 Stepping up to the scale of Covent Garden.
5 The symmetry of Covent Garden.

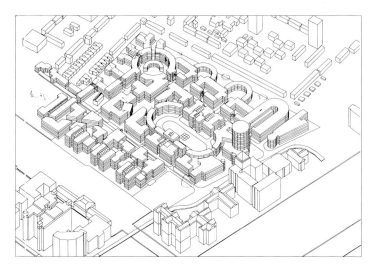

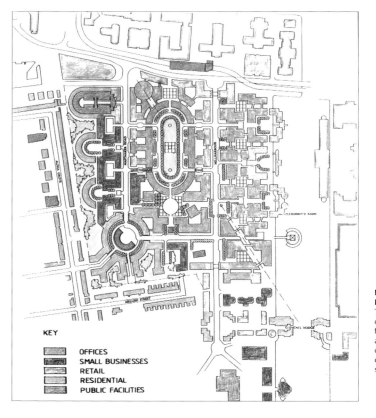

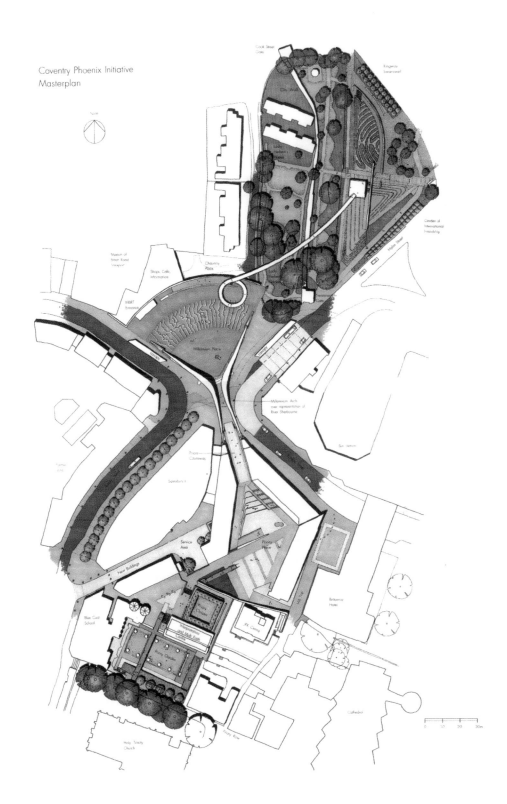

Coventry Phoenix Initiative
Masterplan

Millharbour development proposals, LDDC, London (1989, left)
The redevelopment plan set out to define a central business district fringed by supporting functions, including small businesses, retail and residential, equivalent at this scale of development to the relationship between the city of London and its hinterland of supporting small businesses and amenities.

KEY

	OFFICES
	SMALL BUSINESSES
	RETAIL
	RESIDENTIAL
	PUBLIC FACILITIES

Phoenix Initiative, Coventry (1997-2003)
The masterplan links the cathedral to the Transport Museum via new gardens, visitors centre, housing, cafes bars and the new fan-shaped Millennium Place.

Similarly, in Durham, the practice was responsible for the creation of Millennium Place, a new terrace bounded by a theatre, cinema and conference complex. A new library and council offices complete the street frontage, severed by a 1960s road cutting. The development provides improved pedestrian connections and gives Durham a new social and civic focus.

The BBC project for Broadcasting House also relates back to the work for Spitalfields market. Here there was an ambition on the part of the client to create a building with a strong interface between its function as a broadcasting organisation with a public responsibility, and its need to create a face to the world with which the public can engage. Like the Spitalfields' masterplan the centre of the site is mainly taken up with the core activity, in this case broadcasting, but is penetrated by an arcade which gives access to the radio theatre and other public facilities and links the public space behind the church to Portland Place to the west and Langham Street to the east. Hitherto the area of Langham Street to the north of the church gave access to a service yard. The proposal created a new public space facing south, lined by cafes and shops with a central meeting place that can also double as a performing arts venue.

1 Understanding Transactions, Architectural Review (March 1994) and Anatomy of London, Built Environment (vol 22 1996).

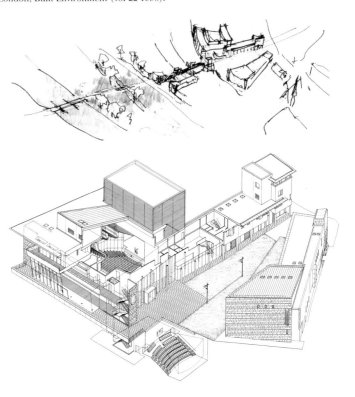

Durham Millennium City Project (1996-2001)
A library, tourist information centre, theatre and council offices are grouped around a new public space – Millennium Place.

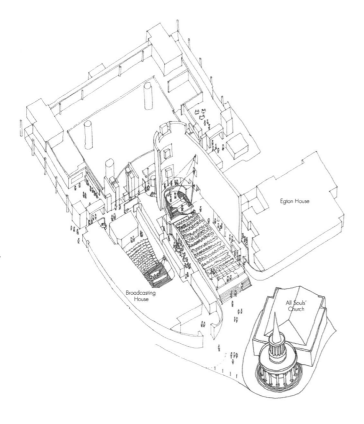

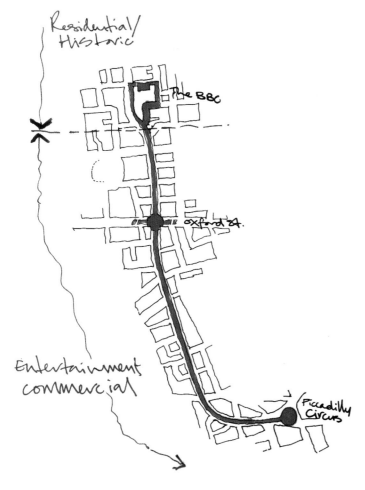

Residential/
Historic

The BBC

oxford st.

Entertainment
commercial

Piccadilly
Circus

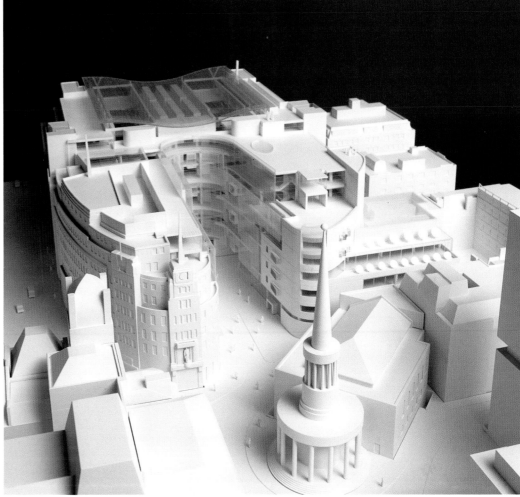

BBC Broadcasting House (2000-06)
Model and axonometric showing the public
space behind All Souls, lined by cafes and
shops, which can be used as a performance
space. The sketch shows the ground floor
public arcade. The diagram illustrates how
BBC Broadcasting House sits at the nodal
point between three urban quarters; the
commercial area of Regent Street and Oxford
Street, the creative industries to the east and
the professional district to the north.

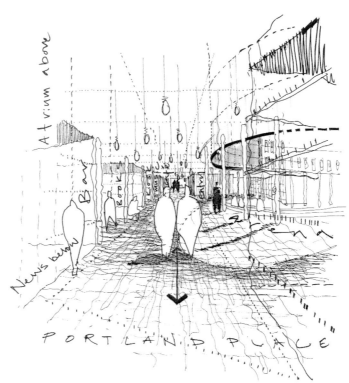

Atrium above

News below

Bar

PORTLAND PLACE

The architecture
of learning

The architecture of learning

Margaret Richardson
The buildings of MJP resonate with learned historical and cultural references.

Architects who trained in the late 1950s and 60s were still taught to respect history, although not necessarily in an imitative way. This was also a period when different ideas of architectural expression were emerging to challenge what Robert Venturi had called 'orthodox modern architecture' in his influential book Complexity and Contradiction in Architecture (1966). In his search for a variety in visual experience he was one of the first, for example, to admire as many complexities in the work of such historical figures as Soane, Hawksmoor and Lutyens as he did in the work of Le Corbusier, Aalto and Kahn.

Richard MacCormac's studies at the Cambridge school from 1959 to 1962 were followed by two years at the Bartlett in London. Throughout his career he has openly acknowledged the value of history and his wish to connect with the past, saying at his inaugural address as president of the RIBA in 1991 that 'to regain public confidence modern architecture needs to relate to the past, evoking tradition without compromising authenticity.'[1] Certainly his term as president was the most civilized for a very long time as he tried to promote architecture in its best sense, rather than other political or parochial issues.

In 1981 the Architects' Journal devoted a whole issue to Architects' Architecture, inviting thirty leading architects to select, in different categories, the buildings that had inspired or interested them. In the category Remembrance of the Past, MacCormac chose Sir John Soane's Museum; in the Golden Age he selected Wright's Prairie houses – and particularly the Robie House – as well as Aalto's municipal buildings at Saynatsalo; and in The Present, Hertzberger's Centraal Beheer. Of the Soane, which has continued to inspire him, he said 'this building… is a precedent for much I enjoy in the architecture of Wright, Kahn and Hertzberger'. Of Wright he said 'I must admit to an almost obsessive interest in Wright's Prairie houses, most of which I have visited. Their geometric language combines an extraordinary abstract power with a delicate understanding of how the houses will be inhabited. This contrast with the European Modern Movement struck me first in the small Thomas House in Oak Park, in which the arrangement of the rooms seemed completely apt and natural.'[2]

MacCormac has written extensively about his work and, unlike many architects, has been completely open about the sources that have inspired him. I first came to know his work in 1985, when I became the assistant curator at the Soane Museum, and his interpretation of the light and spaces in the building helped me to appreciate an historical icon in abstract terms. I had read his article on the Art of Invention, describing Soane as 'an architect who hovered between a relationship to history and architectural ideas which released themselves from the straight classical conventions. Such a position is interesting today because I for one consider that one of the present obligations of architecture is to reconnect backwards while not forsaking obligations to inventions.'[3]

MacCormac has a deep knowledge of Soane's work and, like Venturi, is able to interpret the forms and layered spaces of his buildings in abstract terms. Many of these Soanian elements have been creatively evoked, but not literally imitated, in his own buildings. For example, the elevations of New Court at Fitzwilliam College, Cambridge (1987) are defined by a series of aedicule-like projecting bays symmetrically arranged on either side of each entrance. These bays, with precast concrete columns and entablatures, stand outside the student rooms giving a wonderful sense of enclosure from within and – according to the Architectural Review – have a 'metaphorical balcony status depending upon the absence of visible structure between the balustrade below and the small roof above. MacCormac has likened them to the way in which the stone facade of Soane's house stands in front of the brick construction behind, creating a small internal balcony space on the second floor.'[4]

But the most influential aspect of Soane's work on that of MJP has been his spatial and lighting effects. Describing the Breakfast Room at Lincoln's Inn Fields, MacCormac suggests that 'here the shallow vault defines the expected space but this has been extended by walls placed beyond the limits of the dome. The house is full of such tricks which keep offering unexpected extensions of space.'[5] MacCormac has evoked Soane's lighting effects, created by lobbies at each end of the room sliding up to invisible rooflights, in a number of his schemes. For example, in the Fitzwilliam Chapel at Cambridge (1992) light floods down the curved inner walls from a hidden source, as it does, equally effectively, from light slots along the north and south oak-panelled walls of the senior common room at St John's College (2005). He also likes to use light in imaginative ways, inspired by Soane's coloured lighting effects at the museum and at Dulwich Picture Gallery – the picturesque lumière mystérieuse. This can be seen in his design for the staircases at Fitzwilliam New Court which he visualised as 'cores of light'. Each staircase divides at first-floor level beneath a tall, cruciform lightwell. Then, as EM Farrelly has written 'the stair continues as two separate flights up towards a very skilled deployment of mirrors which contrives to give the impression of a high and airy continuous rooflight, while concealing the fact that much of the roof space is dedicated to service ductwork. This is MacCormac at his most inventive and spatially ingenious combining an inherited Cantabrigian concern for geometry with a Mackintosh-inspired liking for visible construction and an acquired Soanian admiration for the little miracles of space and light that can be brought about by the imaginative fuse of form, colour and, of course, mirrors.'[6]

In recent years MacCormac has also come to value a relationship between art and architecture in the Arts and Crafts sense. His interest in the work of the space and light artist, James Turrell, inspired the 'big blue space' in the Welcome Wing at the Science Museum (1997). Working with the lighting designer Rogier van der Heide (who also worked with MacCormac in designing the exhibition Inspired by Soane at the Soane Gallery in 1999), his intention was to create an interior which had the 'cool blue radiance of a night sky, to induce a sense of elation and wonder (the eighteenth century's 'sense of the sublime') – an appropriate frame of mind for approaching an exhibition of modern science and biotechnology.'[7]

Perhaps the most learned of MJP's buildings to date is the Garden Quadrangle at St John's College, Oxford (1990-91). The towers of the residential buildings, like those at the Bowra Building at Wadham College, Oxford (1988-92), evoke the Elizabethan prospect towers at Hardwick Hall, but the most exciting spaces are those below the raised terraces. On either side of a central, circular atrium, which is open to the sky – like a Piranesi ruin or the amazing demolition images of Soane's Bank of England – are a sunken auditorium to the west and a dining room to the east, both with shallow domes and pendentives, conscious references to Soane's Breakfast Room. Although located at ground level, these are romantically gloomy subterranean spaces, lit indirectly by oculi and glazed screens facing the central atrium.

While MacCormac's work at St John's employs history in a creative way, it is nonetheless perhaps the most literal of all his schemes. The dining room in particular can be compared with the way Juan Navarro Baldeweg reinterpreted Soane's Breakfast Room in his suspended concrete canopy for the cultural centre at the Molinos del Rio Segura in Murcia (1984).

By contrast, the Ruskin Library at Lancaster (1996) is more metaphorical than literal in its use of history. In MacCormac's words it symbolises a 'keep… a refuge for Ruskin's bequest, appearing as a secure tower and fulfilling the verb keep by preserving the collection.'[8] The appropriateness of this image, coupled with the quality of the built work and the craftsmanship of the interior fittings and furniture, resulted in one of the finest small museums in Europe.

MacCormac's work, like that of many contemporaries in Europe, attempts to draw out the historical resonances within the respective culture. Just as Mario Botta's Casa Rotondo echoes a tower for spiritual retreat in the Ticino, MacCormac's towers at St John's evoke memories of Elizabethan England. Above all his ability to be inspired by history but to be inventive at the same time can be seen at its best in his interior spaces and in his experiments with light.

Margaret Richardson is an architectural historian; she was Curator at Sir John Soane's Museum in London from 1995 to 2005. Her publications include Architects of the Arts and Crafts Movement (1983) and John Soane Architect: Master of Space and Light (Margaret Richardson and MaryAnne Stevens, Royal Academy, 1999), as well as numerous contributions to books and magazines.

1 Quoted in Geoffrey Tyack, Modern Architecture in an Oxford College: St John's College 1945-2005 (Oxford 2005).
2 Architects' Journal, 1981, vol 173, pp146-182.
3 Architects' Journal, 1985, vol 181, pp40-41.
4 Architectural Review, 1987, vol 182, pp28-37.
5 Architects' Journal, 1981, op cit.
6 Architectural Review, 1987, op cit.
7 Architectural Design, 1997, vol 67, July-August, p45.
8 Richard MacCormac in Architecture, Memory and Metaphor, (Architectural Review, 1996, vol 200, pp79-81).

4 The Architecture of Learning

The theme for the British pavilion at the 1996 Venice Biennale was the 'architecture of information'. MJP's Ruskin Library, then under construction, was exhibited alongside Foster & Partners' Carré d'Art in Nimes, Colin St John Wilson's British Library, and Nicholas Grimshaw & Partners' Eden Project in Cornwall. The Ruskin Library, with its structural and material references to Ruskin's passion for Venice, had a special resonance. The exhibition catalogue explained that, despite their aesthetic and functional diversity, the four projects were chosen because of their focus on 'the collection, storage, retrieval and transfer of knowledge – concerns at the heart of the information revolution that will undoubtedly be one of the mainsprings of our propulsion in the twenty-first century.'[1]

In the previous year MacCormac had contributed an essay for the Royal Fine Art Commission publication entitled Fulfilling the Purpose of Architecture in Higher Education in which he wrote of the aspirations shared by architecture and higher education. 'Architecture', he suggested, 'should serve as the visible expression of educational values… Universities, of all the commissioning institutions, have a special obligation to this idea… because architecture and higher education share equivalent ideals and face similar difficulties. Both have a commitment to nurturing and promoting particular kinds of public value and to enabling people to achieve the fullest experience of life. The universities, within limited budgets, have to balance training with education, science with art, and the needs of a productive society with intellectual fulfilment. Architecture involves analogous judgements within equally limited resources and, of course, a similar commitment to the pursuit of excellence. It should serve as the visible expression of educational values.'[2]

In designing university buildings over many years, the practice has been encouraged by clients who appreciated that the practical and aesthetic should be coincident rather than additional to one another. 'Architecture should be a marvellous manifestation of intelligence', says MacCormac, 'engaging, challenging and drawing us out, exactly like education itself.' In an earlier essay, The Presence of the Past,[5] MacCormac cites Worcester College, Fitzwilliam College, St John's College and Cable & Wireless as buildings that intentionally demonstrate the client's commitment to excellence in their fields. 'Education with this purpose is itself a form of patronage in the sense that the word means to defend and promote a legacy of values and accumulated knowledge.'[5]

Combining social and teaching spaces
MJP's first design for a teaching building was the Faculty of Arts at Bristol University (1979). Here the architects were presented with a row of nineteenth century villas, set in a conservation area, which were to be restored and incorporated into a new masterplan. The intention was to devise a relationship between old and new which would allow for phased construction and accommodate changes in departmental and faculty requirements.

The competition brief assumed that the departments would be housed within the villas and that faculty space would be provided in the new building. The architects recognised that such a strict distinction would be unlikely to work well, and that for the scheme

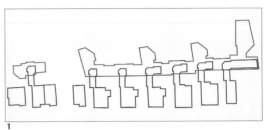

Bristol University Arts Faculty (1979-86)
1 Red: faculty, blue: departments.
2 Red: timeshared faculty lecture space, blue: departmental offfices, green: seminar space, mauve: student common rooms.
3/4 Incremental phasing.

Right View showing the relationship between old and new buildings; staircase to roof-level walkway; corridor with red-stained redwood joinery; view across common room to doors opening onto garden court.

113

to have longevity it would have to offer a high degree of adaptability. This was achieved by linking new and old so that boundaries between the departmental territories and the time-shared faculty space need not be fixed. In short, what was required and delivered was the 'long-life, low-energy, loose-fit' espoused by former RIBA president (and competition assessor) Alex Gordon, who used the mantra long before the importance of sustainability came to be widely recognised.

The design comprises a series of south-facing courtyards within the villa gardens, with one side formed by the backs of the houses and the other two by new single-storey buildings. Common rooms in the angle of the 'L' of the new buildings form part of the primary faculty circulation that faces onto the cloister-like courtyards and serves as 'expansion chambers' – spaces for social and intellectual exchange where students can congregate before and after lectures. This was the first MJP scheme in which circulation was handled in this way. The flexibility of the design meant that individual phases could be contained within single or multiple walled gardens, thus avoiding the sense of incompleteness often experienced during a long-term building project.

The design for the Cable & Wireless College in Coventry was also generated by the organisation of the circulation and social space (see chapter three). However, the competition brief and the site – four hectares within a business park overlooking the Warwickshire green belt – presented quite different challenges. The company was moving its entire training operation from the coastal village of Porthcurno on the tip of south-west England, a remote location derived from the transatlantic cables that arrived there. There were clear strategic reasons for the move, and it gave the company the opportunity to build a bespoke facility to encompass learning, technical and residential accommodation. The client wanted the affiliation with other companies on the business park, such as Barclays, Powergen and RSA, but they wanted the architecture of the college to be distinct. The new building had to establish a clear corporate presence and provide a range of diverse learning spaces alongside residential and social facilities for up to 300 delegates. The MJP design gave Cable & Wireless its own front door on the edge of the green belt and they even rented the surrounding fields in order to secure the 'rural' setting. The building was hailed by Jonathan Glancey in The Independent as 'one of the best buildings in Europe'.[6] The RIBA Awards jury commended it as 'a model of intelligent corporate design', while journalist Andrew Brister emphasised that what is important for blue-chip companies is that landmark buildings 'are designed so that the client is left with a building it can easily manage, one which has low energy costs and minimal environmental impact. The Cable & Wireless College scores on all these counts'.[7] It is, said critic Colin Amery, 'quite simply one of the best and most thoughtful new buildings to have been built in England for some time'.[8]

Cable & Wireless Technical College, Warwickshire (1990-93)
The curved blue ceramic roofs lend the building its characteristic identity. The entrance faces south overlooking the green belt countryside.

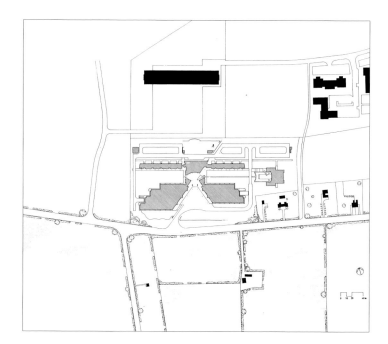

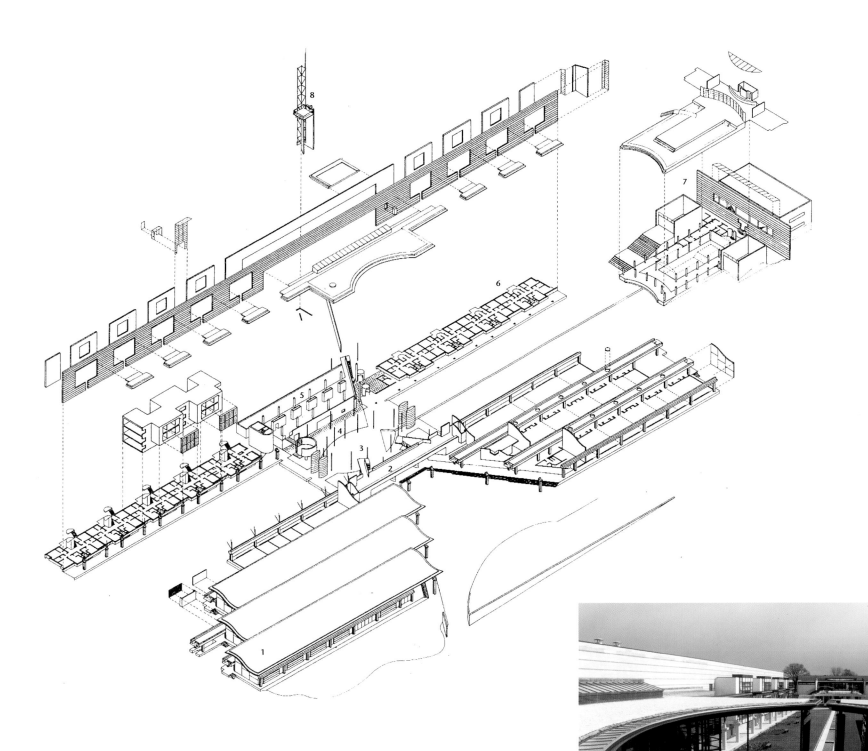

Exploded axonometric and view over ocular court. The key characteristics of the campus comprise: **1** the teaching wings are sheltered by self-ventilating curved roofs; **2** the library forms a bridge between teaching east and teaching west; **3** the ocular court forms the focus of circulation; **4** shared spaces and refectory; **5** administration spaces overlook the refectory; **6** residential accommodation forms the 'back wall' of the campus; **7** the sports/leisure pavilion terminates the end of the east court; **8** the telecoms mast terminates the entrance axis.

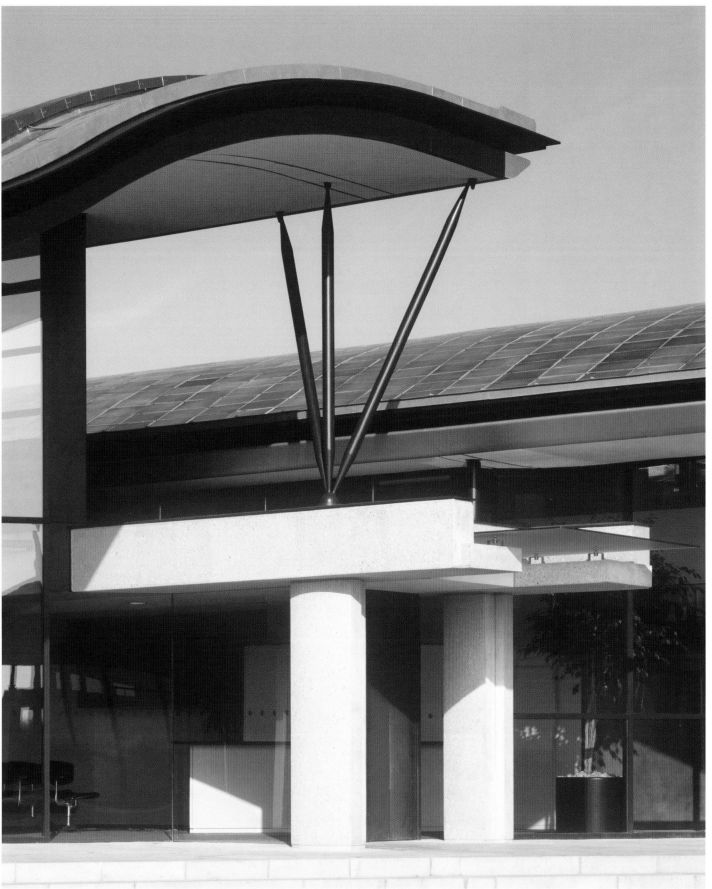

Underside of the Cable & Wireless College wave roofs with glass canopies marking the entrances to the teaching wings.

Double-height refectory at the Cable & Wireless College, looking west and showing the bridge that links administrative offices with the boardroom.

Construction section through the teaching accommodation showing north light and opening lights to achieve cross ventilation beneath the double-curved roof.

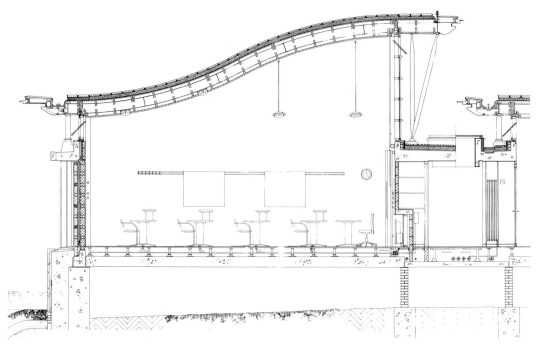

View west towards the ocular court.

Views east towards the sports and leisure pavilion.

Back in remote Porthcurno, MJP was commissioned by Cable & Wireless to carry out a study for the regeneration of the village, which included new communication facilities as well as proposals to generate jobs and tourism centred on a Museum of Submarine Telegraphy. The museum, set in a warren of second world war tunnels built into the hillside, houses telecommunications memorabilia, and was tele-linked to the Science Museum in London and the Cable & Wireless museum in Hong Kong.

Like workplaces, university teaching requires flexible, adaptable and often open-plan spaces alongside more permanent elements. At the Informatics Teaching Laboratory for Queen Mary & Westfield College (now Queen Mary University of London), begun in 1987, the highly visible staircase, rising through the void in the middle of the building, introduces an unexpected social quality into an economical rectilinear building. Open-plan floors arranged around the staircase promote a high degree of social awareness. The efficient design of this simple building was driven by the client's desire for an open-plan space, inspired by their visit to MJP's offices. To minimise the initial capital cost, lifts and air conditioning were omitted but the design contained provision for them to be added later, with an empty lift shaft and a fresh air ventilation system in the raised floor included in the initial construction. The standard six metre grid office floor plate allows for predominantly open-plan space, within

Pothcurno Museum of Submarine Telegraphy (1997-98)
Site plan, aerial view and interior of exhibition space.

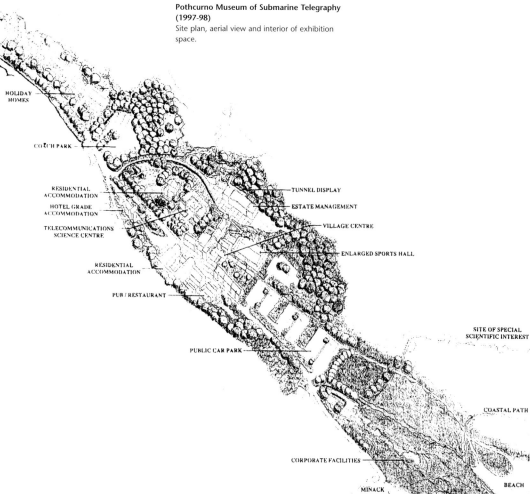

120

which are islands of workstations and a number of seminar rooms. The arrangement challenged conventional thinking for the design of computer laboratories, and encouraged the practice of 'hot-desking' some years before it became the orthodoxy.

MJP's 'box' of course, is anything but boring, as testified by the client Professor Richard Bornat: 'We think this building is wonderful, as nice as we had dared to hope it would be… it expresses the sort of image the department wants to project to its students and visitors… We think it is the only truly pretty building on the Queen Mary College campus… The architects studied the department and its haphazard way of working and produced a flexible building which we can use in all sorts of unplanned ways.' [7] It is, he says, a fantastic space for parties, and the large window on the entrance elevation facing West Square looks best when lit from inside by pulsating disco lights.

MJP later worked with the University of Warwick's Library Services on a series of projects to develop new places for study and research. The aim was to optimise the innovative use of new technologies for independent learning and teaching, while creating social spaces that would promote the exchange of knowledge and ideas. MJP designed vibrant, relaxed, flexible spaces that students and staff could adapt and 'own'. These included the award-winning Learning Grid and the refurbishment of the main library.

Queen Mary & Westfield College Informatics Teaching Laboratory, London (1988-89)
The large expanse of glazing on the entrance front reveals the triple-height space and open-plan layout behind.

University of Warwick Central Library remodelling (2006-)
The reading lounges employ flexible furniture arrangements and use of colour to encourage a sense of ownership among the students.

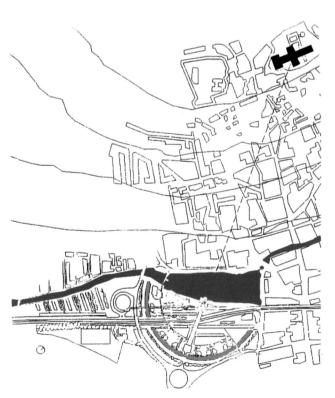

University of Lincoln Masterplan (1993)
Site plan and aerial view showing sight lines to
Lincoln Cathedral.

University masterplans

MJP's track record in designing university buildings has resulted in
several commissions for campus masterplans. The first, in 1993, was
for a new university in Lincoln. David Prichard carried out an
appraisal of two sites identified as possible locations, taking into
account initial accommodation requirements, the phasing of the
development and the potential for future expansion. As with many
of MJP's schemes, the concept for the university on the Brayford
Pool site was a response to the topography. Here, a necklace of
buildings formed an arena looking up the slope towards the
cathedral. Although not commissioned to build their scheme, MJP's
recommendation to use this site within the city was adopted in
preference to the out-of-town campus option reminiscent of post-
war universities, which would have hindered the integration of
'gown' into 'town', essential for a twenty-first century campus.

Back in the capital, MJP's history of working for the London
School of Economics includes a residential building in Myddelton
Street, Finsbury and the refurbishment of the entrance hall and
lecture theatre of the Old Building in Houghton Street. The
practice was also appointed to carry out a strategic analysis of the
Aldwych campus in central London. Although unrealised, the
scheme prompted the client to look more carefully at issues of
circulation and public space. One of the main problems with the

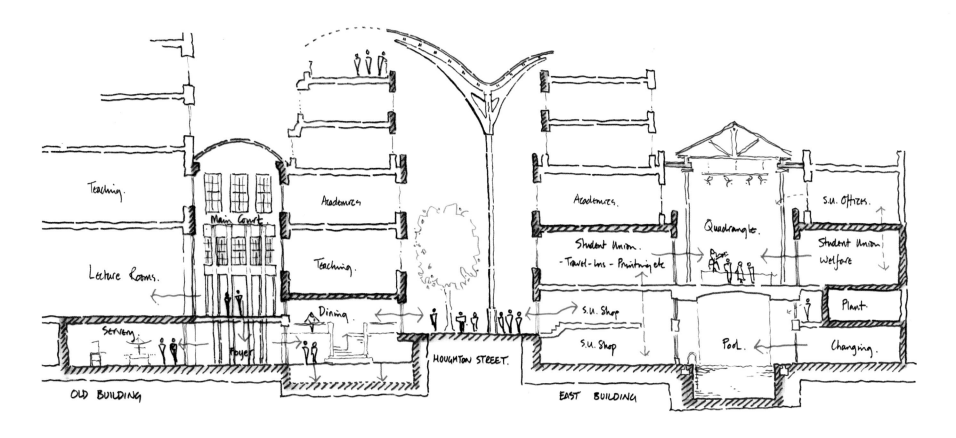

Teaching.

Main Court.

Academics.

Lecture Rooms.

Teaching.

Dining.

Foyer

Servery.

HOUGHTON STREET.

OLD BUILDING

Academics.

Student Union.
- Travel-Ins - Printing etc

S.U. Shop

S.U. Shop

Quadrangle.

Student Union
Welfare

Pool.

S.U. Offices.

Plant.

Changing.

EAST BUILDING

LSE campus is the density of the seven- or eight-storey buildings, with limited vertical circulation and horizontal circulation mostly at ground level. Houghton Street, the forum in the middle of the campus, is overcrowded and oppressive. MJP therefore proposed that instead of perpetuating the congested, vertical circulation that separated departments into vertical stacks, departments could be ranged horizontally, extending through several buildings at the same level via link bridges.

This horizontal arrangement had its origins in the scheme for the Faculty of Arts in Bristol. As at Bristol, MJP looked at the topography of the departments and considered how the circulation spaces might be associated with social and administrative focuses along the route, linking together the teaching and staff rooms. The LSE proposal (partly followed in the realised scheme) included moving the most intensively used social spaces, such as cafes, from the upper floor down to the ground level, with the intention that social spaces would line one side of a central concourse, with the most heavily used lecture theatres on the other side. The lightwells between the buildings were to be enclosed by glazed roofs, with further social spaces branching off from them.

London School of Economics Campus (1993)
Proposals for the LSE campus involved relocating major social functions and a lecture theatre at ground and first-floor level and glazing in light wells to create new social spaces to alleviate the congestion in Houghton Street. The new cafeteria (left) defines the edge of John Watkins plaza.

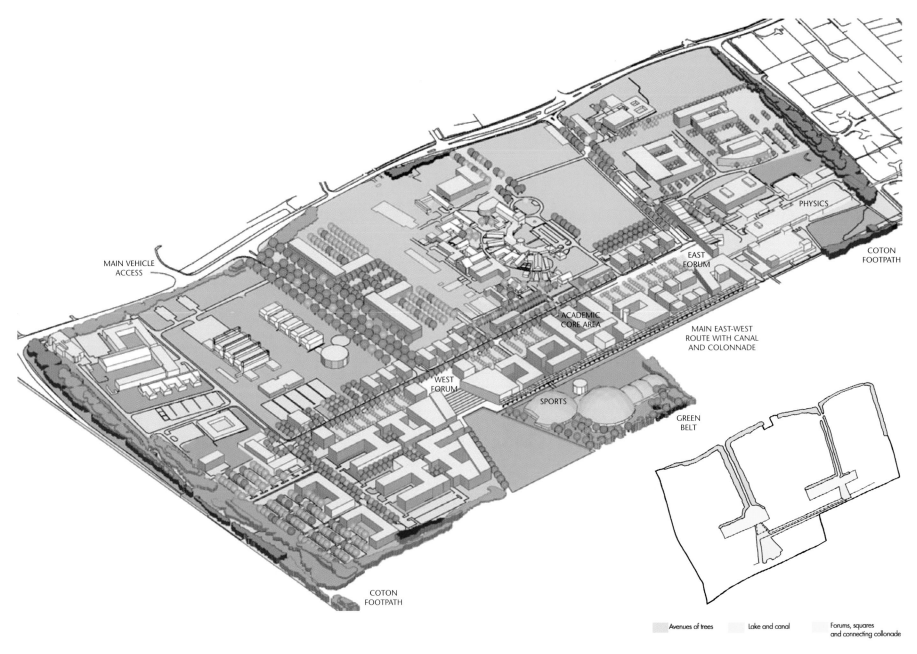

MAIN VEHICLE ACCESS

PHYSICS

EAST FORUM

COTON FOOTPATH

ACADEMIC CORE AREA

MAIN EAST-WEST ROUTE WITH CANAL AND COLONNADE

WEST FORUM

SPORTS

GREEN BELT

COTON FOOTPATH

Avenues of trees   Lake and canal   Forums, squares and connecting collonade

West Cambridge masterplan (1995-2020)
Aerial axonometric showing key elements; aerial view of site. The masterplan draws on the form of the landscape and buildings in the historic city centre.

In 1995 MJP was commissioned by the University of Cambridge to prepare a masterplan for the West Cambridge site on the outskirts of the city. Although there were already several academic and research facilities, most of the 66 hectare site was open, windswept farmland typical of the flat countryside surrounding Cambridge. For the university's academics, used to the physically and intellectually rich setting of the city centre and historic colleges, it felt remote and unwelcoming. 'MJP's desire to create a vibrant environment, with a strong sense that the site was a part of the university, became the key aspiration', explains director Liz Pride. 'We wanted to make a place that would encourage social and academic interaction, and support the exchange of knowledge and the development of new ideas among the academic community.'

MJP's masterplan created a lively environment in a number of ways; first, by incorporating a varied mix of activities. The brief focused on providing academic departments for teaching and research, alongside facilities for commercial research, but it also included social facilities, a sports centre and residential accommodation for staff and postgraduates. Crucially, this range of activities was distributed across the site. Second, MJP identified a core area to give a focus for the social and intellectual life within the site. The aim was to create an environment with the density of the existing university sites in the city centre, but to avoid the dispersed

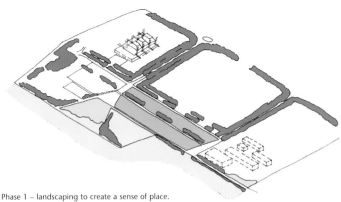

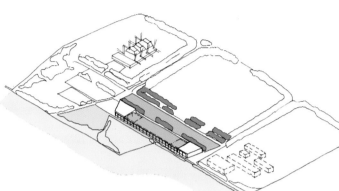

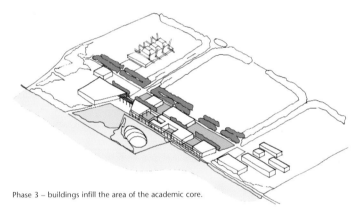

Above right MJP's residences are designed to address the public realm; phasing diagrams.

character of a typical science park, where the separate buildings can be isolated by a no-man's land of informal landscaping and parking.

The masterplan included a rich landscape of squares, avenues and water, with a formal character that integrated the large science buildings and gave coherence to the site, while drawing on precedents from the courts and gardens of the historic university. Pedestrians and cyclists were given precedence, with parking limited to the periphery of the core area. The two major public spaces formed at the intersection of key routes were named the East and West Forums, the former providing the main entrance into the site for cyclists and pedestrians, while the West Forum is located at the end of the main vehicle route into the site.

MJP located the university core area on the south side of the site to tie the existing Department of Physics into the new development and to exploit views of the greenbelt countryside on the south boundary. Significantly, this location also allowed MJP to form a strong connection to the existing Coton Footpath which led to the city centre. This route was extended into the site, penetrating to the heart of the new university core area, entering at the East Forum and running through the West Forum. This key route would be enhanced with landscaping and sheltered by a 380 metre long colonnade, providing a striking visual symbol for the site. A canal, similar to those on the Cambridge 'Backs', would run alongside.

The east/west route, canal and colonnade created a clear, formal edge to the core area of development. MJP located the new sports facilities, designed by Arup Associates as a series of green-roofed mounds, to the south of the route; the inherently different form of this building allowed a transition to be made between the dense, urban science buildings to the north and the greenbelt countryside to the south.

The university's funding dictated that the site be developed slowly over a 25-year period. The colonnade offered coherence during the phased development by forming a long 'screen' on the southern frontage. MJP also proposed a simple landscape of grassed terraces to be formed in the core area of the site as a temporary feature that would unite the early phases of development and indicate the forthcoming transition from farmland to developed site. Strategies for the landscape and ecology formed an integral part of the masterplan and another means of creating a sense of place.

MJP designed two new residential buildings within the West Cambridge site. Residential use had been included in the development to ensure that there would be activity throughout the day, so semi-public courtyards were incorporated in both schemes to provide an interface between those working and living on the site. In addition the schemes provided a nursery and social facilities to serve the whole site.

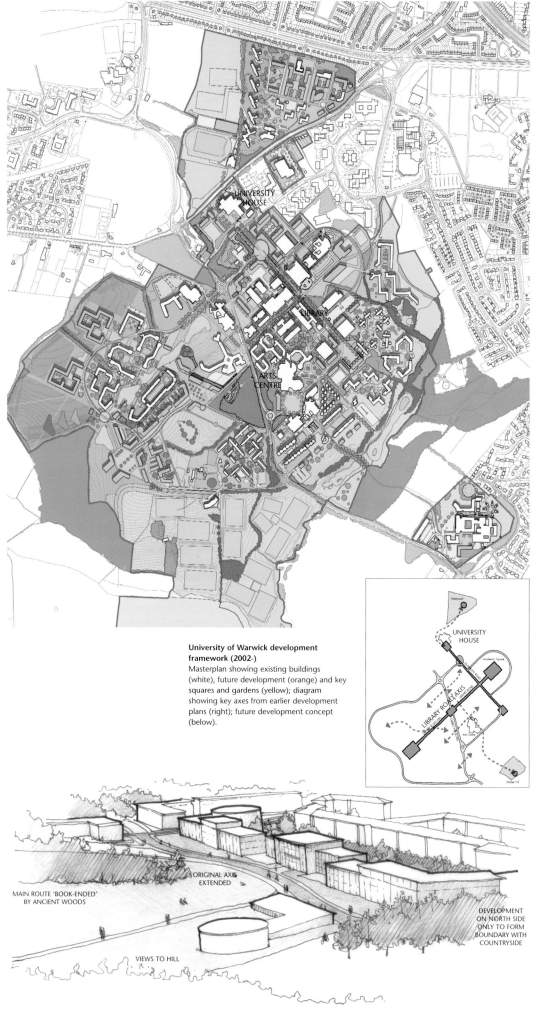

University of Warwick development framework (2002-)
Masterplan showing existing buildings (white), future development (orange) and key squares and gardens (yellow); diagram showing key axes from earlier development plans (right); future development concept (below).

In 2002 MJP was appointed to prepare a development plan for the University of Warwick which would build on past plans and incorporate the university's current needs in a time of considerable growth. The last in a series of development plans, prepared by Casson Conder, was due for review by 2004. Unlike the project for West Cambridge, Warwick encompassed the whole university, but there were many similar issues to be addressed. As at Cambridge, a key aim for MJP was to create an environment that would foster a sense of an academic community.

The campus had some similarities to the West Cambridge site: it lay on the edge of a city and was partially developed but it had large areas of open land running out into the green belt. As director Liz Pride explains, 'there were similar problems of a lack of connection between different parts of the campus and a need to make "remote" development sites more palatable to the academics who would move there. However the Warwick campus was split in two by a public thoroughfare, Gibbet Hill Road, which marked the edge of the green belt and also an administrative boundary between Warwickshire and Coventry. This split was reinforced by the different character of the campus on each side of the road. The Coventry side was already developed, with academic and social buildings ringed by student residences, set in a flat, formal, parkland landscape. The Warwickshire side had rolling open countryside with woods, fields and long views. It had a long history of human occupation and a hill and wood next to the main campus were of archaeological interest. The main developments here were long blocks of student residences which, lacking social facilities, felt remote from the lively centre of the campus.'

Warwick was a relatively young university, one of the 'Shakespeare Seven' established across England in the 1960s.[8] The campus was built on the outskirts of Coventry, with an emphasis on efficiency and modernity. The original YRM masterplan had laid out the university on a rigorous grid of roads rolled out across the green field site, with white-tiled modernist buildings fronting onto streets to give them a public presence, in direct reaction to the private, inward-looking courtyard form of the old universities.

The YRM masterplan was extensive and had not been fully built. It was succeeded by a series of masterplans and developments which largely rejected the framework of the original plan, setting up alternative arrangements of informal courtyards, freestanding pavilions and angled forms, so that by 2002 the campus lacked a clear organisation and felt dislocated and incomplete. The university needed to be able to expand onto the Warwickshire side of the campus into the green belt. MJP wanted to ensure that this expansion would create a lively place, with a mix of university activities.

A key decision was whether to impose a new masterplan structure on the campus or to draw on one or more of the existing plans. Although the succession of plans had not produced a coherent form for the campus, MJP believed that they represented a record of Warwick's development which also reflected changing ideas about university education and planning in the second half of the twentieth century.

'Our approach', says Liz Pride, 'was to revitalise the existing campus plan, consolidating development and increasing density on the Coventry side, while drawing on the strong central axis of the

original YRM plan – Library Road – as a basis for expansion across Gibbet Hill Road into the Warwickshire land. We developed ideas from our work at West Cambridge to form a legible framework of routes linking public squares and gardens. The aim was to unite the disparate parts of the campus, using a lively public realm as the venue for social and intellectual interaction, so reinforcing the sense of an academic community and reducing the perception of distance and separation.'

The size of the campus made it appropriate for there to be a number of focal points. The university's arts centre and student union already provided a social hub, while the main library formed an academic focus. MJP used the newly acquired University House to create a new meeting point for students and staff with plazas that linked the northern extremities of the campus back to the centre. Similarly, new squares were proposed along the Library Road axis extending into the Warwickshire land, forming 'stepping stones' of activity linking future development to the existing campus. The axis route purposely introduced a more formal landscape to the Warwickshire land, appropriate to the future academic buildings. It was designed to relate to existing woods and the hill which were important features on this side of the site. Development was ranged on one side of the route defining a boundary with the open countryside to the south.

Bridging the physical and psychological barrier of Gibbet Hill Road was important to facilitate the expansion into the Warwickshire side of the campus. Proposals to improve pedestrian routes included traffic calming and the formation of broad landscaped crossings spanning the road. The barrier effect was further reduced by opening up views into the campus from the roads and marking the entrances to the university with striking landscaping to increase its public presence.

MJP's framework formed the basis for a diverse range of strategies that encompassed every aspect of campus development including transportation, landscape, ecology, art, heritage and archaeology, services and phasing. It worked with a team of consultants including Arup and Churchman Landscape Architects. Over the period that the development plan evolved there was a huge growth in initiatives and new technologies to improve all aspects of sustainable development. Proposals for renewable energy, with combined heat and power plant were integrated into the plan and expressed in the landscape design with areas of biomass crops ranged between the new buildings. The landscape design incorporated swales and ponds for sustainable drainage and, as at Cambridge, the public realm was designed to promote walking and cycling.

The history of the development of Warwick University provided MJP's team with a stark reminder that university masterplans are rarely completed. 'This was further reinforced through the duration of the project by the impact of shifts in government policy, funding opportunities, and the world economic climate, which made it almost impossible to predict how development would be phased', explains Pride. 'It was essential that the masterplan should provide a very flexible framework for development. The uncertainty also underlined the importance of university masterplanning as a process, as well as a goal. Masterplanning provides a forum for discussion about the nature of a university community and the physical environment that will support it, allowing consensus to be built within the university and the wider community.'

MJP went on to work as masterplanners for UCL in London and the University of Birmingham. These very different institutions and estates provided further opportunities for the architects to develop their understanding of the university estate.

Services
Academic
Central facilities
Residential
Post-experience
Potential sites

Successive masterplans reflect changing ideas about academic campus development. Top to bottom: 1966 (Yorke Rosenberg Mardall), 1974 (Shepheard Epstein), 1994 (Casson Conder), 2006 MJP Architects.
MJP's refurbishment of the student union (above) is designed to enliven the public realm.

Lancaster University Library (1995-96)
The suspended glazed west wall, incorporating fixed brises-soleil, brings extensive daylighting to the triangular double-height reading room. Informal working and meeting balconies overlook the atrium

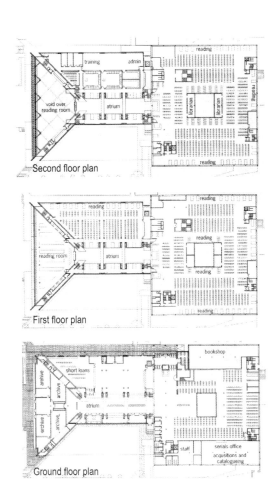

Second floor plan

First floor plan

Ground floor plan

The classification of knowledge

In the last decade information technology has had a major impact on the design of new academic buildings, not least of libraries. The digital information revolution has meant that designers have to accommodate alternative learning methods and facilities alongside book stacks, and university libraries and learning resource centres can provide a social focus within a geographically dispersed institution.

The extension to the Lancaster University library (the first phase of which was completed in 1996) provides deep-plan flexible space that accommodates the broad range of facilities needed, while anticipating what might be needed in the future. As well as reading areas and book storage, facilities include a fully integrated information technology department with seminar and group reading suites, open learning areas and multimedia facilities. Social space is provided by the top-lit atrium, in which potentially noisy activity takes place, leaving the perimeter free for quiet reading areas.

The design draws on ideas about local and foreign transactions. The reading room is a dramatic triangular space with a glazed west wall (with a fixed brise-soleil) – a 'trumpet to the outside world'. While the atrium embraces person-to-person transactions the reading room 'opens up to the wider world, metaphorically and literally, symbolising both the role of the university within society and the new, non-topographic developments in learning and information technology…'.[9]

King's College, Cambridge (1988)
For Richard MacCormac this unbuilt project relates to the Ruskin Library in that it expresses 'the idea of protection through the use of curved walls and consisted of buildings within buildings'.

Ruskin Library (1992-97)
Exterior view; the reading room is dominated by the oak and bronze bound archive; a toplit glass and slate floor leads to the reading room.

MacCormac recalls that initially he was surprised by the lack of conflict between the requirements for paper-based information and those for electronic information. The book stacks require the physical structure to support their weight while the computer technology requires raised floors to accommodate the wiring. At Lancaster, these requirements are met by the slab design and the raised floor is also used for the integration of a ventilation system derived from that developed for the QMUL Informatics Teaching Laboratory. [10]

The library for King's College, Cambridge (1987, unbuilt) and the Ruskin Library at the University of Lancaster (1993) are both buildings that physically symbolise the status of the information within. The intended contents of the King's College library were comparable in importance to the Ruskin project, but the architectural solution was the inverse: the 'archival' element was placed on the outside, rather than inside the building. At King's College the intention was that the library should incorporate an undergraduate reading/lending library, a reading room, a reference library and an archive. The overt distinction between temporary and permanent knowledge was to do with the specific environmental conditions required for the storage of ancient manuscripts and papers. The three metre thick stone 'ark' containing the archive was described by the architects as 'an ossuary of permanent knowledge', enclosing a three-storey high timber structure for the undergraduates' library – 'a rookery of temporary knowledge'.

MacCormac recalls, 'it was very monumental and later caused me to reflect that this word comes from the Latin "monere" – to remind – and the proposed building was to be a great storehouse for remembered information… the library itself was to be above ground while the space beneath was intimately related to the adjoining garden. There was thus an upper and a lower world – a quasi-crypt with a church-like space above – which had a certain historical resonance about them. The architecture was firmly of the late-twentieth century but was aimed at expressing something of the content of the building and its temporal character'. [11]

The Ruskin Library inverts the distinctions made in the King's College library scheme between permanent and temporary space, but it is also concerned with that word, monere. The Lamp of Memory, the sixth chapter of John Ruskin's Seven Lamps of Architecture, sets out his belief that, without architecture, we cannot remember. The chapter is dense with words such as monument, memory, history and story, which are associated with the idea of recall.

Unusually, the Ruskin library has to accommodate the triple roles of archive, exhibition space and reading room. In MJP's design the permanent object, the archive, occupies the heart of the building, with the spaces for temporary exhibitions around the perimeter. This concept grew out of an initial idea for the King's College scheme in which a great treasure chest was buried under the terrace in front of the library, and made visible, through a raised oculus, to those walking above.

MJP's initial design of the Wellcome Wing for London's Science Museum envisaged galleries around a central void, but it soon became apparent that the linearity that follows the classification systems of libraries was inappropriate to the kinds of exhibitions envisaged by the museum. An influence here was Thomas Markus'

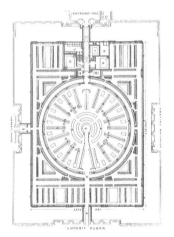

Left to right The British Museum Reading Room (Sydney Smirke, 1854-57), interior view and plan; the Wren Library, Trinity College, Cambridge (Christopher Wren, 1676-84).

book Buildings and Power,[12] which describes how the development of libraries and museums, such as Wren's 'stall-with-wall' Trinity College Library and the circular British Museum Reading Room, has been bound up with ideas about classification and how the fit between knowledge and building form could fail, in the Natural History Museum for example, where the taxonomy of the original layout was made redundant by Darwin's theory of evolution.

There is no attempt in the Wellcome Wing to classify but, perhaps paradoxically, it was influenced by a technique for memorising represented by Giulio Camillo's sixteenth-century memory theatre in which knowledge was replaced by tiers suspended like galleries and viewed from a stage. The extent of what is on offer could be grasped by the visitor in an immediately dramatic way. Likewise, the Wellcome Wing was envisaged as a 'theatre of science'.

The approach gallery to the Wellcome Wing, designed by Wilkinson Eyre Architects, is home to the world of the physical sciences. Here objects with a powerful physical presence are strongly lit and dominate the space. MJP's design for the display of the electronic information within the Wellcome Wing provides a striking contrast. The space is dematerialised in response to the largely interactive and ephemeral subject matter. Unlike the traditional galleries, the Wellcome Wing had to be highly adaptable, with carefully controlled lighting providing the low background

**Science Museum Wellcome Wing
(1997-2003)**
Early computer-generated presentation image illustrating the blue interior and translucent exhibition 'trays'.

Left The slot of space between the west window and the exhibition 'trays'.

Right The upper galleries seen from beneath curved IMAX cinema with the blue wall behind.

Below Perspective view showing the 'trays' and underside of the IMAX cinema; section.

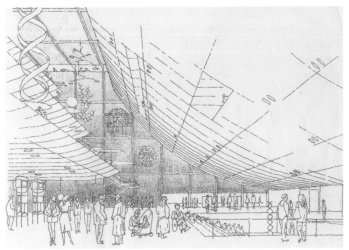

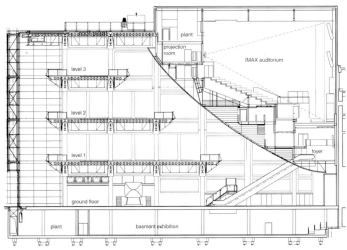

Above View across galleries from escalator.

Left Section showing the exhibition 'trays' and cantilevered structure.

Right The entrance to the Wellcome Wing from the existing museum is marked by an orange 'lightbox'.

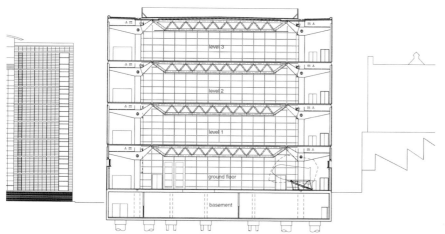

luminance required for the screens and optical devices. Elsewhere in the museum the hovering aeroplanes and enormous steam engines provide the spectacle. Here, the space itself has to provide an inherent sense of drama and, as in the work of the artist James Turrell, space and light seem to have merged. Visitors enter through an orange portal and are drawn into the deep blue space. To add to the sense of drama the underside of the suspended IMAX cinema curves up overhead and seems to compel the visitor to move forward. The profile of the curve is echoed by the three exhibition 'trays', galleries each a little narrower than the one below. Access to the IMAX is via an escalator, which penetrates, says MacCormac, like 'a gangway into a spaceship'. The most ethereal – if not celestial – aspect of the Wellcome Wing is the west elevation, which is also the only external public face of the project. The 30 metre square window, which reveals little of what lies beyond, glows at night and bathes the interior in a luminous blue light.

A key strategy in the competition-winning scheme for the extension to the Science Museum was the accommodation of one of the main functional components, a conference centre, in a separate building facing onto Queensgate. The Great Exhibition site has four boundaries; Kensington Gore to the north, Exhibition Road to the east, Cromwell Road to the south and Queensgate to the west, which retains a grand domestic character until it meets the corner of

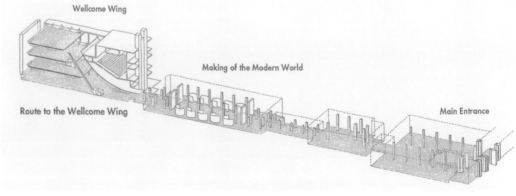

Above Circulation through museum from Exhibition Road to Wellcome Wing.

Left 'Space ship' concept sketch by Richard MacCormac.

Wellcome Wolfson Building, Science Museum, Queensgate (2001-03)
Elevation facing the Wellcome Wing.

Below Phasing diagrams showing the Science Museum Wellcome Wing and the Wellcome Wolfson Building Conference Centre on Queensgate.

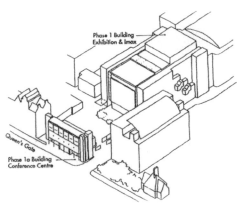

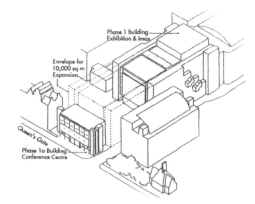

Cromwell Road where the view opens up to the monumental scale of the Natural History Museum. By separating the conference centre from the IMAX and exhibition functions MJP allowed the client to phase the development and funding of the conference centre and provided a pretext for a different scale building to address the existing architecture of Queensgate.

During the early stages of the design process the function of the Queensgate building evolved into a complex mixture of inter-related uses. The Dana Centre occupies the lowest floors, providing an interactive forum aimed at young people interested in scientific debate; the middle floors accommodate offices for the Science Museum administration and the top floor provides an apartment for its director. 'From the outset,' explains director Matthew Dean, 'it was a shared ambition between designers and client to limit energy use and provide an example of a sustainable mixed-use development.'

The diversity of use and the sensitivity of location prompted the design team to find different responses to context, climate and function, resulting in a highly articulated building which nevertheless acknowledges and respects its neighbours. The west elevation, facing onto Queensgate, is given a strong vertical emphasis with the brick panel to the escape stairs and bay window to the office space. This echoes the architecture of the adjacent Omani Embassy, and also acts as a bookend to the Victorian terrace. The centre of the building is arranged axially with Queen's Place (a secondary street joining the western side of Queensgate) and adopts a more monumental scale in response to the longer views afforded by this alignment. The forum space of the Dana Centre is expressed as a blind box at first floor, while the brise-soleil of the office space forms a giant grillage above. The west elevation ends with a large blank brick panel subdivided by subtle terracotta soldier courses – a muted echo of the polychrome Natural History Museum and the striated facades of Richard Norman Shaw's Albert Hall Mansions.

From the south the Queensgate building is revealed as two blocks arranged around a central circulation spine, with the glazed stair tower making the transition to the more open architectural language of the east elevation. The prospect of the building from the Wellcome Wing is of a more forthright expression of function and technology – primarily glass and aluminium with the Dana Centre auditorium punching through the lower levels supported on white concrete columns.

Although the Wellcome Wolfson Building accommodates three distinct functions and responds to the different aspects of its location with appropriate courtesy, its technology is robust and adaptable. The interior of the offices and the public areas of the Dana Centre are characterised by the use of exposed in-situ concrete. The flat slab and circular columns are used to absorb the heat generated by the users while the prominent aluminium grillage of the south, east, and west facades helps reduce solar gain. Because of the location, next to a busy central London thoroughfare, a mixed mode or natural ventilation strategy would have been very difficult to achieve. Instead the chosen strategy of displacement ventilation with exposed thermal mass to absorb heat gain, augmented by external solar shading, obtains an optimum balance between the comfort of the user and the energy consumption of the building.

Above Principal elevation on Queensgate.

Left/below Office spaces feature exposed in-situ concrete; section.

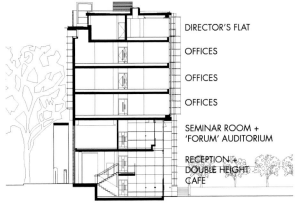

DIRECTOR'S FLAT

OFFICES

OFFICES

OFFICES

SEMINAR ROOM + 'FORUM' AUDITORIUM

RECEPTION + DOUBLE HEIGHT CAFE

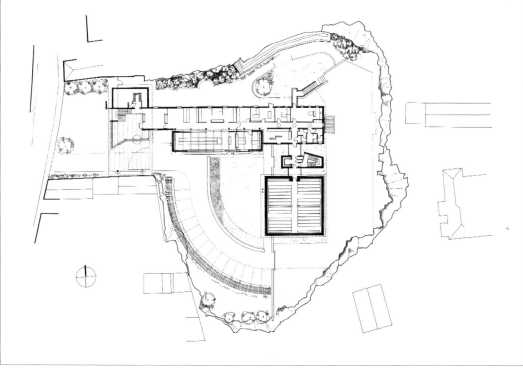

For the Jersey Archive in St Helier, begun in 1996 and built with local practice BDK Architects for the Jersey Heritage Trust, the design challenge was primarily environmental. David Prichard and his team had to 'reconcile the contradiction of absolute control and security of the artefacts with the essential public building criteria of accessibility – both physical and intellectual'.[13] The resulting design incorporates one of the largest repositories in the world to use a passive environmental control system. A range of distinctive buildings, which define three outdoor public spaces with integrated public art works, all employ innovative construction based on technologies familiar to the island's builders and tradesmen.

The repository is a large, mute cube. Situated at the back of the site in a former quarry, it reads as a 'secure' container linked to the 'open' administrative and public elements of the scheme. The L-shaped building and its landscaping contrast with the rugged beauty of the surrounding rock face. Material and form are articulated to make the elements of the scheme immediately legible to visitors, with the blank, white cube set over the stone-walled timber-clad reading room and transparent exhibition space. 'The reading room where the researchers' acts of discovery take place is a treasure chest – a metal-banded oak box with its lid (the roof) open to permit entry of north light and thus literally illuminate the process.'[14]

Jersey State Archive, St Helier (1996-2000)
The archive complex is contained within the rocky bowl of a former quarry. The archives are housed in a white, cubic repository.

Right/below Security levels; sections through courtyard and education/reading room block.

Left The entrance courtyard is overlooked by the glazed reception block; site plan.

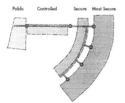

Public   Controlled   Secure   Most Secure

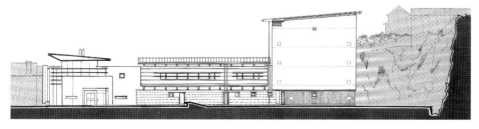

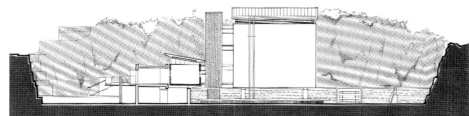

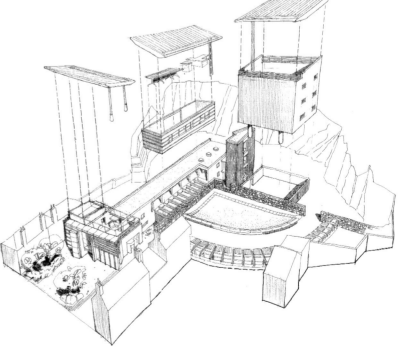

Boathouse 6, Portsmouth Historic Dockyard (1999-2001)
South front with glazed rotunda.

Opposite New splayed steel columns contrast with the original cast iron structure; west-east section before and after conversion showing the new auditorium set within the bomb-damaged east end.

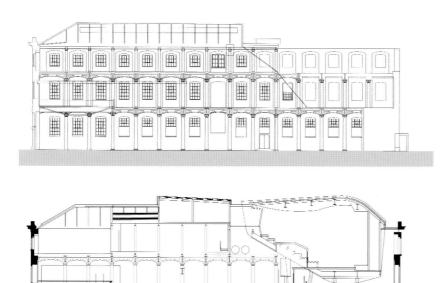

At Boathouse 6 in Portsmouth Historic Dockyard (2000) the challenge was very different – to integrate a new visitor facility into an 1843 iron-framed brick-clad building that was originally used for the storage and repair of boats. Aesthetics counted for little when the east end of the building had been patched up following wartime bombing. Now that the naval base is a major tourist attraction – home to the Mary Rose, HMS Victory and the Royal Naval Museum, among others – attitudes have changed, and Boathouse 6 has become a scheduled ancient monument.

The lottery-funded Action Stations project has transformed the boathouse into a visitor facility, providing a link between the history of the dockyard and the twenty-first century navy, with film and interactive technology to engage visitors. The repaired exterior of the original three-storey building was painstakingly restored to match the original design, with the addition of the prominent glass stair tower. A new 275-seat auditorium and cinema has been placed – seemingly miraculously, like a ship in a bottle – into the east end, leaving what remains of the historic fabric relatively unaffected. There are parallels with the suspension of the IMAX cinema in the great space of the Wellcome Wing, but here, the structure is necessarily independent of the original building. Splayed steel columns, painted black to distinguish them from the cast-iron originals, support the auditorium box, providing a thrilling display of structural gymnastics. The rest of the ground and first floors accommodate interactive displays plus a cafe and shop. The second floor is given over to Portsmouth University's new Institute of Maritime and Heritage Studies, with direct access to the top floor via a glazed lift and staircase tower attached to the southern flank of the building.

As early as 1979 MJP was exploring ways in which to blur departmental and faculty boundaries and make the best use of circulation space, as at the Faculty of Arts at Bristol University. More recently, the changing needs of universities have been reflected in building types and environments at the West Cambridge site, and at the University of Warwick.

At Warwick, MJP has been involved in the Learning Grid project, which is housed in University House, a building purchased recently from the National Grid. MJP had previously prepared a development plan for the university, and had identified this building as a possible link between the two disparate sites of the campus. The project includes the surrounding landscaping, which helps tie the building back into the campus.

The projects discussed in this chapter display a huge variety in their appearance and character from the vibrant interiors of Boathouse 6 and the Wellcome Wing to the calm, purposeful quality of Lancaster Library or the Jersey Archive. However, in every project, MJP's aim was to understand the particular requirements of the people using the building and create an environment to engage their interest, support their learning, and inspire their ideas.

1 Andrea Rose, The Architecture of Information, British pavilion catalogue, 1996 Venice Biennale.
2 Richard MacCormac, Fulfilling the Purpose of Architecture in Higher Education, RFAC, Design Quality in Higher Education Buildings (1995).
3 Richard MacCormac, Architecture: Art and Accountability, RIBA/Interbuild conference, Birmingham (2002).
4 Lord Evans (The Council for Museums, Archives & Libraries), New Statesman Arts Lecture 2001, quoted by MacCormac in Architecture: Art and Accountability.
5 Richard MacCormac, Presence of the Past, essay in catalogue for the Five Buildings exhibition (1994).
6 Jonathan Glancey, The Independent (15 June 1994); Andrew Brister, Building Services Journal (Nov 1993); Colin Amery, Financial Times (13 June 1994).
7 Richard Bornat, Queen Mary & Westfield College client report, Building (23 Feb 2004).
8 Stefan Muthesius, The Postwar University (Yale, 2000); the term was coined by Edward Boyle.
9 Richard MacCormac, Learning with Pleasure, Architects' Journal (18-25 Dec 1997).
10 See references to MJP's libraries at Lancaster in Libraries and Learning Resource Centres, Brian Edwards with Biddy Fisher (Architectural Press, 2002).
11 Richard MacCormac, Ruskin Today: Building the Ruskin Library, Ruskin and Architecture (Spire Books with The Victorian Society, 2003).
12 Thomas A Markus, Buildings and Power (Routledge 1993), p175.
13 David Prichard, An Integrated design: the Jersey Archive, ARQ (vol 5, no 3, 2001).
14 ibid.

Structure and materiality

Structure and materiality

Peter Davey

Since its first projects MJP has engaged both with the materials from which buildings are made and how they are put together.

In the early 1970s Richard MacCormac took me to see the newly completed residential complex for children with learning difficulties at Westoning Manor in Bedfordshire. 'It's just a normal log village', he remarked offhandedly. In fact, it was very far from being a normal anything. Construction of the boarding houses for this visionary enterprise was adapted from a prefabricated Scandinavian system – such things were quite popular for private housebuilding in those days. The building method was chosen for cheapness and speed of erection, but one of the most important reasons for deciding on the system was surely the fact that few young children could possibly object to living in a log cabin – however much the finished result was influenced by Soane and Wright. Not only was the result picturesque, with echoes of the Alps and the Wild West, but the log system offered possibilities of creating forest-scented, warm and comforting spaces at scales appropriate for children.

Similar combinations of criteria, simultaneously pragmatic and poetic, have determined MacCormac's choice of materials throughout his career. Site and context have often played a large part in decisions on materiality. For instance, the brick elements of the housing at Shadwell Basin were chosen to evoke the massiveness of London's Victorian docklands and to address the great pool of water they enclose in a way reminiscent of Telford and Hardwick's St Katharine's Dock. But at Shadwell, heavy almost brutal masonry is relieved by passages of lightweight glass and metal that front the larger rooms of the apartments and offer wide views of the basin. Just as at Westoning, MacCormac tells stories with his materials; here is Victorian toughness and scale, echoing the might of the original docklands (now sadly mostly destroyed), but we are modern and live our lives in the sunlight and security that technology gives us.

Scale has been a major factor in all MJP's residential work, particularly in additions to Oxford and Cambridge colleges that, since the inception of the practice, have constituted a large proportion of the workload. In the Garden Quadrangle at St John's College in Oxford for example, a combination of buff brickwork panels and perfectly formed white precast concrete structure is organised to express the fact that a college is a community of individuals, with each room or set of rooms gently but firmly articulated against the whole mass. The concrete strips form abstracted strings and cornices, and signal recesses and bays in a way that evokes the medieval and classical rhythms and scale of earlier quads.

Similar articulation of brick by concrete strings is seen in the curved liver-coloured brick walls of the chapel at Fitzwilliam College, Cambridge (the strange brick colour was a homage to Denys Lasdun, who designed most of the court in which the chapel is the focus). The curved walls of the chapel embrace a volume that looks out past the altar onto huge mature plane trees in the college garden through the great bronze-framed glass east wall. Within the space floats the body of the chapel, a finely honed wooden platform hovering over a ground floor crypt. In a conventional church, this space would be called the nave (the ship) and the whole wooden interior structure has been formed to evoke the notion that the main part of a church is the ship of faith. Nowhere are nautical analogies made explicit, but the joinery is executed with marine economy and elegance – and the craftsmanship is immaculate – for instance, the thousands of brass screws that fix the oak boards around the central space are turned to exactly the same angle. The ship story, proposed by MacCormac (a passionate sailor) to celebrate one of the oldest myths of Christianity, is given presence by the materials and their handling, down to the last turn of a screwdriver.

MJP have always been associated with traditional or natural materials like wood, brick, slate and stone (often in the guise of precast concrete). In an Arts and Crafts fashion, materials are honestly exposed and allowed to speak for themselves. But in the 1990s new ingredients were added to the palette such as render and claddings, including polished and perforated metal and large-scale sheets of glass. At Southwark underground station on the Jubilee Line Extension there was no alternative means of manipulating the spaces than by cladding the fixed volumes created by civil engineers. The architects' aim was to create a subterranean landscape that would both ease circulation and give clues about your place in the labyrinth by using different wall finishes and lighting.

The station has three main areas. The Blackfriars Road entrance hall (above ground) has a shallow Soanian dome, and the drum it caps is daylit by a clerestorey of glass brick reminiscent of Charles Holden's canonical

1930s tube stations. The intermediate concourse is top-lit by a crescent roof light. From it, escalators descend through Piranesi-like tunnel entrances in a wall of polished concrete blocks. Opposite, a sloping wall follows the curve of the skylight and is clad in triangular panes of blue enamelled glass. Designed in collaboration with the artist Alexander Beleschenko, the panes have a pattern of blue lines at different angles and tones that change from sparkling at the top under the curved rooflight to deep indigo at the lowest level. As you walk around the space, and as the sun moves in the sky, the concourse continually changes in character. Down at the lower concourse, where no daylight can penetrate, tunnels are clad in polished stainless steel panels to maximise the luminance of the blue filtered uplighters.

Blue dominates the spaces of the Wellcome Wing at the Science Museum in London. The addition to the nineteenth-century museum was designed to house interactive displays for interpreting twenty-first century science and technology. By their nature, the displays are constantly changing and MJP wanted to create a space that can accommodate change. The volume is filled with muted blue light intended to evoke the electronic age, a light that allows the exhibits to speak for themselves but a luminance that changes with external conditions. A composite screen was evolved to form the fully-glazed west wall with an outer layer of perforated aluminium that allows 16 per cent of solar heat and 40 per cent of daylight to pass. About a metre behind this perforated layer are triple sandwich panels in which the inner leaf is the sort of blue glass used to make eyewash cups. In the cavity are mirrored aluminium louvres that block direct sunshine for all but 90 seconds in December. Extensive modelling and prototype experiments ensured that the wall works as predicted. The architects and consultants radically rethought materials to form components that seem to make light itself into a building material.

The Wellcome Wing led to further experiments with glass and transparency such as the fritted and acid-etched glass cladding of the BBC's Broadcasting House. But for me, the most moving and poetic use of materials in MacCormac's entire oeuvre is in the Ruskin Library at Lancaster University when it was offered the largest collection of material associated with the great Victorian critic John Ruskin, the author of The Stones of Venice,

perhaps the greatest cultural polemic ever written. Even from the outside, the little building has references to Italy, with its sparkling curved white concrete block walls striated with thin bands of dark green block in memory of Sienna. Between the curved walls is a double-height glass panel into which the bronze door is set, and through the glass are glimpses of the warm interior.

Inside the references are all to Venice. An enlargement of one of Ruskin's daguerrotypes of St Mark's, abstracted onto a big glass panel by Alexander Beleschenko, mistily dominates the foyer. The archive is contained in a building within the curved outer carapace: a strongroom of plaster polished Venetian red and bound with oak strips connected by bronze clasps. On each side of the red box, a path of slate slabs leads like stepping stones over a glass floor that is gradually becoming like the turbid waters of the lagoon as the scratches of use turn it translucent. The analogy is reinforced by dressing the battered walls on the sides of the seapaths with linseed oil, giving them the dark, slippery quality of canal masonry exposed by low tides. The paths culminate in the reading room, a double-height space dominated by a wonderful view through its great west window (an echo of the glass panel round the front door). Vast, ever-changing Morecambe Bay, the place in England most like the Venetian lagoon, is spread below. In the reading room, tables of solid oak inlaid with walnut attended by high-backed oak and leather chairs help create a closeted and comfortable academic atmosphere in contrast to the wide wild wilderness of the bay.

MacCormac's richly allusive architecture never involves the kind of coarse, literal quotations popular among contemporary postmodernists and neoclassicists. Instead, it draws sensitively on the past and on the essence of particular place to tell narratives about history and the world and our place in it. The stories are moving, yet not verbally explicit, a quality of architecture understood by Ruskin, but by few critics since. In MacCormac's work, the tales are always reinforced and elaborated by sensuous, poetic and craftsmanly use of materials, which is why the narratives are so penetrating and poignant.

Peter Davey is an architect, critic and historian. He studied architecture at the University of Edinburgh before joining the staff of the Architects' Journal in 1968, from where he moved to its sister publication the Architectural Review, first as managing editor, then as editor (1982-2005). Davey's books include the definitive study Architecture of the Arts and Crafts Movement (1980), and he has contributed to numerous other books, compendia and international magazines. From 1995 to 1997 he was publisher of the Architectural Research Quarterly. Davey has been jury member of many international competitions and awards; in 1991 he received a Knighthood of the White Rose of Finland and in 1998 he was awarded an OBE.

5 Structure and materiality

Underlying MJP's architectural approach is a concern for the crafted manner in which buildings are put together, and this is well exemplified in the early residential projects such as the log houses of Westoning Manor and the brick and timber housing of Chapter House, Oakwood and Duffryn. These buildings reveal the influence of Frank Lloyd Wright's early work, in particular as interpreted in Henry Russell Hitchcock's book, In the Nature of Materials,[1] as well as contemporary American architects such as Greene and Greene, Schindler and Maybeck. A parallel strand of influence – most clearly traced in the notion of rooting a building on a plinth and floating the roof above – originated in China and Japan, but was reinterpreted by not only Wright but also Jørn Utzon (see, for instance, Platforms and Plateaus: Ideas of a Danish Architect, Zodiac 10, 1962).

While the interest in craft has continued to influence both the structure and use of materials in MJP's architecture, from college residences to the Cable & Wireless College and city office buildings, there has been a growing fascination over the last decade in the unique qualities and 'immateriality' of glass, as evidenced in the Wellcome Wing at the Science Museum, Southwark underground station and Broadcasting House. These buildings provided an opportunity to explore the ambiguous, diaphanous qualities of glass as well as its more evident volumetric, crystalline properties. Director Duncan McKinnon stresses that MJP's work is not 'just a concern with structural expression; in fact, it's the opposite of high-tech. The engineering is always harnessed in the service of creating great spaces, and as a way in which to appreciate other aspects such as form and colour.'

The varied combinations of concrete, stone, steel, glass, brick and timber are striking in the work of the practice, as are the ways in which structure is used to express extrinsic ideas, such as the 'underworlds' of some Oxbridge residences and BBC Broadcasting House. By exploring new forms of construction the practice is able to conjure up a sense of theatre and magic in the most surprising building types. The striking blue wall of Southwark underground station, for example, not only resolves the constructional geometry of an elliptical cone, but also refers obliquely to Schinkel's stage set for the Queen of the Night aria in Mozart's The Magic Flute, creating an unexpected sense of theatre within the station. Appropriately it been used, much to the surprise and delight of the architects and public alike, as a setting for performances by the London Sinfonietta of Fraser Trainer's specially-commissioned composition Line-up. In the Wellcome Wing, the overtly high-tech structural expression is, more importantly, a means of creating the illusion of exhibition trays floating in the ethereal blue-lit space.

Above left
Westoning Manor, Bedfordshire (1972-75)
Oakwood, Warrington (1977-78)
New Court, Fitzwilliam College, Cambridge (1983-86)
Cable & Wireless Technical College, Warwickshire (1990-93)
Southwark Underground Station, London (1991-99)
Warwick Court, Paternoster Place, London (1996-2003)

Above right
Chapter House, Milton Keynes (1974-77)
Sainsbury Building, Worcester College, Oxford (1980-83)
Bowra Building, Wadham College, Oxford (1989-92)
Crown Place, Clifton Street, London (1995-98)
Wellcome Wing, Science Museum, London (1996-2000)
BBC Broadcasting House, London (2006)

Right Sainsbury Building, Worcester College.

Hampshire County Council offices, Havant (1984-89)

Windows, walls and roofs

One of the earliest MJP projects in which window bays were employed was for a community of houses for children with special needs and their carers at Westoning Manor, Bedfordshire. The unusual brief by MacIntyre Schools' first director Kenneth Newton Wright, to build a 'normal log village', resulted in two pinwheel plan timber log houses (of the six planned). The architectural response was a surprising mix of references to Scandinavian construction and materials, and the work of Frank Lloyd Wright and Greene and Greene. Despite the somewhat eccentric brief, Richard MacCormac and Peter Jamieson enjoyed developing the project with what proved to be a very articulate system, made up of pieces that came together as 'large toys'. The low-pitched grey-blue slate roofs, crowned with glazed lights, overhang solid log walls that provide the internal and external finish. The detailing could be very straightforward because the roofs' overhang protected the vertical surfaces from rain, while the interlocking nature of the construction was expressed at the corners with projections.

'Externally the window personifies the building and affirms the human presence, whether in the domestic tradition, represented by Dutch painting, or in the medieval bay or the classical tradition of the window as the vestige of the little house, the aedicule of the god in the Greek temple', writes MacCormac. 'This idea comes from the late Sir John Summerson's marvellous essay, Heavenly Mansions, in which he propounds the theory of aedicular architecture. This inhabited window, or little house, finds its place in much of the practice's work, in the bay windows of the Sainsbury Building at Worcester College, Oxford, and in the aedicular bays of the New Court at Fitzwilliam College, Cambridge. Windows signal the human presence.' [2]

According to Prichard, MJP's preoccupation with the expression of windows is partly a response to the limitations of the curtain wall but, more importantly, it is to do with exploring and manipulating the conceptual status of the window in relation to the wall and roof. Windows are variously treated as a straightforward aperture in a masonry wall; as a void, relating to the Wrightian Chinese/Japanese notion of the roof floating above a masonry base; and as an object within a strongly expressed architrave. At the Chapter House in Milton Keynes the ground-floor brickwork, perforated by windows, rises to the level of the first-floor sills. Above, the first-floor walls are framed in timber which supports the roof. The glazing slots directly into the timber frame, obviating the need for separate window frames and resulting in an architecture in which the roof is seemingly suspended above the brick plinth.

Though far removed from Frank Lloyd Wright, MacCormac cites the work of Alexander 'Greek' Thomson as a key influence, not least the double villa in Glasgow (1856), in which the 'immaculate Greek detailing of the trabeated window/portico opening is visually and memorably undisturbed by the sheet of plate glass behind'.[3] Examining a series of models of Greek Thomson facades made by students at the Mackintosh School of Architecture, MacCormac saw that it was possible to incorporate a sequence of window forms within one building; window as aperture, window as object, and window as continuous void. The building that most clearly exemplifies this exploration is the hostel for the London School of Economics in Myddelton Street. The plinth is punctured by small window openings that light communal rooms, above which the upper storeys rise as a series of planes of brickwork. Within these the projecting brickwork of the plinth is extended up to form window cases that are articulated with reconstituted stone lintels, corbels and cornices. At the uppermost level the wall is set back to reveal planes of glass within a framework of reconstituted stone, finally revealing the underlying framed structure of the building.

Greek Thomson's influence is also evident in the offices for Hampshire County Council in Havant in which the idea of embedding the columns of the first floor into the wall below, and for changing the materiality of the wall from floor to floor while maintaining the same-sized window openings, came from Thomson's now-demolished Cairney Building of 1860. At Havant the roof structure is exposed and the larger offices at first floor level are lit by the translucent glazing panels in the gables. The administrative core for each department is housed in the double-height 'clerical hall' around which are clustered two floors of executive offices, inverting the assumption that 'servant' functions should be in the back rooms with the executives in the grander spaces. The unexpected interior layout is hinted at on the exterior by the barrel-vaulted roof and the glazed umbrella over the staff entrance. 'The articulation of the ground and first floors continues the practice's long-standing exploration of the Wrightian theme of roofs floating over a solid masonry base.'[4]

The use of pitched roofs was becoming more widespread in the early 1970s, partly as a result of the failure of flat roofs and their association with social deprivation, and for MJP the authentication of pitched roofs by the American Arts and Crafts architects of the early twentieth century. Richard MacCormac recalls a comment once made to him by the critic Charles Jencks: that in general either walls or roofs should dominate an architectural composition. At Westoning, Chapter House and Worcester College the idea of the floating pitched roof is dominant. Chapter House has straightforward pitched roofs. At Worcester College's Sainsbury Building, which MacCormac described as 'a piece of ordinary housing that's been composed in a very complex way and

LSE Student accommodation, Myddelton Street, London (1992-93)

Below Cairney Building, Glasgow, by Alexander 'Greek' Thomson (1860).

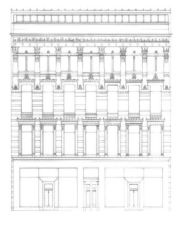

which could be read as a stack of Utzon court houses', a brick building is also covered with simple pitched roofs. The projected eaves have strongly declared rafters and the roof is split, so daylight penetrates into the middle of the building through a glazed ridge, expressed in a broken pediment. Corner bay windows appear at the building's extremities. The clusters of rooms (three in each L-shape, with six rooms sharing a central kitchen) are arranged to be entered on their long side, with daylight entering from the corner.

New Court, a residential building for Fitzwilliam College, Cambridge, represents a shift away from the dominance of the roof towards the articulation of the wall. 'The first change', explains MacCormac, 'is that the roof is subsumed into the top of the brick carcass; the second is that the wall construction and post-and-lintel, or trabeated, bay windows incorporate the wooden bays of Worcester into a masonry system of brick and precast concrete.'

Although the three dimensional organisation of New Court is a logical development of its predecessor at Worcester, its architecture is new. The bay windows are set into concrete-framed aedicules, like miniature buildings with their own roofs. The slender precast structures contribute an entirely different, more urbane, aesthetic to the facade than would have been the case had they been made in timber. The glazed, trabeated openings are articulated in a similar way to those at John Soane's house in Lincoln's Inn Fields, forming a series of shallow steps and layers. The architecture and materials of the facade refer with respect to the neighbouring wing, designed by Denys Lasdun in the 1960s as part of his 1959 masterplan for the college, reflecting the bands of brick and concrete and the mix of wide and narrow windows. But New Court has calmer, more rhythmic symmetries and the white concrete courses help to describe the stepping and layering of the facade.

New Court set off ideas within the practice of trabeated construction and it anticipated the structure and compositional form of the Oxford buildings at Wadham College and St John's College. However, there is also something of the commission for the second, unbuilt, Worcester building in both these schemes which was to develop a kind of hybrid of terraces and pavilions that emerge as prospect towers to create a lively skyline. The second Worcester proposal also develops the combination of precast piers and courses combined with brickwork that emerged out of New Court and characterise both the Bowra Building at Wadham and the Garden Quadrangle at St John's. In each case, the courses bind together complex architectural composition.

At St John's, MacCormac explains, 'we broke the corners of the brickwork to produce slots at the front of the rooms on each side, which back-light the window wall, to reduce the contrast with the light level seen through the window.' In the Jowett Building for

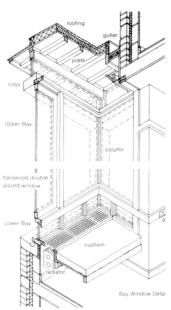

New Court, Fitzwilliam College, Cambridge (1983-86)
Detail of aedicule, bay window detail, oblique view showing the stepped and layered facade that adjoins Denys Lasdun's 1963 building. The front and rear elevations (right) address a court and a street.

Top John Soane's house, Lincoln's Inn Fields, London (1812-34).

151

Balliol College, Oxford, this idea reappears with a game of layering and unpeeling at the corners, where the towers slide up behind layers of brickwork in an allusion to Edwin Lutyens's Castle Drogo in Devon. As at St John's, where the courses articulate the complex profiles of the structure, the brick courses of the Jowett Building articulates the form.

Burrell's Field at Trinity College, Cambridge, is another descendent of New Court, in which the bay achieves a new degree of assertiveness. MacCormac describes the 'explicit 45 degree geometric relationship between the cubic brick construction and the glass and lead-coated steel construction which intersects it; The large volumetric bays imply the corners of glazed cubes, locked into their brick counterparts. In addition, small punched windows sustain the plasticity of the brickwork.'

Project architect Mike Evans described the experience of sitting in one of the bay window seats as being 'beyond the masonry enclosure of the building and out in the landscape. From this position, mirrors set at 45 degrees on either side of the fireplace reveal a fictive space corresponding exactly to the room opposite, reaffirming from inside the counter-geometry of the glass and metal elements expressed in the elevations.'[6] These undergraduate buildings are two- to three-storey high boxes from which emerge 'prospect towers'. They are linked together by walls and paired precast concrete columns, again reminiscent of New Court, which create colonnaded and continuous pergola-like structures that form a boundary. In places they are roofed over to house fellows' sets and common rooms, with the glazing set behind as a continuous screen.

Although gridded curtain wall systems are the norm for wrapping commercial buildings, MJP's preference is for combinations of stone, concrete, steel and glass, applying similar ideas about layering and the plasticity of materials as in its domestic and collegiate work. Interviewed by the RIBA Journal in 1998 about the newly-completed 10 Crown Place office building in Clifton Street, London, MacCormac admitted that the opportunities for innovation and experimentation were limited, but they were still there. Offices, he said, 'are not a dramatic building type. It's essentially a question of how to put windows into a structure.'[7] As with so many building projects in the City of London, the immediate concern was planning consent. The Shoreditch conservation area is characterised by nineteenth century warehouses with powerfully articulated facades. MJP analysed the relationships in these facades between the primary structural piers and the secondary horizontals, which represent the floors with stone or iron lintels, often supported by the tertiary element of a minor central column. MJP reinterprets this grid at Crown Place with paired grit-blasted reconstituted stone columns representing the primary structure and secondary horizontals, and shot-peened

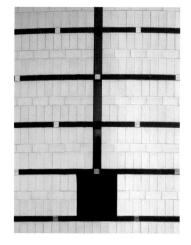

Top to bottom
Edwin Lutyens' Castle Drogo (1910-31) inspired the tower rooms and parapets of Jowett Walk.
Hardwick Hall, Derbyshire, by Robert Smythson (1590-97).
Ruskin Library detail – the exterior is 'encrusted', to use a Ruskininian term, with white masonry and dark grey-green courses, joined with stainless steel bosses, the equivalent of visible fastenings used in the cladding of Italian buildings, which Ruskin called 'confessed rivets' (footnote 5). The courses and spiralling stainless steel plates amplify the sense of curvature.

Right Bowra Building, Wadham College Oxford (1989-92).

Top Garden Quadrangle, St John's College, Oxford (1990-93).

Above The Jowett Building, Balliol College (1994-2004). Pavilions, linked at corners, fulfilled the brief for incremental development. They form three-sided courtyards looking out over the playing fields, an adaptation of the traditional Oxford quadrangle. The organisational diagram is similar to Bowra (Wadham) and St John's Garden Quadrangle, with shared accommodation on the ground floor and residential accommodation above.

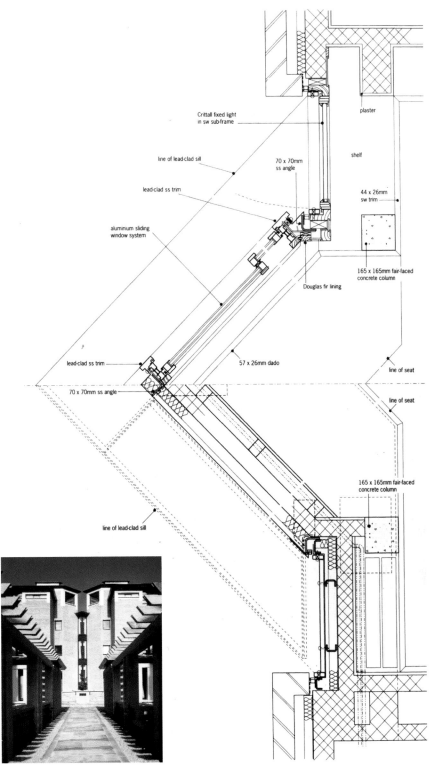

Burrell's Field, Trinity College, Cambridge (1989-95)
Section through the bay window showing the internal concrete profile of the window seat, which is detailed so as to maintain the glazed character of the envelope at intermediate floor levels.

Left diagram labels:
- Crittall fixed light in sw sub-frame
- plaster
- line of lead-clad sill
- shelf
- 70 x 70mm ss angle
- lead-clad ss trim
- 44 x 26mm sw trim
- aluminium sliding window system
- Douglas fir lining
- lead-clad ss trim
- 165 x 165mm fair-faced concrete column
- 70 x 70mm ss angle
- 57 x 26mm dado
- line of seat
- line of seat
- 165 x 165mm fair-faced concrete column
- line of lead-clad sill

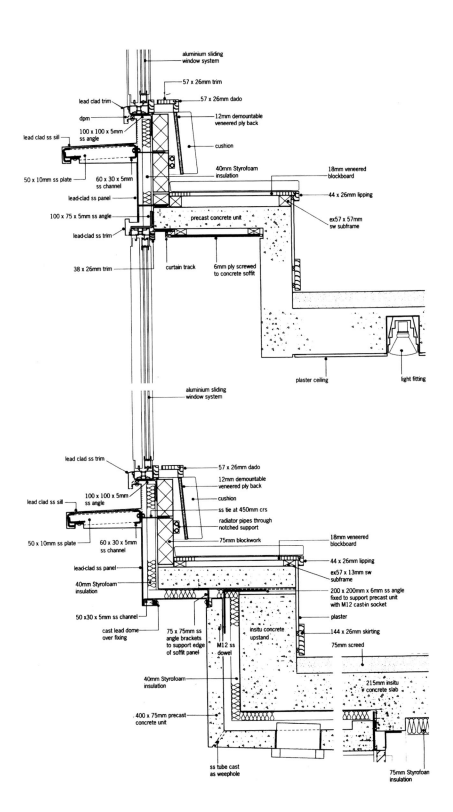

Right diagram labels (upper):
- aluminium sliding window system
- 57 x 26mm trim
- lead clad trim
- 57 x 26mm dado
- dpm
- 12mm demountable veneered ply back
- lead clad ss sill
- 100 x 100 x 5mm ss angle
- cushion
- 40mm Styrofoam insulation
- 18mm veneered blockboard
- 50 x 10mm ss plate
- 60 x 30 x 5mm ss channel
- lead-clad ss panel
- 44 x 26mm lipping
- 100 x 75 x 5mm ss angle
- precast concrete unit
- ex57 x 57mm sw subframe
- lead-clad ss trim
- 38 x 26mm trim
- curtain track
- 6mm ply screwed to concrete soffit
- plaster ceiling
- light fitting

Right diagram labels (lower):
- aluminium sliding window system
- lead clad ss trim
- 57 x 26mm dado
- 12mm demountable veneered ply back
- lead clad ss sill
- cushion
- 100 x 100 x 5mm ss angle
- ss tie at 450mm crs
- radiator pipes through notched support
- 75mm blockwork
- 50 x 10mm ss plate
- 60 x 30 x 5mm ss channel
- 18mm veneered blockboard
- lead-clad ss panel
- 44 x 26mm lipping
- 40mm Styrofoam insulation
- ex57 x 13mm sw subframe
- 200 x 200 x 6mm ss angle fixed to support precast unit with M12 cast-in socket
- 50 x30 x 5mm ss channel
- plaster
- cast lead dome over fixing
- 75 x 75mm ss angle brackets to support edge of soffit panel
- insitu concrete upstand
- 144 x 26mm skirting
- M12 ss dowel
- 75mm screed
- 40mm Styrofoam insulation
- 215mm insitu concrete slab
- 400 x 75mm precast concrete unit
- ss tube cast as weephole
- 75mm Styrofoam insulation

155

stainless steel intermediate columns, the tertiary element between. The clear glass bays lie in the frontal plane of the building.

At Warwick Court, in Paternoster Square, the facade is significantly more complex. 'The five storeys below cornice level have a carcass of stone, strongly expressed as projecting frontages at each end of the long facades', explains MJP director Jeremy Estop. 'Emerging through the flanks of this stone envelope is a layered composition of precast concrete, metal, glass and red sandstone which sets up a complex, syncopated rhythm. It is ordered by the primary structure of columns and beams, into which a secondary grid of metalwork and glass bays is woven. The fifth floor is fully glazed, set back behind a narrow balcony. The secondary grid extends up to support the projecting balustrade.'

David Prichard believes that the success of the design for Cable & Wireless is due to the harmonious nature of the composition and use of materials, despite the conjunction of different building types to accommodate learning, residences, leisure and administration facilities. The fundamental idea for the teaching areas – arranged in two wings of parallel strips to the south of the site – is that the roofs are separated from the concrete structure. A clear distinction is made between the concrete materiality of the robust piers which support the long corridors and the lightweight roofs that float above and overlap each other both in section and in plan.

The powerful linearity of the overlapping wings is in stark contrast to the composition of St John's Garden Quadrangle, which is its contemporary. At Cable & Wireless, the striation created by the blue-green stripes of polished precast courses in the masonry of the back wall are, says MacCormac, 'to do with sustaining a quality of surface over about 200 metres of blockwork. It would have been difficult to sustain the effect of that wall if it wasn't speeded up in some way, with what we called "go-faster stripes".' The Architectural Review considered the workmanship here as 'immaculate and the blockwork, normally such a dreary medium, acquires a kind of nobility'.[8]

The roofs over the teaching areas, which are constructed of curved steel beams and bespoke ceramic tiles, are the most dramatic and memorable element of the scheme. As well as a strong aesthetic they provide a practical solution to lighting and ventilating the teaching spaces. Working with engineers Ove Arup, the undulating roof form was laboratory tested to show that warm air that accumulated under the highest part of the curve would be naturally displaced by cool air entering windows on the lower side.[9]

The architecturally distinct character of the groups of rooms in the long residential terrace to the north of the site is linked to the curved roofs of the teaching spaces by the flat roof which spans the central common rooms and dining room, and defines the oculus. Whereas at New Court the bay windows express the individual rooms, at Cable & Wireless whole groups of bedsitting rooms are pushed through the plane as metal and glass bays, held up by insitu concrete columns, representing a radical change in scale. Between the bays, canopies, supported by tapering steel struts which rest on the top of the columns, allow for the continuation of the sheltered colonnade beneath. These canopies establish a cornice line, level with the teaching wings eaves, that unites the two differently scaled buildings.

Planar architecture
Above Crown Place, Clifton Street, London (1995-98), features a precast facade and glazed bays.

Below/left Warwick Court, Paternoster Square, London (1996-2003), a precast concrete, metal, glass and red sandstone facade facing onto Paternoster Square.

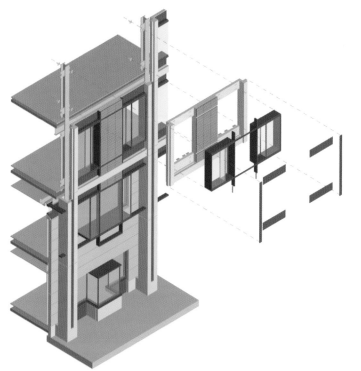

Cable & Wireless Training College, Warwickshire (1990-93)
Roof detail showing the turquoise ceramic tiles located with stainless steel rigging; detail showing bands of custom-made green blocks.

Rendered planes

The Jersey Archive is characterised by its combination of materials and architectural languages, with the disparate elements of the building composed in a picturesque manner. 'The non-geometric forms, which are unusual in our work, were driven by the rugged site, with the quarry walls becoming a part of the architecture of the scheme', explains project architect Neil Deely.

The scheme consists of three elements: a reception and exhibition pavilion, a public reading room (which resembles an oak-panelled chest), and a repository, a four-storey white rendered box, partly resting on two white precast columns. The choice of materials and the construction techniques – in particular the rendered blockwork walls and insitu concrete structure used for the main spine and much of the repository – reflect those available on the island. The Jersey Archive introduces a new theme in the practice's work – the use of render to explore the idea of planar surfaces – and this recurs in the longitudinal walls of the Templewood Avenue house in Hampstead and the rendered elevations of Friendship House in Southwark.

Conceptually, the campus-like design for the British Embassy in Bangkok is a logical progression of the Oxbridge work. Jeremy Estop explains that the new building 'is treated as an inhabited wall around the garden'. The architecture contrasts the solid in situ concrete construction with fine 'furnishing' of light metalwork, hardwood screens, windows, doors and pergolas. The scheme includes embassy staff residences, a club and sports facilities as well as domestic staff residences, arranged around an enclosed garden, that provides an oasis in the middle of this frenetic city. The residential building consists of a terrace of loadbearing concrete cross walls infilled with light glazed screens and timber louvres on the garden elevation and solid fenestrated walls on the elevation to the boundary to resist bomb blasts.

The compositional idea of Bangkok has been likened to a musical score, with the crosswalls establishing a rythmic beat and the variety of accommodation, houses and apartments, introducing a series of subthemes with combinations of internal and external spaces, terraces and greens within a constant discipline of concrete crosswalls and piers. The crosswalls and piers represent the primary and secondary structures and spatial subdivisions are intersected laterally by the service zones for built-in furniture. The material quality of the scheme resides in the contrast between two kinds of construction, the rendered concrete walls and the internal and external joinery, a furniture of screens, louvres and pergolas.

The lateral approach to the existing ambassador's residence from the new entrance on Wireless Road is in the tradition of the English country house, where the landscape and the residence are revealed gradually through a sequence of views and spaces.

**British Embassy, Bangkok
(2005-09, above and right))**
White rendered walls with terraces, balconies and timber louvred windows create a rhythm to the facades and a screen to more private rooms set deeper in the plan.

Left Jersey State Archive, St Helier (1996-2000); Templewood Avenue, Hampstead (1995-99); Friendship House, Belvedere Place, Southwark (2001-03) with narrow horizontal bands of turquoise mosaic tiles at each floor level to provide relief to the white render.

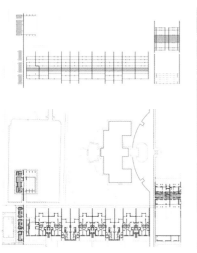

Above Sainsbury Building, Worcester College,
Oxford (1980-83).

Below Bowra Building, Wadham College,
Oxford (1989-92).

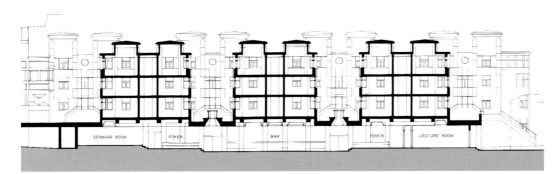

SEMINAR ROOM   FOYER   BAR   FOYER   LECTURE ROOM

Underworlds

The notion of an underworld that contrasts with an inhabited
world above appears initially in the Sainsbury Building at
Worcester College, where the common room is positioned at water
level below a terrace. 'It is our first building that makes an
architectonic distinction between the residential superstructure
and the common room in the base', says MacCormac. 'It also
refers to Aalto's MIT dormitory in Cambridge, Massachusetts,
where the white concrete common room is constructed as a post
and lintel structure in contrast to the sinuous brick superstructure
of the student accommodation above.'

In the drawings for the second Worcester College building there
is a 'crypto porticus' or underground passage, which runs through
the plinth as a processional route from the auditorium to the
fellows' meeting room. Special views into the garden would have
been seen from this cave-like space.

The site for the Bowra Building at Wadham College was an
urban rather than semi-rural location, with more public
accommodation than in either of the Worcester buildings. As a
result, the whole of the ground level is given over to a series of
public rooms, including a sunken gymnasium, creating an
underworld of columned architecture and large spans. As at
Worcester College, this is a concrete underworld, spatially
independent of the configuration of student rooms above.

At the Cable & Wireless College, the client's late introduction to
the brief of a leisure pavilion, in combination with the local
planners' height restrictions, pushed the pool and sports hall into
the ground. David Prichard chose to exaggerate this by creating a
hillock out of which the pool hall emerges – an otherwise Roman-
like underground chamber with a barrel roof, massive columns
and grotto green mosaic linings. The grotto introduces the theme
of water for the whole campus.

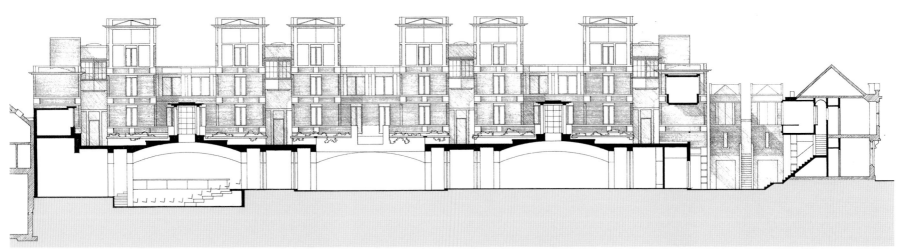

St John's College Oxford, Garden
Quadrangle (1990-93, left and right)

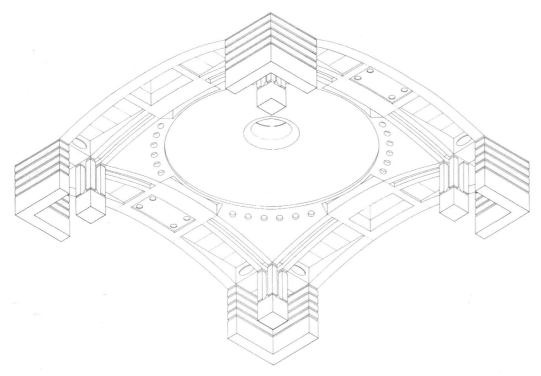

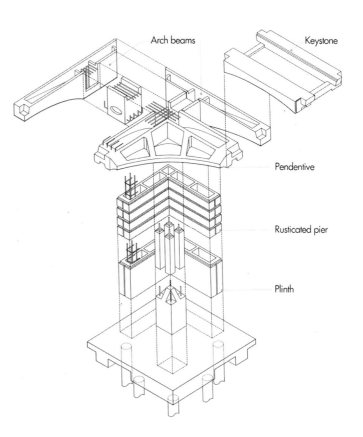

Arch beams

Keystone

Pendentive

Rusticated pier

Plinth

At MJP's St John's College project the contrast between the worlds above and below is even more dramatic. Three cavernous spaces, which perhaps originate in the design for the mall in the final masterplan for Spitalfields market, support towers and gardens above. This is the most striking instance of an underworld in the collegiate projects, anticipating the much greater scale of the proposed newsroom in the BBC redevelopment. It combines hollow keystones, very large precast concrete elements weighing up to 20 tonnes, with articulated and variously finished concrete elements such as the heavily point-tooled piers and the highly polished columns and grit-blasted pendentives that support the shallow domes. The entrance to the underworld, through a large arch at the south of the building, leads to a sunken circular forum at the heart of main east-west axis. The dining room, to the east, and the auditorium, to the west, are expressed at terrace level by circular lanterns providing lighting to the interiors, inspired by the work of John Soane. The sense of mystery in these underground spaces is anticipated by the magnifying lens in artist Wendy Ramshaw's gate, which gives access from the fellows' garden. Alex Beleschenko's glass screens veil and partly conceal the interiors.

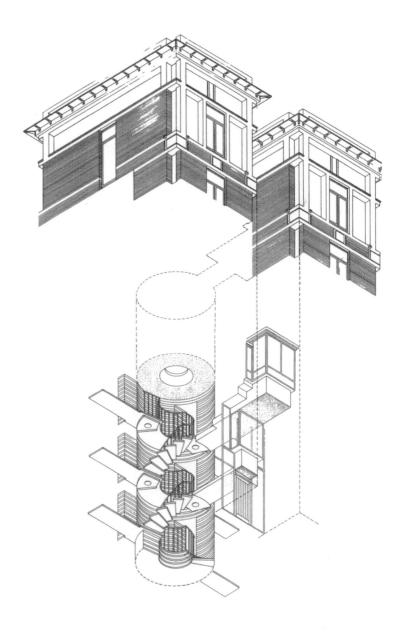

St John's College Oxford, Garden Quadrangle (1990-93)
MJP's most structurally complex Oxbridge building is a puzzle of interlocking pieces with services cast into the precast concrete, including air conditioning fed into the pendentives of the domes. Its realisation, says Jeremy Estop, 'relied upon our collaboration with the structural engineers, Price and Myers, and their commitment to the job. Constructing one building type on top of another was always going to be difficult. It was achieved by using precast concrete, which limited the risk and potential delays'. Drawings show the roof vault dome structure over the auditorium and dining room, the precast concrete roof support assembly, and the staircase.

Right Alex Beleschenko's glass screen and Wendy Ramshaw's gate at St John's.

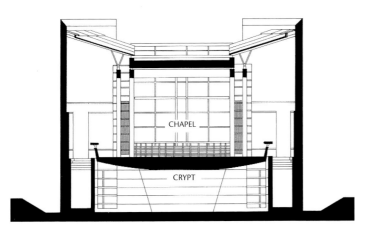

The Fitzwilliam College Chapel in Cambridge, however, is the most succinct expression of the idea. Here the underworld is the crypt, and the world above, the congregational space, consists of a timber vessel suspended between piers, which in turn support the four paired columns and the roof. Richard MacCormac's ideas for the chapel were reinforced by a visit to Antoni Gaudi's incomplete Guell Chapel in Barcelona. Other influences include various buildings that house ships, such as the Vasa in Stockholm and Viking vessels in Oslo, where the planked wooden hulls contrast with the smooth curved surfaces of their enclosures. Although the Ruskin Library is self-evidently a direct development of the Fitzwilliam Chapel, the underworld there is virtual and publicly inaccessible. It is only possible to glimpse the basement space through the glass floor which runs from the entrance at ground level, where it suggests the lagoon and the canals of Venice.

Fitzwilliam College Chapel, Cambridge (1989-91)
Cross section through the chapel 'upperworld' and crypt 'underworld'.

Right Detailed sections through the 'vessel' balustrade showing the glazed 'water line' sealing the gap between the vessel and the wall that separates the stair from the crypt.

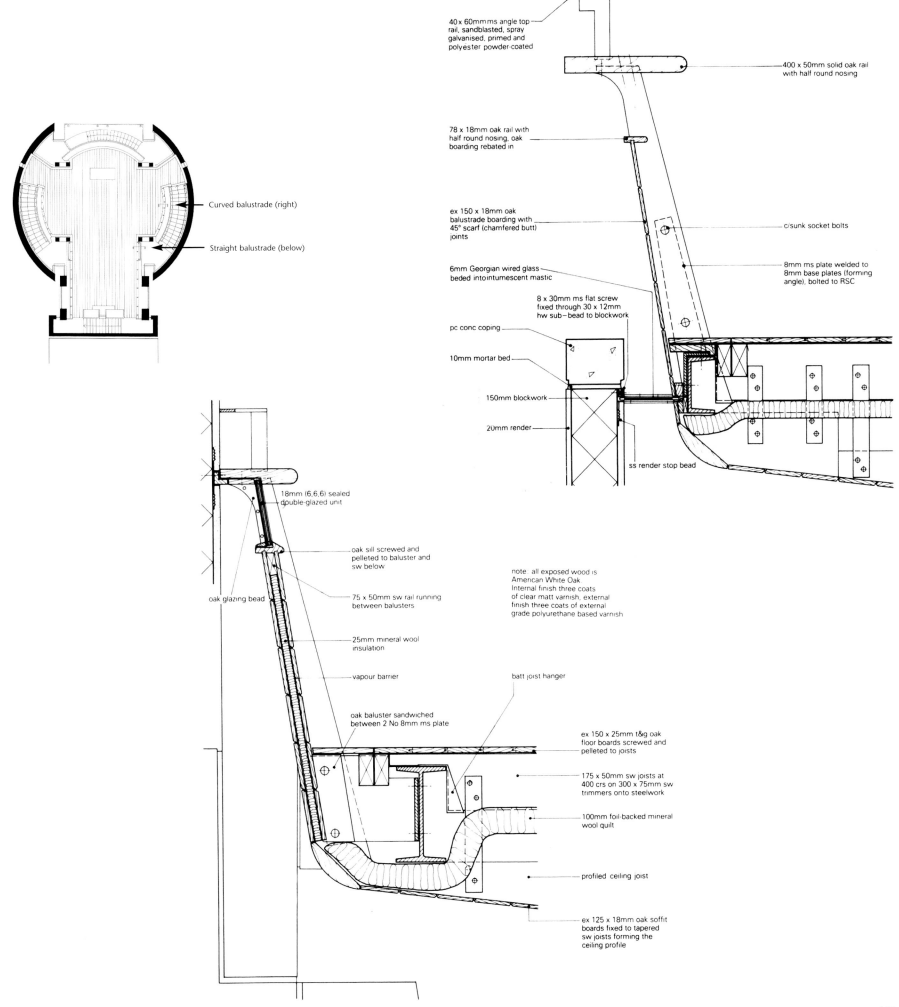

40 x 60mm ms angle top rail, sandblasted, spray galvanised, primed and polyester powder-coated

400 x 50mm solid oak rail with half round nosing

78 x 18mm oak rail with half round nosing, oak boarding rebated in

ex 150 x 18mm oak balustrade boarding with 45° scarf (chamfered butt) joints

c/sunk socket bolts

6mm Georgian wired glass beded into intumescent mastic

8mm ms plate welded to 8mm base plates (forming angle), bolted to RSC

8 x 30mm ms flat screw fixed through 30 x 12mm hw sub-bead to blockwork

pc conc coping

10mm mortar bed

150mm blockwork

20mm render

ss render stop bead

Curved balustrade (right)

Straight balustrade (below)

18mm (6,6,6) sealed double-glazed unit

oak sill screwed and pelleted to baluster and sw below

oak glazing bead

75 x 50mm sw rail running between balusters

25mm mineral wool insulation

vapour barrier

batt joist hanger

oak baluster sandwiched between 2 No 8mm ms plate

note: all exposed wood is American White Oak Internal finish three coats of clear matt varnish, external finish three coats of external grade polyurethane based varnish

ex 150 x 25mm t&g oak floor boards screwed and pelleted to joists

175 x 50mm sw joists at 400 crs on 300 x 75mm sw trimmers onto steelwork

100mm foil-backed mineral wool quilt

profiled ceiling joist

ex 125 x 18mm oak soffit boards fixed to tapered sw joists forming the ceiling profile

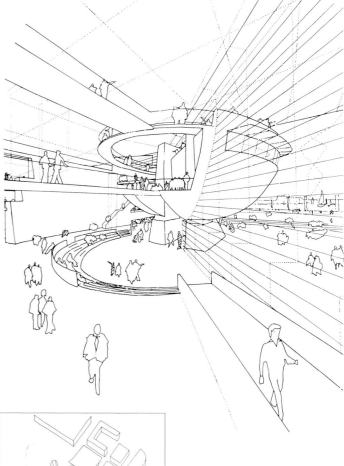

Gathering and enclosure

Addressing the pierhead

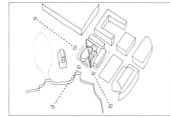

Facing the world

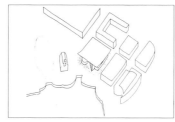

Inclusive roof

Welsh Assembly competition, Cardiff (1998)
The central concept of MJP's competition scheme for the Welsh Assembly was that the assembly chamber (left) should be raised, visibly held aloft as a vessel, rather than sunk into the podium. The patinated bronze-clad chamber is in the form of a vessel which alludes to the maritime history of its location, and to the idea of politics as a rite of passage. The geometry of the scheme generated a prow in the form of a terrace with a large public half landing above. The public areas were enclosed by a curved slate-clad wall, reminiscent of a slate quarry (tactile, and resonant of Wales), to separate it from the members' offices. Shutters would come down over the continuous strip window at the back of the public gallery when the assembly is sitting. The whole structure played a fundamental role in the energy strategy for the building. The cloud-like roof was designed to admit a gradation of daylight and controlled sunlight which would increase in intensity towards the back of the space. The interior would have given a strong feeling of being outside, enhancing the landscape metaphor. The roof, with a continuously perforated soffit, was designed to be highly sensitive to changing conditions of daylight and sunlight, so that those in the public space of the building would experience the changeable weather of the bay.

In MJP's scheme for the redevelopment of the BBC's Broadcasting House the great newsroom that occupies the ground and lower ground level of the new development allows for maximum uninterrupted floorspace, but it is also a physical representation of the importance of news at the heart of the corporation's output. The weight of the building is drawn down onto the branches of huge tree-like transfer columns, enabling the centre of the newsroom to be column free. By flooding the space with daylight from two atria above, the architects wanted to ensure that journalists, producers and technicians would not experience any sense of working below ground.

Newsroom, BBC Broadcasting House (2006)
'Another architect might have set out to design the transfer structure over the Broadcasting House newsroom as an overtly expressive structure. We are always trying to surprise and delight, rather than overly explain how things work' (Duncan McKinnon). In this case the structural expression is about forming a volume which encapsulates the activity of the newsroom in a great central space.

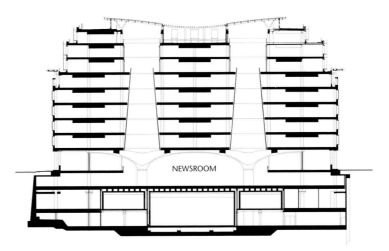

NEWSROOM

'Furnishing' a building

For MJP 'furnishing' is not so much about placing movable utilitarian objects in a building, but finely crafting the individual elements that relate a building to its users, and which can comfort, surprise or delight them. Often these elements achieve an architectural identity of their own. As early as the Chapter House project (1973-77) the timber staircases are seen as a subordinate architecture that is conceived as furniture. This, says MacCormac, was partly influenced by conversations with Philip Dowson of Arup Associates in the early 1970s about the Thomas White building for St John's College, Oxford, and also by the architecture of Louis Kahn in which the scale of the primary structure contrasts with the elements with which the user has direct contact.

In the Sainsbury Building at Worcester College the staircases and kitchens are conceived as large pieces of timber furniture with a strong visual identity. This idea was developed further, using polychromy, in the interior of New Court at Fitzwilliam College where the windows are like cabinets fitted into the precast structure. At Fitzwilliam, the Bowra Building at Wadham College and St John's, student kitchens are planned as pieces of exquisite cabinetwork suspended over the entrances. At the Bowra Building the kitchens are pushed out from the elevation plane at first floor level, so that students can look sideways up and down the lane. At St John's they appear to be dramatically suspended between twin towers, perched like crow's nests between first and second floor levels. At Cable & Wireless the staff rooms form balconies that project over the circulation routes and the residences' staircases are like a nest of boxes – the south-facing bays express a cluster of rooms, within each room is the lobby expressed as a red box, inside which is another aedicule, the jade mosaic shower cubicle.

The theme reaches a logical conclusion with Fitzwilliam College Chapel and the Ruskin Library where the 'furniture' provides the focus of the main space, creating a building within a building. The predominant materials in the chapel interior are white render and white concrete. These are finished with stone-like rustications at the lower level, with slender highly polished columns and beams above, contrasting with the honey-coloured oak vessel that forms the principal floor at the centre. The wooden underside is curved like the hull of a boat and appears to be detached from the outer curved structure. Oak stairs follow the curve of the cylindrical outer walls, finished in white render, with string courses relating to those on the exterior. Like the treatment of the columns and piers, the courses develop from rusticated strips at the lower level through to lines simply incised into the internal render, which represent the daywork joints.

Top to bottom
Exeter Library, New Hampshire, Louis Kahn (1967-72).
Thomas White Building, St John's College, Oxford, Arup Associates (1970-75).
Kitchen at Worcester College, Oxford, MJP.
Organ doors closed at MJP's Fitzwilliam College Chapel.

Right
Fitzwilliam College New Court staircase from top-floor landing. The large spherical uplighter acts as a 'light fountain' to throw light up to the Soanian-ochre ceiling.
Striped ash veneer staircase from the ground floor lobby.

Appropriately the Ruskin Library is dominated by the Ruskin archive, a three-storey-high piece of furniture reminiscent of the building-like cabinets of William Burges and crafted in a similarly elaborate manner with oak, bronze and polished red Venetian plaster. The inspiration for the archive, and the idea of the separate identity, range from the choirs in medieval cathedrals to Richard Serra's Weight and Measure sculpture. The poetic manipulation of light in the library, with shafts dropping vertically through dramatic slots, highlights the relationship of the archive to the outer ark, and has its origins in the Fitzwilliam College Chapel. 'Daylight filters down through the whole three-storeys, separating the archive structure from the galleries on each side, just as it separates the centre of the Fitzwilliam Chapel from the periphery.' [10]

**Ruskin Library, Lancaster University
(1992-97)**
Detail showing the oak and red Venetian plaster and a glimpse of the Beleschenko glass.
Drawing of Ruskin Library interior revealing the central archive.
Interior detail looking through a glass bridge which connects one gallery to the other.

Southwark Station (1991–99)
Intermediate level with blue cone wall by Alexander Beleschenko; detail showing the fritting pattern on the triangular glass panes.

Right Ascending the escalator from the platforms to the intermediate concourse.

Materiality and immateriality

By the time MJP won commissions for the Jubilee Line Extension underground station at Southwark, the Wellcome Wing at the Science Museum and Broadcasting House they had already explored, says MacCormac, 'the crystalline and volumetric qualities of glass which can forcefully represent the volume of a building'. The language of bay windows developed in the college buildings had been refined in the robust character of the bays in the offices buildings at Clifton Street and Paternoster Square, where glass came to be used in a tectonic manner.

However, in these more recent buildings the practice also began to explore the diaphanous qualities of glass. At Southwark the glazed lining to the intermediate concourse, when first encountered obliquely from the descending escalator, appears to be a brittle, reflective material. Conversely, when seen from the ascending escalator that emerges from the lower concourse, it appears almost transparent. 'The architecture of St John's and Cable & Wireless was highly tectonic', says Richard MacCormac. 'They're about constructional ideas. But we decided that the Jubilee Line Extension station at Southwark wasn't going to be a demonstration of bravura engineering, rather it was to be about surface, light and artifice, to create unexpected atmospheres – a lumière mysterieuse perhaps, which defies the experience of being underground.' In contrast, the subterranean architecture of Hopkins Architects' Westminster JLE station is rooted in the expression of structure and cavernous engineering.

At Southwark the curving glass wall on the intermediate concourse level brought together 'art, architecture, engineering, computing and manufacturing technology to stunning effect.' [11] Initially the geometry of the wall presented problems in the choice of cladding as it seemed impossible to design a system that could employ a repetitive panel. In collaboration with engineer Hanif Kara (then with YRM Anthony Hunt) and artist Alex Beleschenko, MJP developed the idea of using a pattern of triangles that varied in size and shape (with narrower triangles towards each end of the wall). The material of choice was glass, since the panels could be cut to shape with comparative ease. The refinement of the triangular tessellation, the development of the surface and the final specification included four print designs in four different rotations, giving a multiplicity of fritting patterns.

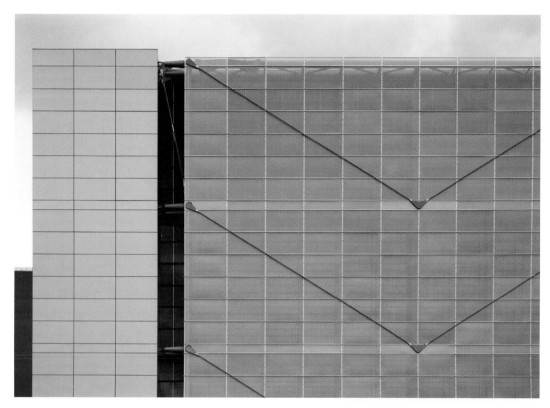

Tectonically the Wellcome Wing is very clear – a series of insitu concrete columns with great steel cantilevered gerberettes which support the huge trusses of the exhibition trays and hold aloft the Imax cinema. But at the same time the building seems to defy structural understanding, with these giant structures veiled from below by steel grillage which creates a sense of weightlessness. Fibreglass mesh scrims hung on the north and south sides obscure and seemingly dematerialise the lateral walls and concrete columns. Rogier van der Heide, then principal of lighting designer Hollands Licht and a key collaborator on the project, accentuated the effect by washing the white-painted surfaces behind the scrims with blue light, dislocating the spatial boundaries.

The blue west wall, now the defining hallmark of the Wellcome Wing, comprises an outer skin of clear glass and an inner layer of blue glass with polished aluminium solar louvres in the cavity. An additional outer shield of perforated aluminium panels helps to reduce solar gain and sunlight penetration. The glass is supported by a lightweight steel structure supported by three pairs of V-shaped, high-tensile steel bracing rods which direct the loads diagonally to pairs of support points at the top of each end of the curtain wall. Though impressive, the structural engineering is barely visible, a paradox perhaps, but simply a means of achieving a dramatic, dematerialised context for the new world of information and biotechnology.

Wellcome Wing, Science Museum, London (1996-2000)
The Blue Wall creates an electric glow evocative of the electronic age in which we live. The only sign of the structural gymnastics are three pairs of V-shaped cross braces.

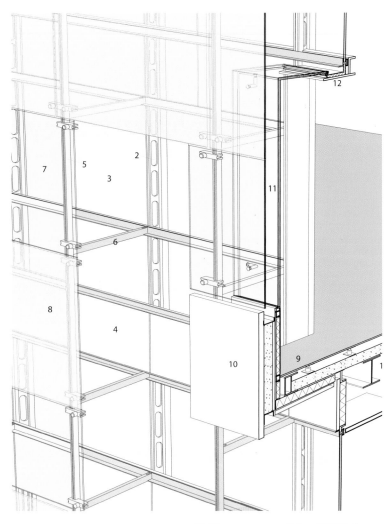

Faced with the prestigious yet daunting commission to extend the BBC's Broadcasting House at the north end of Regent Street, MJP gave careful consideration to the approach. The original 1932 building, Richard MacCormac points out, 'is a highly abstracted stone envelope made up of screens of Portland stone wrapped around a steel frame. Rather than the rational, declared precast structure of Crown Place and Warwick Court, the architectural character of the original Broadcasting House triggered a response that was also quite abstract.' The elevations along Portland Place to the west, Hallam Street to the east and the north elevation between the two are clad in Portland stone, but the south elevation required a specific response to provide a new backdrop to Nash's grade-one listed All Souls' Church on Langham Place. The solution took the form of a glass concave screen that made a clear distinction between the old and new buildings, wrapping around the space and locking into the new stone facade on the east side.

A polarity is set up between the assertive convex solidity of Broadcasting House and the receptive concavity and lightness of the suspended facade. The solar screen of laminated glass is etched in a pattern of vertical strips on the outer face and a ceramic frit on the outward-facing surface of the inner laminate, with a grid of small squares on the same horizontal module as the etched strips. The ceramic frit is chromatically and tonally matched to the Portland stone facade at the north-east corner of Broadcasting House. In daylight the patterned areas of the screen appear relatively opaque and comparable to the Portland stone of Broadcasting House. At twilight, the facade is transformed like a theatre scrim, becoming increasingly transparent as the daylight levels drop below those inside the building. The night time transparency can be reversed or varied by external floodlighting or

BBC Broadcasting House, London (2006)
Designed by MJP in collaboration with structural and facade engineer, Whitbybird, the aim was to create a calm uncluttered facade, minimising movement joints. The two seven-storey skins are hung independently from cantilevered brackets. A 1.2 metre gap in between allows access for a cleaning cradle, so there are no maintenance gantries. Very low wind speeds mean diagonal bracing can be eliminated by using rigid connections.

Glazed facade (drawing by Graham Bizley):
1 Main building structure
2 Internal skin structure
3 Internal skin glazing
4 Internal skin solid panel
5 External skin structure
6 Wind-load restraint
7 External skin – clear glazing
8 External skin – fritted glazing
9 Balcony floor
10 Balcony external wall
11 Balcony internal glazing
12 Balcony gutter

Above Full-size mock up of façade used for lighting tests.

Below Photos of a model showing results of lighting tests.

by projecting images onto the facade.[12] Sophisticated lighting design is needed in order to pull off the trickery of immateriality and, in this case as for the west facade of the Wellcome Wing, the concept lighting design was entrusted to Rogier van der Heide.

Lighting tests of the glazed facade were carried out in 2002 in a studio at BBC Television Centre in Shepherds Bush with BBC technicians and van der Heide. A full-size one-storey high two-metre wide module of the solar facade and building envelope was constructed using combinations of clear, etched and printed glass with elements of the ceiling, floor and back wall. The appearance of the facade was examined in a range of daytime and nightime conditions with a range of internal lighting levels. The tests included lighting the cavity between the external solar facade and the building envelope and using blue light to illuminate the back wall and ceiling downstand.

The solar facade consists of transparent strips of glass, which allow views out, alternating with larger areas of printed and etched glass, which moderate the daylight. The interlayer of the lamination, with a 64 per cent opaque pattern of squares, is over-laid by an etched pattern of vertical strips, which convert some of the transparency into translucency. The non-reflective and opaque characteristics of the facade are most apparent when seen obliquely, and will appear similar to Portland stone during daylight. There was an intention for light artists to work on the appearance of the building at night and the tests demonstrated the potential effect of blue light which would create a dramatic backdrop to the floodlit spire of All Souls.

1 In the nature of materials: the buildings of Frank Lloyd Wright 1887-1941, Henry Russell Hitchcock (1942).
2 Space and Light, Richard MacCormac. Modern Painters (Summer 1993).
3 The past and MacCormac, Dan Cruickshank. Architectural Review (May 1989).
4 County Classic, Richard Weston, Architects' Journal (20 Sept 1989).
5 The Ruskin Library, Lancaster, Richard MacCormac, Architecture of Information catalogue, British pavilion, Venice Biennale (1996).
6 Distinguished pavilions, Michael Evans, Architects' Journal (1 Feb 1996).
7 Beyond the fringe, Jeremy Melvin, RIBA Journal (Dec 1998).
8 Only connect, Peter Davey, Architectural Review (May 1994).
9 Green Buildings Pay, ed Brian Edwards (Spon 1998).
10 Ruskin Today: Building the Ruskin Library, Lancaster, Richard MacCormac, Ruskin & Architecture, ed Rebecca Daniels and Geoff Brandwood (Spire 2003).
11 Rhapsody in Blue, James Macneil, Building (5 June 1998).
12 See Light House News, Richard MacCormac, Architectural Review (April 2004).

Test one shows the facade in daylight when external light levels are sufficient to reduce dependence on artificial light internally. This is the condition when the facade is most opaque, but the Portland Stone in the building envelope behind the solar facade is still perceptible.

Test two shows the facade in an overcast sky. Internal lighting causes slightly more transparency (the warmer tone is caused by the colour value of the dimmed light, representing the sky).

Test three shows the facade at twilight. Transparency is greater because of relatively higher internal light levels.

Test four shows the facade at night with some external floodlighting and some lighting between the facade and the envelope. The relationships between internal light levels, external light levels and lighting in the cavity offer a high degree of control of the backdrop to All Souls at night.

Test five shows the facade at night. Because the concave facade directly to the north of All Souls does not front production areas with high light levels (350 lux) it will be possible to reduce lighting on floors and working surfaces to 150 lux. Non-reflective surfaces will keep ambient levels low with the objective of restricting the reflective light levels of soffits seen from below.

Art and
architecture

Art and architecture

Richard Cork
MJP's reading of architecture as a cultural activity has led to many productive artistic collaborations.

For much of the twentieth century, adventurous artists and architects regarded each other with a mistrust bordering on outright disdain. Artists bridled at the traditional idea that architecture was the 'mother of all the arts'. They hated the thought of continuing to play a subservient role outside or inside buildings, and the word 'decorative' became anathema to most artists involved with modernist aspirations. As for architects, they aimed increasingly at the creation of self-sufficient structures no longer reliant on an artist to lend them aesthetic credibility.

Viewed in this embattled context, the enlightened outlook developed by MJP seems almost miraculous. Far from shunning all contact with the pollution of artists, Richard MacCormac and his colleagues became open in their willingness to consider an admirably wide range of possibilities for art. Backed by the informed enthusiasm of Vivien Lovell, a prodigious number of artists including Antony Gormley and Howard Hodgkin were approached when MJP started working on St John's College Garden Quadrangle in Oxford. Lack of funding from its alumni meant that, in the end, only Alexander Beleschenko, John Howard and Wendy Ramshaw were able to carry out commissions there. But Beleschenko's translucent glass screens play an integral part in the spatial

experience offered at St John's, and Ramshaw's iron gate with its fish-eye glass lens was a breakthrough which led her work into new areas.

Unlike so many architectural practices, MJP have never been loath to pinpoint the stimulus provided by artists. Take the Wellcome Wing at the Science Museum in London, where the luminous impact of the great blue wall was inspired by Yves Klein and James Turrell. Both men had been given outstanding exhibitions at the Hayward Gallery, and the blueness they explored there became an essential part of the potency achieved by MJP in the Wellcome Wing.

The eloquence of colour grew even more spectacular when a team led by MacCormac tackled the designs of two major London exhibitions: Ruskin, Turner and the Pre-Raphaelites at Tate Britain, and Surrealism: Desire Unbound at Tate Modern. Boldly escaping from minimal whiteness, both shows were transformed by coloured light with filters. The emotional drama of Ruskin's life was reflected in the design's intensity, culminating in a deep purple room exploring the traumatic moment when he finally went mad. And the audacious colours deployed throughout the Surrealism survey proved equally powerful, whether in the embryonic shock delivered by pink light at the entrance or the central area of darkness signifying sadistic aggression.

The tragic legacy of full-scale destruction provided a formidable challenge at Coventry, where MJP and Vivien Lovell devised a regenerative scheme enriched and articulated by artists at every turn. No arbitrary constraints were placed on the media they employed or their modus operandi. At one extreme, sound elucidated the vision of David Ward who made powerful, poignant use of the city's oral archive in the eleventh-century Priory Cloister which was recreated with pleached lime trees. Elsewhere, in the aptly named Garden of International Friendship, Kate Whiteford devised a maze fragment whose outermost edge is defined by a bronze text taken by the poet David Morley from the Coventry Mystery Plays. As I have argued elsewhere,[1] MJP can achieve a genuinely heartfelt sense of catharsis. Nowhere more hauntingly than at the new Broadcasting House, where all the people who have died working for BBC News are memorialised in Jaume Plensa's steel and glass cone projecting words as elegiac as 'silence' and a defiant beam of light high into the sky at night.

Richard Cork is an art critic, historian, broadcaster and exhibition curator. He read art history at Cambridge, where he was Slade Professor from 1989-90. Formerly editor of Studio International and art critic of the Evening Standard, The Listener and The Times, he now writes for the Financial Times and a range of international art magazines. He has curated exhibitions at Tate, the Royal Academy, the Hayward Gallery, Barbican Art Gallery and the Serpentine Gallery. His books include studies of Vorticism (1976), Art Beyond The Gallery (1984), David Bomberg (1987), A Bitter Truth: Avant-Garde Art and the Great War (1994), and four volumes of critical writings on modern art (2003). In 2009 he curated the exhibition Wild Thing at the Royal Academy, which focused on the radical work of sculptors Epstein, Gaudier-Brzeska and Gill. His book, Mercy, Madness, Pestilence and Hope: A History of Western Art in Hospitals, will be published in 2010.

1 Richard Cork, A Redemptive Alliance: Art, Architecture and Landscape in the Renewal of Coventry, Phoenix: Architecture–Art–Regeneration (Black Dog 2004).

6 Art and Architecture

The Art and Architecture conference held in 1982 at the Institute of Contemporary Arts (ICA) in London was a defining moment. At the time architects, and indeed clients, had a reputation of fighting shy of meaningful collaborations with artists. Among clients, art was often regarded as an unnecessary and extravagant expenditure, while architects played up to their reputation as the guardians of design for whom the idea of aesthetic collaboration was anathema. As a result public art was limited, with very few exceptions, to self-contained works sitting in or near major public buildings. If the art was moved elsewhere, the building would lose little of its meaning or identity. Today, the most successful public art programmes are unique and inspired by the site and, in many cases, public art has become as much about contributing to public space as enhancing architecture.

The ICA conference brought together politicians and environmentalists as well as artists, and ideas of interdisciplinary collaboration, and the principle of the funding mechanism Percentage for Art, gathered pace. The Arts Council came to back the scheme, and the Royal Society of Arts set up the Art for Architecture scheme, which until 2004 supported the early involvement of artists in building schemes. Nowadays planning authorities often play a role in encouraging public art as an integral part of new buildings.

Despite an initial reluctance to work formally with artists on the design of their buildings, MJP nevertheless embraced exposure to artists and their work from the very earliest days. When the office was based at 5 Dryden Street in Covent Garden, many of its fellow tenants were artists, and when MJP set up the Spitalfields Workspace in Heneage Street, they sublet space to artists and made the foyer available for exhibitions of local artists' work. The practice also instigated fortnightly Monday evening previews, which brought many artists to the office.

When Richard MacCormac first started considering collaborations with artists he was concerned with 'rediscovering a spatial relationship between works of art and architecture'. Historically the role of art within architecture had been quite clearly defined – the frieze on a temple, the decoration of a lintel or carved detail on a staircase. 'One was reassured that art had its place, and that the relationship between artist and architect was mutually understood.' MacCormac had originally felt that art should be at the service of architects, to amplify the architecture. What would happen, he asked, 'if you took the artist away from the autonomous work of art? How would an essentially private message sit in the public realm, and would it require the presence of the artist to explain the concept behind the work?'

In retrospect, MacCormac sees the ICA debate as anticipating a loosening of boundaries, recognising the limitations of the message projected by much British architecture. 'People began to realise that architecture could be about things; that it has its own language which is quite distinct from its functionality and technology. The crossover between art and architecture was, and is, exhilarating and for artists it was a release from what some might have called the tyranny of Cork Street.' Over the years initial doubts by MacCormac and his colleagues about working with artists have evaporated. 'The fact that the relationship between architecture and art has no fixity at all is very exciting. Secondly, the issue of what the art should be about is ultimately up to the artist themselves – the architect cannot second guess it.'

Vivien Lovell of art consultant Modus Operandi has been highly influential in the ways in which the practice has considered working with artists. She first met MacCormac at the ICA conference, when Lovell was Visual Arts Officer for the London Borough of Tower Hamlets. Soon afterwards she was invited to visit the office to look at some of MJP's work and it became obvious to her that 'there was the potential for artists to be involved in many of MJP's projects, though sadly in the early days by the time the thought had occurred to them it was usually too late to do anything about it.'

St John's College, Oxford

Almost a decade after the ICA conference, MJP's client for St John's College Garden Quadrangle in Oxford was keen that artists should be involved in the project. MacCormac invited Lovell, who had by then founded the Public Art Commissions Agency, to collaborate and together they looked at seven potential commissions. Since 1633, when Hubert Le Sueur created bronzes of Charles I and Queen Henrietta Maria for the Canterbury Quadrangle, St John's had enjoyed a long history of commissioning a wide variety of art. The new artworks were considered not as stand-alone pieces but as art that would become an integral part of the architecture and enrich the public spaces.

James Horrobin and Wendy Ramshaw were invited to propose designs for decorative gates and railings for the new building; painter Simon Lewty and sculptor, poet and performance artist Brian Catling were considered for art commissions relating to the history of St John's. Richard Devereux also responded with a text-based work; designs for decorative glass screens were submitted by Alexander Beleschenko, Jane McDonald and Elizabeth Ogilvie; Antony Gormley, Peter Randall-Page and Vincent Woropay were asked to consider sculptural works for the new courtyard at the south-west entrance; Beleschenko and Ramshaw were also invited to submit designs for chandeliers for the auditorium and dining-reception area; Howard Hodgkin was asked to consider the potential for a series of screens for the stage in the auditorium, and the printmaker John Howard was commissioned to document the progress of the new building's construction.

In the end, funding was available only for Wendy Ramshaw, Alexander Beleschenko and John Howard but these commissions, particularly the first two, marked a turning point in MacCormac's understanding of how the practice might collaborate with artists.

The idea of commissioning a jewellery designer for the gate fascinated MacCormac, particularly because of the attention to detail this might bring to the commission. The iron gate, which leads from the new building though a medieval wall and into the college garden, is a finely crafted work in which the artist's skill and creativity in small-scale design is brilliantly translated into a delicate yet functional sculptural piece. At the centre of the gate, at eye level, is a double-lens through which the whole of the Garden Quadrangle is framed; the technicalities of bringing the design to life were reconciled by a blacksmith, Richard Quinnell.

St John's College, Oxford,
Garden Quadrangle (1990-93)
Glass Screens by artist Alexander Beleschenko
in which thousands of pieces of worked
colourless glass were incorporated to create a
suggestion of water running over the surface
and a play of transparent and opaque qualities
that modulate the light for the interiors.

At first MacCormac was uncomfortable with the asymmetry of the design but the client remained convinced and ultimately the architect was won over. 'I learned two important lessons on this job', says MacCormac. 'One was a new willingness to recognise the autonomy of the artist, and the other was to see the gate as much a part of the landscape as of the building, so I relinquished my claim on the gate as overtly architectural.'

'What is most delightful is the way in which MacCormac has brought the work of two contemporary artists into the building seamlessly', wrote Jonathan Glancey in The Independent. 'The glass walls that march around the undercroft courtyard – where entrance is gained to the meeting rooms and theatre – are a small triumph.' [1] The glass walls or screens are by Alexander Beleschenko who trained as a painter at Winchester and the Slade before turning to glass in the mid-1970s. The screens are constructed of thousands of individual pieces of handmade and hand-treated glass, forming translucent and transparent walls which filter light into the densest part of the building. MacCormac and Beleschenko immediately understood and respected each other's work, and the artist has worked on three subsequent MJP commissions – for the Ruskin Library, Southwark underground station, and the glass fins of the spiral bridge at the Phoenix Initiative in Coventry. 'Beleschenko proves that art into architecture does not have to be mere tokenism… his glass is a part of MacCormac's architecture and each gains from the other.' [2]

Artist Fleur Kelly also worked on St John's, but the commission came directly from MacCormac rather than through Lovell's programme. Kelly decorated the inner surfaces of the pair of saucer domes with subtle sky frescoes.

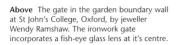

Above The gate in the garden boundary wall at St John's College, Oxford, by jeweller Wendy Ramshaw. The ironwork gate incorporates a fish-eye glass lens at it's centre.

Above right St John's lecture theatre with its dramatic Soane-like saucer dome Buon Fresco by artist Fleur Kelly.

Luminosity – Wellcome Wing, Southwark station and Sutton Walk

The influence of contemporary artists on MJP's work can be seen even in buildings where there was no formal artistic collaboration. For example, two exhibitions at the Hayward Gallery – on light artist James Turrell (1993) and colourist Yves Klein (1995) – significantly influenced MJP's design for the blue wall in the Wellcome Wing at London's Science Museum. 'Visual and aural influences on an architect are never premeditated and only become apparent subsequently. In retrospect, two exhibitions at the Hayward Gallery seem to have been important for the Science Museum project… Klein Blue is so saturated that one looks into, rather than at it, as though into space. At the Hayward, Turrell exhibited work using light to achieve an extraordinary dissolution of boundaries, and a pursuit of evanescence… In the Wellcome Wing project the intention in the use of colour is psychological – to create an interior which has the cool blue radiance of a night sky, to create a sense of elation and wonder… so as to create an appropriate frame of mind for approaching an exhibition of modern science, of biotechnology.' [3] MacCormac had wanted to ask Turrell to collaborate on the Wellcome Wing, but the limited budget coupled with enormous time pressure left little room for experimentation.

Two other projects that share with the Wellcome Wing a preoccupation with luminosity, are Southwark underground station and the 'image wall' at Sutton Walk in Waterloo. The invitation to Alexander Beleschenko to work on the cone wall at Southwark came directly from MJP despite the fact that there was no budget for artistic collaboration, 'We took on Beleschenko as our cladding consultant to take advantage of his expertise in glass technology. He was commissioned to design a print pattern which would act as a counterpoint to the very precise geometrical expression of the triangulated elliptical/conical wall. Importantly, glass is inherently more adaptable than precast concrete, and therefore came in at a significantly lower cost. Here the huge advantage as far as we were concerned was that our cladding consultant also happened to produce a work of art.'

The intricate pattern of glass triangles cladding the sloping wall on the intermediate concourse level encapsulates MJP's interest in surface, light and artifice. Hard and reflective surfaces seen obliquely contrast with transparency.

Sutton Walk, a key pedestrian route to the South Bank Arts Centre in London, runs under a railway viaduct. MJP worked with Alberto Duman, whose work ranges from printmaking and photography to installations, to produce a 50 metre glass image wall, based on a photograph of the existing wall, and installed under the Hungerford Bridge. Opposite, a free-standing monolith, made up of mirrors which light up and become transparent when triggered by passing pedestrians, marks the Waterloo entrance. The idea sprung from the artist's belief that two of the consistent elements in the making of a metropolis are light and people, and the relationship between privacy and exposure.

Top Wellcome Wing at the Science Museum (1996-2000) where the colour was influenced by the work of Yves Klein and James Turrell.

Above Alexander Beleschenko's Blue Glass Wall (1999) on the intermediate concourse at Southwark Station (1991-99); fritted glass triangles reflect sun and daylight from above.

Left Alberto Duman's Monolith, a freestanding mirror at the Waterloo entrance to Sutton Walk (1999-2001), with six light-sensitive panels triggered by the movement of passers-by; the title refers to the film 2001: A Space Odyssey.

Below Duman's glass wall at Sutton Walk, a 12mm-thick glass screenprint of a life-size photograph of the original wall behind.

Ruskin, Turner and the Pre-Raphaelites
exhibition at Tate Britain (1999-2000).

Exhibitions at Tate Britain and Tate Modern

MJP's involvement in the art world extends beyond working on building projects. A small team, led by Richard MacCormac, has also designed two exhibitions for the Tate galleries in London – Ruskin, Turner and the Pre-Raphaelites was held in the newly refurbished Tate Britain at Millbank in 2000, and Surrealism: Desire Unbound, at Tate Modern, challenged the convention of gallery space as a white cube. MacCormac argues that the fashion for displaying art in stark, white spaces 'isn't a neutral convention; it's culturally obliterative, a way of belonging to a sect and buying into a kind of clinical, minimalist world.' These ideas are echoed in the book of essays Inside the White Cube – the Ideology of the Gallery Space, by Brian O'Doherty,[4] in which he investigates 'what the highly controlled context of the modernist gallery does to the art object, what it does to the viewing subject, and, in a crucial moment for modernism, how the context devours the object, becoming it.' In the light of such a strong belief in the way in which exhibitions should be contextualised and given life, both Tate exhibitions were thoughtfully lit and highly coloured – colourist Jocasta Innes and lighting designer Rogier van der Heide collaborated with MJP on both exhibitions.

MacCormac was invited by the critic Robert Hewison to design the Ruskin exhibition, partly as a result of his work on the Ruskin Library (of which Hewison was a trustee). The polychromatic interiors reflected the Victorian era and the architecture of William Butterfield and William Burges, as well as giving expression to Ruskin's fluctuating temperament throughout his life. By opening up the intersections in the strict grid of partitions, diagonal views were offered to visitors, at some points revealing as many as five different colours. The palette ranged from the entrance 'decompression chamber' in black, through yellow, red, damson and deep purple, reflecting the turbulent, even violent, mood of Ruskin in his final years.

For Surrealism: Desire Unbound at Tate Modern the concept was to use colour and lighting less as a means of evoking a mood or 'weather', and more as a tool for creating the appropriate atmosphere for the diverse and often challenging subject matter. What resulted was a dream-like sequence of rooms, each painted in colours to complement the characteristic palette of the artist on show, with oversized, black-framed portals. The entrance was bathed in pink light, partly to shock and partly to evoke a sense of a womb and a heartbeat. The dark space at the centre of the exhibition reflected the violent, often sadistic, nature of the work.

Surrealism: Desire Unbound exhibition at
Tate Modern (2001)

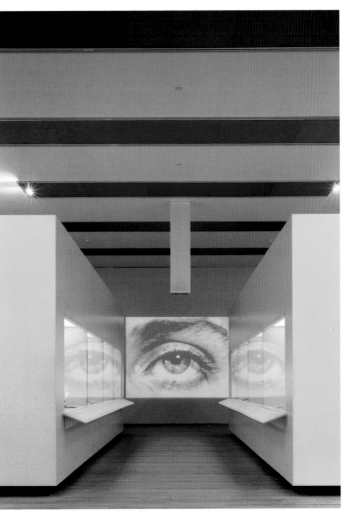

Coventry Phoenix Initiative (1997-2003)
Time Zone Clock (2003) by Francoise Schein, seen beneath the Whittle Arch at Millenium Place.

Below View over Priory Cloister towards the twin spires of Coventry Cathedral and Holy Trinity Church. Priory Cloister includes the spokenword artwork Here by David Ward.

Coventry's Phoenix Initiative

The MJP scheme which has so far involved more artists than any other to date, is the Coventry Phoenix Initiative, which was short-listed for the 2004 Stirling Prize. Although MJP built new buildings within its masterplan, including the Visitors' Centre, Youell House and a redevelopment of the entrance to the Coventry Transport Museum, it is the public art which defines the scheme, and which resonates with both the city's past and its future. 'The aim was to create a collaborative process not just between design professionals, but uniquely to invite artists to make a new place – or series of linked places – redeeming a fragmented site. Through artists' interventions, disparate areas could be given identity, not by some grand formal gesture, rather by way of an episodic journey through a series of places, highly contemporary yet informed by history, and unique to Coventry.' [5]

Project architect Toby Johnson recalls that the design team had just three months to put together a revised masterplan for the site, after the city's initial proposal for a national centre for human achievement was turned down for funding by the Millennium Commission. The city's desire was to reclaim and regenerate three hectares of the city. 'Coventry could afford a series of public spaces with a major public art programme, built around a route which links Basil Spence's cathedral, through the eleventh century Priory to the Transport Museum and ultimately, the Garden of International Friendship.'

Before MJP's appointment, Vivien Lovell had been commissioned by Coventry City Council to write a Public Art Strategy for the city as a whole. Following consultation with MJP and landscape architects and urban designers, Rummey Design Associates, Lovell wrote a strategy specifically for the Phoenix, outlining the curatorial vision and thematic starting points, identifying potential sites within the masterplan that would lend themselves to public art works, and short-listing artists who might be considered. Various selection procedures were employed, from an open call for regional artists, an invited competition for Priory Cloister, competitive interviews for Priory Place, Millennium Place, the Garden of International Friendship and an artist's lighting commission, and a direct invitation to Jochen Gerz.

A proposal was also invited from the poet David Morley, who was head of creative writing at the University of Warwick, and whose subsequent work focused on a reworking of the Coventry Carols and Mystery Plays with local people. Chris Browne was awarded a residency with the city's archaeology department leading to a commission for the Priory Gardens. David Ward was appointed to the Priory Cloister and his eight sound posts, Here, take extracts from the city's oral archive, creating 'whispering trees' among the pleached limes. In addition, his concept for blue lighting flooding

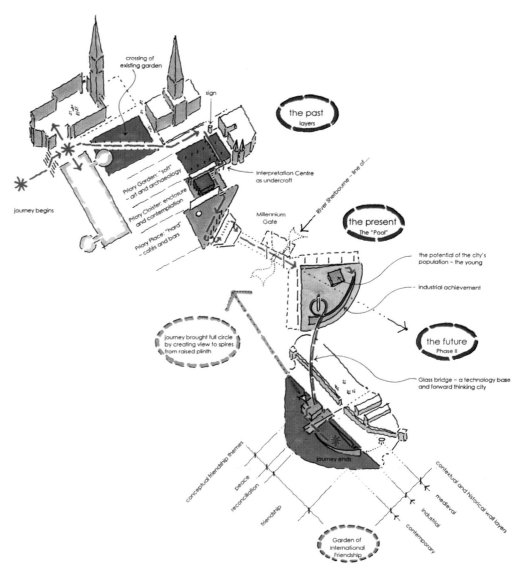

Above Millennium Place from the spiral ramp looking towards the Whittle Arch.

Right The Journey, 1988 concept sketch by Dominic Scott of Robert Rummey Design Associates.

Below Priory Garden at night looking north towards the Visitors Interpretation Centre.

Below right Waterwindow (1998-2003) by Susanna Heron with the Priory Cloister behind.

the cloister walls was realised in collaboration with lighting designers Speirs & Major. Priory Place is introduced by Susanna Heron's Waterwindow, which reflects the animated nature of the space. At Millennium Place, the largest new space, Francoise Schein's Time Zone Clock makes reference to Coventry's clock-making history and maps its twin cities. Unlike the other artists, Jochen Gerz was given an open brief, as it was central to the artistic plan to invite this established German conceptual artist, known for his 'counter-monuments' and invisible memorials, to carry out a major work or works within the area of Coventry that had been blitzed. 'The Phoenix Initiative's choice of Jochen Gerz to work alongside other artists in Coventry is particularly appropriate… [his] twinned projects, Public Bench and Future Monument, have a deep link to Coventry's role as a "site of memory". As England's first bombed city, Coventry takes its place in an international network of sites marked by the dialectic between ruin and pain, reconstruction and reconciliation… Gerz's works are exemplary public commissions in terms of their consultative processes, and as "public art" involving "public authorship" they symbolise transnational, personal, and indeed private stories; stories of the anonymous and the disappeared which will never be known. At the moment of inauguration and at a time of Britain's involvement in new wars, his complex project, with its historic roots in post war Germany, deserves further consideration.' [6]

Public Bench and Future Monument provide further artistic interest at Millennium Place, alongside Schein's clock. The Bench invites public interaction through the placing of red vinyl plaques each bearing two names, that of the active participant and a chosen companion, hero or heroine, living or dead, along the back of the seat. The monument is more controversial. It 'addresses the taboo of issues like history and the necessary infidelities of memory', explains Gerz. Members of the community were asked to name nations who had previously been enemies of their country, and who are now its friends. Plaques declaring the friendships are inlaid in the ground around the brightly lit obelisk.

The client had assumed that the programme would include traditional public art in the classical tradition, such as life size bronzes of famous Coventry citizens. Instead, MJP and the team of artists promoted what MacCormac calls a 'democracy of monumentality and memory which is to do with eventfulness and the way in which cities collect people together. In Coventry, the citizens literally imprint themselves on the place with hundreds of vulgar red plastic tabs. The vulgarity of the material is deliberate on Jochen's part.'

This exhilarating artistic and historic journey through the site culminates in the Garden of International Friendship, which is dominated by a fragment of a maze by Kate Whiteford. Poems selected by David Morley are engraved into the stone walls. Pedestrians arrive in the garden via a dramatic spiral ramp and bridge, designed by MJP and engineer Whitbybird with glass balustrades by Alexander Beleschenko.

Top Future Monument (1998-2003) by Jochen Gerz is intended to represent tolerance, reconciliation, peace and change.

Above Public Bench (1998-2003) by Jochen Gerz, a 45-metre long bench with red acrylic plaques featuring the names of the citizens of Coventry and people chosen by them.

Right The Garden of International Friendship designed by RDA and Kate Whiteford. The top of the curved walls has an inset bronze text extracted from the Coventry Mystery Plays, by poet David Morley.

Broadcasting House

Speaking at the Context and Collaboration conference organised in 1990 by the Public Art Commissions Agency in Birmingham, the Seattle-based artist Jack Mackie shrewdly described public art as 'the art of making places public', and this was exactly the intention of the public art programme for Broadcasting House, devised by Vivien Lovell with MJP.

A key objective of the BBC headquarters redevelopment was to make it more accessible and visible to the public, creating a destination at the top of Regent Street that embraces passers by, rather than turning its back on them. Art was to reflect the culture of the BBC, including that of communication and internationalism, as well as Lord Reith's mission to inform, educate and entertain. The need to involve a broad range of artists and art was therefore paramount. The commissioning of art as an integral element of new developments had been part of a public art policy, and often a condition of planning permission, within Westminster City Council since 1994. Clearly MJP would have wanted to collaborate with artists even if it hadn't been obligatory, and Modus Operandi were appointed to oversee the commissioning for the project.

The original Broadcasting House set an impressive precedent, with its Eric Gill sculptures on the Portland Place and Langham Street elevations and entrance, and work by leading young designers of the 1930s, including Serge Chermayeff, Wells Coates and Raymond McGrath, which brought style and diversity to the interior spaces. With the new project, the BBC was keen to restore its reputation as a patron of great art as well as architecture.

Modus Operandi devised a public art plan comprising four strands: permanent commissions, a temporary programme, an artists-on-site scheme, responding to the transformation of Broadcasting House, and artist-led education and community projects. Artists of all disciplines, from painters and sculptors to poets and sound artists were offered the chance to collaborate on both permanent and temporary art works. After researching a list of between 12 and 18 artists for each project the BBC's public art group, which included senior figures from across the organisation, refined it down to four or six names, from which several were selected.

Wide diversity was achieved in the selection, both in terms of types of artistic expression and the locations, visible and invisible, of the artworks. The artists included Richard Wentworth and Ruth Maclennan, who were involved in an outreach project working with nine-year-old children from the nearby Gateway School on a video and sound project. Antoni Malinowski was appointed as an artist-consultant during initial discussions on colours and surfaces throughout the building. A photographic documentation of the exterior and interior of the original building was produced by John Riddy. Catherine Yass made a film from the viewpoint of flying over the roofs of the original building, partly as a historical documentary, but also as a way of revealing the secret life of the building. A video, Presence, was shot by Brian Catling in the old drama studio inspired by and using objects from the former sound effects store. Tom Gidley also filmed various aspects of the building, including the Radio Theatre and Drama Studio and the site of the original Room 101, made infamous by George Orwell in

BBC Broadcasting House (2000-06)
The variable lights of the Cyclorama create the nightime setting for All Souls church. The model shows the effect of natural and artificial light on the curved glass screen. The colour and opacity of the glass changes from day to night, acting as a foil to the Portland stone and steel structure.

Right Unititled – Room 101 (2003) by Rachel Whiteread; Eric Gill working on Ariel and Prospero (1932), which was installed above the entrance to Broadcasting House.

Below All Soul's lighting and artist Liz Rideal's temporary hoarding Kerfuffle.

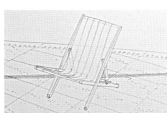

BBC Broadcasting House (2000-06)
At the heart of the development is a new open air space, featuring a major new artwork, World, by the Canadian artist, Mark Pimlott. Mixing texture, light, text and discreet audio, World will create a unique and reflective public arena.

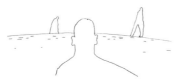

Nineteen Eighty-Four. Rachel Whiteread, invited to respond to Room 101 before its demolition, chose to cast the entire void of the room and the result, Untitled: Room 101, was installed for nine months in the Cast Courts at the Victoria & Albert Museum. 'The idea of a public art programme for Broadcasting House, which incorporates not only physical public space but public space on the airwaves, fascinates artists and has triggered a further debate about the nature and scope of public art.' [7]

The most immediately apparent and permanent public art works are Breathing, a collaboration with Jaume Plensa; World, in collaboration with Mark Pimlott, and the lighting of the glass screens behind All Souls. MJP developed the idea that the building's appearance could change through day, ultimately becoming a screen onto which images might be projected at night. Tony Cooper and Martin Richman developed lighting proposals for the church of All Souls, relating it to the facade of the original Broadcasting House.

The site of Mark Pimlott's competition-winning proposal World is the Langham Street Public Space. The architect-artist describes the surface of the public space as 'a portion of a sphere that people can walk across and stand on a terrain that evokes the world. The surface is lined with markings, like lines of latitude and longitude and the names of towns, cities, and regions across the world are engraved randomly into the surface. This globe is not a map, but a calling together of all places in the world within the reach of the BBC.' [8] This artwork in particluar is intended to make the new Broadcasting House the primary destination north of Oxford Circus. Just as importantly, it represents the interface between the corporation and its global audience. The strength of Pimlott's proposal encouraged the BBC to apply to Westminster City Council for permission to close Langham Street to traffic, with the aim of making it a truly public space and one where events and performances could readily take place.

Breathing, by the Spanish artist Jaume Plensa, is also certain to attract a huge attention both inside and outside the BBC. The artist was appointed on the basis of his potential to create something dramatic and inspiring, rather than his initial proposal for a giant question mark hovering above Broadcasting House. Breathing is the result of a number of variations on the theme of a cone rising through the heart of the building. MacCormac had independently been thinking about incorporating an inverted cone within the new building, and this metamorphosed into an idea to push the cone up through the building, possibly as a means of creating a lightwell. In collaboration with Plensa the idea evolved into a slim steel and glass cone which projects out of the top of the building, to become the third spire – an inversion of the spire of All Souls', perhaps, and a complement to the spire on

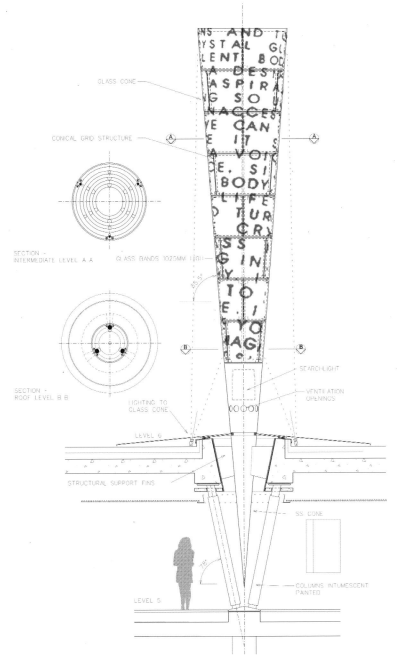

LIFE TURNS AND TURNS ON THE CRYSTAL GLASS BREATHING IN OUR BODY

SILENCE IS A VOICE, OUR VOICE
SILENCE IS A BODY, OUR BODY

LIFE TURNS AND TURNS ON THE CRYSTAL GLASS BREATHING IN OUR BODY

I INVITE YOU TO BREATHE
I INVITE YOU TO LISTEN TO THE SILENCE

Broadcasting House – from which a vertical beam of light projects one kilometre into the night sky. Breathing, a poem written by Plensa is etched into the glass surface, fragments of which can be viewed from different parts of the building, but the poem is legible in its entirety only at ground level.

'What is fascinating about working with artists', says Richard MacCormac, is that so often you find that the process has an unexpected outcome, as with Breathing, which has become a memorial, as well as an art work.' The success of the original idea can be measured by the enthusiastic way in which the BBC took ownership of it, suggesting that the spire might be dedicated to correspondents and crew members who have lost their lives while covering wars around the world.

The sculpture-as-memorial inspired another poem, by James Fenton, whose conversations with Plensa informed the final version of his memorial poem which will be located in the public arcade alongside a small version of the sculpture Breathing.

John Simpson, the BBC's senior foreign correspondent, responded enthusiastically to the artwork and Fenton's poem: 'It's a couple of years since I started campaigning for a memorial to the people who have died working for BBC News, and the result is far better than anything I had hoped for. To have commissioned James, who isn't merely one of the best poets writing today but also knows from his own experience what it means to be a reporter working in dangerous circumstances, was a stroke of real excellence. [It] touches, with great delicacy, on the precise condition of each of the people who have died, and their relatives and friends will feel that James has understood and expressed exactly what happened in every one of their cases. I cannot think of a better memorial, and I am very proud of the BBC for its ability to summon up a production as inspiring as this.' [9] Simpson read James Fenton's poem at the opening ceremony of Breathing on 16th June 2008, when it was inaugurated by United Nations secretary general Ban Ki-Moon.

1 Through a glass lightly, Jonathan Glancey, The Independent (26 January 1994).
2 ibid.
3 Blue Space, by Richard MacCormac, in Frontiers: Artists and Architects Architectural Design (vol 68, July/Aug 1997). See also Space and Light, Richard MacCormac, Modern Painters (Summer 1993).
4 Thomas McEvilley, from Inside the White Cube – the Ideology of the Gallery Space, Brian O'Doherty (University of California Press, 1999).
5 Richard MacCormac and Vivien Lovell, from Phoenix: Architecture – Art – Regeneration (Black Dog, 2004).
6 A stranger with secrets: Jochen Gerz, Future Monument, Public Bench, by Sarah Wilson, Phoenix Architecture/Art/Regeneration (Black Dog, 2004).
7 Vivien Lovell, in Building the BBC (BBC/Wordsearch, 2003).
8 From the artist's proposal.
9 Correspondence from John Simpson to BBC.

Right Jaume Plensa's poem Breathing is etched into a glass cone from which is projected a kilometre high beam of light; James Fenton's poem Memorial was read at its inauguration.

MEMORIAL

WE SPOKE, WE CHOSE TO SPEAK OF WAR AND STRIFE –
A TASK A FINE AMBITION SOUGHT –
AND SOME MIGHT SAY, WHO SHARED OUR WORK, OUR LIFE:
THAT PRAISE WAS DEARLY BOUGHT.

DRIVERS, INTERPRETERS, THESE WERE OUR FRIENDS.
THESE WE LOVED. THESE WE WERE TRUSTED BY.
THE SHOCKED HAND WIPES THE BLOOD ACROSS THE LENS.
THE LENS LOOKS TO THE SKY.

MOST DIED BY MISCHANCE. SOME SEEMED HONOUR-BOUND
TO TAKE THE LONELY, PEERLESS TRACK
CONCEIVING DANGER AS A TESTING-GROUND
TO WHICH THEY MUST GO BACK

TILL THE DRY TONGUE FELL SILENT AND THEY CROSSED
BEYOND THE REALM OF TIME AND FEAR.
DEATH WAVED THEM THROUGH THE CHECKPOINT. THEY WERE LOST.
ALL HAVE THEIR STORY HERE.

Anthology

NOTES ON THE ROLE OF FORM
IN THE DESIGN PROCESS

Richard MacCormac

Arena, May 1967

This essay was the result of having to evaluate propositions about architecture which might have been taken for granted had they not been exposed to the opposite view. It was provoked by the experience of two very different, perhaps complementary, educational environments, the School of Architecture at Cambridge and the Bartlett School at University College. Broadly speaking these represent respectively those who believe in the primacy of form and synthesis, and those who emphasise analysis in the belief that architecture is sustained by a broad base of knowledge; a host of interrelated subjects replacing 'architecture' as a unique subject.

The danger of the former attitude is that form may be considered for its own sake, isolated from the forces that generate it. The priority of aesthetic goals may be assumed[1] and little effort made to counter those who believe that such preoccupations are in direct opposition to the effective solution of the urgent physical requirements of our society.[2]

The danger of the analytical attitude is less easily defined. Directing attention away from solutions back to the disciplines that contribute to them, sociology, psychology, ergonomics, engineering and so forth, has enabled architecture to tap developable sources of knowledge instead of wallowing in rapidly obsolescent aesthetic theory.[3] But this very classification may mean that those areas of mental activity not readily accessible to analysis are sieved out and ignored. The word 'architecture' itself may become an empty title because it seems to have obscured the assembly of subjects found to be its real content.

Arriving at the Bartlett in 1963 after three years at Cambridge, some of us adopted a partisan stance in favour of 'architecture' in the rather confused sense that we understood it. We were aware that we had inherited a 'lore' acquired empirically through the spatial and formal experience of studio design, rather than a systematic body of knowledge. Our aesthetic preoccupations soon convicted us of 'formalism', but our relative success in solving organisational problems prompted us to consider whether the architects' traditional concern with pattern, order and simplicity was not effective in solving physical as well as aesthetic problems. We also wanted to know more about our compulsion to achieve elegant solutions, which contrasted with the cold-blooded approach of our Bartlett contemporaries.

In a lecture to the ICA Dr Ross Ashby made an interesting hypothesis.[4] He suggested that there may be 'survival value'

for organisms that perceive 'simplicities'. Perceiving pattern, form, structure, allows us to translate many stimuli into a number that can be more readily handled by our intelligence: the nervous system, he suggested, is arranged to seek simplicities,[5] and when it succeeds we experience pleasure, as we do when we indulge in other activities designed by nature to prolong or procreate our species. Within this hypothesis one might consider production for aesthetic ends as an essential playing or exercising of vestigial survival mechanisms which require gratification in the same way as aggressive and competitive energies are sublimated in sports and games.

Jonathan Miller's talk to the AA, The Shape of Size,[6] interpreted our formal motives another way. From clinical observations of patients suffering from atrophy of the brain he deduced that we resort to making models of order in our immediate environment when we are unable to order the world at large. Patients tended to simplify the appearance of their personal possessions as far as possible, clothes folded in squares, eating utensils arranged at right angles.

Professor Wilhelm Worringer interpreted the geometric art of primitive man in a remarkably similar way: 'he snatches from the uninterrupted flow of events the individual objects of the outer world which he wishes to secure by fixing them intuitively. He frees them from their disquieting environment… and reduces their varying modes of appearance to certain decisive and recurrent characteristics, and these he translates into his abstract linear language… making them absolute and inevitable.'[7]

Each of these interpretations suggests that our aesthetic tendency is deep seated. What is critical in a discussion of the design process is whether such an urge works in the direction of useful rather than purely aesthetic ends. Certainly at University College it was generally held that the scientific solution of problems could hardly accommodate such apparently emotional predilections. This attitude perhaps fails to recognise that science itself has often depended upon the postulation of elegant constructs as well as on empiricism. John Rogers (Lecturer in Philosophy at the University of Keele) has suggested that the innovations made by Galileo, Kepler and Copernicus were the product of aesthetic theory rather than experiments; their own sense of harmony and order led them to make certain hypotheses in spite of the lack of empirical evidence.[8] Copernicus' criticism of the Ptolemaic system was in terms of elegance: 'it

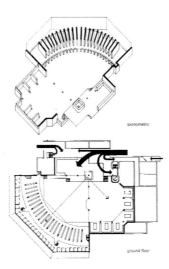

axonometric

ground floor

Above Cambridge University History Library, by James Stirling (1964-67)

seemed neither sufficiently absolute nor sufficiently pleasing to the mind' and he argued that the problem could be solved with 'fewer and more simple constructions'. Kepler was apparently 'delighted by Copernicus' and 'perceived how clumsy in many respects is the hitherto customary notion of the structure of the universe'.

Rogers pointed out that information sought subsequent to the hypothesis is of a quite different kind, and more effective, than that sought for its own sake prior to it. Dr Abercrombie has made an analogous point about the perceptual experiment with 'the Hidden Man'.[9] Until the face in the picture appears we could endlessly attempt to classify the black and the white patches. As soon as we recognise the head and shoulders of a man we are able to be discriminate about the kind of information useful to us.

A conceptual approach to architecture has similar consequences; as soon as we impose a system upon a range of requirements the system modifies the kind of information we need. If we accept this it means that we should attempt synthesis at the beginning of the total design process so that we can collect the right kind of information, instead of frittering away time in an all-embracing analysis which is proved largely redundant when the solution is achieved.

In the examples that follow, the designer has recognised in the range of information before him some critical requirement which could determine the general form of the building. The forms adopted in each case have an immediate aesthetic appeal; they are generic, either linear or centroidal and the concept dominates the whole solution

to the problem.

The first example is a Bartlett fourth year design project for a joinery works by Robin Webster who had been at Cambridge until Intermediate. We were presented with an existing building consisting of two sheds which shared a common slot of space. The designer proposed to use the first shed as the machine shop and the second for joinery and its attendant machines and it was perceived that common to both these requirements were several linear systems. These included trunking to extract sawdust and carry it to the boiler, and timber stored on a continuous rack served by a gantry immediately adjacent to both machines and joinery benches. The 'one off' nature of different jobs meant that priorities in the production and assembly of joinery changed from day to day. There would always be unfinished components standing by machines and being overtaken by other more urgently required orders; the result, in the existing joinery works, being considerable congestion. Complicated attempts were made by some students to analyse these fluctuations, but in this example it was observed that the linear form enabled the machines to be separated out from the parking of trolleys carrying components, and the single line of machines in echelon enabled components to move down the line by passing those which were inappropriate and visiting any machine without being swivelled through more than 45 degrees, an important requirement with long pieces of timber and one which would not have been met had the machines been arranged in parallel ranks. In this way the linear theme provided an appropriate spatial model for several processes.

The Marina Towers in Chicago take similar advantage of a centroidal form. The problem was to provide shelter for people and cars with the most direct communication between them on a small site. The solution was remarkably elegant because it was found that both kinds of accommodation and their respective kinds of access could be provided by the geometry of the cylinder. The flats utilise the radial segmental characteristic of the circle, the cars its projection into a helix, and the structure, services and communication between flats and cars are accommodated by a cylindrical core.

The discovery of a form which can meet a number of requirements simultaneously seems to require two distinct faculties. In the first place the designer must be able to project alternative

spatial models for organisational requirements and, subsequently, be able to recognise that the form chosen can accommodate systems to suit others.

In the limited competition for the new history library at Cambridge, James Stirling's building was favoured because all the book stacks could be supervised from the reception desk. The radial form which achieved this was found to meet other organisational needs. By associating the entrance with the reception desk and arranging the supplementary accommodation, staff rooms, seminar rooms, common rooms and so forth, radially along two sides of the reading room, all the main destinations can be perceived and reached directly from the same point, which became a reference for the whole building. In addition the galleries overlooking the reading room provide visual contact between the supplementary functions and the raison d'etre of the faculty.

The roof structure is a product, rather than a determinant, of the form. As the volumetric expression of the radial idea the value of its shape is obviously aesthetic rather than utilitarian.

But one feels, nevertheless, that it was the result of the same kind of recognition as that which correlated the physical systems of the building. The radial property of the form has been employed for both useful and expressive ends: there is correspondence rather than conflict between functional and aesthetic intentions.

The simplicity[10] of these schemes suggests a hypothesis: if several systems have to be accommodated by a design there is a greater probability that a simple form will provide for all, than will a highly determined form derived exclusively from one set of criteria.

If this is so the designer should be ready to sacrifice individual requirements initially, if in so doing there is less sacrifice than would otherwise occur in their mutual interaction. This is presumably the principle which lies behind the completely uniform gridded master plan proposed for Loughborough University by Arup Associates, and the similar system proposed for the Oxford University laboratory sites by Sir Leslie Martin.[11] It is these generalised systems which are best able to provide for unpredictable growth and change.

The other implication of this hypothesis is that the powerful aesthetic motive toward formal simplicity and conceptualisation should not be considered an obstruction to solving practical problems but a valuable, if little understood, aptitude.

THE ANATOMY OF
WRIGHT'S AESTHETIC

Richard MacCormac

Architectural Review, February 1968

Although no general theory could be deduced from such elementary and rather specialised examples the relation between visual clarity and the order of structure, services and circulation, which they illustrate, suggests that any theory of form in architecture should be as much concerned with the role of form in the design process as with the way in which the final product is perceived.

1 See for example Towards an Understanding of Form, Peter D Eisenman (Architectural Design Oct 1963), one-time research student at Cambridge, which is concerned with the symbolic and perceptual attributes of form.
2 See for example the Young Fabian Pamphlet by Paul Thompson with the remarkable title Architecture: Art or Social Service? (Fabian Society, March 1963).
3 Lord Llewelyn Davis: Inaugural Address, The Transactions of the Bartlett Society, vol 1, 1962-3 (UCL 1964).
4 Art and Communication Theory, a talk given by Dr AW Ross Ashby to the ICA, 7th April 1960.
5 cf Gestalt perceptual theory.
6 See Arena: Architectural Association Journal (Jan 1966).
7 Form in Gothic p18 (Tiranti, 1957).
8 The Hypothesis of Harmony, The Listener (Feb 18, 1965).
9 MLJ Abercrombie, Arena: Architectural Association Journal (June 1966).
10 See Rudolph Arnheim's discussion of Simplicity in Art and Visual Perception, pp37-50. On p41 he says 'In a relative sense a thing has simplicity when it organises complex material with the smallest number of structural features.' This could be a definition of effective design.
11 Architectural Design (Dec 1964).

Frank Lloyd Wright's acknowledgment of his kindergarten experience and outward resemblance between his buildings and the illustrations of the 'gifts' in the Froebel manual are already well known [1] (see Grant Manson's Wright in the Nursery, Architectural Review, June 1953). Though remarkable, these comparisons did little more than indicate the source of Wright's characteristic 'style.' Closer investigation – at the level of intention and organisation rather than simply of appearance – suggests that the kindergarten was of a much more radical significance for Wright, that it provided him with a philosophy and with a design discipline to realize his architecture.

Froebel did not intend his patterns merely to have aesthetic appeal. He conceived them as the instrument of a system of education based upon a pantheistic conception of nature. The aim of this was two-fold, intellectual and spiritual; an understanding of Natural Law would simultaneously develop the powers of reason and convey a sense of the harmony and order of God: 'God's works reflect the logic of his spirit and human education cannot do anything better than imitate the logic of nature.'

Froebel identified the governing force of nature as 'the Divine principle of Unity' and found a medium for conveying this metaphysical ideal during his study of crystallography (he studied several natural sciences in an effort to substantiate his preconceptions). The geometry of crystallography, which he supposed was typical of the structure of all matter, became the basis of the patterns in the kindergarten handbooks.[2] The Froebel gifts were presented to children as sets of wooden blocks packed in cubic boxes and accompanied by a text describing the purpose of each. By modern standards, the requirements of the manual are extraordinarily strict. The theme of unity becomes a moral discipline; only complete symmetrical patterns are allowed, and the child is encouraged to feel that their pleasing effect is a reward for respecting 'order… Heaven's first law' while 'arbitrariness' is condemned as being against nature.

Such a discipline must have made a deep impression upon Wright. It presented him with a comprehensive vision in which aesthetics were inseparable from universal principles of form. In the light of such an inheritance we may appreciate his extraordinary confidence in the absolute validity of his architecture as an expression of Natural Law and his almost messianic belief in his role as an architect. The extent to which he was indeed affected becomes apparent if one

compares extracts from the text of the manual and examples from the exercises with some of his own characteristic statements.

'The child is first taught to take the cube out of the box undivided in order to inculcate alike the sense of order and the idea of completeness… In life we find no isolation. One part of the cube, therefore, must never be left apart from or without relation to the whole. The child will thus become accustomed to treating all things in life as bearing a certain relation to one another.'

'Any building should be complete,' said Wright, 'including all within itself. Instead of many things one thing… Perfect correlation, integration is life. It is the first principle of any growth that the thing grown be no mere aggregation… and integration means that no part of anything is of any great value except as it be integrate part of the harmonious whole.'

In each of the Froebel patterns the parts have to some extent surrendered their identity to the whole to which they contribute (1). For Wright this was a basic recognition; parts added, porches, verandahs and balconies, should not be sensed as additional but should seem intrinsic, as extensions of inner structure. To help the child arrange the blocks, the kindergartener could provide a table-top ruled with a grid.[3] The discipline of a grid, combined with modular components, engenders the kind of correlation described. Wright appreciated this in his

own planning: 'What we call standardization is seen to be fundamental groundwork in architecture. All things in nature exhibit this tendency to crystallize… The kindergarten training, as I have shown, proved an unforeseen asset… a properly proportional unit system kept all to scale like a tapestry, a consistent fabric of interdependent related units, however various.'

Given these disciplines, T-square and set-square were the obvious tools of Wright's aesthetic. It is characteristic of his sketch plans that they are matted with explanatory lines – a mesh refined and tightened to correlate appropriate parts. 'This principle of design was natural, inevitable for me. It is based on the straight line technique of T-square and triangle. It was inherent in the Froebel system of kindergarten training given to me by my mother.'

Some of the exercises are composed with rectangular blocks rather than cubes, and these set up a tartan, rather than an even, modular grid. A typical pattern consists of two interpenetrating cruciforms, breaking through a square (2), establishing an interdependence of interior structure and external shape comparable to that in Wright's work. In fact it is surprising to find Froebel anticipating one of Wright's most fundamental propositions; for the handbook claims that the gifts 'enable the child to strive after the comprehension of both external appearances and inner conditions' and emphasises that the outward shape of

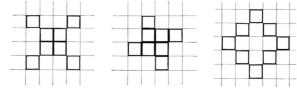

1 'In the Froebel patterns the parts have… surrendered their identity to the whole.'

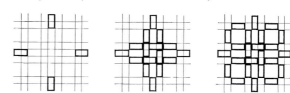

2 'A typical pattern consists of two interpenetrating cruciforms breaking through a square.'

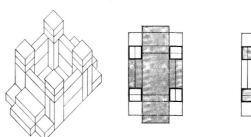

3 'the characteristic intersection of square and cruciform into three dimensions.'

the patterns is conditioned by the geometry of the whole. Similarly, the exterior forms of Wright's buildings usually project internal spaces, the precedent of the Froebel excercise suggesting that he started from a geometric premise rather than from some personal spatial insight: 'This sense of the within, or of the room itself, or of the rooms themselves, I now saw as the great thing to be expressed as architecture. This sense of interior space, made exterior as architecture, transcended all that had gone before… Hitherto all classical or ancient buildings had been great masses or blocks of building material sculpted into shape outside and hollowed out to live in.'

Comparisons of this kind, between flat patterns and architecture, must take into consideration the perceptual difference between seeing the whole pattern from above and grasping the overall form of a building from its perimeter. Wright understood this problem when he wrote, 'I have endeavoured to establish a harmonious relationship between ground plan and elevation of these buildings; considering the one as a solution and the other as an expression…' This is aptly illustrated by one of the models in the manual, which is an alternative to the flat patterns. The rather unbelievable 'bath' translates the characteristic intersection of square and cruciform into three dimensions (3). The overall structure is conveyed by the elevational distinction between the two figures; the interplay of steps and podium at each end depend upon a similar expression.

The approach to Wright's Prairie houses, which follows, has been developed from the preceding analyses. The evolution of typical features of the period, the overhanging roofs, the podia and the projecting cubic forms, is considered as an extension of the kindergarten system rather than simply the invention of a personal idiom. Wright's architecture, often supposed the most impervious to formal analysis, reveals a surprising geometric rigour. The plan of the George Blossom house of 1892 is, for example, obviously analogous to the intersecting squares and cruciforms of the patterns (4). Elevationally the plan is conveyed by the recessed central bays, which suggest that the entrance porch and balcony are extensions of the plan rather than additions. In comparison, the front and side elevations of the Winslow house of the following year are far less explicit (5). They obscure the grid extending through them, making no response to the main entrance and porte cochère. In this respect, the august exterior of the Winslow house seems to have

made little contribution to the main stream of Wright's development. The interior, on the other hand, heralds his future spatial technique. At the centre of the house the entrance hall, a deceptively simple box, is ingeniously integrated with the rooms to which it gives access. Its constituents – fireplace, doorways, balustrades and steps – provide a substructure corresponding with the dimensions of adjacent spaces (6).

The plan of the Isidor Heller house (1897) is similarly conditioned (7). Here the dining room and living room are related across the entrance hall by a common axis. The dining room, like the entrance hall of the Winslow house, is substructured to integrate with the spaces serving it. The access slots and dining area are consequently distinguished and a served-servant hierarchy suggested – an early precedent for that currently fashionable idea. This subdivision in plan enabled a distinction to be made between loadbearing wall and window. Wright had been dissatisfied with the windows which simply appeared as holes in the walls of the Winslow house ('I used to gloat over the beautiful buildings I could build if only it were unnecessary to cut windows in them.') Here the position of the windows is determined and they express the cruciform organization of the plan – a step towards the complete interdependence of exterior and plan in the living area of the Joseph W Husser house, two years later. The exterior of the Husser house is in this respect the antithesis of the front elevations of the Winslow house. No longer conceived as a separate entity wrapped around the plan (8), it is the product of the various components which make up the interlocking volumes of the interior; this is the crux of the idea which Wright's architecture inherited from the kindergarten.

It will be seen that the Husser house is developed from an underlying grid. From the plan of the Charles S Ross house of 1902 it is possible to abstract a perfect tartan (9) and from this the volumes of the building can be projected exactly, in the same way as in the case of the Froebel bath. The predominant figure is a cruciform with another contained within it, comparable with the Froebel cruciforms on a tartan grid (2). This kind of figure was to be the basis of most of Wright's later houses. In this example, the inner cruciform is expressed with porches and balconies and the outer with the roofs, which are extended geometrically from the main cube of the house. The raised portion of

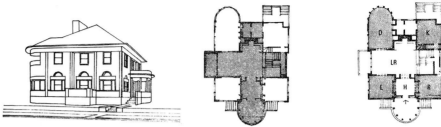

4 'the plan of the George Blossom house (1892) is…analogous to the intersecting squares and cruciforms of the patterns.'

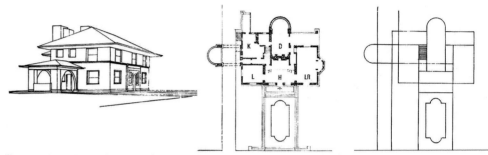

5 'In comparison, the front and side elevations of the Winslow house of the following year, are far less explicit.'

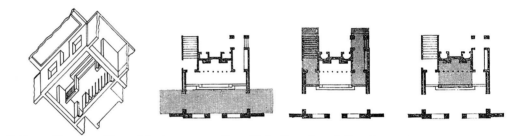

6 'its constituents provide a substructure corresponding with the dimensions of adjacent spaces.'

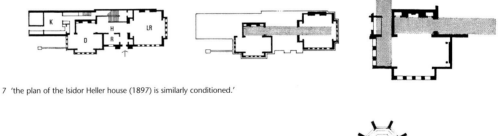

7 'the plan of the Isidor Heller house (1897) is similarly conditioned.'

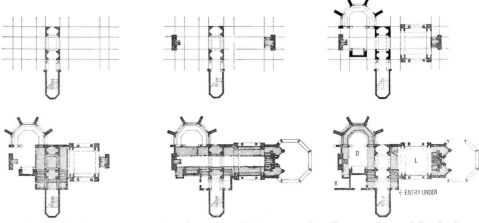

8 'The exterior of the Husser house… is no longer conceived as a separate entity wrapped around the plan.'

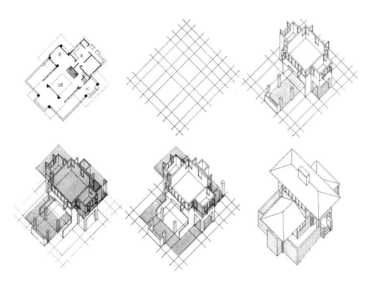

9 'From the plan of the Charles S Ross house of 1902 it is possible to abstract a perfect tartan.'

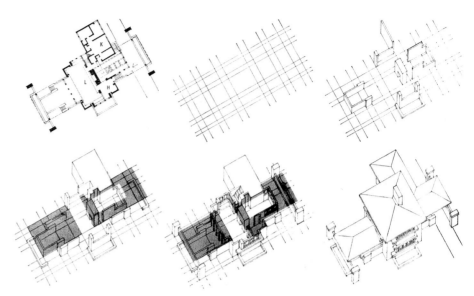

12 'The detached corner piers of the Robert Evans house of 1908... suggest the main volume of the building "stands" within the grid rather than around it.'

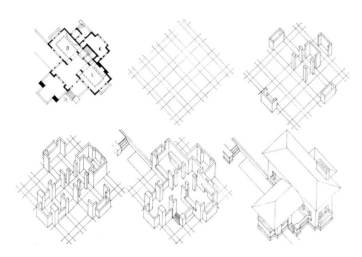

10 'The same grid underlies the little Barton house of the following year.'

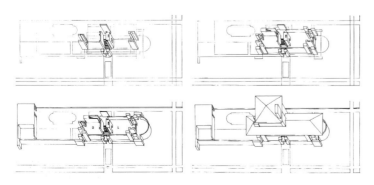

11 'The EE Tomek house of 1907 is another variant of the same theme.'

the living room ceiling and bedroom casements also correspond with the inner grid. The podium further develops the theme of modules contained one within another by expressing a yet wider module, which is related to the volume it surrounds as the eaves are to the volumes beneath them. The same grid underlies the little Barton house of the following year (10), distinguished by a more consistent structural discipline which perhaps reflects Wright's preoccupation with the large scale structure of the Larkin Building at this time. The plan is again composed of crosses, one within another, the exterior walls and main piers of the porch representing the outer figure, and the bay window of the kitchen, the living room flower boxes and the extended verandah of the porch representing the inner one. Other components submit as rigidly to the pattern; the living room windows, with their large flat cills, and the chimney and dining room sideboard expose the wider module of the tartan, the lesser module being taken up by the structure throughout. The grid also relates the house to the adjacent Martin house, with which it forms a larger group.

The EE Tomek house of 1907 is another variant of the same theme (11). The grid, not so explicit or so readily comparable with Froebelian precedents, engages the sidewalks of the suburban corner site and integrates them into a circulation system continuous inside and outside the building. In the living areas,

a distinction is made between 'served' and 'servant' spaces which recalls the Isidor Heller dining room. Although it can be interpreted as a cross penetrating a rectangle, the Tomek house illustrates the longitudinality which Wright had begun to adopt in preference to the symmetrical cruciform plan. The organisation is revealed frontally as a succession of layers standing one behind another. In previous examples, the inner modules of the plan have been revealed by successive projections at the extremities. Here, in addition, the screen wall and non-structural piers in the foreground suggest that a layer has been stripped away to reveal the actual external wall in the middle. By disintegrating the perimeter wall in this way, Wright was able to expose further cross references between the extremities of the plan, and to suggest that the main volume of the building stood within the grid rather than around it.[4]

The detached corner piers of the Robert Evans house of 1908 have the same effect (12). To use an analogy with the kindergarten, it is almost as if they defined the extent of the ruled table top within which the pattern stands. Wright's progress can be measured by comparing the Evans house with the Blossom house based upon the same cross-in-square plan sixteen years before. The windows of the Blossom house conform to an elevational discipline unrelated to the interior. Those of the Evans house express the cruciform component projecting

between the blank corner units which establish the square. The tentative projections of the Blossom house have become, in the Evans house, the cantilevered roofs of verandah and porte-cochère. Beneath these the inner modules of the grid are represented by components of various heights, flower boxes, balustrades and bay windows arranged so that they overlap but do not obscure one another. With this assembly of parts, characteristic of the mature Prairie period, Wright translated the patterns of the kindergarten into a three-dimensional system of architecture.

1 The Kindergarten Guide – an Illustrated Handbook Designed for the Self-instruction of Kindergarteners, Mothers and Nurses, by Maria Kraus Boelte and John Kraus (E Steiger, 1877). All quotations are from this edition.
2 'As late as 1898 Herbert Spencer (whose works Wright was to read avidly) could still assert that the growth of crystals and organisms was "an essentially similar process".' See Peter Collins, Biological Analogy (Architectural Review, Dec 1959).
3 At the end of the eighteenth century Durand was providing his students at the Ecole Polytechnique with an array of abstract room-shapes that could be arranged on squared paper to make ideal symmetrical designs. There is no evidence to suggest that Froebel was familiar with this technique, though he was, for a time, apprenticed to an architect. See Peter Collins, Changing Ideals in Modern Architecture (1948).
4 Grids and intersecting forms in the work of Le Corbusier are discussed in a joint article by Colin Rowe and Robert Slutsky, to which the present study is indebted (Transparency: Literal and Phenomenal, Perspecta 8, 1963).

HOUSING AND OLD PEOPLE'S HOME
BURGHLEY ROAD, LONDON NW5
LONDON BOROUGH OF CAMDEN
DEPARTMENT OF ARCHITECTURE

Richard MacCormac

Architects' Journal, 26 January 1972

Kentish Town, in which Burghley Road is situated, is characterised by the scale and consistency of the nineteenth century system of terraces and streets. Although the fabric of the houses remains permanent they are capable of a subtle expression of changing occupancy, through the decay and renewal of their exterior finish. Variations of social class or ethnic group take place cell by cell to give richness and variety within the uniform scale and organisation of the whole pattern.

Public housing is being introduced into large clearings in this system, and in contrast to the nineteenth century builders the architects of the new schemes have not arrived at a consensus about the appropriate form of housing. Consequently each new estate is like a fragment of an ideal city set apart as a social and aesthetic oasis and disconnected from the remains of the nineteenth century context.

The housing at Burghley Road has the quality of an unprecedented solution to a specific problem – a new invention. The first impression is dramatic and unforeseen after the humdrum brick and stucco of the surrounding Victorian streets. Hidden behind existing houses the scheme comes suddenly into view revealing the successive silhouettes of cluster blocks and the tower. The effect of the clusters is castle-like rather than domestic. 'Like fortresses, you could defend them against an army,' to quote one of the children there. This exciting but forbidding character is confirmed by the dark russet bricks in black mortar, which unify the whole scheme. Even the window frames are painted brown.

Site planning and density
Admittedly the site does not invite integration with the surrounding area. Previously allotments and railway land, it is isolated by the railway along the north side and falls precipitously towards back gardens of Lady Somerset Road and Burleigh Road to the south. With no frontage on to a through road and vehicular access limited to one end, it is a back land. Even so the particular way in which the site is developed makes few concessions to the surroundings. The cluster blocks, conceived as independent units to cope with the abrupt changes of level on the hill side, fit their own grid of north/south culs-de-sac and transverse pedestrian routes. In terms of figure and ground the blocks are positive and the spaces between residual. The consequence of the grid is a variety of fortuitously shaped areas at the edge of the site, which insulate the scheme from the world beyond its boundaries.

Because of the very steep slope along the south side, the site area has been reduced for the yardstick calculation, to give a density of 165 bed-spaces per acre instead of 117 which would be the density taking the whole site into consideration. The cluster blocks depend upon the higher yardstick figure, but it is questionable whether the notionally reduced site area, which still has open space up to the boundary, is as critical for site planning as an actually smaller site would be. The discussion of alternative building forms, which concludes this appraisal, suggests that the site might accommodate low-rise housing with densities of about 100ppa (247 people per hectare).

Road access children's play
Road access was limited to the single entry from Ingestre Road; from this the main distributor is drawn in a line towards the other principal point of pedestrian access but this seems to be the only option given the gradient along the south edge. The drawback is that the terrace houses and tower are cut off from the rest of the scheme in which pedestrian segregation has been largely achieved. It was striking to see the whole width of the road used as a pedestrian mall, particularly by young children who felt no compulsion to stay on the pavements.

Generally the roads are enclosed as culs-de-sac within the cluster blocks, a system which would have been achieved throughout the site had not the old people's home been brought into the brief after the original site plans had been determined. As a result three clusters were displaced to expose lengths of road each side of the old people's home. Although the number of cars is limited, the effect is visually disrupting. Generally the spaces between buildings are conceived as level plateaux enhanced by carefully detailed paving. The two culs-de-sac intrude into this pedestrian scene with the borough engineer's aesthetic of cambered surfaces, black macadam and radiused curbs.

The steep changes of level of the site have been manipulated into a series of interlocking plateaux, connected by ramps and steps, upon which the buildings stand and in effect much of the hill has been levelled and cut into a continuous substructure. As a result the series of parallel footpaths which connect and align the cluster blocks offer a variety of experiences which might not be expected from the plan. Level walks drop suddenly into precipitous canyons of steps or become galleries overlooking sunken courts. Children enjoy this, for

the changes of level around the buildings offer alternative routes for chasing on foot, roller skating and bicycling. It is possible that the fortuitous nature of the spaces around the buildings is inherently stimulating for children and the provision of play equipment in specific and rather obscure parts of the site seems almost superfluous.

Cluster blocks
The cluster blocks are the main constituent of the scheme; the other building types seem to be introduced expediently, the terrace houses take up the slot of space by the railway and the tower puts back, in a limited area, the accommodation displaced by the old peoples home. Back to back stepped sections of this kind are a device for optimising the conditions of light and view between blocks as well as providing sheltered parking, enclosed street access instead of a gallery at second floor level, and patios for the upper units on the roofs of those below. Conceived as groups of 16 dwellings which can be arranged in basically three kinds of section, the cluster blocks are intended to mediate between the need to adapt to different site gradients and to present the direct labour organisation, which built the scheme, with replicating construction. When considering the basic land use properties of cluster in relation to other building forms, this argument about site layout appears to be misconceived. What is startling about the cluster blocks and apparently perplexing to some of the residents is the huge scale of the vehicular spaces which they contain. Over the road the height of 14.5 feet (4.42 metres) provides access for fire engines but this is continued over the car-parking on one side to allow the units above a view over those on the ground. These spaces admit more daylight than is usual in internal car parks but they are 'gloomy', to quote one of the residents, and their cavernous scale makes them too conspicuous for their modest function.

Access to the upper level
Access to the upper units in the clusters is by ramp or stair. Along the southern edge of the site the ramps overhang the falling ground and climb above the tree tops. The effect is elating on a fine day but must be bleak in rainy weather for a mother with two children and the week's shopping. The ramps are wonderful in a bloody-minded Corbusian way and an expensive attempt to improve the access to the upper units.

The milieu of the second-floor street is sympathetic; it is superior to a single-sided access deck because of its enclosed

feeling and sense of occupancy conveyed by the just perceptible sounds of radios, voices, and the clink of washing-up. The little entrance yards, which allow each family to express possession of their territory with planting, contribute in the same way. The details withstand scrutiny; the raked joints, boot lintels, brick sills and wooden gates give a robust and friendly impression. Between adjoining blocks the streets briefly and dramatically become bridges revealing penetrating views through the scheme or over the roof tops of Kentish Town.

Upper level units
In each cluster block variation the upper level units are the same, consisting of terraces of four- and five-person dwellings on each side of the access way. The kitchen conveniently overlooks the entrance yard for the supervision of young children, and the front door opens into a rather tight hall from which the stair leads to the bedrooms without intruding into the living area. There are limitations to this conventional arrangement. The kitchen though intended for dining is rather small for five people and the sharing of the single living room by a family of five precludes the pursuit of incompatible activities by different members. Camden's scheme at Fleet Road proposes a better alternative. Children's bedrooms and dining/kitchen are associated together at entry level, while the living room, with nuances of 'front parlour' or 'drawing room', and the parent's bedroom, becomes a refuge from the untidyness and noise of the children. Such arrangements allow bedrooms to become extensions of living areas at a later date. As well as the entrance courts, enclosed roof terraces extend from the living areas of the five-person units and from one of the bedrooms of the four-person units. Potentially the whole roof area of the lower units might be used as a terrace for those above. Unfortunately, the cost of concrete slabs instead of timber joist construction has restricted the size of the open space leaving a bleak area of asphalt where the roof is unused. Advantage of this limitation has been taken for an aesthetic game. The terrace screen walls reflect the projecting kitchens and coincide. with the walls of the bedrooms below, contributing to the overall effect of interlocking volumes upon which the appearance of the clusters depends. The heavy brick masses are carefully distinguished from the concrete frame which supports them; the quality of construction is good and the general impression is that the buildings have

been thoughtfully put together. Combinations of two- and four-person units at ground level enable the clusters to adapt to different conditions. An unexpected characteristic of these units is that they are dual aspect relying on small and rather dark voids or patios for daylight. The four-person units combine a living room and bedroom on each floor but do not provide openings for these rooms to be. used together. Access for pedestrians is top-lit by the alternating voids between the bedroom at first floor level. Sometimes the access way is below car level, but it is ironical that where the levels are the same, GLC Petroleum Acts require an intervening wall which obstructs direct entry from car to house.

The two-person units, planned as small patio houses, enable the cluster blocks to provide for two generations of a family. Entry is from outside through a projecting lobby which contributes to the visual theme of brick volumes. But again it could have been through the patio directly from the parking area if GLC regulations had allowed.

Terrace houses
Although next to the access road and exposed to the noise and visual intrusion of passing cars the six-person terraced houses do not have integral garages. The conventional two-storey arrangement gives a spacious 27x12 feet (8.2x3.7 metres) living room on the ground floor which can be divided with a folding screen. It would be interesting to know whether tenants prefer this option to two acoustically separate rooms which a three-storey house with an integral garage could provide.

The glazed entrance porch which provides space for bins, meters and children's toys also satisfies the need for a sheltered threshold from which small children can make sorties into the world outside. The glazed roof and rough finishes also suggest how a cheap conservatory might provide more living space for children for the same cost as a conventional fully finished Parker Morris living room. After all children are the main users of houses.

Tower block
The architects feel that the form of the tower is justified socially because it accommodates only two-person units and four-person units with children over 15 years old. Only a user survey would reveal whether residents accept the isolation. The large central lift lobbies on to which most of the front doors of the flats face would seem to maximise the chances of people on each landing

meeting each other.

The relation between the building and its site is unconvincing. As well as being cut off by the access road, the tower overlooks car-parking to the north. These hard surfaces all round attract children whose shouting may irritate those residents who either have no children of their own or have children who have out-grown the noisy stage. The worst consequence of the site is that half the bedrooms face north towards the railway and are exposed regularly to the cacophony of goods trains.

Old people's home

One of the most important aspects of the old people's home is administrative rather than architectural. As elderly people are also accommodated in the ground-floor flats of the cluster blocks and in the tower, the old people's home represents a decisively different attitude to a proportion of the elderly on the site. In this case the distinction may be justified. Those in the cluster blocks and tower are still capable of looking after themselves while those in the home inevitably subject to the tidy-mindedness of the institution of which they are part are mostly physically handicapped. The architects have integrated the building into the estate by giving it a central position and a chunky form which relates it to. the cluster blocks. With roads on three sides the outlook for much of the building is bleak and noisy but it may be that the bustle of people and cars is enjoyed by residents. For those who want peace there is the view on to the central courtyard, and some get the best of both worlds in the rooms facing into the sunken courts adjoining one of the main pedestrian routes.

The dining hall, the communal focus of the home, is exposed intentionally in a public situation on the south side. Its largely glazed volume contrasts with the small windows and castellated aspect of the rest of the building. It is difficult to know if this is a success. At first children stared in at the residents eating and the building seemed to offer inadequate privacy. On the other hand every resident is encouraged to come out from the privacy of his room into a semi-public world where he may meet old people from the flats and in fine weather may be tempted to stay on the open entrance terrace facing south.

The home accepts the current DHSS practice of bringing all residents together for meals in one place and dispersing sitting rooms around the plan for small groups to meet casually. It deviates from DHSS in its scale - 60 residents instead of

the recommended 35. The number of residents and the centralised eating facility set the architects a problem which is inherently difficult to solve in terms of the current objective of small scale domesticity.

Perhaps inevitably, access to rooms on both floors is from a central corridor but this is alleviated where it becomes a gallery overlooking the central court and a bridge above the north-east entrance. The sitting rooms introduce punctuations of light and subdivide the community into smaller groups.

Building form analysis

In conclusion an entirely different approach to the appraisal of Burghley Road will be considered briefly. Having discussed the detailed effects of the building as it has been designed, the choice of building type will be questioned in terms of a theoretical approach to building form.

This is not an abstract exercise without a basis in user requirements. Inevitably the criteria by winch Burghley Road and other high density schemes are judged tend to be those which can be fulfilled with terraced houses – pedestrian access at ground level, integral garages, private open space with earth for planting and direct access to public open space. These conditions can be met economically by buildings with a maximum of three storeys, so the relevant question to ask is whether there are alternatives to the clusters which can disperse the four-storey accommodation in low rise at the same density.

In a recent paper[1] for the Centre for Land Use and Built Form Studies, Lionel March has advanced a mathematical modelling technique for the study of built form to replace, with mathematical argument, what he sees as our 'well intentioned but wrongly conceived design rules'. Theorem 4.1 is vitally relevant to housing design and specifically to the solution at Burghley Road. It states: 'Comparing infinite arrays of rectangular built forms controlled by a given angle of obstruction, the floor space index of an array of continuous courts is always greater than that of an array of streets, which in turn, is always greater than that of an array of pavilions for any given number of storeys.'

In other words, at Burghley Road, it is probable that linear forms, terraces and streets with the same distance between them as the clusters would achieve equal density with fewer storeys, while courts would achieve the density either with more space between buildings or lower buildings. It would be presumptuous to

'This housing scheme is an instructive example of some of the problems which London boroughs encounter on difficult sites. It is a composite project, comprising cluster blocks, tower and terrace housing, with an old people's home in the centre; cohesion is achieved by a limited range of materials.'

attempt to propose a resolved design alternative to the scheme built but diagram R illustrates how a three-storey 12 feet (3.66 metre) frontage terrace scheme, with slightly less space between blocks, can give the same accommodation with private gardens and integral garages for all family dwelling and three-storey walk-up two-person flats. Clearly the costs of adapting terraces to the changing site levels either with extensive fill or earth moving would be high, but it is unlikely that they would be higher than the concrete floors, concrete frame, dispersed drainage arrangement and peculiar foundation loading of the clusters. Planning a continuous convoluted court form can gain more space between buildings while maintaining the same density and corresponding more closely to the site contours.

Research into building form has a number of ramifications. It demands the attention of practising architects who should test the applicability of elementary models to the specific content of housing. It underlines the importance of making the right basic choice of form if the architect is not to spend his inventive energy unwittingly trying to compensate for the effects of a misconception.

As well as having quantitative advantages, street and court forms readily match the existing pattern of housing stock, which we no longer wish entirely to replace. In particular the development of site perimeters to gain density implies careful adaptation to the conditions around sites. Instead of being withdrawn and isolated on their own land, housing estates could be hardly distinguishable from the context into which they are inserted.

The final point concerns density. The traditional terrace adapted to incorporate garages can be built at densities up to about 100 ppa (247 people per hectare). From 100 to 150 ppa, evidence suggests that stacked arrangements are necessary, and although the cost yardstick increases it does not sustain the amenity offered by houses on the ground. Gardens and convenient access are denied and the private plot with its expression of family identity is replaced by some kind of megastructure which symbolises the unpopular intervention of government. Is it really worth building public housing much above 100 ppa?

1 March, L, Land Use and Built Form Studies Working Paper 56: Some elementary models of built form (Cambridge University School of Architecture, 1970).

THAMESMEAD: PART ONE

Richard MacCormac

Architects' Journal, 11 October 1972

Superficially, it seems absurd to build a new community at Thamesmead, on 20 feet of peat, next to a major sewage works and under an umbrella of pollution from Barking and Belvedere power stations (on the north bank), which is obnoxious enough to prohibit building above 200 feet.

Yet, since 1965, when the surplus Royal Arsenal land was bought from the Ministry of Defence, the good sense of the Greater London Council's decision has been confirmed. The choice of wasteland gives Thamesmead the topical virtue of resource conservation unlike its unrealised predecessor Hook, which would have swallowed several thousand acres of agricultural land. Instead of being an isolated community in an unwholesome industrial area, it now looks as though it will become part of a general redevelopment of the river east of the city on a line between London and Foulness.

The inflation of the value of building land makes the original price of Thamesmead land seem incredible. At £170 per dwelling, the cost is low enough to offset the exceptionally high development cost associated with piling buildings, roads and drains, so that the total costs are comparable with those of developing an inner London site.

The context of Thamesmead

Apart from its scale and the daunting technical problems of the site, the distinguishing objective of Thamesmead is that it should be a multi-class community with its own services, employment and amenities rather than a residential dormitory. It follows the social concepts of Hook and sets out to avoid the monolithic one-class society of the huge pre-war estates such as Dagenham.

Yet, unlike the new towns, Thamesmead is part of the existing matrix of south-east London. It has to come to terms with the eight-lane penetration of Ringway 2 and the six lanes east/west of the Woolwich/Erith road, both of which impose severe acoustic and visual constraints upon the site. Once the position of Ringway 2 was decided the outcome of the bridge versus tunnel argument became crucial to preserving the town's linear form along the river. The east/west road, on the other hand, was accepted on the Thamesmead site rather than further south (as originally planned) because the design team realised that it could be accommodated in a new situation with less injury. Even so, the basic form of the town is fundamentally, and I think adversely, affected by the status of the road.

These roads are also Thamesmead's lifeline. Since the closure of the Woolwich Arsenal in 1965 and the unexpected closure of the AEI factory in 1968, there has been a lack of skilled employment in the area and a feeling of industrial depression and isolation. Residents of Thamesmead travel far afield to work at present and, if both husband and wife work in central London, this will add an annual fare bill of more than £150 to the already high cost of shopping and rent.

The recent curtailment of the ringway system gives priority to Thamesmead's section and will connect the town with the area north of the river where there is currently labour scarcity. The east/west road should similarly open up a hinterland of employment. Conversely these improved connections should encourage the establishment of new industries and offices in the area. It is important that they do so, for British Rail's North Kent line, the only railway connection to central London, is already overcrowded.

Thamesmead's own shopping provision is complicated by the existence of the Woolwich and Erith centres, a conflict with whose interests brought about a public inquiry in 1968. The outcome was to restrict the size of the new centre to 200,000 square feet to be implemented in two equal phases. Although the road system is designed to serve more than twice this area, Thamesmead is restricted, for the time being, to district rather than 'strategic' status.

There is another, different, sense in which Thamesmead is subject to its context. Although the first generation of residents have come from dense substandard housing, the general housing densities in the Woolwich/Erith areas do not go much above 50ppa. To respond effectively to housing needs, Thamesmead was planned to double this density. But ultimately the accommodation it offers will be judged in relation to the surrounding areas of pre-war speculative housing and the GLC's post-war Abbey Wood estate at 70ppa. In terms of density this remains a predominantly suburban rather than urban area.

The masterplan

The identity of Thamesmead is therefore ambiguous. As a sudden administrative tour de force springing up out of marshland it is distinct; but to the residents who go to the cinema in Woolwich or work in Dagenham it is probably only part of an extensive personal schema of locality.

The evolution of the masterplan to some degree reflects this dilemma. The GLC planners' brief to the architects in

May 1965 proposed a centre on the north/south axis of Harrow Manor Way, which would have linked with the railway station and a subcentre at Abbey Wood; one of the objectives was the integration of the existing Abbey Wood estate.

In the published report (Woolwich-Erith: a riverside project, GLC) of March 1966 other criteria have prevailed: 'the need to seize the visual opportunity that the Thames waterfront offers' has become a priority. In the 1965 draft plan the half-mile wide band of housing along the river is not structured by density, whereas the 1966 published masterplan proposes a high-density spine along the front 'giving the new town a firm riverside identity, and creating a scale of development to balance the structures on the north bank'. The centre is also located along the riverfront at the densest part of the spine where shops and communal buildings become part of the river promenade and overlook a yacht station for the Port of London Authority.

One detects two changes of emphasis in the plan, both of which continue to determine the nature of the present development. It is responsive to the particular quality of the site, flatness, water and dramatic scale; and it has become more independent of its context having a completeness of form on the north side of the sewer bank which leaves the first stages and Abbey Wood as appendages.

The subsequent plan remains much the same except that the centre has reverted to an axial form so that the spine should shelter it from the severe winds which blow up the river; and the system of one-way distributor roads looping round the environmental areas has been transformed into a district distributor along the north edge of town making half loops through the middle of the environmental areas with culs-de-sac off them. Pedestrian routes and local roads converge in 'crows feet' at the junctions between environmental areas to create areas of high activity, for the location of pubs, shops, offices and bus stops, in association with the high-density housing spine. In contrast primary schools are associated with low-density housing and amenity areas for recreation. Playing fields and public open space buffer the low-density fringe from the east/west road.

Clearly the most important concept in the Thamesmead plan is this density structure and the most critical, the spine building which forms the skeleton of the town. The arguments in favour are elaborate and interlocking, and need to be scrutinised one by one.

The visible form of the town

Already stages I and II dramatically illustrate the visual intentions of the plan. In the otherwise flat landscape, the spine buildings progress northward like trains towards the future centre of the town. In Kevin Lynch's terms (in Image of the city) they are an artificial topography which identifies the places of highest activity, the vehicular and pedestrian routes to the centre and the environmental areas between them. They enable the whole scale of the town to be understood from the open space at the south edge to the hard protective definition by the river. This is impressive and must overcome the kind of monotony which one experiences in large, dense, low-rise schemes such as Albertslund. But a difficult question of values becomes apparent. At what cost and what sacrifice to residential amenity has a grand visual idea prevailed? Would it have been possible, with a low-rise scheme, to have achieved a structure through changes in the scale of open space, like the eigteenth century use of parks, squares, streets and mews? The architects think not, principally because their open space resource is largely allocated to noise protection. They also feel that the high buildings are needed for the town to hold its own against its neighbours, the power stations. This is true in a grand conceptual sense, but perceptually a row of apple trees 30 feet from a ground floor window could obscure the horizon.

Spine buildings and the road system

The district distributor road along the north edge of the site will carry between 500 and 2000 vehicles an hour and the spine buildings are intended to protect the environmental areas from traffic noise. Although the chosen hierarchy of roads may be an inherently good one it is also clearly the result of the density structure preferred for visual reasons. Without this structure the town could have been served by a more even mesh of less loaded and noisy distributors. One objection would be more frequent severance of environmental areas. But in fact, although the development plan seems to resemble a large Radburn diagram, the local distributors do penetrate residential areas. If the highway engineers have their way and apply their standards, the severance will be considerable in any case.

The use of medium-rise buildings as high-density acoustic barriers is also inherently difficult. To be effective they need to be single aspect; the greater frontage halves their density and increases cost. In stages I and II distributor roads do not generate much noise and dual aspect

buildings are probably satisfactory. In stage III the yardstick has determined that part of the spine building is dual aspect. The consequence is the opposite of the intention; instead of protecting dwellings from noise, the spine building exposes the maximum proportion of the population in a dense strip.

The deck system

A number of factors have contributed to the idea of the deck system contained in the spine buildings. In the first place the old bye-laws of Bexley prescribed that no habitable room should be below the level of 8.5 feet above Newlyn datum, which affected the design of stages I and II. This constraint no longer applies now that a decision on the upstream Thames barrier has been made and river wall defences are to be built. The idea was sustained as an obvious device for vehicular/pedestrian segregation and as a way of getting over the sewer barrier to the north. By putting cars underneath, dwellings in the spine building open off a narrow paved street and face out onto private balconies. The deck is made into an almost continuous upper ground plane which in stage I runs along the terrace houses as well. Finally, what sustained the deck in a physical sense was probably the belief that, at this density, deck access was necessary anyway and that it should be a continuous integrated system instead of a series of isolated galleries serving individual blocks.

As important as these physical factors were the social qualities which the architects believed could be effected by building form. The Woolwich-Erith report speaks of 'linking the community by high-density spines of dwellings' which 'will give the town a basic skeleton around which the people will live' and concludes that this approach will 'bring into being a new environment and life... of considerable urban merit'.

Ideas of this kind were most coherently expressed by the Smithson's proposals for deck housing and the cluster city in the early 1950s which the Team 10 Primer exposed to a wide audience in 1962. Their argument rejected the arbitrary social subdivisions of slab and tower blocks and sought forms of physical organisation, equivalent to street and district, which would really represent the new scales of association in modern society.

For sociologists the defect of this approach to urbanism is the same as that of the neighbourhood theories it set out to replace. It equates community with physical form whereas people increasingly inhabit a non-place community, identified by patterns of consumption, careers and loose social networks related to work colleagues and recreation rather than district.

There is evidence, among community workers, that the deck system succeeds as a medium for renewing and perhaps making acquaintances, principally for women and children, for men have less reason for using it. But it is important to realise that this is a function of the route being limited, rather than raised, and could equally occur on the ground.

Intensity of use depends on the facilities to which the route offers access and on its continuity. The architects have been thwarted; in stage I the brewer wanted the pub on the road not the deck; Bexley insisted upon a separate primary school associated with its playing fields; the old people's clubroom is separate; and the youth club has joined the school. Unfortunately, the vision of a village street in the air, alive with corner shops, occasional small industries, nursery schools and so on, has not been realised.

More serious is the difficulty of achieving continuity. Even within stage I the deck system is broken by Yarnton Way and one detects an inherent problem in combining the spine building with the road layout. In the masterplan the spine building is usually shown as a continuous band progressing towards the centre, but in its detailed working out the highway requirements can explode and offset the connections. Stages I and III are separated by the junction between the Woolwich/Erith road and Harrow Manor Way, and the connection between the two parts of stage III coincides with a local distributor junction.

Within stage III the yardstick has had its emasculating effect and the main pedestrian deck fails to cross the access roads which penetrate the spine. This seems a disaster; either the deck system should be sustained as a convenient route or the principle should be abandoned.

The pedestrian system through open space
An alternative to the deck is a system of paths which will pass through the low-density housing areas and public open spaces and along the canals. For some of the residents in the lower-density areas, this will be a more direct route to the centre now that it is clustered on a north/south axis rather than arranged along the river. The architects have described what they hope will happen on these routes: 'stopping to rest; looking at surroundings, river, sunset; watching children at play'. It promises to be delightful and the pleasures are already appreciable

Vision of an urban landscape with the highest density concentrated along the river (from Woolwich–Erith report).

at stage I where the lake and exceptional landscaping make the kind of place where it is good to be on a Sunday afternoon in summer.

Density and building form
The planned density for Thamesmead's housing was originally 100ppa with a proportion of 6 per cent public housing to 35 per cent private giving a total of 60,000 people on 600 acres of housing land.

The Thamesmead reappraisal, published by the GLC earlier this year, revealed that private developers would be unlikely to build at a density higher than 15 houses per acre and that the occupancy rate for private houses was much lower than the one person per habitable room assumed for public housing. Thirty-five per cent of private housing will now take up 50 per cent of the land and bring down the total population to below 50,000. With public housing remaining at 100ppa there will be rather obvious distinctions between the private and public sector – an urban environment for the workers with the majority in flats and maisonettes and suburbia for the owner occupiers.

It is worth briefly considering certain ideas about building form which could help blur these distinctions. The density of 100ppa is an interesting one, being about the maximum which allows terraces with the suburban amenities of private gardens, integral garaging and a proportion of public open space. The public housing at Thamesmead could be the same kind as that offered in the private market even though the frontages would be less.

Another Thamesmead statistic which is relevant to the pattern of land use, though less conclusive, is the ratio of residential land to open space. The combined acreage of recreational and educational land to open space in the master plan, before reappraisal, was about 500, not far short of the area of housing itself. What is interesting about this, as Sir Leslie Martin has demonstrated,[1] is that as the proportion of open space increases in relation to housing, the housing form can be less constrained without loss of density. For example housing and school land are usually arranged separately, but if the housing is converted into a ribbon around the school and the school playing fields are dual use, views are opened up and private gardens have access into a park. A further development of this argument, which needs investigation, is that because of the large area of recreational land adjacent, it may no longer be necessary to provide public open space within the residential area. With little loss of density private plot sizes can be increased by absorbing a greater proportion of the residential band into private ownership. The argument advanced by the GLC against using recreational land to disperse housing is that much of the land is already allocated as an acoustic buffer along the spine road. This land would be freed if the insulation were achieved instead by an earth embankment. Studies of the kind illustrated suggest an environment with a less dramatic image than Thamesmead which could be entirely in three-storey housing at 12 foot frontage or 75 per cent at 16 foot frontage. The GLC have argued that such an approach would be 'oppressive' in the flat landscape of Thamesmead. This assumes that the physical image has greater significance than the amenity which terrace houses and gardens gain over flats and maisonettes, and the levelling of social distinctions which a multi-class low-rise scheme implies. Anyway, Amsterdam is a good place and the ingredients are basically the same.

Thamesmead belongs to the period of Willmott and Young's Family and Kinship in East London, Jane Jacob's The Death and Life of Great American Cities and Roger Mayne's photography of the East End. It represents a reaction by architects against the middle-class values of suburbia and the feeble aesthetics of the mark one New Towns in favour of a bold act of communal architecture which conceives the town as a building and preserves the values of street life.

The intention is noble and the result in stage 1, spared the discipline of the yardstick, is spectacular and highly accomplished if the premises are accepted. But, with the easy wisdom of hindsight, it is difficult not to feel that something altogether more modest and private might have been achieved, appropriate to a potentially suburban situation, without betraying social and aesthetic ideals. The masterplan represents an image of a high-density town rather than a strategy, and this commitment is becoming increasingly difficult to sustain as it is assaulted by the yardstick, changing attitudes about community and new facts about housing form. The plan also assumes the public authority distanced from the user in order to speculate about his needs and engineer his social environment. Over the next decade this situation must change as the paternalism of local authorities is challenged by tenants associations and co-operatives articulate about their own values.

1 Education without Walls (RIBA Journal, August 1968).

THAMESMEAD: PART TWO

Richard MacCormac

Architects' Journal, 18 October 1972

Driving from London, the first buildings of Thamesmead to come into view from the new Woolwich–Erith road are the spine blocks of stage I, which immediately establish the town's distinct identity in contrast to the surrounding area. To the south the housing is a typical outer London mixture of inter-war semis and Victorian terraces, drab but adequate. To the west the Greater London Council's Abbey Wood Estate, in the London County Council's pitched roof and brickwork people's vernacular of the early 1950s, with grass and tidy front gardens presents a polite and vacuous kind of suburbia.

The new Thamesmead buildings stand out as a spectacle which demands your attention and response before you turn away. The architecture is persistent – sharp and invigorating or tiresome and obtrusive, depending on the weather, or your state of mind. It announces uncompromisingly that this is a new community whose surroundings will be an artificial environment of streets and alleyways enclosed by concrete, and symbolically separated by the spine block and the north – south distributor road from the encroachment of suburban fantasy.

Planning structure

Stages I and II are not typical of the general form of Thamesmead because of their separate position south of the sewer bank. The environmental areas along the river will be defined by the district distributor along their north edge where the higher densities occur and decline into lower densities towards the south to fringe the linear park. Stage I is defined on the north side by the east – west spine road and along the west side by the existing position of Harrow Manor Way and split in two by the distributor road (Yarnton Way) which bounds stage II. The position of this road, coinciding with the existing alignment of Eynsham Drive, divides stage I into two distinct parts and severs the northern higher rented housing, already isolated on three sides by water and open space, from the southern area of public housing.

The distribution of open space in stage I is distinguished by the balancing lake, located in the lowest part of the site, which drains the surrounding area and discharges water via the canals at low tide through one-way valves at Cross Ness. The lake penetrates the housing and fronts the spine block to give it the same watery prospect as the future spine building along the river front.

In other respects the location of open space in stage I conforms to the general concept of the master plan. The primary schools inserted in fingers of space opening off a greenway at the east edge to which the low-rise housing has access.

The intentions behind the structure of stage II are less distinct and its context is even less characteristic than that of stage I. It lacks the advantage of the lively effect of water, but to compensate for this the spine building has a view over the greenway. This must be delightful for its residents but contradicts the principle of density structure adhered to elsewhere. What makes this unsatisfactory in terms of the masterplan argument is that the low-rise housing and one of the primary schools associated with it abuts land safeguarded for industry, when one might have expected a spine building to perform the task of visual and acoustic protection. Another inconsistency is that the spine building does not continue towards the town centre, but stops short. It is interesting to note that the masterplan did not propose any high density housing in stage II, suggesting that it might be considered an appendage of stage I (see previous essay for analysis of masterplan).

The road system

The distributors related to stage I and II will remain to some extent isolated from the main distributor system of the towns. Nevertheless, these are fast roads and their isolation from the environmental areas feels appropriate even if one disagrees, as I have done in my previous article, with the measures which achieved this. Traffic swishes past on Yarnton Way which is not pleasant to cross, and one feels exposed on the limited width of pavement. In contrast, within the southern area of stage I pedestrians generally take precedence and the pace and sound of traffic is successfully diminished.

Access roads

In stage I the access roads are placed at the edges of the low-rise housing areas and run along the west side of the northern part of the spine block. In these positions they do not sever the pedestrian movement within the housing areas and towards the shops and local centre but they do, to a small extent, intercept the north-south movement between housing and the two primary schools which could well have been within the mini environmental areas defined by the access roads. The two rows of tower blocks are also severed from the low-rise housing – not inappropriately as their occupants, mainly without children, are in each case potentially cut off from the noisy children's environment to the south.

In stage II the access roads into the low-rise area are rather differently arranged as culs-de-sac running east-west, and subdividing the housing into strips. These roads are long and straight, encouraging vehicle speeds incompatible with the 'soft' green spaces within the housing courts intended for toddlers, which' are exposed to their noise and danger.

Culs-de-sac and car parking

One of the difficulties encountered in designing higher density housing is the greater proportion of space taken up by car parking and the road hierarchy. In the case of the tower blocks and the spine buildings this is solved by decking over the garages and the roads serving them. This is effective in conserving space, but inherently bleak and disproportionately expensive and wasteful of resources given the yardstick for this density. The proof, in the low-rise parts of stages I and II, is that terrace housing can meet this problem without resort to such gestures.

The culs-de-sac in stage I are exceptionally narrow, 26 feet from face to face of the houses, a dimension which is not usually permitted by planners on grounds of privacy but which seems to be acceptable to the majority of tenants. Separate pavements have been discarded and the scale is tight, like a mews in which completely hard surfaces are acceptable, and the atmosphere is far better than the decked-over parking. The provision for first-floor access allows two car spaces per dwelling, but as only a proportion of the houses back onto culs-de-sac, the total percentage of car provision within them is about 100 per cent; additional space is required beside the access roads for visitors.

Pedestrian routes, recreational space and children's play, and the spine-block deck system

In the first part of this study I looked at the factors which generated the deck and concluded that it was a dubious solution to the problems stated. But it is well worth looking at because, although it may be unreasonable, it largely succeeds in realising its subjective intentions. The unreasonableness is an important ingredient, for logically the deck should be straight like the access roadway underneath and the only purpose of the alternating permutations of dwelling types is to effect a constantly changing pedestrian environment. This is a place which excites people and which the rationale of modern architecture does not produce. It epitomises a dilemma for architects for on the one hand we sense that people enjoy this kind of thing and on the other we are slightly disgusted that they respond to the derivative and picturesque rather than to the products of logic. The deck is a medieval street and the architects are not ashamed to say that as well as Parkhill and Habitat, Thomas Sharpe's Anatomy of the Village was a source of imagery during the design.

The village idea makes itself felt in a number of ways. It is good to find front doors left open and to have the street affected by music and chatter from inside the dwellings – reassuring domestic sounds which we find when we go on holiday to old villages by the sea. But it's a pity in terms of this particular fantasy, that living rooms or kitchens do not front onto the street.

With the front doors open, children scamper along the deck from house to house, leave their toys outside, ride bicycles and chase dogs, and people stop to chat in the way that was intended. Under foot the surface alternates from paving to brick, fortuitously, so the quality of the street is subtly altered as you walk. But how strange it is that it should be necessary to fall back upon devices of this kind, which reflect the disorganisation of pre-industrial society, in order to disguise our own logic and administrative capability!

Access in the stage I spine blocks is not entirely charming in this way. The galleries connecting the upper level maisonettes and flats are rudimentary, with asphalt underfoot and elegantly detailed glazed wind screens which are acquiring the patina of old bus shelters, only partially protecting the pedestrians from the vicious winter winds which blow down the Thames. However seductive the subjective quality, deck access remains inconvenient and draughty both as a means of private access from car to dwellings and as a means of access to public destinations. In stage II economy has ruthlessly simplified the section so that the deck in the spine building runs for 1600 feet on the east side of the building. No longer a village street, this reformed version evokes Corb's references to the promenade deck of the Aquitania – and it's boring.

The pedestrian environment in the low-rise housing

The now obsolete Bexley bye-law, which required all housing accommodation in stages I and II to be 8.5 feet above Newlyn Datum suggested the deck access idea, not only for the stacked dwellings, but for the low-rise houses too. The architects originally envisaged a continuous system on first-floor level which would enable pedestrians to reach all destinations within stage I without descending to the ground. Eventually this proved too expensive to execute and the terrace houses are only linked in groups across the site at right angles to the principal direction of movement towards the spine block and the centre, the bus stop in Harrow Manor Way and the bridge across Yarnton Way to the local centre.

So the upper level system does not offer a direct route which avoids stairs, for mothers with children, prams and shopping, which should have been its justification. Its practical advantage, already mentioned, is that the space consuming slots leading to front doors between garages, usually necessary to three-storey housing, can be taken up with cars. Its subjective advantage is to complicate the environment and make it labyrinthine and explorable, particularly for children, to whom it offers another dimension for chasing games On the other hand it is confusing, for the houses perceived as groups at ground level are not necessarily connected at deck level and consequently the house numbering is difficult for visitors to grasp until they notice the colour coding of doors and gates. The housing manager was originally very unhappy about the deck and the architects agreed that if it proved unpopular they would convert it into private balconies. The secretary of the tenants' association says that the residents do not feel that the deck violates their privacy. This is surprising, for visitors may feel that they are continuously trespassing on personal territories and dislike the free view down into private gardens.

The deck fulfils the rather special values of Thamesmead which put community before privacy. The individual identity of the houses is subordinate and it is difficult to imagine them in private ownership.

The main pedestrian areas at ground level in the stage I low-rise housing run east-west connecting the spine at one end and the linear park at the other. The feeling of moving in from the access roads and culs-de-sac at the edge of the housing to the vehicle-free oasis at the centre is very pleasant and the accompanying change from the tight scale of pedestrian alleys and mews to the series of courts along the centre is good too. Visually, one responds to the intention of a tightly knit urban environment which is so much better resolved, in its own terms, than the litter of terrace houses along access roads in the Abbey Wood Estate. Even so, one has reservations about this urban rather than suburban scale. Where it is too small for grass, the hard surfaces make it acoustically harsh. The incessant and inescapable noise of children dominates the spaces between buildings during the evenings, holidays and weekends.

Stage II is more open and the pattern simpler, but it will probably be less easy for the pedestrian to grasp, because the access roads do not define the edges of the housing areas but penetrate it like the pedestrian ways and the housing form is the same in each case. There are even pedestrian culs-de-sac off the east-west pedestrian ways – paved and used by children – which are little different from those serving cars.

It would be interesting to compare the social milieu of the low rise housing with that of the spine block in stage I. The latter consciously attempts to achieve the neighbourly qualities of street life by removing the road from between the houses. On the other hand the building form which achieves this denies other media for social interaction which exist in the low-rise situation. There is no house-to-house link on the garden side to give children access to each other without going through the house; kitchens do not overlook the street so the passing faces do not become familiar; and the garages are completely detached from the dwellings, so that car cleaning rituals which can be a social focus in a cul-de-sac are likely to take place amongst strangers.

Recreational space

One of the best things about the east-west pedestrian ways in stage I is the glimpse they offer, through a succession of openings, of the open space on the east side. This is a raised grass mound (made up of excavated material from the lake) which stretches south towards the park and Lesnes Abbey, with which it will eventually be connected by a bridge over Abbey Road. This is a marvellous concept. The connection with the park is highly effective and the raised open space dramatic and unexpected. Walking along the top gives a feeling of exhilaration and children race up and down the grass slopes.

The other amenity associated with stage I is, of course, the lake on which it is possible to sail or row. Promenades along the edge of the lake link with the shopping centre and the linear park, so it is possible to walk around the stage I housing area experiencing an unusual variety of environments with virtually no conflict with vehicles. One gets the impression at Thamesmead that these open spaces are interesting enough to bring people out to stroll or relax, like Primrose Hill or the river front at Richmond.

The local centre in stage I

All the dwellings in the immediate vicinity of the local centre, the spine block,

Bridge over lake with tenants' clubroom and health centre beyond – 'an artificial environment of streets and alleyways enclosed by concrete'.

tower and old people's flats are at first-floor level or above, and the bridge over Yarnton Way, from the southern part of stage I, also introduces an upper level. So the shops are also located at first-floor level and service access is introduced underneath, with garaging for the adjacent tower blocks under a forecourt which is perforated by light wells ingeniously cut out of the interstices between the pedestrian routes criss-crossing the space. From ground level, by Yarnton Way, the court is reached by a seemingly ceremonial flight of steps across the full width of the forecourt which probably helps to give a feeling of accessibility to the upper level – although it seems a massive gesture for the benefit of people coming from the bus stop only.

The good qualities of the centre are due to its surroundings and the approaches to it – over the lake, by the future children's paddling pool, past Derek Stow's distinguished health centre, and through the unexpected and pleasant grassed court behind the shops onto which the old people's dwellings look.

The dubious aspect is the complexity of structure for such a small place and the subterranean environment of the parking, a refuge for derelict cars, shop litter and children kicking Coca-Cola tins. The scale and the techniques are those of a multilevel urban centre, of which it

attempts to be a microcosm.

Dwelling types: the point blocks

As the architect points out, the high-rise buildings were a response to the housing manager's requirement that the majority of small dwellings, two- and three-person, should be sited away from the larger noisier family dwellings. On the site plans of stages I and II the 13-storey point blocks stand in lines, as though they have been directly substituted for spine buildings.

One feels that they abruptly contradict the general intentions of the master plan by their visual independence representing a social independence – or isolation. Yet this may not be inappropriate; the small and presumably childless families in them are likely to be more mobile and less socially dependent upon propinquity than those with children. The point block offers a quiet environment, with views perhaps of the Thames and more civilised access than an open gallery if the lift is respected and decently maintained

The point blocks (which are based on the standard GLC design 'PFG') make obvious use of the Balency system, with floor-by-floor repetition of a limited number of wall components which elegantly and sharply express the quality of their assembly. They are popular with the site labour force because the floor by floor progress of construction has a

rhythm and rate which can gradually be improved as operations are repeated and skills acquired.

External wall panels are loadbearing, with windows made as openings within the panel or at the corners of the building. Floors are cast in situ to give effective jointing between the floors and tops of the vertical units and structural continuity over them. This combination of precast walls and in situ floors, which distinguishes Balency from most other heavy concrete systems, has needed only minor modification in the design of the reinforcement in the floor slabs to conform with the standards imposed after the Ronan Point disaster.

The exterior design displays some ingenious and quirky details, such as the continuous re-entrant angles of steel which run vertically up the corners of the building holding the glazed wind screens to the balustrades, and the horizontal slots between the balcony balustrade components, which become in the middle of the entrance elevations ventilators to kitchen cupboards. At the top the precast facing panels project up establishing that the building is composed of planes and the corner kitchens become little glazed boxes.

All this is enjoyable but the environment on the ground suffers. Wind speeds in the shopping centre and at the edges

of the housing are increased just where walls of buildings should have given protection and the provision for under-deck car parking is costly and bleak.

The spine blocks

The spine block in stage I gives the impression of a continuous random pattern but, like a clever wallpaper design, it in fact consists of fourteen 16 foot bay units which are reflected in the next 14 bays, so that the whole pattern only repeats through 28 bays. I find it impossible not to admire this invention. The craggy profile of the building is consistently sustained by indentations of plan and section and the angled projections of balconies, rooflights, ramps and stairs. The quality of concrete here, as throughout the scheme, with white aggregate and white cement, is surprisingly humane and pleasant.

It is like a giant kind of Lego set and seems to represent, visually, the idea of industrialised building as a kit of parts which can be combined in a variety of ways. It is ironical, then, to discover that it was not carried out in the Balency system. In preliminary studies at tender stage, Cubitts found that the design (which like the whole of stage I was conceived without any particular IB system in mind) was not economic in Balency. The numerous panel types would have been inordinately expensive in the special Balency steel moulds and were instead made in timber moulds and hung on an in situ concrete frame. The complexities of the design would also have posed difficulties for site management and for a labour force whose satisfaction is not in overcoming new difficulties each day but in seeing progress. In fact the construction of the spine block separately proved an advantage for it enabled a start to be made on stage I before the completion of the IB factory.

Taking a cooler, analytical approach, one notes, as the architects mention, that the spine block has a density little different from that of the three-storey low-rise housing. Each 14-bay unit accommodates 107 people. In a double row of terrace houses each side of a cul-de-sac, the particular dwelling mix in the spine block would give 4.5 people per unit frontage of dwelling, at a total of 126 people over the same length. If the spine blocks were arranged in rows, there would be more space between them but the angle of obstruction would be greater and the subjective effect more dense.

The reason for this similarity is that the spine blocks are not effectively two-sided streets. Half the bedrooms in the maisonettes have to have an outlook

RIBA Journal, November 1973

across the centre of the block, so they either stand opposite a complete void or overlook a single-storey dwelling. The spine block offers dwellings with more difficult access and smaller gardens at greater cost than the houses.

The spine block in stage II is a poor thing by comparison, straightened out to bring down the cost, but still with balconies, which may not be achieved within the yardstick in stage III. Its redeeming feature is its magnificent relationship with the rolling grass hump of the linear park, against which it lies like a ship in the trough of a wave.

Terrace houses

The terrace houses are 13 foot frontage for four-person families and 15 foot 9 inches to accommodate further bed spaces for five- and six-person families. These three-storey houses are really two-storey houses raised off the ground. They lack one of the usual merits of three-storey houses, which is that the entrance gives access to the stair and hence to all rooms without loss of privacy. With the access gallery at first-floor level they suffer the disadvantage of the front door opening straight into the small dining area.

The larger houses have integral garages, the smaller houses, not related to culs-de-sac, instead overhang sheltered covered ways at ground level. In both stage I and II these make very pleasant cloisters of main pedestrian routes. But, in terms of yardstick penny pinching (which didn't apply to stage I and only partially applied to stage II) the duplication of covered routes at two levels, and the decision not to use such an obvious space for garaging, would seem very extravagant.

Under the other side of the house there is a covered open space, extending into the garden. Now that the by-law no longer applies this is potential space for expansion and garden rooms which some tenants have anticipated with personal arrangement of trellis work which the architecture is strong enough to accept.

Like those of the spine blocks, the elevations of the terrace houses consist of two horizontal panels hung as cladding, rather than a single loadbearing panel with windows in it, like the towers. Floors are precast and internal cross walls give lateral rigidity to the party walls.

The strata of window and wall which characterise the spine blocks and terraces gives Thamesmead's housing a crispness and serenity absent from the hole-in-the-wall window convention typical of the continental application of Balency. The windows themselves are peculiarly arranged. At bedroom level cedar mul-

lions are set in a varied module, containing metal casements and enamelled infill panels. The effect is to distinguish the individual cell of space behind the concrete facade, implying that the dwellings are made with more transient and manipulable – and hence more 'human' – elements than the systematic megastructure which supports them. This message is reassuring but a deceit in so far as the system in fact rigidly determines the internal layout of the dwellings and will not readily allow the changes in plan and section which are possible in traditional construction.

At living room level normal centre pivoted windows are introduced underlining the superfluousness of the wooden mullion system above. Surely a universal system of fenestration could have been devised consisting of essential elements, which might have survived the economics which have removed the mullions from stage II and left the elevations partially unresolved.

Density of terrace houses and patterns of land use – a hypothetical alternative

It is interesting to find that the net density of these terrace houses, in the most elementary street layout is 154 ppa, a density which exceeds the average for Thamesmead. An objection to using solely terrace houses in this way would be the monotony of a large area. But if we take the Martin/March technique of arranging housing around open space and apply this to the site area of stage II we find that low rise housing could be disposed in a band around the two primary school sites, which would be less deep and therefore in a simple sense less monotonous than the areas of low rise housing in either stages I or II*.

To achieve this, accommodate access roads, hammerheads and additional car parking and open space within the housing site area, the average house frontage would probably have to decrease though not to less than 12 feet ** In this example the ratio of open space to housing is about 1 to 5. If the open space is proportionately increased, which it could be theoretically, given the proportion in the masterplan, the housing layout could open out and plot sizes increase in the way that was demonstrated in the previous article.

This arrangement reduces the depth of vehicular penetration of the housing area and brings all the housing into close contact with open space, so that people might feel they were at the edge of a park rather than in a tight urban area. More fundamentally, it dispenses with all that concrete construction which has been so

ingeniously and expensively devised to hide cars under decks, raise dwellings off the ground and provide ramps, stairs and bridges to give access to them.

This appraisal has been critical where it has been concerned with alternative strategies rather than simply with the quality of what has been accomplished. It would be quite wrong to dismiss Thamesmead either because of this or because the 'style' of its architecture seems, in a very superficial sense, out of date. Thamesmead is industrialised building on a marsh; the achievement so far is that it has transcended the grim image which this combination evokes and invented a new environment. It is, in many ways, deeply considered, humane, even passionate, and this is largely what architecture is about.

* For further discussion of the properties of layout patterns see Lionel March, An examination of layouts, Built Environment (Sept 1972 p374) and Richard MacCormac, Pollards Hill: The evolution of the design, Architectural Design (Oct 1971 p617).
** It would be fair to point out that five- and six-person dwellings at 12 feet frontage need ground-floor living space which would have originally been prohibited by the Bexley by-law.

The advantages of houses are that they offer easy access, garages can be integrated with the dwelling, and private gardens can be provided for children, as can related public open spaces for the easy supervision of young children.

There are other equally important but less tangible advantages of houses. They continue a social tradition which is peculiarly English and classless, and local authority tenants' houses need not be distinguishable from those of private owners – unlike local authority flats, which inherently symbolise the intervention of government in the housing process. Houses create a more friendly environment than flats through the opportunities for social contact offered by streets, and through private gardens and garages associated with the houses. They also offer a more easily maintained environment, because the house and its surroundings are identified with the people living there.

The net density of terrace housing can be surprisingly high. Fig 1 shows a possible arrangement of parallel three storey terraces of 3.66 metre frontage with 120 per cent car provision, giving a net density of 440 pph. Measured in this way, the density of the terraced houses in stage 1 at Thamesmead, for example (fig 2), is more than 375 pph (150 ppa), which is half-again as much as the overall density of the town. Conventionally, it is not possible or even desirable to have such high densities, because of the lack of view and open space which such an arrangement would entail if it covered a whole site. But Lionel March's mathematical demonstration of the advantages of court rather than street forms indicates one way to avoid this result (fig 3). He argues that, for a given angle of obstruction, the floor space index of an arrangement of courts is greater than that of an arrangement of streets, and therefore one can deduce that courts will achieve the same density as streets with larger spaces between buildings (fig 4).

When this theory of built form is implemented in actual housing design, a problem of vehicular access becomes apparent, because an arrangement of courts has to be broken into to admit vehicles, and therefore loses density. So a modification of the court form has to be devised which reconciles vehicular access with the maximum continuity of building. Figs 5 and 15 show such an arrangement, which originated in the London borough of Merton architect's department. Here, the perimeter of the 16-acre site (6.5 hectares) is developed as a series of alternating vehicular and pedestrian spaces with an unbroken terrace, which maximises length like an intestine.

It is interesting to compare this site and its three storey courts (fig 6) with another site in Camden – Burleigh Road (fig 7) – where the density is about the same (250 pph) but the buildings are largely medium rise. The Burleigh Road site could have used the perimeter principle (fig 8) and so limited the building height to three storeys.

If a site is very much deeper than these examples, you may ask how the court idea can be used without vehicles breaking through to reach the centre of the site. One answer is to insert another land use, which should be open space (school or park land), into the centre, as at Pollards Hill in the London borough of Merton (figs 9 and 10). Here, 33 acres of housing (13.3 hectares) have views and access to seven acres of park land. Vehicular access is limited to perimeter culs de sac. There is segregated pedestrian access to shops, and the density is sustained at 288 pph (115 ppa).

It is again interesting to compare this with stage 2 of Thamesmead (fig 11): a mixture of towers, middle and low rise housing, and two primary schools. The proportion of housing to school land is about the same as the proportion of housing to park at Pollards Hill (5:1), and thus a similar perimeter scheme would be possible there (fig 12), giving all families houses with gardens.

There is a further statistic to do with Thamesmead which maybe relevant to other local authority and new town developments. The combined sum of recreational and educational land in the original master plan of 500 acres (200 hectares) was almost equal to the land allocated to housing: 600 acres (240 hectares). If we take the initial perimeter diagram (fig 5) and string the 16 acres of housing around the area of adjacent school land, the layout unfolds like a concertina, and every house has a direct view and direct access to open space (fig 13). At least theoretically, it seems possible that Thamesmead could have been a garden city composed of 16 acre (6.5 hectare) parks, containing pitches and playing fields, much like Parkers Piece in Cambridge. The contrast with the concentratedly urban image of Thamesmead is obvious (fig 14).

If housing adjoins recreational land, it may no longer be necessary to provide public amenity space within the housing area : either more houses can take up this space to give a higher density, or the density can remain the same and greatly enlarged private plots can be provided (fig 16). Because private gardens adjoin open space rather than other buildings,

1

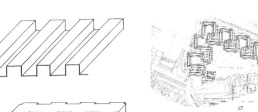

2

3

4

5

6

7

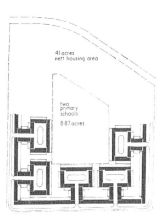

8

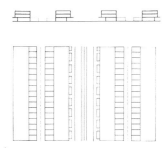

9

10

11

12

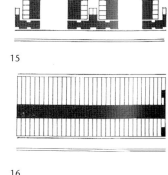

13

14

15

16

they can be built on, and the community is free to alter the boundary between public land and individual plots. This is a new and useful concept of 'ribbon development'. The ideas discussed here originated in research at the centre for land use and built form studies in Cambridge, and have been developed in local authority work. Clearly, research and practice can sustain each other more in this way. Here are some of the issues raised:

Though the cost yardstick increases for densities above 250 pph, it fails to compensate for the loss of amenity when dwellings are raised off the ground. If we agree that houses are more desirable than flats and can be built at densities up to about 250 pph, should not this be the top limit of densities, and why in the London area do architects continue to suffer tortuous design problems with densities of 340 pph (136 ppa)?

Conversely, if houses can be built at densities up to 250 pph, is there any good reason for continuing to build flats and medium rise buildings up to this density, as many authorities still do?

Both theory and practice show the advantages of considering several land uses simultaneously if the best housing is to be achieved. Planning should surely take housing layout strategies into account at its inception.

The separate administration of parks and school land in local government tends to perpetuate the very problems of high density housing which these recreational land uses were supposed to ameliorate. How can the organization of local government overcome this? Perhaps the concept of the community school is crucial here.

If good high density housing relies on the association of housing with recreational land, the suburbs might be the best place for such building.

It appears that ribbon development gives the largest plot size for a given density, but the diagram shown (fig 16) assumes a substandard access road with car access directly from it. Perhaps we need to challenge so called 'highway standards' if we are to gain the best overall advantage for housing itself.

The Architect, March 1975

Newport Borough Council propose developing 158 hectares of land at Duffryn for housing and associated communal and commercial facilities. The land is located within two miles of the town centre and near the western end of the M4 motorway.

Apart from a few houses at the northern perimeter the site is completely clear of existing buildings and consists of flat farmland drained by a complex system of storage greens and water courses with woodlands which divide up the area for the first phase of the development. To the northwest lies Tredegar House which the council has acquired and the site forms part of the large estate formerly managed from this fine mansion. St Joseph's Roman Catholic comprehensive school is located to the south east of the house and a further secondary school, Duffryn High School, lies at the south east corner of the development area. Thus the development provides a rare and challenging opportunity to create a completely new suburb consisting of 4000 houses together with shops, schools, community facilities and open space.

The council appointed the Mouchel Consortium after assessing four submissions from invited consortia, for the design, supervision and construction of a first phase programme of 1000 houses in a designated area of 38.5 hectares.

The brief

The brief included the following schedule of accommodation at a density of 185 people per hectare and 2.3 parking spaces per dwelling.

Bed spaces	Dwellings	Relative %
4* **	260	26%
2	180	18%
5	500	50%
61.7	60	6%

* inc 10 bungalows for disabled persons
** inc 50 bungalows

Within the designated area the following land uses were defined for the first 1000-house phase of the development:

Nett housing:	approx 22.5ha
Public open space:	3.0ha min
Primary school:	2.9ha min
Retained woodland:	8.2ha min
Total:	36.6ha

In the planning brief the first phase was to put in the framework of a highway and pedestrian system which would allow access to further phases of development and relate to existing pattern of the area. At the same time the brief emphasised

that the uncertain phasing of future development required the first stage to be an entity in its own right with the necessary facilities and services including a District Centre.

Concerning the existing landscape, the brief emphasised the quality of the exceptionally fine woodland in the Phase I areas and the fundamental importance of relating access routes and housing to this in a meaningful way and developing an appropriate landscape design policy.

Pedestrian routes were to be conceived hierarchically, distinguishing between subsidiary routes within housing areas and principle routes (and cycle tracks) linking the whole Phase I area without conflict with roads. The provision of public open space was principally intended for childrens play located to minimise disturbance to residential areas.

Although the brief was specific about a maximum building height of four storeys and certain relationships and distances between dwellings, pedestrian and vehicular routes, the choice of building forms was left to the consortium. However concern was expressed that the layout should 'foster social and community development' as it was felt essential 'that residents shall be able to identify themselves with their own part of what will be a very large development'.

The theoretical approach to the design

The design was developed from a theoretical approach to housing form which has now been fairly extensively described elsewhere and originated in the Department of Architecture at Cambridge University in studies by Sir Leslie Martin and Lionel March.[1, 2, 3] Perhaps most relevant to the Duffryn project was Sir Leslie Martin's contribution to the 1968 RIBA Cambridge conference on education where he proposed that the density of housing in terrace form could be maximised if housing land was arranged around another land use such as a school instead of being considered in isolation.[4]

This speculation was put into effect and its value demonstrated in schemes in the London Borough of Merton such as Pollards Hill where the density of three-storey housing was as high as 288 persons/hectare (16 persons/acre). The reason for this effect is that within bands of housing land of certain dimensions threaded around or between other land uses it is possible to devise geometrically efficient patterns of layout based on the court form which maximise both the space that housing takes up and the dimensions between opposite terraces.

All the houses within such a band can have access and most a view of the public open space which the band adjoins, so the need for communal space within the housing area is not as great as it would otherwise be.

As housing densities go the Duffryn density of 185pph is not particularly high but the Consortium's planners felt that the location on the fringe of Newport would be used to the best social advantage if the environment and houses offered suburban amenities not usually achieved at even this moderate density

So, in this instance, the intention of the layout geometry was not so much to achieve high density as at Pollards Hill, but wide-frontage houses restricted to two storeys with large front or back gardens and space for a car within their curtilage.

The site plan and response to the environment

The area designated for Phase I has a clear natural form. At the centre is Kennel Covert, the old game covert for the estate. The core of the covert consists of elms, around which are spruce and larch with a fringe of varying densities consisting, on the west side, of rhododendron and laurel. The overall effect is of layers of foliage, changing colour and form as they rise from the laurel edge to the crowns of the elms.

The edge of the site is no less clearly defined by a woodland belt which encloses the north west and north east sides of Phase I and by Tredegar cutting, a deep drainage channel which defines the south east boundary towards Duffryn High School. The only edge remaining closed by such strong natural features is that to the south west adjoining the land reserved for the further phases of development. Although the site is a distinct entity, strong visual connections exist between it and landmarks such as Tredegar Fort, the copse on Coed y Defiad and Tredegar House itself. The relationship of the covert to the perimeter divides Phase I into three areas, large scale landscape rooms with a common reference to the centre of the site, each with distinct shape and quality. This remarkable natural form lent itself readily to the idea of perimeter development. The borough's proposed distributor road system already took account of the landscape and skirted the edge of the site and it was apparent that a housing band adjacent to this would free the central area of Phase I exclusively for pedestrians. Initial calculations showed that the 22.5 hectares for housing could

be arranged as a band about 105 metres deep, including a perimeter access road and that this would reinforce the three landscape rooms which would consist of areas designated for public open space and the primary school.

The geometry of the housing layout itself was considered simultaneously in terms of the theoretical approach already outlined. The first and most crucial design idea was to introduce the 45 degrees angle into the planning of the cul-de-sac groups. This device enabled the terrace form to be continuous around corners without losing garages or back gardens on the inside of the corner. In a rectilinear court, flats in the corner can overcome these problems and maintain density. Here the number of small units was insufficiently high for this, but in any case the large proportion of elderly people in small units would have been poorly situated in an environment dominated by families with young children.

The geometry of the typical cul-de-sac was very tightly constrained to achieve the density required by the brief. The minimum length as well as relating to the overall area for housing land, as already described, was also dictated by the ubiquitous refuse vehicle turning circle and the minimum of two houses needed in the 'throat' of the cul-de-sac. The cross dimensions were similarly determined by the turning circle with garage plus hardstandings in front of them so as to achieve two car spaces within the curtilage of every dwelling. The dimension between houses on the garden side being the minimum of about 20 metres between the windows of habitable rooms stipulated in the brief.

Within these constraints the terrace form in the Duffryn design has the maximum possible length to achieve a particular balance between density, and frontage, and, as a by product of the form the district heating mains can be accommodated in the continuous roof space rather than in expensive underground ducts.

It is interesting that the density cannot be increased. Even a reduction of house frontage is impossible because, on the inside of the corner the back gardens become pointed and therefore inaccessible and similarly on the other side the hardstandings overlap. So paradoxically the wide-frontage house which was required in any case, was found to be an essential component of this particular design strategy.

Another effect, to be expected from a basically court form of layout, is the relatively generous scale of the spaces; the distance across the base of the 'green' cul-de-sac (on the garden side) being about 50 metres. The width of the green itself is nearly 25 metres, quite sufficient as space for young children, but only about 5 per cent of the total housing area. So, conversely, assuming a spatially economic road layout the form maximises the space allocated to house and garden, the plots averaging about 7x18 metres.

The hierarchy of the open space
This low proportion of open space within the designated housing area depends upon the perimeter relationship of housing to public open space in two ways: geometrically it depends upon the definition of housing land, for yardstick purposes, along the back of the access road and along the front garden fences adjoining the public open space. There is little of the residual land which often accounts for a large proportion of open space in housing layouts.

Socially it depends upon the free access to recreation which the large public areas adjoining the housing allow for children, taking the pressure of their activities away from the vicinity of the houses, where consequently noise and wear are diminished.

The distinction between open space within the housing area and that designated for public open space is significant in other respects; the public open space. in which the main pedestrian system and cycle ways are located, is clearly the realm of the community at large and maintained by it; the greens within the housing, on the other hand without public routes through them are identified with the groups of houses around them and could be administered by their own tenants' associations. The two kinds of space also meet different children's needs, the smaller, sheltered and more secure greens in the housing (without direct links to the access road) being appropriate to the younger children, as an extension of their own gardens, the larger areas to older children's more independent and energetic activities.
On one part of the site to the north of the proposed District Centre, these relationships do not apply. Here the housing form is changed to suit mainly small families, couples and single people. Although two-person dwellings are scattered throughout Phase I the majority have been collected in this location, slightly removed from the recreational areas and therefore from the noise and disturbance of children and in easy reach of commercial and communal facilities.
The courtyard system is a response to the lower level of car ownership expected

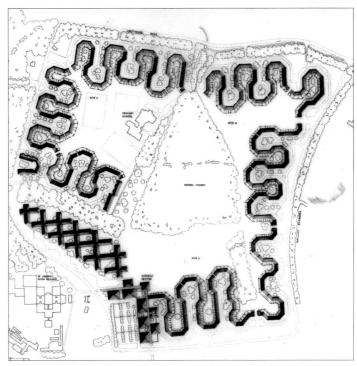

Plan diagram of Duffryn.

and the need to protect the environment of the flats from casual access rather on the principle of almshouses.

The road hierarchy
In a perimeter scheme the open space and road systems are on the counter-form of another, interlocking in the housing band. On the outside the distributor road system, linked with the country highway system not only serves the housing but improves access to existing sub-regional facilities such as the two secondary schools and Tredegar House. The access roads are designed as a series of culs-de-sac to which the individual housing culs-de-sac are attached. Thus there are no through roads penetrating housing areas where children might be endangered by relatively fast moving traffic, the culs-de-sac being analogous to harbours in which the movement of the car is tempered. In this way the car is brought to the house and garage courts, with their problems of misuse, are avoided.

House types
The family housing consists broadly of three types related to location in the court. Larger houses for 5, 6 and 7 persons generally surround the end of the cul-de-sac where the back gardens are largest and the smallest four-person units, of narrow frontage generally take up the straight sections of the terrace. With this variety the housing manager

can offer various choices to prospective tenants. Those who do not wish to participate in the communal arena represented by the green court can face out into public open space. Those more socially minded and interested in making a show of front gardens may appreciate being at the entrance to the cul-de-sac where their gardening will contribute to the quality and life of the whole scheme.

The wide frontage houses have a number of advantages: every house, except one type of 4-person unit, has both living rooms relating to the back garden and one living room dual aspect to overcome problems of orientation. They have potential flexibility of use on the ground floor with separate living rooms or open plan. Kitchens generally overlook the back garden so that the housewife is easily able to supervise young children in the garden or in the play space beyond. Bedrooms generally face towards the rear to avoid disturbance from the cul-de-sac at night. Alternative plans locate the living room on the first floor with the master bedroom and substitute childrens bedrooms for the living room on the ground floor. This enables young children's bedrooms to double up as play spaces during the day within control of mum in the kitchen and with direct access to the back garden.

The houses and two storey flats have been generally developed from the NBA range of metric shells. The 'squint' wall

occurs at the end of the plan opposite the service areas to minimise non recti-linear components, and the whole family of plans are being correlated so that although there are 11 house types (excluding flats) to offer consumer variety the number of components making up the plans is limited so the superstructures are well suited to timber frame systems as well as traditional construction.

Duffryn represents a stage in our continuing research into the relationship between housing layout and the general pattern of land-use at various densities. Such an approach merges the roles of architect and planner, and requires the close co-operation of the sometimes competitive departments of local government. The Duffryn scheme reflects the interdisciplinary nature of the consortium team and their working relationship with their opposite numbers in Newport Borough Council.

The scheme design is by a consortium led by LG Mouchel & Partners, in association with Land Use Consultants Planning Consultants, MacCormac & Jamieson Architects, Wales & West Design Group Architects, Hoare Lea & Partners Consulting Engineers, Gleeds Quantity Surveyors and PA Consultants Management Consultants

1 Pollards Hill Merton – the Evolution of the Design, Richard MacCormac (Architectural Design, Oct 1971).
2 An Examination of Layouts, Lionel March (Built Environment, Sept 1972).
3 Housing Form and Land Use New Research, Richard MacCormac (RIBA Journal Nov 1973).
4 Education without Walls, Leslie Martin (RIBA Journal, Aug 1968).

OFFICE FORM, ENERGY AND LAND USE

*Dr Dean Hawkes, Richard MacCormac,
Dr Francis Duffy, Paul Townsend and
John Herbert*

RIBA Journal, June 1978

In this joint article, Dr Dean Hawkes, of the Martin Centre at Cambridge, examines the energy implications of the office form which started as a speculation in the firm of MacCormac and Jamieson, and the urban and future design potential of the idea are described by Richard MacCormac who, with David Prichard, has developed some working studies. Dr Francis Duffy has acted as office layout consultant. Paul Townsend, of the Martin Centre provided costings and John Herbert of Land Use Consultants provided landscape information.

This a hypothesis about the design of office buildings which started from an enthusiasm for the quality of rooflit courts, ambiguous inside/outside spaces, such as that in Wright's Larkin building (1), or in Aalto's Rautatalo building (2), in which the convivial activities of the city, shops and cafes are introduced into the sheltered environment of the surrounding offices. Such buildings propose a kind of urban space as apt for northern climates as the piazza is for the south.

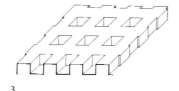

1

2

This qualitative appreciation of courts is supported by quantitative attributes of density and environmental behaviour. The studies outlined here are a further investigation of the primary theme of architectural research at Cambridge – the comparison of alternative built forms. They specifically address what might be called the 'classical' comparisons between 'court' and 'pavilion' forms of building. Earlier studies have demonstrated the advantages of the court in terms of the efficient use of land and these have had effect in the field of housing layout,[1,2] but whereas for housing the courtyard array (3) poses problems at the intersections, for offices

3

the intersections offer a location with vertical circulation and services. As with housing, the concept offers the potential of dual land use, sustaining the plot ratio of office accommodation while offering the courts for public use.

Here, the potential of the court as an efficient user of energy is the main subject of examination and forms a critique of the conventional wisdom that the most efficient built form, thermally, is that which is 'more cube-like', continuing earlier work at Cambridge.[3,4]

The present work opens with a speculation. The question is can we achieve a balance between the variables of the built form which would offer both the inherent economies of a daylit and naturally ventilated building and the low external surface area of a deep-plan

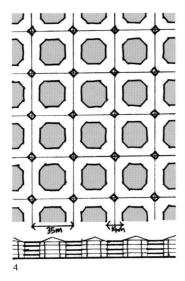

arrangement? The study begins with an investigation of an array of glazed courts (4), surrounded by a band of daylit space, and concludes with two worked examples, one rural and one urban.

Investigation of a Generic Form

Initial studies concentrated on a single court and the space associated with it (5). First, the daylighting question was examined. Studies using scale models showed that adequate daylight for most office activities would be achieved in most of the building during the summer months. These considerations determined the basic dimensions of the court. Conversion of measured daylight factors

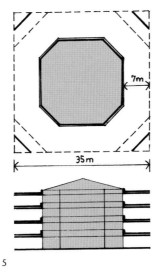

3

5

6

into absolute illuminance indicated that levels exceeding 100 lux would be achieved 5 metres from the windows on the lowest floors at the beginning and end of the working day in the months of April and September (6).

Next, the summertime thermal conditions were studied by estimating mathematically, by the BRE Admittance Method[5] the temperatures which were likely to be reached in both the court and office space on a hot sunny day. The results showed that the temperature in both spaces would be acceptable provided that most direct solar gain could be effectively excluded from the court. This could be achieved by a variety of means and detailed analysis showed that a 'reversed north-light' configuration would offer an acceptable compromise between solar control and the admission of daylight. With this, the peak temperature in the court would be of the order of 25 degrees Celsius and in the top floor offices less than 24 degrees Celsius.

At this stage, the form could be seen to offer a satisfactory visual and thermal environment in the summer months without the use of substantial energy consuming systems. Having established this, the next step was to calculate its winter energy consumption. These calculations were based on a 'standard' court and its associated office space. It was assumed that the office roof was well insulated (U = 0.5W/m²degC) and that

the glazed court roof was double glazed (U = 3.0W/m²degC) and that the walls between the office space and the court are single glazed (U = 5.6W/m²degC) The temperature difference between indoors and outdoors was taken as 20°C and a ventilation rate of 5 air changes per hour was assumed. The analysis showed that the temperature in the court resulting from heat loss to it from the offices would be of the order of 13°C and that the heating requirement, under steady state conditions and allowing for occupancy gains would be 35.5W/m². These calculations did not make any allowance for the effects of heat gains from lighting or machinery, nor did they allow for the benefits of passive solar gain in the winter months.

The next step was to make an estimate of annual energy consumption using the 'degree-day' method.[6] This showed that, for locations in the London area, with the building occupied eight hours a day for five days a week, the heat requirement would be a little over 230MJ/m² per annum. After making an allowance for a small amount of energy consumed by mechanical ventilation the total would be of the order of 250MJ/m² per annum.

To put this figure in perspective, a typical figure for a 'conventional' air-conditioned office building would be 1300MJ/m² per annum and, for recent deep-plan offices of the Integrated Environmental Design type typical energy consumption is around 800MJ/m² per annum.[8]

Towards application

Most buildings will of course be restricted, by site constraints and the brief, to a small number of courts. In these cases, the edge condition will inevitably increase the energy consumption of the building as a whole. The worst case must be that of the single court surrounded by a further 7 metres wide band of office space (7a). The behaviour of this outer band is taken to be like that of a notional double banked corridor of offices in a conventional slab block with 50 per cent glazing in the external walls, double glazed (U = 3.0W/m²degC) and well insulated wall construction (U = 0.5W/m²degC) which calculations show as being likely to have an annual energy consumption of about 625MJ/m² per annum. The effect of an outer band, with these characteristics, is to raise the annual energy consumption of the single court to around 500MJ/m² per annum. All other cases would be superior to this and analysis for the two and four court

forms showed that they would consume approximately 450MJ/m² per annum and 400MJ/m² per annum respectively (7b, 7c).

These results show the economies of scale which one would expect from those forms which maximise court-side office space relative to perimeter space. It is possible, however, to attend to the problem of the building for a small site by the use of a simple tactical device. If the generic court were to be completely enclosed by a windowless wall with good insulation (U = 0.5W/m²degC) – a 'teacosy' – it would offer annual consumption of approximately 300MJ/m² per annum (7d).

The result endows the whole system with enormous potential by allowing the designer to choose appropriate combinations of generic courts with or without perimeter space to suit any particular set of circumstances whilst, at the same time, preserving part of the energy conserving properties of the generic court. A small number of the possibilities based on four courts are illustrated (8). For a glimpse of the immense combinatorial possibilities beyond this, the reader should see the work on The Animals of Architecture by March and Matela.[9]

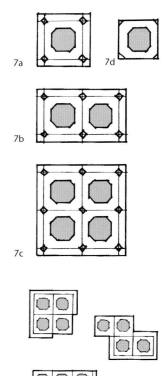

7a

7d

7b

7c

8

In essence, the environment in these buildings would be characterised by its variability, within limits, and by the ability of the occupants to exercise a degree of control over their own local conditions. A fluorescent lighting installation would give general background lighting after dark and each workplace would have its own individually controlled task lighting. The narrow cross section makes it unnecessary to use complex air-handling systems for heating, with their associated service zones, a simple hot water heating system with radiators or convector units would be adequate and would, again, allow a degree of local control. Mechanical ventilation would be required to provide permanent extraction from the service cores at the junctions between courts and this would be used to provide the primary wintertime ventilation. Air would be drawn from outside, through the court, into the office spaces and out through the cores. This arrangement would mean that incoming air would be pre warmed by its passage into and through the court before entering the office spaces. In the summer months, the mechanical ventilation of the cores would continue, but the office space and courts would rely more on natural ventilation through opening lights and controllable openings at the edge of the court rooflights.

Rural study

The lack of external constraint in this hypothetical open site (9, 10) allows this example to be generalised and its main characteristics are shared by the second example on an urban site. It might represent the headquarters of a large private or public organisation accommodating up to 5000 personnel in a total area of 70,000 square metres.

Implicit in the scheme is an attitude to the recent evolution of office building design and in particular to the two acute problems facing office planners in the aftermath of 'burolandschaft' – firstly to retain the freedom of the open plan and yet create identifiable places within it and, secondly, to invent building forms which have the capacity to be either highly cellular or, to a high degree, open. Hertzberger showed the way to solving the first problem in Centraal Beheer. The concept illustrated here reflects the same concerns as Hertzberger but has the potential to solve the second problem. Office space of relatively narrow depth which is punctuated by courts and held together by a grid of circulation can offer cells, small areas and deeper spaces five or six work-

places deep, provided it is possible to shift the bands of circulation from one side of the office space to the other, so the scheme can offer advantages of planning flexibility quite apart from any environmental considerations.

At ground level, the courts are connected by a mall which offers a primary circulation route through the building. Given the population, this would generate some of the characteristics of an urban street relating to shared amenities such as restaurants and shops or creches. A principle of this scheme is that no office space is more than one court from the edge and that accommodation looks out as well as in. In energy terms, it is about 425MJ/m² per annum (7b, 7c).

9

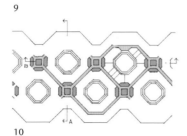

10

11

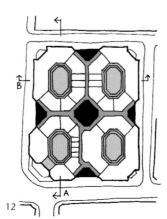

12

Urban study

This study takes as its context a half hectare redevelopment site in Covent Garden. The crucial test here is that the concept offers a commercial plot ratio. A scheme consisting of four courts with only single banking of accommodation around the outside offers a plot ratio of about 4:1 in five storeys (11, 12) and about 5:1 in six storey-construction. The generic form has been distorted to suit these conditions while maintaining its essential advantages.

The single banking of accommodation around the outside allows the scheme to be heavily 'wrapped' in insulation on its road elevations, with limited glazing for views, while admitting daylight and ventilation to the working areas from the internal courts. Consequently, the building gains the maximum benefit from its court arrangement (7d). Assuming a building with a total floor area of 18,000 square metres the annual energy costs can be estimated as being about £30,000, which might represent a saving at current costs of £60,000 per annum over a totally air conditioned building consuming 1000MJ/m² per annum.

Apart from the performance of its office environment, the particular interest of this example lies in the contribution which it makes to the repertoire of urban space and form. While maintaining its high plot ratio, it offers to the community the same kind of sheltered space as the traditional glazed markets of Covent Garden (13). Assuming basement car parking, it opens up a proportion of the site to the public for use as gardens or as access to ground-level restaurants and shops. As an urban form, it preserves traditional urban scale and proposes a planning convention that is the reverse of that which has recently dominated and destroyed the structure of our towns. For instead of isolating buildings from one another as pavilions surrounded by draughty channels of open space, it suggests an opposite stereotype of building against a notional party wall or site boundary of given height to create useful sheltered space within the site and continuity of urban form without.

Future research and development

The purpose of these initial studies has been to test a hypothesis. The results show that a built form based upon a relationship between a glazed court and adjacent daylit, naturally ventilated space offers the prospect of creating a very acceptable office environment at an annual energy consumption considerably lower than that achieved in much recent construction. The worked examples

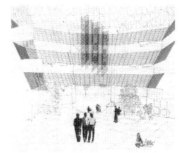

13

demonstrate the way in which the theoretical studies may be used as a spring board for realistic designs for particular circumstances.

In the future, the potential of these studies may be extended both theoretically and in application. Further theoretical analysis would place precise limits upon the dimensions of the generic form within which its inherent performance characteristics are maintained.

Combinatorial studies would spell out explicitly the relationships between energy consumption and an extensive set of forms based upon the generic case. These would also provide the basis for detailed investigation of the relationship between the built form and capital, costs and costs in use.

The application of these studies is not restricted to questions of office building design alone. The underlying principles and performance characteristics would hold when applied to any other building type whose dimensions and functional organisation related to those of the generic form. Educational buildings, libraries, shops, some industrial uses and some health buildings come to mind as likely subjects.

1 Martin, L and March, L, Land Use and Built Forms (Cambridge Research, April 1966).
2 MacCormac, R, Housing Form and Land Use: New Research (RIBA Journal, Nov 1973).
3 March, L, Elementary Models of Built Forms, in Martin, L, and March, L, (eds), Urban Space and Structures (Cambridge University Press, 1972).
4 Hawkes, D, Modelling the Environmental Performance of Built Forms, in March, L, (ed), The Architecture of Form (Cambridge University Press, 1976).
5 This method is outlined in the IHVE Guide 1970, Book A.
6 These calculations were based on the data presented in the IHVE Guide 1970, Book B.
7 Milbank, NO, Energy Consumption and Cost in Two Large Air-conditioned Buildings, IHVE/BRS Symposium: Thermal Environment in Modern Buildings (Building Research Station Current Paper 40/68).
8 This figure is derived from data giving the measured annual energy consumption of two IED buildings.
9 March, L, and Matela, R, The Animals of Architecture: Some Census Results on N-omino populations for N-6, 7, 8 (Environment and Planning B, 1974, vol 1, p193-216).

HOUSING AND THE DILEMMA OF STYLE

Richard MacCormac

Architectural Review, April 1978

The ideological void in which architects find themselves in the aftermath of the Modern Movement continues to provoke speculation, in these pages and elsewhere, about the meaning that architecture should now have. Underlying such discussion, there is usually an assumption, or at least a hope, that the subject is coherent and that the question of meaning is common to the range of building types. Consequently there is a tendency for the discussion to be somewhat abstract and illusive. The purpose of this essay is to consider housing as a particular building type with attributes which give the modern/vernacular dilemma a special significance and intensity. Behind the aesthetic and technical characteristics of style lies a contentious but highly relevant sphere of social attitudes of which, on the whole, we remain unconscious and which the Modern Movement ignored. Reviewing this background does not reveal panaceas but may disturb some prevailing assumptions, particularly the rather stale acceptance of 'vernacular'.

Sketch by Kenneth Browne after the retouched 1940 postcard depicting the Stuttgart Weissenhofsiedlung (1927) as an Arab village.

There are two respects in which housing is peculiar as a building type; of the whole range of buildings, only houses are essentially private and this distinguishes how they are perceived, both by the public and by the resident, whether owner or tenant; the other less definite and related characteristic is technical. In spite of the assertion of the Modern Movement that housing should be part of a homogeneous building technology, it is evident that the building industry itself has evolved house-building techniques which are quite specific; pitched tiled roof, gang-nail truss and brick-clad walls.

The characteristics of English housing in relation to other building types are most clearly revealed in the new towns and in particular Milton Keynes. The techniques assumed by the Modern Movement, steel or concrete frame, flat roof and infill cladding either transparent or opaque, prevails in the design of buildings for commerce or industry. The offices and shops of the city centre of Milton Keynes are a scintillating development of American Mies and the [Milton Keynes Development] Corporation's speculative buildings for industry, whether flat roofed or portal frame, are knowing celebrations of the qualities of the big industrial box, astringent and evidently economic.

Housing in Milton Keynes, on the other hand generally eschews both the techniques and the materials of industry, though there are important exceptions which enable this argument to be elaborated. The preferred materials of the house building industry (in which I include funding institutions, public and private) now lend themselves to a self-conscious revival of traditional house forms, small windows, steep pitched roofs and lean-to's which in some instances are almost indistinguishable from eighteenth century buildings.

So the cityscape of Milton Keynes, in which industry and housing are more generally mixed and more closely associated than in the earlier new towns, offers a remarkable alternating display of the two cultures of home and work. Nearly half the working population of the city live within a grid square distance of their employment and so experience an almost instantaneous shift of environment each day.

One way of interpreting this dichotomy is see it as a continuation of the nineteenth century reaction to the industrial city: 'The early romantic suburb was a middle-class effort to find a private solution for the deprivation and disorder of the befouled metropolis: an effusion of romantic taste but an evasion of civic responsibility and municipal foresight. Life was actually in danger in this new urban milieu of industrialism and commercialism and the merest counsel of prudence was to flee.' Housing remains deeply affected by that reaction. It continues to reflect the separation of work and home life, the former impersonal, disciplined and insensate, the latter for most people an outlet for personal fulfilment and aesthetic experience. These assumptions underlie a continuing vision of the garden city in which industry is segregated and utilitarian, and the matrix of landscape contains housing and keeps up the traditions of the romantic park, an unproductive amenity rather than cropable pasture or forest land. Attempts to homogenise the urban milieu are fraught with difficulties because of this and other deep-seated attitudes. Let us consider, in particular, Bean Hill, the Milton Keynes housing scheme by Foster Associates. Here, in planning terms, is a thoughtful interpretation of 12-to-the-acre suburban housing. The single-storey solution offers the traditional advantages of the bungalow, adaptability with minimum physical alteration and ease of management with a young family. The road layout is economic, residual space is avoided and the gardens are large.

Technically and aesthetically the scheme extends the firm's approach to larger industrial buildings. The same concern for manufacturing economy involved initial consideration of portal frame construction clad completely, walls and roof, in corrugated sheet. Eventually, a timber-frame system was designed and clad in black finished corrugated aluminium so that the whole scheme consisted of man-handable lightweight elements, rapidly assembled.

These were the technical intentions, innocent of extraneous and unintended meanings. The problem with schemes such as these (I include work that I have been involved with in the public sector such as Pollards Hill) is that they provoke a certain hostility to the materials and style which was not envisaged at the time of design. An explanation for such reactions is developed in the account of social behaviour by the Chicago economist Thorstein Veblen in his attack on nineteenth-century American society, The Theory of the Leisure Class [1899]. His argument is that aesthetic attitudes to domestic surroundings and furniture are deeply meshed with value judgments of other kinds, principally economic and social. He sees the goods and environment with which people surround themselves as signals of social status. From this point of view, machine-made goods are particularly problematic, their very ubiquitousness denying the possibility of expressing social distinction and their evident economy implying low financial status. The terms used by the middle-class to describe such goods, 'cheap' and 'common', do not discriminate between social, aesthetic and economic values, though usually the person making the judgment assumes that it is an aesthetic one.

Conversely, handmade goods are especially valued for their characteristics of imperfection and rarity. Veblen develops a nicely ironical attack on William Morris and his propaganda for a return to handicraft and household industry. For, within the context of mass production, Morris's goods, because of their relative crudity, rarity and labour-intensiveness, will demonstrate the special ability of the purchaser to consume conspicuously, conforming to a social structure in opposition to Morris's intentions.

Veblen's thesis allows us to understand the very limited middle-class patronage of the Modern Movement in both architecture and product design in England and other advanced industrial societies. (The same problem may not have existed in recently industrialised societies which did not have a nineteenth century middle class, namely Denmark, Sweden, Norway and Finland, where modernist architecture continues to be unselfconscious.) The essential economy of means as exemplified by say the Pavilion de l'Esprit Nouveau, the plain walls, bare light fittings, skeletal steel stair and mass-produced furniture was, in Veblen's sense, disreputable. This disreputability was confirmed by public sector commissions. In this sense the Peckham Health Centre, rather than disseminating a taste for the new architecture and furniture, as it was expected to do, probably had the opposite influence and with pristine works canteens and pithead facilities equipped with tubular furniture identified the new architecture with the working man's environment. One concludes that the possibility of a universal democratic style hoped for by the critics at the time could only be conceivable in either an ideal classless society or one which does not employ goods and the physical environment to signify its social structure.

This problem is particularly acute in public sector housing, ironically because of the success of public architects in imposing the style which never prevailed in the private sector. As a consequence, rented housing and modern architecture are almost synonymous in the public mind and the aesthetic of economy, whether expressed through the white architecture, the concrete of the New Brutalism, or overt prefabrication signifies public tenancy with all its associations.

The architecture of housing is like clothing, an outer layer which communicates identity. The form of expression is highly sensitive and to be deprived of choice is to be partly depersonalised into submission or truculence. The haircut and issue of a uniform which initiates military service illustrates the principle. Philippe Boudon in his study of Pessac describes the feeling voiced by inhabitants of being prisoners in a baffling environment which came to be known locally as the 'Sultan's District' or the 'Moroccan Settlement'. Nazi propaganda again – the International Style played on similar public reactions in the faked postcards depicting the Weissenhof exhibition as an Arab town complete with palm trees and camels.

The alterations to the Pessac houses made by the residents can be considered either as a search for individual expression or for alternative social identity. Many commentators tend to emphasise the need for freedom of expression, underestimating the extent to which conformity to a chosen image is voluntary. In suburbia, or the Nash terraces around Regent's Park, uniformity, even monotony, confirms a satisfactory achievement of social equilibrium. So the need for individual expression in housing may be inverse to the acceptability of the overall image. Looked at in this light, Habraken's concept of 'supports', which is the most developed approach to housing flexibility, becomes ironical; for arguably, it is only his massive undifferentiated collective image of housing which requires a high degree of choice and flexibility to alleviate it.

The now general rejection of the Modern Movement in housing and the supposed revival of vernacular would seem to resolve these difficulties, for pitched roofs and 'natural' materials sustain the old suburban illusions and the vestiges of a craft aesthetic as a kind of social camouflage. Ralph Erskine's partly public tenanted and partly private housing at Eaglestone, Milton Keynes, proves such housing to be both marketable in the private sector and economic in the public. But the whole phenomenon has a slightly depressing sense of déjà vu. We seem to be experiencing the early 1950s in reverse; the 'people's detailing', of the first phase of the Roehampton Estate, which was supplanted by the 'heroic' second phase, has emerged again and we have the same alternatives of, on the one hand, acceptable images without syntax and, on the other, syntax without acceptable images. Our present situation is distinct if we reject the idea of one architecture simply substituting for another in this way. The alternative evolutionary model is represented by Wright's early Chicago period. Here emerged a new sense of architecture within the recognisable 'dress' of American suburbia. For all the elements of Wright's houses, the free plan, strip windows and extended parapets and roofs already existed, as Vincent Scully has documented in The Shingle Style: In the Language of Wright's Prairie Period, there was sufficient conventional usage to make his new syntax accessible.

This model suggests a less passive notion of vernacular than that currently fashionable, assuming that architecture is to be innovating rather than simply conservative. The degree of conventional use need only include those meanings

THE RIGHT MIX

Richard MacCormac

Architects' Journal, 9 July 1980

which make the work recognisable. In the housing of Span, for example, the terrace layouts and the use of brick and tile and painted windows allude to eighteenth century terrace housing being re-colonised by the middle class at this time. The gardens suggest the spaciousness of Victorian and Edwardian suburbia, but the whole conception is a new chemistry of these ingredients, catalysed by the Modern Movement.

In the realm of interior design, Conran's Habitat has succeeded where Isokon failed to disseminate modern design in the 1930s. Photographs of the first Habitat shop in the Fulham Road in 1964 showed designs by Breuer and Eames set within the context of Thonet chairs, Chesterfield sofas, quarry tiles and country cooking utensils. This sudden enthusiasm for basic but not necessarily inexpensive design and environment (once termed 'conspicuous thrift'), finally established a milieu within which the values of modern design were absorbed and given social significance.

Although the current return to vernacular in housing reflects a concern for context and conservation, it should also be seen as a movement which could re-establish the public convention of architecture. In terms of information theory, this familiarity of convention raises the probability of communication, while a full break with style (Pessac) so diminishes it that there may be almost complete misunderstanding. 'If only the most probable combinations appear, the work lacks originality and corresponds to the norm we usually call the "style". Less probable combinations define the originality of the work relative to the style.' In housing and domestic design, these conventions express highly sensitive social information with which architects have lost contact through lack of patronage and the interlude of the Modern Movement. We have to embrace these conventions partly as a subterfuge to engage society, like Wright in Oak Park. Vernacular should be a Trojan horse whose acceptable exterior hides other less expected meanings.

It is increasingly obvious that, in the immediate future at least, most major urban development initiatives will have to come from the private sector. The problem will be, as it was during the last excesses of private enterprise in this field, to reconcile the rapaciousness of the developer with the needs of the community. Below, Richard MacCormac describes a study his practice, MacCormac and Jamieson, has undertaken of the Spitalfields area of east London. Here, based on an analysis of part of Venice, undertaken with Ove Arup & Partners, he has produced a scheme which demonstrates how a modern development with a high plot ratio and large proportion of office space can conform with the scale and duplicate the rich mix of uses that characterises the area. It proposes that mixed use and glazed atria offer overall energy savings and speculates that atria and malls encourage a conviviality of public life. The study was presented in April 1980 at the Centro Culturale (Tre Occi) in Venice Radiotelevisione Italiana.

Spitalfields is a decayed area of mainly eighteenth and nineteenth century development dominated by Nicholas Hawksmoor's Christ Church (1725) currently being restored and used for the performance of Baroque music. The market site, which forms the subject of this study and which has an uncertain future, is a short walk from Liverpool Street Station and is connected to Bishopsgate by Artillery Lane, a shopping street of interest and quality. The area is characterised by a lively multiplicity of uses: housing, offices, shops, workshops, restaurants, pubs and the streets are used for markets. Buildings are generally four or five storeys high defining streets of various width.

A conventional developer would wish to maximise the area of office space on the site up to the permitted plot ratio of about 3.5:1. A conventional approach would be to stand a tower on a podium. To achieve the plot ratio the tower would be 15 to 20 storeys high with a base of two to three storeys. Such a monolithic scheme would be out of scale with the surrounding area, would affect the local climate with downdraughts and turbulence, and would contribute nothing to the street system, either in form or content. It would deny the multiplicity of activities which are characteristic of areas like Spitalfields and deprive its own users of any sense of participation in their surroundings.

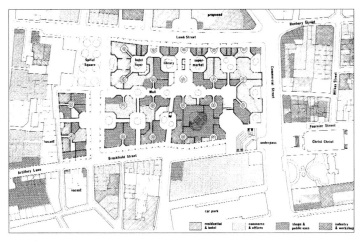

Spitalfields ground plan showing rich mix of uses and new routes relating to the existing streets.

Venice as a comparison

Venice is an exemplary European city not only because of its canals and the quality of its facades, but because it offers a system of public, semi-public and private spaces in which a multitude of public and private activities are inter related and reconciled.

Our study of a typical area of the city revealed a high plot ratio (3.5:1) but the buildings generally have a street scale. The public experience of the city was not of buildings as solid objects, but of the spaces enclosed by the surfaces of the buildings. These spaces were found to be arranged in sequences of public, semi-public and private enclosures, in which deliveries and refuse collection mingle unobtrusively with pedestrians. An analysis of uses showed offices, shops, workshops, housing and services such as banks, co-existing in various combinations of plan and section. Large public buildings such as churches, and theatres, in which the activities do not relate to the street, were sometimes buried in the fabric of other uses and announced themselves in the street facade emblematically with pediment or portico.

The public spaces of Venice were seen to be each a forum of public life in which people meet.

There were also in Venice a number of semi-public spaces in the form of glazed atria which were the courts of former palaces. These included the post office building, the Coin Supermarket, the Grassi Art Gallery and the sumptuous interior of Danieli Hotel. Each is an extension of the environment of the building around it. Space may be ambiguously external and only partially heated, as in the post office, or ambiguously internal and completely heated as in the Danieli. Daylighting varies from the brightness of the post office court and the Grassi to the dim Gothic opulence of the Danieli.

Spitalfields proposal

In terms of building form, our proposal is an inversion of the conventional developer's planning stereotype of the 1950s and 1960s. Instead of a tall building set back from the boundaries of the site or on a low podium our proposal goes up to the existing street lines and invites spaces and entrances to be carved out of it in response to the surrounding street pattern. Although the plot ratio is 3.5:1 the scale is only five storeys like adjoining streets. It offers a series of glazed courts and malls adaptable to many public and semi-public functions.

To test its urban qualities we have subjected our Spitalfields study to the same series of analyses used for Venice. The block diagram of the ground floor illustrates how the overall form is fragmented. The routes between the blocks render the whole site accessible and link the scheme to existing roads.

The spaces in the buildings are of three kinds, public, semi-public and private. Private subdivisible space is within the blocks; the principal public space is the longitudinal mall developed as a covered route between the corner of Brushfield Street and the proposed arena beside Commercial Street. The glazed courts on each side of the mall are precincts, comparable with the spaces contained within the city blocks of Venice. They are interpretable either as tributaries of the public thoroughfare or as semi-public spaces for particular uses such as foyers, exhibitions and so forth. They are the 'light wells' of the scheme and as such are equivalent to the windy residual areas out side conventional developments which enable them to conform with light angles. Here they increase the ground floor of the building by about 20 per cent while the cost of the fabric enclosing them remains largely attributable to the surrounding office space.

Servicing by vehicle is envisaged at a semi- basement level so that deliveries can be brought close to shops and work-shops and double handling is limited.

The GLC survey of 1972 shows Spitalfields as a mosaic of different uses, residential, offices, shops, workshops. Our proposal continues this pattern of multi-use through-out the ground floor, fronting the malls with shops, workshops and studios. The semi- public courts offer such uses as a hotel foyer, supermarket, banking hall, post office, library, exhibition space, restaurant, wine bars, and theatre. Each court is a forum or arena around which are office spaces like galleries. The inhabitants of the upper levels become spectators and participants in the activity which the building contains, as in traditional squares or piazzas.

Architectural intention

Architects have tended to classify visually and spatially and to be more interested in buildings as containers than in the animation of the spaces they contain. Now there is a move away from the cool abstraction of the modern movement towards the idea of building as a framework for the experience of activity as exemplified by Hertzberger's Centraal Beheer.

The scheme is like an artificial hill, its south side and top layered with housing to take advantage of passive solar gain. Where it faces onto Brushfield Street, the housing is a rough brick crust through which the smooth ceramic-faced construction of the commercial accommodation is glimpsed. The housing articulates the entrances to the courts and mall and to the theatre buried within the scheme.

To the west we have suggested how the development might relate to an adjoining site. To the east the offices are protected from the noise and fumes of Commercial Street by a series of glazed arboreta and to the north there is the suggestion that the elevation might break down in the centre and avoid over shadowing Lamb Street to offer a formal cue to future development to the north.

Energy control

The scheme minimises energy consumption through the following design strategies which were devised in conjunction with Ove Arup and Partners.
A compact form with minimum external periphery.

The use of 'free' ambient energy sources. Predominantly south-facing housing acts as an external crust to the scheme and takes maximum advantage of winter passive solar gains. Energy consumption by the offices is minimised by admitting natural light through glazed courtyards and gallerias.

The use of buffer environmental zones between the external climate and the internal controlled areas. Environmental conditions within the glazed courtyards vary with external conditions and are only controlled when sedentary activities take place.

Energy transport between different uses. Certain users have energy spill particularly at inter-seasonal periods. We have hypothesised a mix of uses when the excess energy spill from offices, restaurants and shops can be utilised to heat the dwellings. The scheme offers planning gain for the public while satisfying development criteria. Its potential lies in the inter-relationship of different uses to offer energy economy and the high plot ratio of office development with a traditional urban form could provide for a low rent mixed uses on the ground floor.

SUBURBAN SYNTAX

Richard MacCormac

Architectural Review, October 1985

Current theories of urban design are preoccupied with the forms and values of eighteenth- and nineteenth-century cities, and disdainful of suburbia which remains without respectable discussion. The wishful thinking implicit in this is curiously reminiscent of the Modern Movement; for whereas the Modern Movement proposed an ideal new world to convert society from its suburban aspirations, the new urbanists, such as the Kriers, propose an idealised old world.

The reality is that suburbia has become the residential convention of the twentieth century, just as the terrace was of the eighteenth and nineteenth. So, paradoxically, some of the most pressing issues of urbanism are really suburban ones, and it is to the language of suburbia that we should be addressing ourselves. Some would argue that the essence of suburbia is its formlessness and to suggest that it has its own language is to contradict its fantasy of escape from the community of the city. But that vision of concealment in arcadia has been degraded into the pot-pourri of repetitive and monotonous individuality, for which suburbia is reviled.

Both the laissez faire of speculative development and the public initiatives of the New Towns have failed to offer a convincing alternative vision, particularly in relation to densities which have increased in response to higher land costs. There is no landscape theory comparable to the Picturesque, but instead massive planting is intended to veil the repetitiveness. The common experience of the traveller, particularly in the later New Towns such as Milton Keynes, is of a continuous semi-rural nowhere through which buildings appear haphazardly until an estate is reached itself a large cul de sac.

The phraseology of New Town planning is peppered with terms like 'urban design philosophy', 'sense of place', and 'visual order', yet it was only at the end of their abruptly truncated development periods that the designers of such New Towns as Warrington and Milton Keynes came to realise the significance of roads as the key to suburban experience.[1]
The descending hierarchy of road systems is the latent structure of suburban design, and the purpose of my argument is to explore how that system may be visually represented, so as to fulfill, with quite specific images, such vague terms as 'visual order'.

In taking the roads as the basis, the highway engineers' assumptions are both accepted and subverted. Vehicles are accepted as dominant on major roads which are distinguished from roads where people live. This, so far, is the conventional wisdom, but beyond this we have to question the extent to which the criteria of travel should prevail over the criteria for making places in the road system as a whole.

In the conventional hierarchy of district distributors local distributors and access roads, only about one third of road frontage is directly accessible from buildings and it is this factor more than any other which determines the relative diffuseness of modern development. We must ask ourselves whether the road as street can claim a greater proportion of the system than current highway engineering allows. Our study suggests that it can.[2]

What follows is not a prescription; suburban planning can take many forms, it is just one possible kind of invention, and this belief underlines the fact that planning should be a process of design fired by an aesthetic, not a rule of thumb promoted by geography graduates.

The sense of being nowhere in suburban road systems arises from the dominance of travel over destinations and the assumption that only the destinations are 'places' , the roads between them, not. In Kevin Lynch's terms, there is no 'artificial typography' to tell you where you are in relation to the system as a whole except in the crude sense that the roads get narrower and slower. The. illusion of landscape associated with major roads is usually insufficiently deliberate and the exits to where people live are unexpressed. There is a failure to distinguish between the different places in the hierarchy and the thresholds between them.

The road hierarchy

In conventional road planning the major distributor (the equivalent of the grid road system in Milton Keynes), is connected to housing by local distributors, A. Our proposal is to eliminate the local distributors and substitute boulevards directly fronted by buildings, connected at intervals of about 350m to the distributor, B

For this to work these connections must not be too frequent to compromise the efficiency of the distributor or too far apart to overload the boulevards. Our proposal challenges existing standards in both respects, increasing journey time by only a few minutes. But it is likely to save about .75m.of road and associated infrastructure per dwelling (about £500/dwelling). The boulevards offer a 'street' system continuous like the distributor, but slower so as to be attractive to users, rather than travellers, and associated with the highest density and lowest car ownership, with bus routes, shops and light industry and accommodation mainly for those without cars.

The access roads connected to the boulevards are more conventional. But the pattern suggested is a cellular one. Such a cellular system offers the continuity which a system of cul-de-sac estates does not. Devices for reducing vehicle speed, such as constrictions of width and changes of surface ensure that such access routes are less attractive to travellers than the boulevards. Interestingly, such a pattern of roads fits the pattern of perimeter development around schools and recreational space which we have proposed elsewhere, C. Even if only 20 per cent of the total developable land is 'public open space' (including school land), it is possible for all dwellings to be within about 150 m of it, a real garden city relationship. The road pattern itself is not only exceptionally economic but the distinctions between different parts of the system are easily made recognisable and views of 'open space' are readily obtained through the housing to help orientation and create surprise.

Places and thresholds

The set of drawings which follows proposes an architectural repertoire capable of describing the places and thresholds latent in the pattern of roads. Instead of roads being the boundaries of sites, A, each site should straddle a road to contain it as a place, B, C. Consequently the boundaries of the sites are parks and common land so each site demands an interpretation of this quintessentially suburban situation, D.

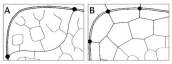

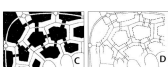

The main distributors

The image is of a road through landscape. The junction is made an urban intervention in this arcadia to herald the entrance to a community. For this to work the illusion of landscape must be complete, and the contrast deliberate, E, F.

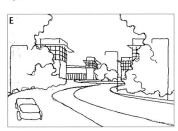

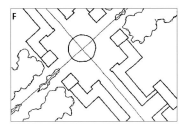

The boulevard

Instead of more landscape verges, this is definitely a street, potentially dense and relatively urban if fronted by flats in three to four storeys rather than houses with less scale. It is a place of arrival as well as a road to travel along, where you would expect to find some local shops, small businesses and a bus route, G, H.

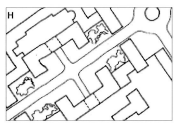

Cross roads

Towers mark the main axis of the road. End houses are adapted and mitred to frame the junction, K, L.

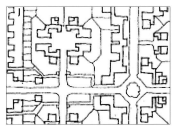

Entrance to a residential area

Flats form a gateway through which the diminished scale of family housing is discovered. Parkland is glimpsed beyond this threshold and offers another point of reference, I, J.

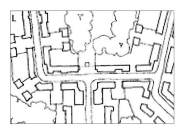

A street opens into a green

The end houses turn the corner. Their facade brickwork becomes a brick retaining wall which engages the entrance porches of villas around the green, M, N.

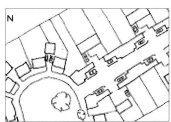

Entrances to vehicle courts

Semi-detached or end of terrace houses form the gateways to the final vehicle destinations of the scheme around which houses and gardens are clustered, O, P, Q, R.

1 Hugh Canning, Chief Architect and Planner of Warrington, wrote of the 'city building' function of roads in his introduction to the Warrington project, (Architects' Journal, 13 Sept 1978).
2 Terence Bendixson broached this issue in 'Slow Speed Roads (Architects' Journal, 10 Oct 1977).

FITTING IN OFFICES

Richard MacCormac

Architectural Review, May 1987

Offices, once the exemplars of Modernism, have become the Frankenstein monster of architecture. With the tower block of housing, the office block represents what most people dislike about modern architecture and architects. In part this reaction is the result of a strange but influential coalition; on the one hand there is the conventional left-wing view that offices are offensively capitalist, and on the other the conservative fear of change and the loss of the familiar.

Whereas the context of North America enables office building to be spectacular, brashly symbolic, and able to characterise new kinds of place, in Europe and perhaps particularly in Britain, it has failed to create convincing new environments and is seen simply to have eroded the qualities we value in urban surroundings. With highway engineering the office building has been the main cause of dead public places; places in which the function of motion takes priority and which have no significance of their own.

Much has been written about the urban shortcomings of modern architecture, particularly as epitomised by the office block surrounded by residual space. The sense that the European city is about public places, not about buildings as objects, excepting monuments, has led to a revival of eighteenth-century urbanism as exemplified by the work of the Kriers.

Office and public realm

This work is important, but one can go further and see through the appearance of eighteenth-century urbanism to its intention. This was (to paraphrase Richard Sennett) to hold the values of public and private life in balance. Transactions in the public realm engendered civility and were seen to transform the human animal into a social being. The eighteenth century city was a 'cosmopolis' with pleasure gardens, coffee houses, theatre and entertainment open to a wide public. Streets were specifically designed for pedestrians and from these malls and boulevards arose the idea of the covered arcade, the Parisian 'passage' culminating in the great glazed public spaces of the nineteenth century such as the Milan Galleria.

Although such ideas of public life continued through the nineteenth century, powerful forces were set against them. The scale of cities made them more impersonal and created the new problem of vehicular traffic. Functions became separated into special areas – an idea subsequently endorsed by CIAM.

'The City' of London is such an area, virtually without life except that created by its business cycle. Such disintegration continues in new ways and tends to be supported by conventional financial institutions. The specific social milieu of Fleet Street now appears to be breaking up as technical and economic requirements of the newspaper business prevail over traditional human relationships. Similar priorities appear to have prevailed in the BBC's proposed move to the White City.

Another complementary pressure in England during the nineteenth century was a moral one; the public domain was dangerous and disorderly. This Protestant ethic tended to confine personal experience to the place of work (which took on a deliberately industrial character) and to the sanctuary of the family – safely removed to the suburbs. It is this above all which has distinguished London from Paris.

Office and local economy

Local planning authorities express the problem of the office in relation to local needs as one of balance, particularly in relation to small businesses which are supposed to be endangered by large ones. One way of considering this is financial and makes a distinction (as is made throughout this essay) between the business transactions of the offices themselves and the transactions of employees and others outside them.

An office development employing 6000 people will generate local demand for many services. If the daily expenditure on food and drink was to average £2 per head, the annual expenditure on this alone would be in the order of £2.5m. If other shopping and service industries are taken into account the financial turnover may be several times this sum. Quite apart from the advantages of rate income and potential employment, offices create a vast opportunity for the local and small-scale generation of wealth. This is a matter which has been overshadowed by less definable though important questions of social balance, and planning gain.

Apart from size, the main distinction between large organisations in office buildings and most small businesses is their relation to locality. Offices are generally concerned with transactions which are regional, national or even global whereas small businesses, particularly retailing, restaurants, bars and markets offer transactions to the local community and to visitors through their street frontage. In this immediate sense, large offices have nothing to offer locality, however important their role in

A canal covered by an arcade could form the spine of the development.

employment, in priming the local economy and supporting the rates base. Their transactions are foreign.

In between the scale of the large office and that of the small retailer there is a growing sector of small businesses which, while specialist, are themselves street related. They may be commercial or professional, like Hatton Garden or the Inns of Court. They suggest the idea of specific hinterlands of business concentrating their own milieu and advertising it through the places they surround and make their own. They are an important component of the argument about balance, but tend to be overlooked in institutional investment and by planning policies, which do not recognise them as a separate class of use.

Offices and streets

We respond to places in cities which offer something and we unconsciously sense their civility even if we do not wish to take immediate advantage of their offer. Such places do not engage us through an abstract quality or through allusion. Their spatial enclosure is latent like an unfurnished or undesignated

room and becomes significant through the content of its faces and what these present. The difference between, say, London's Charlotte Street and its extension to the north into Fitzroy Street is not spatial – it is a matter of use. The traditional mix of Charlotte Street offers local residents, workers and visitors goods and services such as food, DIY, newspapers, restaurants and pubs, whereas Fitzroy Street has been gradually invaded by professional and commercial offices whose transactions are not local and whose facades 'are themselves isolated from the pavement by basement areas and car parks.

Similarly the advance of the City of London into the East End has resulted in the destruction of street frontage and street-related activities and their replacement with hermetic buildings set back as isolated blocks which accommodate regional or national functions. Small businesses are also burgeoning but these are moving into existing buildings and for reasons I have described are not seen as complementary to the larger functions.

Reshaping the office to make it more city-like

Cities are structures which reconcile public, institutional and private use. Traditionally the institutional functions also defined and provided symbols for the public domain. The public world, contained by the facades of the private one could be represented, and was real and imaginable as Palladio's Teatro Olimpico at Vicenza testifies. Nolli's map of Rome is also a reminder. In such cities, between the purely public and purely private domains, are intermediaries, colonnades, arcades, market halls, churches and precincts, to which might be attributed various kinds of activity. The institutional office, as a building type, has proved quite incapable of contributing to such a range of urban distinctions. One historical explanation is that the office, in the guise of the Chicago steel frame of the 1880s, which modern architects have inherited through Sullivan and Mies, is a descendant of the cotton mill. Even the interior layout mimics that of the machines. Such buildings predicate only two kinds of territory for the city: that of the workstation and that of the street outside – the street as passage not place-and they are essentially separate. There is a coercive utilitarianism implicit in this. The office block itself represents the discipline of work, its hermetic form safeguarding its productivity from the disorder of the world outside.

The future civility of city and workplace depends on the insubordination of this idea. The space and activity of the city must assert itself as the public domain which office space encloses and protects and the office as a social organisation must find characteristics in itself which make it more city-like.

Several modern buildings establish precedents. Aalto's Rautatolo brings the city into the core of an office complex with shops and restaurants around a glazed courtyard. Although Wright's Johnson Wax building is isolated from the context of Racine, it has characteristics of a city in microcosm, its own urban topography consisting of a central square of administrative services surrounded by workstations. Similarly Centraal Beheer has the characteristics of a small town – an administrative kasbah rather than a mill.

Small offices as communities

Before considering the problem of locating large office buildings so that they do not supplant local transactions, we ought to think of building forms which relate small businesses to the public and which suggest what the hinterland of large organisations might be like if they are not parts of the large organisations themselves.

Office organisations offer their own social topography. The clerical and reception areas are the places of exchange. In our project for Hampshire County Council, the district offices for the social services department cluster the teams of social workers around a double-height 'clerical hall', a great luminous volume which forms the point of reference for the organisation as a whole. The two other departments, education and careers, are interpreted analogously. In particular, careers, arranged around a double-height hall, will find itself in a new version of its current accommodation in an Edwardian house, in which the private offices and interview rooms are clustered around a two-storey high hall and staircase, a publicly accessible place.

Our own offices which we share with a number of small businesses and an art gallery, represent a shift in this idea. Although not a public building it is not really private either; it is a cul-de-sac off the street in which a number of enterprises co-exist and as a consequence of being under one roof do business together.

This idea has been developed further in a hypothetical project for St John Street, Smithfield. In this a community of small businesses surrounds a galleria. The suggestion of Centraal Beheer is fulfilled by making its streets into a public place with shops and restaurants at ground level and offices looking into the glazed street. Like the nineteenth century versions, such as the Burlington Arcade, the intention is that this would be a named place from which the businesses would gain their identity. The arcade belongs both to the business community and to the public.

Such a building brings the idea of office closer to that of market. It becomes an emporium in which the services of the participants are shown to be available to each other and to the public. It depends upon 'inlook' rather than outlook and if it is pressed up against the perimeter of its site, will yield a good plot ratio in relation to building height.

Large offices In traditional urban structure

The horizontal dimensions currently required for dealing floors are compatible with eighteenth- and nineteenth-century residential block sizes but not with the medieval subdivisions of the City of London. For moderate plot

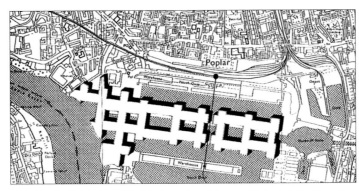

Dating from the time the Canary Wharf development was first proposed for London's Isle of Dogs, this exercise transposes the street grid of Bloomsbury into a building grid 50 metres deep, achieving the equivalent floorspace of the Canary Wharf plan, but within a maximum of five storeys.

ratios (say 4:1) the requirement for dealing floors could encourage buildings of a height compatible with traditional street architecture. An analysis of the Canary Wharf proposal (Architectural Review, February 1987), for example, shows that if the site area is superimposed on part of Bloomsbury and the residential blocks and gardens are filled with office space from street to street, all the floor space can be accommodated in seven-storey construction.

An interesting geometric transformation is to reverse figure and ground and form a grid of deep offices around a series of urban squares. Building height is down to five storeys. The Milan Galleria has been taken as a model for a great retail and business arcade containing a canal, which connects Greenwich with the City. The covered canal would be animated by shops and small businesses or local water-borne transport. The squares beyond could form a deliberately quiet hinterland for the large businesses, green, temperate and modestly-scaled, like Grays Inn.

Significance of office buildings

There has been a failure in urban design to find a context for offices - beneficial to urban functions as a whole, in which offices are acceptably significant. Great nineteenth-century commercial institutions, like the Royal Exchange, succeeded in symbolising themselves through their Classical form as well as responding to locality by incorporating small businesses and shops in their periphery.

Modern speculative office building has not only disregarded its context but also lost the capacity to represent the idea of commerce except by height. Venice was a commercial manifestation, its splendour emanating from the palaces of the mercantile families, in which residence, office and warehouse were combined.

So part of the problem of office design

is to recover the architectural means of representing commerce while subsuming the form within the disciplines of urbanity. City institutions achieved this in the nineteenth-century by taking the palazzo as their image. These conformed with streets but impressed through their individual presence. Lutyens' Britannic House powerfully represents itself, fronting Lombard Street, while also contributing to the shape of Finsbury Circus.

Large buildings like law courts, churches and theatres have, traditionally, embedded themselves in the urban fabric acknowledging their limited claim on frontage. They appear emblematically on the skyline and street, freeing the rest of the block for residential, retail and small business use. Perhaps the most important effect of the glazed central court in current office design is that it releases office floors from their reliance on outlook and enables other functions to claim the perimeter.

Spitalfields

Our project for Spitalfields sets out to place great commercial institutions in the context of these ideas. The office buildings do not appear as objects, for it would be impossible walking around them to view them as such. They appear emblematically around a central circus, where the commercial presence is the space itself.

Only here is office activity presented at ground level in the form of foyers. Elsewhere, like the Royal Exchange, each of these office buildings has embedded around its perimeter a continuous array of shops and small businesses, whose economy it sustains.

The glazed courts enable the office buildings to be inward-looking rather than relying on the surrounding streets. To the south and east, to Brushfield Street and to the extension of Crispin Street, flats claim frontage at the upper

levels and retailing on the ground complements that under the offices and faces into a continuous glazed arcade.

From this the glazed office courts are glimpsed as dramatic internal landscapes.

These arcade and perimeter buildings mediate between the function and scale of the offices and the function arid scale of the surrounding eighteenth- and early nineteenth-century buildings of the conservation areas. To the north an arcade for small businesses fulfils a similar role. Here the arcade is likely to establish its own milieu as a concentration of special services in which coffee shops and bars help catalyse a publicly accessible community of small businesses.

These businesses, with residential accommodation over them, are integrated into the new housing which adopts the scale and form characteristic of the adjoining conservation area. To the east is a public square, museum and performance building, consisting of a theatrical space at upper level with a public performance area below. In the evenings the circus becomes the vehicular setting-down point, the foyer for these public activities, to ensure the liveliness of the place after working hours.

Offices here become the containers of a lively and well tempered locality.

PUBLIC AND PRIVATE DOMAINS

Richard MacCormac

Urban Design Quarterly, July 1988

The opportunity to undertake an urban design proposal for Spitalfields fulfilled in a practical way ideas which we have been looking at in an academic manner for perhaps ten years. These were ideas about the nature of cities, what makes cities agreeable places to be in, ways in which it is pragmatically possible to reconcile the intentions of private development and large office buildings with the kind of environment which we enjoy being in.

One starts from images of the 1960s like the Euston Tower at the end of Tottenham Court Road, buildings which really have made the office building as a type almost the symbol of a failure of modern architecture and of modern cities. Big buildings quite out of scale with the European city, though perhaps not out of scale with the nature of American cities, which cause problems of micro climate, have very little to do with street either in terms of the activity that goes on in the buildings, or the way in which they come to the ground. They are often surrounded by traffic, and together with the effect of road engineering these buildings have made cities very hostile, so that spaces around them are spaces through which people are passing and there is no sense that you would wish to stay there.

Local and foreign transactions

If you look at images of cities in the past, such as Palladio's Little Theatre, at the Teatro Olympico at Vicenza, it is fascinating to see that the permanent stage set of the theatre is a street in a city so that it is natural, unquestionable perhaps, that man saw himself on the stage of life in a city, and that is where the action is played out. It is that image of the city that we have to retrieve. Even quite well mannered buildings, in a stylistic sense, can be bleak, they are too large in scale for the idiom in which they are designed, but principally I think because they don't have anything to do with the streets which they stand by, and to which they don't relate. It seems to me that the problem is that the activities that go on in them are foreign to the place and I would like to introduce a way of thinking about cities which is a new kind of terminology which distinguishes between what I call foreign transactions and what I would call local transactions.

There is a range of different transactions that we can consider. The foreign ones are ones that don't have to do with the immediate place – things like large banks and large international organisations. At the other extreme perhaps something like a street market is the most intensely local kind of activity so that the thing that is going there relates immediately to the passer-by. It may be that we like those latter kinds of environment, not because *we* necessarily are going to make a purchase, but because we know instinctively that it is possible that we can be furnished with what we require by that environment. It is rather like analogies with natural environments and we know instinctively, probably through evolution, that we can be sustained in certain environments. We couldn't be sustained in desert, we can't be sustained in the middle of the sea. We are sustained probably, or sense the possibility of being sustained, in the most ecological1y rich conditions perhaps on the edge of an escarpment where there is a forest and a valley below, with a river in it which is most people's idea of beautiful countryside. I suspect it is instinctively responding as a kind of supportive ecology, and I think cities are like that; it is possible to think of them as having these changes of ecological condition with the edges being the interesting bits.

A street, which I think is rather like that, is Charlotte Street in London and it is interesting because the bottom end of it has this ecological richness. It has a number of different sorts of businesses, but at ground level the businesses are of a local transactional kind, they are small shops, restaurants, pubs and so forth, and the upper levels are less transactional: they are offices and some residential. The north end, where Charlotte Street becomes Fitzroy Street, has been gradually colonised by professional and commercial activities large offices set back from pavements, sometimes with basement areas, and the change for the pedestrian is from the place at the southern end where you feel you could obtain what you need from the city, and the northern end where the pedestrian then passes through, knowing that in a way that is not relevant territory. It is the territory of a specialist group, professional people, mostly engineers and architects, as it happens, just as in the same way the City of London is also the territory of a special group.

Glazed courtyards

One stimulus to this way of thinking was work that we carried out with Dean Hawkes at Cambridge University School of Architecture into the environmental effects of glazed courtyards; there were a number of outcomes of this - the energy aspects and the density and plot ratio aspects were particularly interesting. Rather as the Fresnel square approach to housing shows you could get high densities in low rise, so in a similar way the courtyard office was found to be a form that could reconcile the European scale of cities and low rise buildings with quite high plot ratios. But there was another aspect to it that was interesting which was the notion that in one enterprise there would be different sorts of territories, there would be private territory in the buildings and in the courtyards there might be public territory. Instead of the residual space left over around the edges of large buildings which characterised the approach of the tower in the 1960s, this approach contains and makes space a positive figurative component of the scheme. It has latent in it the possibility of a deliberate public space-making tactic, and it implies interesting kinds of negotiation of planning gain.

We did a small study of the IPC site in Covent Garden where we found we could get four glazed courtyards in that site, and buildings of seven or eight storeys, rather then the building that has been built, which is not a bad building but it rises to about 12 storeys and it offers no public space. What we were doing was really extending the notion of Covent Garden as a series of tempered public spaces which is what the market buildings provide. They were contained within the private domain of the offices and would have shops at ground level.

Spatial images

I am going to refer to a number of prototypes which give one a very rich range of images for buildings of this kind: the first one is opposite the Kremlin, where the Gum Store covers I believe about 14 acres of multi-storey shopping and it is an image of a great covered public environment, though the use is a single one. Another image which has always been important to me was Alvar Aalto's office building in Helsinki, the Rautatalo building, which contains a court in the centre with access to the offices around it and a restaurant and shops, an annexe to the city system open streets, a tempered environment which is very suitable to the type of climate.

Frank Lloyd Wright's Johnson's Wax Building provides a large scale glazed space for the main typing pool; it is not a public space, but a marvellous image for the notion of a great courtyard around which offices are formed. Herman Herzberger's Central Beheer building might be another image of a possible public environment forming a kind of casbah of public spaces within an office context. Soane's House and Museum is another example of this type of environment on a smaller scale, producing intricate and explorable buildings within buildings.

I think in the past cities were made up of a reconciliation of public and private interest which we have got to try and retrieve. The reconstruction of the Stoa in Athens is a marvellous space which was fundamental to the way in which the democracy worked and the way it traded. The Royal Exchange in London is a very interesting nineteenth century building to me because its transactions are those of a national exchange and those transactions are nothing to do with the passer by, so they are in that sense foreign. The scale of the transaction is a great one, and it is contained within a large internal glazed court. It is also an interesting building because it symbolises the status of those transactions in its classical idiom and its great portico. But it also relates to its situation because it plays host to numerous small shops which are tucked around it into its external colonnades, a very elegant section; these shops relate to the passer by and provide for the passer by. So this, in the ecological sense I was describing, is a building whose edges reconcile as it were the inner contained use with the public world outside.

A very interesting example of that kind of building in London is a typical nineteenth century London theatre such as the Coliseum which fronts the street with a brilliant entrance, but the great theatre itself is embedded within the city block, so its transaction which is foreign to the locality like an office or the Royal Exchange, is contained within the block and all around looking out into the streets are small businesses and shops and residential.

We have looked at certain kinds of development condition that is in a way comparable to these examples. At ground level a new development can relate in scale to an existing street which may contain early nineteenth century houses and shops. On its other side, within the new development, it may have shops at ground level relating to that new shopping space and perhaps small businesses immediately above which are someway between local and foreign transactions as I have termed them. Further within the scheme itself there is a mall which is the territory of the offices themselves. That is a specific milieu for that specialist commercial world and doesn't compromise the local transactions which characterise the fringes of the block.

Spitalfields

Now we come to Spitalfields itself which is located to the north east of Liverpool Street. Around the site are various conservation areas. To the south there is the tight medieval street pattern of Artillery Passage and Gun Street. To the north is the conservation area centred on Elder Street which is an eighteenth century pattern with a similar pattern of early eighteenth century housing to the east and the great church of Hawksmoor. In that pattern it is characteristic to find mostly very small businesses, shops and small scale family housing. Embedded in this small scale structure are some very large buildings such as bonded warehouses of Cutlers Gardens which are the old East India Warehouses, Trumans Brewery and of course Liverpool Street Station itself. Of course as things stand now, Spitalfields Market, and the Bonded Warehouses, the brewery and the market are foreign transactions. They don't relate directly to the locality. Wholesale markets particularly do not do that.

Development brief

Tower Hamlets produced a Development Brief for the site. One part of the brief concerned the heights of buildings. The Brief proposed a limitation of 12-15 metres for the perimeter of the site and a limit of 30-35 metres for the centre of the site.

Our approach to the development involves in a sense quite abstract urban design considerations of a formal sort, and important issues of content. It may be quite difficult to pick out where the boundaries of the scheme occur and that is intentional because the scheme has around it buildings which in scale and form and function mediate between the core site, which is the main offices and the fringe areas that I described. Furthermore, the street systems on all sides are picked up by streets and lanes that run through the scheme, so in a sense it is rather like repairing a tear in an old rug. The new scheme weaves together the strands which at this moment are left untied around the fringes of the site, owing to the fact that the wholesale market is really a very large private territory.

Content

The important thing about its content is that the centre of the site is very much as I described the earlier hypothetical study. The centre of the site is a commercial hinterland which belongs to the specialist society of office workers, bankers or whoever, that regard this as a kind of annexe of the city. Around that are small shops, small businesses and housing; these local transactions relate to similar activities in all the areas fringing the site and through the whole system is the range of streets I described. The territory, even the commercial territory in the centre, is by no means an exclusive territory and is penetrated by public routes. The residential uses take over from shops on the upper floors of the perimeter structures creating residential buildings around the periphery behind which the office buildings are to some extent screened from the streets. The residential uses relate to housing that exists on the outside of the site boundary.

You could say in a sense the strategy is rather like a game of dominoes. We don't think that an office building is compatible with existing housing round the outside of the site; it is rather like a 6 and a 1. So we then find another building type which is our new housing with shops underneath and perhaps small businesses and that is the domino that has the value which can be reconciled both with the offices within the scheme and with the historic housing on the perimeter.

On the ground floor plan the circus links through to the public square at the east end of the site where there will be a theatre and it also links through to public gardens at the north which form an important open square at the end of Elder Street. In a way one can imagine that this circus would be a bit like the taxi dropping off point at the Savoy Hotel in the Strand; it is a place where people might be dropped off before going to the public space at the east so it becomes not only an actual space but an important annexe and threshold to the most populated part of the site. As we go up through the floor levels, what is happening architecturally is that the very large floor plates of the office buildings gradually decompose into a series of pavilions which are 15 metre wide which are what appear above the housing and form the skyline to the scheme. It is perhaps coincidental that the grander houses in Spitalfields are built in the early eighteenth century also have a 15 metre frontage to them. We have reflected ideas about the Spitalfields weavers attics in the loggias of these buildings which are formed with columns and are glazed at the top of buildings.

There is a strong contrast between the large scale of the office buildings rising through the centre of the scheme, and the continuous colonnades and arcades that run through the offices penetrating them and providing connections to the north, south, east and west.

The streets within the scheme are

deliberately covered by their colonnades or covered with glass vaults. This is because we think that the environment of that sort even though it is not a conditioned environment will be able to gain some radiant heat from the surrounding offices and will be slightly tempered all the year round. In the British climate in winter, narrow streets particularly if they are running east/west never dry out as they are very damp underfoot; these streets will be dry, and rather then having the character of a modern shopping centre we think of them more in relation to somewhere like Leadenhall Market. The biggest glazed space is the space we propose at the east end of the site with a theatre within it. We have been talking to the Royal Exchange Theatre who are located in the old Cotton Exchange in Manchester in a very analogous way; that is a very interesting relationship between theatre as a foreign transaction and various other activities like restaurants which have a symbolic relationship with the theatre and which help to sustain the theatre and are, sustained in turn by it.

Our approach to the scheme reminds me of something I read about Mount Everest and how in Nepal it doesn't have a single name. It's named according to what direction people approach it, and in a similar way perhaps this scheme will have different meanings to different people;, for shoppers, for people who live around it, for people who live in it, people who work in the banks so that it is experienced as a series of places which are all overlaid to reconcile a series of different expectations.

THE OFFICE BLOCK:
HISTORY OF A BUILDING TYPE

Richard MacCormac

Royal Fine Art Commission publication Building in Towns: the Importance of Architectural History for the Successful Developer, 1988.

The office block – a term we all use, and one we use nowadays in a pejorative way, is an expression of the negative feelings about offices which we entertain, but it is difficult to trace the sources of these feelings because the history of the office as a building type is not at all well documented. Nowhere, for example, in the catalogue of the RIBA library is it possible to find a reference to the history of the office. Nikolaus Pevsner's A History of Building Types includes a chapter on the subject of Warehouses and Office Buildings, but fails to recognise the office itself as a topic with which a great architectural historian might concern himself; and, again, in that massive compendium, Banister Fletcher's A History of Architecture on the Comparative Method (1956 edition), the word office is noticeably absent from the index, even though the office building had by that time been the predominant metropolitan building type for perhaps seventy years.

What can one conclude from this? It is quite extraordinary that there should be such a misfit between what interests architectural historians, and what has actually happened. It says something about the values of our society, that it is unable to apportion significance to the office as architecture because perhaps it conjures no feelings of faith, community, pleasure or awe, and it is a revealing insight into our ideas about cities, about work and private interest writ large.

Yet the word 'office' itself is a powerful one. We speak of the 'Papal Office', and of 'high office', and the Vatican, the White House and the Mansion House all have concrete significance to us as symbols of those different forms of office. But our concept of the office as a building type shares none of that majesty or significance. So we need to find a fresh critical approach to consider what it has been and what it might become.

One of the origins of offices is to be found in the world of Italian banking, during the Middle Ages. The Medicis established the first recorded counting-room or office "where they keep the affairs of the Bank" in their Milan palace, at a time when book-keeping was just beginning to be understood as a financial discipline. The Medicis sought to set up a financial system based on bills of exchange in order to service more effectively their basic trade in wool, thus initiating, for the first time in history, a system of trade control that was quite separate from the business of exchanging commodities - a form of financial activity that could be pursued away from the market-place itself, with no direct relation to the citizen on the street.

It is this characteristic which has shaped the development of the office building more than any other. For, unlike open market buildings, offices are closed off to the flow of the public, communicating only between themselves, and not with the outside world. The Medicis, therefore, were amongst the first agencies to develop this segregation of activities, providing offices within their palaces, such as that in Milan, where a manager – one might even describe him as a bank manager – would be installed in apartments on the first floor, or piano nobile. But even before their time, money-lending and other forms of financial exchange had been developing distinct from commodity exchange, with separate locations within the marketplace for their transactions, such as the Loggia dei Mercanti in the square at Bologna. In London, Lombard Street recalls the special activity of Italian money dealers.

As the focus of financial power shifted from Italy to the Netherlands and Northern Europe, these arrangements, where financial dealings were separated from the rest of the market, and took on a hermetic and professional character of their own, developed to create the buildings of the international financial institutions which we know now.

The origins of the term 'Bourse', to describe the Paris Stock Exchange, lay in the name of the Belgian family which built the palace and Place de la Bourse in Bruges in 1641. Today there remains a fascinating correspondence between our modem dealing floors and their historic predecessors. The Bruges place, with its loggias, known as 'factories', where the agents of the dealing institutions, or 'factors', would execute their transactions, is exactly analogous to the London LIFFE Exchange, where we see the 'factories' of the various institutions ranged all around the dealing floor, and the 'factors', dressed up like jockeys in their strange colours to identify themselves, rushing out into the meeting-place to deal, and back into their 'factories' to check their VDUs for the satellite information which supplies them with their power to deal.

Another analogy can be pursued, for these shouting, gesturing characters also represent the mythical successors of the cockney stall-holders on Brick Lane market – a local market in Spitalfields of the old fashioned kind, still related to citizens, where commercial activity continues to follow the patterns which animate cities, unlike the activity on the dealing floor, which, in an architectural and environmental sense, kills cities off. Hermetic and introverted, the dealing floor represents an environment dedicated to transactions quite foreign to ordinary citizens, enclosed in a building that is totally unconnected to people outside its interests – although it may indirectly affect the economy of the locality. By contrast, the old-fashioned market represents the territory of local transactions, springing out of the substance of local life.

This differentiation is recognised very early in documents on office buildings, and in the structures of their time. The earliest public official building recorded by Pevsner is the administrative building of Como, called the Broletto, from the word 'brolium', which means to 'fence in'. The 'fenced in' administrative office is on the first floor for security, with the market-place underneath it, a pattern which was true of subsequent Italian administrative buildings. Various treatises on office buildings appeared in the fifteenth century. Filarete underlines the importance of combining government buildings and commerce in the same place, and some twenty years after he wrote his treatise, the architect Francesco di Giorgio wrote a treatise on offices which provides a description very similar to the sort of brief one might get from a commercial developer today. The building is to be a courtyard building, one might call it an atrium building, with only one entrance, and access to all the rooms from a circulation system around the atrium, on each side of which is a stair. In a sense it is a prototype for a modern office, which seems to suggest not that developers are looking back to Francesco, but that building types themselves are simply not so various as one might think and, inevitably, modern buildings will have much in common with their predecessors. Arup Associates' No 1 Finsbury Avenue, for example, is extraordinarily close to Francesco's example, with a courtyard, or atrium, in the middle, two entrances rather than one, and vertical circulation running up each end. Francesco also refers to a

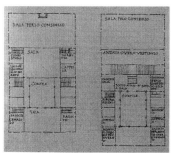

building type which he does not actually draw, called the Casa degli Officiali, and here perhaps is the first use of the term 'office building'.

The Uffizi in Florence, known now as a great art gallery which has held the Medici collection since 1574, was in fact built in 1560 as a comprehensive office building for the administration of Florence and its various officials - the commissioners for the militia, and for public demeanour, mostly concerned with the regulation of prostitution, and the guilds. This building probably provided the pattern for subsequent public office buildings, of which there were not many further examples in Italy, but which started to appear some hundred years later in Northern Europe. The great Town Hall building of Amsterdam (now Royal Palace), built in 1648, is an example, with a marvellous plan based on two courts, divided by a great raised central hall which is reached by a staircase in the centre of the building. Around the courts runs an enormous coffered and vaulted colonnade which gives access to the offices on the perimeter.

The size and scale of this building are such that they would still be impressive in London today, 350 years later. Building scale has become a great issue in planning now, perhaps because we tend to relate size with significance: if a building is very large, we expect it to have commensurate meaning, and if it does not have that meaning, we resent its claim on the public consciousness. Offices, for the general public, do not have that significance which would give them the right to size – but it is not size in itself which is necessarily objectionable. It is intriguing to remember that when, in the nineteenth century, the Church decided to demolish the spires of Lincoln Cathedral, public outcry at the loss to this huge monument was so great that civic disorder broke out in the city, and although the plan was carried through, it was quite clear that nobody wanted the building reduced in size.

The first large purpose-built office in England was Somerset House. Designed by William Chambers, it represented a logical development in the growth of public administration and the buildings which housed its activities. The palaces of Westminster and Whitehall, which had been royal domains before the Civil War, had been swallowed up by administrative offices of various kinds; but Somerset House was the first structure put up expressly to contain such functions, and its plan reveals uncertainty about exactly what kind of animal it is. A very early

Place de la Bourse, Bruges.

example of a corridor building, it nevertheless incorporates staircase arrangements on the lines of the Inns of Court, where the cellular organisation of 'chambers' points to the influence of the monastic and collegiate tradition. To the river front, it has the presence of a palace, with a great rusticated plinth punctured with an entrance for river traffic, the regular fenestration broken by terrific open porticos to bring south light into two narrow courts. The porticos, supported on great arches, were surely inspired by Piranesi's fantasy drawings of Rome.

Perhaps the most astounding public office building ever erected in England, was Soane's Bank of England started some twenty years later, and its demolition must constitute the greatest act of architectural vandalism of this century in this country. But apart from these outstanding examples of purpose-designed buildings, offices at this time generally took a smaller, less grandiose, form - the lawyer's chambers, or the counting room in the merchant's house, where business and domestic activity took place in close proximity. This long tradition of combining commerce, residence and office created the great medieval merchants houses of Europe, which reached their most beautiful expression in Venice. Here the warehouses on the lowest levels, with offices and residential accommodation above, were adorned with splendour by the families who owned and inhabited them to express their status and identity. This tradition continued in London well into the nineteenth century, and is documented in Booth's 'poverty maps' which, surprisingly to us today, show places like Commercial Street and Whitechapel in the East End colour-coded in red to

represent wealth – an indication that merchants were living above their warehouses in an area where the great philanthropists and social observers were simultaneously recording the most dismal conditions.

The other office type, which is so vividly recorded by Dickens in Nicholas Nickleby, Dombey and Son, and Pickwick Papers, was the small professional office based on a range of rooms, as in the chambers of the Inns of Court. But new economic demands were leading to the growth of large bureaucracies requiring appropriate buildings. An early example was Sir Robert Taylor's Stone Buildings in Lincoln's Inn (1774-80). Although incomplete as executed, the plans show that horizontal circulation throughout was intended, representing a deliberate move away from chambers to corporate organisation, and a precedent for the design of the modern commercial office building. These changes were stimulated in part by the enormous expansion in the demand for office floor space during the second half of the nineteenth century, created by the shift away from craft industry into manufacturing industry, introduced by the industrial revolution. It gave rise to the emergence of three new building types: the corporate office, grown out of the civic tradition of the official palazzo, the specialised exchange, developed from the market-place, and then the most radical development, the speculative office itself, intended for no client in particular, and peculiar among building types, because treated as a commodity which, in certain places, becomes shamelessly utilitarian.

Cockerell's Sun Life Building (1841) is the world's oldest insurance office, an interesting example of the corporate headquarters belonging to the tradition

of buildings intended to stand as symbols of their owners or occupants and their affairs. Internally, it has much the air of a large country house, with a series of large and small rooms for specific activities, and none of the sort of flexibility or uncertainty that prevails in present-day offices although, in fact, the number of staff virtually tripled over a period of sixty years. It makes definite architectural statements in a way that is difficult today, and it did so with that demonstrative vigour that we associate with Victorian and Edwardian commercial architecture. A late monument to that tradition is Lutyens' Britannic House in Finsbury Circus. This great building deploys its classical language to bring its repetitive storeys of accommodation into a greater order, of metropolitan scale. Brilliantly composed, it is also responsive, enclosing Finsbury Circus in a gentle curve.

During the twentieth century, corporate scale has increased at an incredible rate, requiring a commensurate scale of enormous organisational buildings epitomised: in London by the Shell Building, on the South Bank, which has a floor area of approximately 42 acres. Shell is a poor building architecturally and is symptomatic of a period when the commercial world in Britain had become utterly disconnected from architecture. Elsewhere great corporate clients still commissioned the best architects to design their headquarters buildings, and many classics of the Modern Movement were born, such as the Lever and Seagram buildings in New York and the Pirelli Building in Milan – buildings which will probably be re-valued when the overcomplex flavours of Post-Modernism become sickly. Some British clients woke up to architecture in the 1960s, but there are few distinguished office buildings in the City. Exceptions are Commercial Union and the P&O Building, now set off against Lloyds, that extraordinary gesture of technical optimism. Foster's Willis Faber building in Ipswich is similarly inspired by a poetry of pure technique. Earlier, in the West End, the Smithsons' Economist building was a successful solution to the problem of accommodating a very high plot ratio, embracing the metropolitan scale of the city, without jeopardising the Georgian scale of St James's, and this remains a demonstration of how large corporate buildings may be related to an historic context. More recently, John Outram's unsuccessful competition scheme for the Financial Times building raises quite different issues in the architectural response to a corporate brief – the recovery of myth in the modern world, expressed through decoration.

The role of companies in shaping the development of an architecture of offices has been significant when they have asked their architects to consider the design in terms of their own organisation. In Frank Lloyd Wright's Larkin Building (1904) in Buffalo, work study theories and the tremendous expansion of low-skilled clerical employment, taken over by women typists, are determinants in the spatial arrangement. The women occupy the galleries, the prototype of the typists' pool, having lost their former status as clerks, and the men occupy the lower floor in one single corporate volume. Around the walls, rather evangelical exhortations to work hard are inscribed in goldleaf, while the typewriter, Gestetner and telephone symbolise the new characteristics of the Larkin mail order business. Later, Lloyd Wright was to design the headquarters for the Johnson Wax Company, one of his greatest, most inventive buildings. The clerical pool is like a great open court in a complex city of executives. I wonder whether the pool, with its inverted tapered columns topped by circular discs separated by reeded glass, was not derived from the huge lily pool which Lloyd Wright made at the Imperial Hotel in Tokyo as if it was seen from underneath. This is a practical commercial building which is also deeply and mysteriously beautiful.

For an insurance company near Arnhem, Herman Hertzberger, a Dutch architect, has designed a maverick and wonderful building where conventional notions of clearly defined office floors are challenged by turning them into a series of almost balcony-like structures, built up within the shell of the enormous overall envelope. The result is a kind of labyrinth of little streets and alleyways in which the employees are curiously free to express themselves in their own furnishing of their individual spaces – a total contrast to the great American environment of infinite ceiling and floor, without particular sense of room or place. This return to making rooms has architectural origins in the work of the American architect Louis Kahn, but it must also reflect political resistance to the deliberately subduing aesthetic of universal corporate power, and the search for more humane and personal working conditions. Colin St John Wilson's unbuilt headquarters for Lucas made this kind of proposition and was followed by two projects by Arup Associates, fortunately both built, offices for Lloyds at Chatham and headquarters for CEGB outside Bristol. Both manage to find a sense of human scale and place

within what are very large buildings.

Quite unlike corporate headquarters, exchanges are market-places and meeting places, places for social activities varying from the scale of the great Stoa in Athens to the original intimacy of Lloyds Coffee Shop now reconstructed in the Lloyds building. In the eighteenth and nineteenth centuries, the exchange became an increasingly important building type, with cellular accommodation around the central collective space. The Piece Hall in Halifax is a typical example of an eighteenth century market-place which can be seen as a prototype for the covered exchanges which are a great feature of English cities, the Royal Exchange of Manchester, or the Corn Exchange in Leeds, or London's Coal Exchange. The latter, a painted cast iron and highly decorated structure, was pulled down in another great act of vandalism. These were buildings of tremendous rhetoric, products of an era capable of making great statements, and stood as powerful symbols of the public acknowledgement of commercial interest, quite unlike most commercial buildings today.

Most offices today are speculative, in the tradition which saw its beginnings in the nineteenth century. Edward I'Anson (1812-88), a commercial architect, delivered a paper to the RIBA in 1864 entitled 'Some Notice of Office Building in the City', which drew attention to the emergence of a new building type, designed on a speculative basis, in a repetitive manner, and consisting of a complex of chambers for rent to small or large businesses. In America, the speculative office building was called a 'unit building', after the repetitive fenestration system which was a characteristic of such blocks, together with the frame structure which allowed for the installation of glass partitions. Classic examples, such as Peter Ellis's Oriel Chambers of 1864 in Liverpool, one of the first iron frame buildings where the frame is expressed without any masonry cladding (not easy to get away with today), already bear a strong resemblance to the modern office block. A number of stone clad metal frame buildings were put up in London at this time, characterised by a rational 'unit system' and a floor plan segmented into chambers, each with their own fireplaces and other facilities.

After Chicago's great fire of 1871, this building type provided the model for the design and construction of huge vertical chambers buildings, such as Burnham's Reliance building, in which the density was such that, by the end of the nineteenth century, the plot ratio in the

centre of Chicago was 20:1, which compares to a mere 5:1 prevailing generally in the City of London today. In Buffalo, in Sullivan's Guaranty Building, again a system of repeated stacked chambers, we see set out for the first time the notion of the modern office building as subsequently crystallised by Mies van der Rohe and SOM, with no attempt at modulation of the facade from the top to the base – a solid base in Sullivan's building, which would have been replaced by piloti in the Mies or SOM version. The Guaranty Building actually has a curiously banal plan, more like an hotel than a compact office block, with a court scooped out of the back to provide cross-ventilation in the days before air conditioning. The invention of air conditioning eventually allowed blocks to be planned with far greater density. Beneath the slender great spire of the Empire State Building is a deep plan structure, with three tiers of offices on each side of the core factory-like conditions of employment, reflecting contemporary ideas about work, and the sharp distinction between places of work and places of pleasure.

So with this inheritance of ideas about offices, what history are we making now in the development of the office block? We can make skyscrapers, or we can make what Demetri Porphyrios has described as 'groundscrapers' – because the high plot ratios of buildings like Centre Point are surprisingly similar to parts of Edwardian London such as Kingsway – medium rise buildings with a high proportion of ground cover. The questions we face are not simply about style, or appearance, despite the importance of our sensuous, visual experience of buildings; more fundamental is the impact of buildings on the places which they surround. That forlorness so typical in office buildings of today is very much a result of the way in which they hit the ground, irrespective of their aesthetic appearance above that level, their style, or age, or any other intention. It is a failing the citizen does not experience in, say, the wonderful loggias around the edge of the Piazza San Marco in Venice, which offer shelter and shade from the sun, but also shops and commercial activity underneath dense repetitive floors and fenestration which could be offices. Or, by contrast, in the exquisite Rautatalo Building designed in the 1950s by Alvar Aalto in Helsinki, there is a great glazed court off the street, a refuge in winter or summer with its public atrium surrounded by shops and restaurants. It is a beautifully detailed, elegant, rather fastidious public place, incorporated

within a large office block.

Office buildings of all kinds have this potential to play host to the citizen, to provide a place for local transactions within the structure setup for making foreign transactions, like the Broletto in Como or the public buildings of Siena with markets beneath them. We can find models in London, like the Piccadilly or Burlington Arcades, which penetrate large commercial blocks. Space offered to the public in this way need not be uncommercial if it provides viable premises for retailing activity. At Broadgate now, the great central rotunda is beginning to develop a public life, and to build up a reputation as a place where things happen. In our own competition proposals for Paternoster Square, we sought to invest the streets with different characteristics, based on contrasts we could identify between the different public places we knew. Thus, East-West streets might be open at the top, glazed over half way down between the offices in the middle, and then covered with open vaults at the bottom, a hybrid between a galleria and Nash's Opera arcade by the Haymarket. North-south streets would not be enclosed, allowing the sun to penetrate. Another idea was that public routes could be taken through under the circulation of the office buildings themselves. The belief that a massive office redevelopment in present-day London can viably incorporate public arcades completely integrated into the office block system, just as at the Milan Galleria, is also the basis for our Spitalfields proposal. Ground level is opened up to small shops and market stalls, and the local things that citizens enjoy.

There is no reason why the office as a building type should not re-invest itself with a sense of belonging to the community, with feelings of pleasure, or a kind of faith, on the part of the public which moves around it. This will be achieved if the office as a building type reconciles the claims of commerce with those of the citizen. But whether this will happen depends finally on the attitude of the developer.

I would like to acknowledge Dan Cruickshank's The Origins of the Office (Architectural Review, Nov 1983], which provides the most concise history of offices in England from the eighteenth century onwards. Pevsner's History of Building Types (Thames & Hudson 1976) must be acknowledged for its information about early public buildings, but the commercial background is marvelously amplified in the second chapter of Mark Girouard's Cities and People (Yale 1985). I am also indebted to Frank Duffy's chapter Office Buildings and Organisational Change in Buildings and Society (ed Anthony D King 1981).

SPACE AND LIGHT

Richard MacCormac

Modern Painters, Summer 1993

Those of us brought up in the rhetoric of the modern movement are familiar with Le Corbusier's definition of architecture as 'the masterly, correct and magnificent play of volumes brought together in light', but it needs little reflection to recognise the abstract, though passionate, platonism of this statement and its underlying assumption of the steady brightness of the Mediterranean sun. This essay is an experiment, an evaluation of architecture in terms of narrative, mood and space, taking light as its theme and referring to painting as a medium for engaging areas of expression which rarely form part of current architectural discourse.

The tradition of painting invites contemplation of effects of light infinitely more complex than that evoked by Le Corbusier. It reminds us that light is significant only in relation to darkness, and that we have become so used to obliterating darkness with the seemingly limitless ambient energy of electricity that we have almost lost any sense of what it was like in the pre-electric age. We have driven the shadows away from our wishful sense of the present. Paintings from the pre-electric past reveal how the small local light source or the shaft of daylight in the otherwise darkened room isolated the event and concentrated the sense of the moment, whether convivial or solitary, and, in the work of Rembrandt, arouse a poignant and precarious sense of mortality.

If architecture is a reflection upon building, then painting is a kind of double reflection incorporating people and time. In particular, paintings remind architects of the meaning of windows, that they are not just holes in walls but make habitable places both in a practical and symbolic sense. In Dutch seventeenth-century painting, the scene often 'takes place' at the window or in the bay. Externally the window personifies the building and affirms the human presence, whether in the domestic tradition, represented by Dutch painting, or in the medieval bay or the classical tradition of the window as the vestige of the little house, the aedicule of the god in the Greek temple. This idea comes from the late Sir John Summerson's marvellous essay, Heavenly Mansions, in which he propounds the theory of aedicular architecture. This inhabited window, or little house, finds its place in much of my practice's work, in the bay windows of the Sainsbury Building at Worcester College, Oxford, and in the aedicular bays of the New Court at Fitzwilliam College, Cambridge.

Windows signal the human presence, the subject often explored in the paintings of Edward Hopper.

The bay window seeks light. It expresses itself as a kind of lantern, but with the function of capturing, rather than emitting, light. It suggests the idea of daylight as a force, fierce and pressing in the south of Europe, gentle and pervasive in the north. In Scandinavia, the winter light, reflected off the snow or water, infuses interiors with a disembodied icy buoyancy, a sensation wonderfully apparent in the Haga pavilion – the little summer pavilion of Stockholm's Drottningholm Palace where reflections off water seem to suspend the mirrored interior in light.

In contrast the Southern interior, isolating itself with its massive shell, is like a pressurised diving bell into which light forces itself through the smallest apertures. Windows become instruments to tune the perception of the interior, which remains cool, separate and mysterious as in the great nave of Le Thoronet, Le Corbusier's inspiration for Ronchamp, where a single circular aperture makes the interior resonant with a blast of light, and in Ronchamp itself where light forces itself through the cleft between wall and roof and through myriad small apertures.

The northern cathedrals of the Middle Ages ~ stand openly in light, are immersed in lucidity. The older constructional tradition of the south, of Santa Sophia, Ravenna and St Marks, Venice, is cavelike, resisting the light, allowing only the illumination of its own mystery. Once admitted, light becomes fugitive, and the art of the mosaic, with its infinite facets, catches fleeting evanescent sparks of reflection which Ruskin described:

'It is lost in still deeper twilight, to which the eye must be accustomed for some moments before the form of the building can be traced; and then there opens before us a vast cave, hewn out into the form of a cross, and divided into shadowy vistas by many pillars. Round the domes of its roof the light enters only through narrow apertures like large stars; and here and there a ray or two from some far away casement wanders into the darkness, and casts a narrow phosphoric stream upon the waves of marble that heave and fall in a thousand colours on the floor. What else there is of light is from torches, or silver lamps, burning ceaselessly in the recesses of the chapels; the roof sheeted with gold, and the polished walls covered with alabaster, give back at every curve and angle some feeble

gleaming to the flames; and the glories round the heads of the sculpted saints flash out upon us as we pass them, and sink again into the gloom...'

Of twentieth-century architects, perhaps only Carlo Scarpa, a Venetian, found that sense of dissolution of surface, with his use of glass mosaic, alabaster and his recovery of antique plaster techniques to give deeply coloured translucent and shining surfaces which absorb and reflect, and excite the retina by confusing the precise depth of focus.

The building of the ancient world which precisely represents the metaphor of the cavern and of Plato's cave is the Pantheon in Rome, in which the disc of the sun makes its daily transit around the interior as a single shaft of light projected on to the shadowy coffering of the dome. The idea of the Pantheon as cave echoes the eighteenth century archaeological discoveries of Pompei, which revealed lost underworlds of the past, unseen and unpenetrated by daylight for centuries. For Piranesi these discoveries offered an alternative reality to be set against the contemporary world. Piranesi inhabited this antique world and glimpsed the contemporary world through fragmented vaults in the Vedute, his views of ancient Rome. But in the terrible visions of the Carceri prison series the real world is entirely excluded, intensifying his metaphoric underworld, from which no escape is offered.

The underground cavern and its opposite, the daylit world above, offer, to architecture, a powerful psychological polarity to which many attributes may subconsciously attach themselves - timelessness, mortality, knowledge, memory, security, secrecy, savagery, incarceration and expiation. This polarity is found in the work of Gaudi, in the cave-like structures under his Barcelona gardens and in the incomplete Guell Chapel where the crypt, a roughly hewn cave, was to support a chapel of light.

The pendentive and domed construction, adopted by neo-classical architects in the late eighteenth century, is associated with secure and windowless building types such as banks, law courts, art galleries and mausolea. Soane's Bank of England (now demolished) consisted of a series of great top-lit cavern-like pendentives and domes. Gandy's illustrations of these, with other images, such as Alexander Pope's grotto in Twickenham, inspired a project of mine, currently building for St John's College, Oxford, where vaulted top-lit public rooms of white concrete structure and

deeply coloured walls lie, concealed, beneath an upper world of planted terraces around which students live.

Soane was influenced by Piranesi and by Turner's use of colour, specifically by his use of translucent coloured glazes. Soane's equivalent to a glaze, to achieve what he called 'lumière mystérieuse', was to use coloured rooflights, usually amber, to wash the interior. This intervention of colour has the effect of isolating the experience of the interior from a temporal sense of daylight and weather. As one would expect, the idea is powerfully evident in Soane's mausoleum at the Dulwich Art Gallery. It is also employed in the museum at Lincoln's Inn Fields, where the coloured roof lights have recently been replaced. In modern architecture, such a mediation of daylight with colour to create a mystery appears in the work of Le Corbusier at Ronchamp and also in the Chapel at La Tourette where the three great 'light canons' bombard the coloured interior with coloured light. Part of the effect at La Tourette is created by projecting coloured light on to surfaces which are at the opposite ends of the colour spectrum, red on to red and red on to blue, so that there are extraordinary contrasts between vividly lit surfaces and those that glimmer darkly.

Such manipulations of light challenge common experience and the expectation of enclosure which buildings usually satisfy. The dissolution of physical enclosure, which gothic architecture strove for and achieved at the Sainte Chapelle [Paris] and Kings College Chapel [Cambridge], appears in the mystical sense of the possibilities of glass in the polemical writing of German architects such as Scheerbart, Taut and Scharoun, visions entirely betrayed by the utilitarian actuality of the glass architecture of subsequent history There are recent exceptions such as Nicholas Grimshaw and Bill Pye's everchanging water wall at the British Pavilion at Seville, Hopkins's Schlumberger tent outside Cambridge, a billowing volume of light, Nouvel's pattern of steel irises transforming the south facing wall of the Arab Institute in Paris into an oriental fabric of steel and glass, Foster's Sackler Gallery at the Royal Academy, or Benson and Forsyth's little oratory in Cumbria, a cylinder of silent translucency.

But the reductive materialism of the modern movement confused literal transparency with what Colin Rowe has called the 'phenomenon of transparency', which, paradoxically, can be more readily obtained with solid

materials, because it is about the illusiveness of the physical boundaries of space. Again with Soane, we can examine this in the breakfast room at Lincoln's Inn Fields. Here, a space is defined by a pendentive dome, but the walls, which might be expected at its perimeter, have disappeared and the room redefined by screen walls beyond, lit from continuous skylights above, giving the impression that they are outside the space of the room itself. In the library, this trick of extending boundaries is realised with mirrors above the bookcases to suggest rooms beyond. In the picture room, walls literally fold away to disclose further spaces; and, in the whole interior of the museum, unexpected vistas, corridors, mirrors, alcoves and glass floors push out through the boundaries of each room to create an aesthetic of relativity.

These effects are related to Piranesi's perception of antique ruins as fragmented – enclosures through which further spaces and vistas can be seen. But perhaps both Piranesi's and Soane's ideas of space also derive from Pompeian wall painting in which rooms are enclosed by painted screens through and over which are glimpsed vistas and perspectives of architecture. The Soane museum can be interpreted as three-dimensional Pompeian wall painting.

The illusiveness of space and its physical boundary is an inherent part of the aesthetic of modern architecture, evident in the early work of Mies van der Rohe and always in the work of Frank Lloyd Wright. It is also found in a diversity of current practice: in the Picasso Museum in Paris, for example, Roland Simounet develops, in the context of an existing structure, a sense of surface which is sometimes palpable and rooted, sometimes shifting and ambiguous, in its layered planes and in the relative reflectivity of gloss and matt surfaces. In Leiviska's church at Myyrmaki in Finland, surfaces seem suspended in space and light, released from gravity.

I will conclude with two projects from my practice's work - the unbuilt chapel for Tonbridge school and the completed chapel for Fitzwilliam College, Cambridge. Both these schemes bring together many of the preoccupations of this essay: the idea of the aedicule, the building within the building, the polarity between the underworld and the world above, and the use of light to create an illusive definition of space.

In the Tonbridge scheme, the building within a building is a kind of ark which contains the congregation, and the gap

Design in Mind, by Bryan Lawson
(Butterworth Architecture 1994;
with permission from Elsevier).

between this wooden structure and the perimeter makes an ambulatory for the choir through which light filters. The design addressed the problem of achieving something of the quality of reflected light in a gothic building, a quality that modern construction cannot easily replicate. In gothic buildings, the intensity of direct clerestory light is usually mediated by the deeply-moulded shafts, ribs and reveals which form an aura around the window opening. In contrast, Victorian and Edwardian 'gothic' buildings (including the original Tonbridge School Chapel before it was burned down) often suffer from glaring contrasts between the brightness of the windows and the shadowy walls. In our proposal the cellular construction of the wall was to be filled with reflected top-light, and similarly the vertical shafts of the clerestory were to be backlit by concealed roof-lights to overcome the glare. For the same reason, daylight was to be cast directly onto the roof structure.

In the little chapel for Fitzwilliam, equivalent effects are achieved in a distinctly different way. Top-light is thrown down the perimeter walls, disengaging their enclosure from the central baldacchino-like structure which defines the congregational space. This space is also defined by a vessel-like timber structure, an ark, which in turn, is not only separate from the perimeter of the building but distinguishes the sacred space from the underworld of the crypt. This building brings together several of the themes addressed in this essay. But it remains virtually monochromatic unlike my next comparable project, the Ruskin Library at Lancaster University.

Richard MacCormac was born in 1938. He studied architecture at the University of Cambridge and at the Bartlett School in the University of London. At Cambridge he was heavily influenced by the work of both Leslie Martin and Lionel March and met his future partner Peter Jamieson. He admits to having an 'almost obsessive interest' in the Prairie Houses of Frank Lloyd Wright which he was awarded a travelling scholarship to study. He continues greatly to admire the work of Frank Lloyd Wright, but has since developed an almost equal respect for Sir John Soane. He set up his own small practice after qualifying in 1969, although the partnership with Peter Jamieson was formed soon after in 1972, and was eventually also to include David Prichard. The practice quickly became known for a series of influential projects all largely at the domestic scale. These included a number of low-rise housing schemes including student accommodation as well as a number of academic university buildings at both Oxford and Cambridge. Richard MacCormac has written and lectured extensively on his approach to architecture, and remains a popular speaker in schools of architecture. He has taught architecture at Cambridge and was appointed George Simpson Professor of Architecture at Edinburgh University in 1982 and has sat on a number of educational committees. He was elected president of the Royal Institute of British Architects in 1991 and his term of office was marked by a consistent emphasis on the quality of design. He has warned of what he sees as the potential harm to the quality of design caused both by 'design and build' and by the British government's recent attitude towards competitive tendering for architects' fees. Richard MacCormac has campaigned to exhibit and explain architecture in a more publicly accessible manner in 'architecture centres'. The end of his presidency was celebrated by the 'Art of the Process' exhibition at the RIBA, which showed the evolution of designs by a series of well-known British architects.

The practice of MacCormac, Jamieson, Prichard has more normally had about 24 staff but has grown to nearly twice that size. Each project has its own design team with up to ten working on the largest projects in the office. The practice has tended to design buildings of a residential scale and has developed what Richard MacCormac describes as 'a sort of vernacular' approach to these projects. MacCormac does not use the word 'vernacular' so much to refer to

the style and appearance of their architecture but rather to the process itself. 'We have established a kind of typological repertoire which is to do with density and the main problems like car parking and so on.'

Richard MacCormac himself has been combining his own practice with his term of office as President of the RIBA. He sees his role in the practice 'to initiate the design process in all major jobs', but here he is particularly referring to those projects which do not fit into the 'vernacular' pattern. One of the other partners Peter Jamieson takes a 'technical and contractual role' looking after problems on-site and reviewing the designs technically. Another partner, David Prichard, is 'very much a job runner' and leads the design teams. Richard MacCormac feels that their organizational structure is not very clearly defined, something which he sees as an advantage.[1]

Richard MacCormac speaks about his role as 'making a series of interventions at different stages in the design process'. He likes to have a degree of detachment from the everyday running of the project which allows him to intervene at what he considers to be critical moments. 'Part of the game is to create a crisis by recognizing that something is not right.'[2] He describes how such a series of interventions work in relation to the practice's design for the new Headquarters and Training Building for Cable and Wireless:

'At the very beginning of the process the centre of the scheme was a circular courtyard, but later I thought this was wrong. By then we had this V idea going in which the building opens in a V shape rather like the wings of a bird… towards this wonderful landscape. Then suddenly I had this idea that the courtyard should be pulled into an oculus, a sort of eye shape which would reflect the dynamic of the whole project.'

This reflects a central theme of Richard MacCormac's approach to design – the struggle to understand an emerging idea, and to recognize and describe it so that it may be may worked out and resolved. He describes how on the same project he and one of his assistants were working over the weekend on the residential section of the scheme:

'I can't quite remember what happened and either Dorian or I said 'it's a wall, it's not just a lot of little houses, it's a great wall 200 metres long and three storeys high… we'll make a high wall then we'll punch the residential elements through that wall as a series of glazed bays which come

through and stand on legs…'[3]

This design concept which emerged from one of Richard MacCormac's self-induced crises eventually revolutionized and organized the whole design. However, this can only be a team activity in Richard MacCormac's view: [4]

'I or somebody else comes up with an originating idea, some idea that seems powerful enough to generate a scheme and to subsume a lot of decisions within it…[5] it needs somebody in the team to pick up the ball and run with it (Dowson and MacCormac, 1990). I find that I seize on somebody in the team who understands what the crisis is… you have to find this person who sees what it is about otherwise it's hopeless.'[6]

Richard MacCormac believes that architecture is what he calls 'a medium of thought' which is 'a kind of analogical or metaphorical way of thinking'. However, he is no abstract philosopher but rather a simultaneously passionate and yet practical man who sees 'the deeper structures of architectural thought as the means of reconciling the methodological and empathetic aspects of architecture'. He is quite cynical about the traditional design brief. 'The real problem is often concealed by the way it is written about as a brief.' This attitude leads him to have mixed feelings about design competitions which, he admits, are simultaneously frustrating and exhilarating, but he worries that they can be 'rather hit and miss' because of the lack of contact between designer and client. 'Often in competitions the winning scheme is the one that tells the client something that they never knew before… something that is terribly important to them and was not in the brief.'[7] He seems fascinated by the mystery of where design ideas originate and frequently refers to the struggle to understand an emerging design idea. 'Issues which are the stuff of the thing often only come out when you try and solve, when you try and produce a scheme, and therefore the design process defines objectives in a way in which the brief could never do.' Richard MacCormac is convinced that design solutions and problems emerge together very much as reflections of each other. He clearly sees analysis and synthesis as closely intertwined processes which between them allow the architect to understand both brief and design concept. 'In our office we design as a means of coming to terms with the brief and recognize a reciprocal relationship between the production of form and the definition of the programme.' This notion of reciprocal functionalism forms one of the principal ideas informing Richard MacCormac's design process. He recognizes that 'although rooted in modern movement…these concerns…are a critique of the slogan "form follows function" and we believe that to some extent, the reverse is and should be true'. He is fond of the journey as a metaphor for the design process, which he claims, like all art, is a reflection of life itself. 'The design process is a journey, an episodic journey towards a destination which you don't know about.' He speaks of the trials of this journey and the need to keep staff 'loyal to the process', and he recognizes the pain that designers suffer. Perhaps in part due to his tactic of creating crises, he openly admits that the journey can become 'terribly fraught… with people literally in tears'. However, it is the 'big idea' that keeps designers going throughout a process which he believes is 'unsustainable unless it's very idealistic':

'This is not a sensible way of making a living, it's completely insane. There has to be this big thing that you're confident you're going to find. You don't know what it is you're looking for and you hang on.'[8]

This emphasis on the idealistic nature of design and the search for a 'big idea' is also backed up by Richard MacCormac's practical side. He talks a great deal about the need to understand this idea and to follow it right through the detailed design stage. 'It's a matter of trying to find the life of the idea in the way it's detailed and made and that is incredibly difficult and hugely important really.' Richard MacCormac goes so far as to say that the detailed design stage is 'where architecture stands or falls'. He feels that the American term of 'design development' is therefore a more accurate description of this critical phase of design. Richard MacCormac talks of the need to maintain continuity between the conceptual stages and these detailed stages of design in order that the 'right connections are made'. This attitude leads him to be concerned about design and build packages which he feels can be disastrous.[9] This argument can be seen very clearly in the development of MacCormac's acclaimed design for the chapel at Fitzwilliam College in Cambridge. Very early in the process an idea about playing round and square shapes together began to emerge. 'At some stage the thing became round but I can't quite remember how.' Eventually the upper floor began to float free of the structure

supporting it. 'The congregational space became a sort of ship.' However, it was not until quite detailed problems were considered such as the resolution of balcony and staircase handrails that this idea was fully understood and the 'vessel' took on its final shape and relationship to supporting structure.

Richard MacCormac has no enthusiasm for technology as an end in itself or as a major driving force generating design ideas, although he admires the work of many 'hi-tech' architects:

'The choices that we make about how we express construction are more to do with aesthetics than they are to do with the technological exigencies of the situation… but I do share with the so-called hi-tech people a sense that what is worth doing is to clarify and make evident how a thing is put together and what its nature is.'

If any consistent set of generators can be seen throughout Richard MacCormac's work it is those to do with basic geometry. There is a strong sense of organization about the work of the practice and this seems to be introduced at a very early stage in MacCormac's thinking about a scheme. He thinks that 'architects try to translate the stuff of briefs into some kind of structure as soon as possible'. In the early years of the practice these ideas were quite explicit and formal and were clearly the result of Richard MacCormac's time studying at Cambridge, where he was particularly influenced by the ideas of Sir Leslie Martin and Lionel March. [10]

'We look for a clear geometric analogy for the content of the problem. All our schemes have a geometric basis, whether it is the pinwheel arrangement of Westoning, the courtyard system of Coffee Hall flats and Robinson College, the specific tartan grid of the Blackheath houses or the circle-based geometry of Hyde Park Gate.' (MacCormac & Jamieson, 1977).

More recently the geometry is becoming more relaxed and informal but it remains a strong generator of design ideas. Richard MacCormac describes in detail how their scheme for the Bristol University Faculty of Arts was based on what he calls a 'grid of relationships'. This scheme required the adaptation of a row of existing houses with new accommodation linking them to the rear. The solution incorporates strong geometrical rules even though these use irregular shapes partly derived from the existing Victorian houses and their garden boundaries. This more flexible geometry allows for a range of

definitions of territorial arrangements from the individual department up to the shared faculty space. 'We saw the design problem as one of discovering an organizational analogy between the brief and what existed.'(MacCormac, 1983).

This illustrates an interesting principle behind Richard MacCormac's attitude towards geometry. He has studied the geometry of architecture in its own right and his thinking and conversation are littered with references to organizing devices such as grids and structures, and to forms such as domes and pendentives. However, in MacCormac's mind these always remain subservient to a greater purpose. 'Geometry is used as a means of making distinctions between one kind of place and another so that different activities take place in situations which have their own identity and, through use, can increase their distinctiveness' (MacCormac and Jamieson, 1977). At Bristol it was the definition of faculty and departmental territory, and in much of the housing it is the organization of family and group territories. 'The motive and incentive, as distinct from the method for this housing work, has been social.' In his often-expressed admiration for the work of Sir John Soane, Richard MacCormac lays great emphasis of the ability of the geometry of architecture to create an environment of light and shade. He describes how his practice makes use of a 'repertoire of tricks' which draw significantly on his study of Soane's work (MacCormac, 1985).[11]

Another lesson which Richard MacCormac has learnt from his study of Soane is that of the importance of drawing. 'All Soane's projects involved an enormous amount of drawing…That process is a fundamental reminder to architects of the thinking pencil' (MacCormac, 1985). MacCormac himself admits to feeling incomplete as a thinker unless he has a pencil in his hand. 'Whenever we have a design session or a crit review session in the office I cannot say anything until I've got a pencil in my hand…I feel the pencil to be my spokesman, as it were.' What is perhaps surprising coming from such a geometrically creative and innovative designer is the admission of just how dependent he is on the act of drawing. 'I haven't got an imagination that can tell me what I've got without drawing it… I use drawing as a process of criticism and discovery.'[12] This leads Richard MacCormac to question whether computer-aided design can ever really replace this process of

drawing as a thinking tool. However, he also sees dangers in allowing the drawing process to dominate the designer's thoughts. He recently organized a weekend urban design workshop on London and found himself working on areas of Bermondsey. 'I was drawing whole chunks of Bermondsey without any feeling for it at all, the felt tip was drawing things that I didn't like at all, it was being a felt-tip pen and not a piece of Bermondsey.'[13]

1 Office size and structure
At its largest this practice would be a similar size to that of Ahrends Burton & Koralek. However, the structure is very different, employing a more corporate system of allocating responsibilities. This method of working where each partner plays a particular role presumably suited to their interests and strengths is different to the form of organization found in the other multi-partner practices reviewed in this book. Stirling and Wilford both operate in parallel and ABK tends to operate almost as three practices. It is interesting to note that Denise Scott Brown and Robert Venturi have recently moved away from this kind of structure.

2 Intervention
This conscious use of intervention to disturb or shake up the design process shows some similarities with the ideas expressed by Richard Burton. Clearly the timing and nature of Richard MacCormac's interventions in this way must be critical to their success. At the time of writing this book Richard MacCormac probably found himself rather more detached from the daily working of the design team than normal, since he was also President of the RIBA!

3 Conceptualising and the central idea
This idea of naming a concept occurred frequently in conversation with Richard MacCormac and can also be seen repeated in much of his writing. Most of the examples to be found here referred to geometrical forms such as oculus, pinwheel and pendentive, or to types of place such as belvedere and walled garden. It seems to be a device to better understand an emerging idea or design concept. Once named in this way, the designers can share all the implications inherent in the idea and work them out in order to test the appropriateness of the idea to this particular scheme. It also serves to keep the design team together, as it were, in ensemble. As Richard MacCormac puts it, 'the right connections must be made'. There are considerable similarities between what Richard MacCormac is saying here and the search for conceptual ideas expressed by Ian Ritchie.

4 The design team
It is very clear from listening to Richard MacCormac talking about the evolution of his designs that he genuinely cannot remember from which member of the design team each idea originates. Indeed, ideas are obviously not born in an instance but develop and clarify over time, with members of the design team contributing to that process. This indicates a very close, almost intimate, method of group working.

5 Primary generator
This seems to be a fairly clear statement of the idea of a 'primary generator'. It can be seen as

a strong organising idea from which a substantial amount of the basic design concepts flow. Richard MacCormac seems to be telling us that once this idea exists, and is understood, then many decisions can be made almost automatically. Thus this represents a device for reducing uncertainty, a way of eliminating alternatives.

6 The design team and the central idea
Richard MacCormac lays great emphasis on the need to have the whole design team understanding and sharing the concept behind the primary generator. This is a recognition of the obvious but often neglected fact that today design on this scale is a team rather than individual activity. This team, like those on the sports field, must 'play together' or 'be on the same wavelength'. A prerequisite for this to happen is the establishment of a sort of 'office culture' to which both Richard MacCormac and Sir Philip Dowson make reference in their discussion on Design Delegation, which contains this particular quotation.

7 Design competitions
Richard MacCormac is known for his criticism of the way some clients use competitions as a means of exploiting designers without giving adequate reward. However, here he seems to be making a most important point which flows from much of what is said in this book about the nature of the design brief. Many of our designers have commented on the frustration of working on a competition without access to the client, and this seems to be strongly linked to the wish of these designers to involve the client in the design process itself, and consequently to see the initial brief as merely a starting point in what Richard MacCormac calls a journey of discovery about both problem and solution. What MacCormac is telling us here is that the competition can be quite a good vehicle through which the client may come to understand their problem better without necessarily establishing the working client/architect relationship. Perhaps a more public and explicit recognition of this role might result in a better use of the design competition.

8 Sense of purpose
This point is also made very strongly by Ian Ritchie. Quite simply, the business of bringing a design idea to realization, particularly in the form of a building, requires a huge amount of determination, patience and perhaps stubborn doggedness. What both Richard MacCormac and Ian Ritchie are telling us is that it is the dedication to the deep underlying ideas behind the design that feeds this process and sustains the designer throughout this long and painful task.

9 Continuity
Richard MacCormac raises this issue frequently in his writing and public speeches. He believes that we must be extremely careful to protect the 'environment of design' to ensure high quality. In particular, he is concerned that unless there is continuity from the earliest phases of design right through design development to detailed design, those important underlying ideas will get lost. All too often books on the design process tend to deal much more with the glamorous early conceptual phases of design, but Richard MacCormac is reminding us of the importance of the detailed phases. How could the continuity of ideas which Richard MacCormac calls for be maintained through a design and build procurement system?

10 Guiding principles

Richard MacCormac clearly brings a continuing interest in geometrical systems into each design process with him. In this sense therefore we can see this as a designer-generated constraint of a formal kind. Since this seems to be a recurring theme in MacCormac's work, and because he has also written about it, we can interpret it as a set of guiding principles. The geometrical devices which result from this in the form of grids and forms become primary generators which structure the problem and solution. However, see also the next note for an elaboration of this idea.

11 Intentions and mechanisms

This seems to be a fundamentally important point that Richard MacCormac is making here which we might use to refine the concept of the primary generator. Although MacCormac's work seems littered with examples of formal constraints as primary organizing ideas, he is suggesting that these geometrical devices are in reality merely mechanisms through which a greater purpose is realized. What we see here therefore is the experience of the designer in knowing how such geometrical devices work and the effects they produce. This might be likened to a composer knowing how certain musical keys and key changes create moods. It reveals the necessity for designers to study these devices in their own right in order to establish their own vocabulary or 'repertoire of tricks', which may then be applied to express the greater ideas behind each design.

12 Drawing

It is interesting to note how many of our designers are apparently quite humble about their own ability to imagine three-dimensional form and space without drawing it. See particularly Richard Burton, Herman Hertzberger and Eva Jiricna's comments about this. Richard MacCormac agrees very much with Donald Schon's delightful image of the designer having a conversation with his drawing, which is also referred to by Denise Scott Brown. There seems a general consensus that the act of drawing during the design process is indeed an extremely reflective one in which the designer 'talks to himself' through the pencil. The idea that it is difficult to think and talk about design matters without holding the pencil is commonly expressed by designers. Just as it is sometimes necessary to 'think aloud'.

13 Drawing

Richard MacCormac is expressing a concern here similar to that voiced by Herman Hertzberger and Ian Ritchie. Essentially, this is the danger of the power of design drawings to take over and lead their own life such that the designer tends to design the drawing and not the real object. This is a tendency common among design students.

14 Speed of working

The image of the designer as a juggler is also used by Michael Wilford, and the need to oscillate very quickly between many issues is also referred to by Richard Burton. The intense concentration needed to keep several moving objects in your eye at once seems to offer a parallel to the need to keep several important but quite separate issues in mind when designing. Like juggling, this requires considerable practice and preparation, and looks easy when done by an experienced practitioner so that we fail to see just how difficult a skill it is until we try it for ourselves.

15 Analysis, synthesis and evaluation

The conventional shorthand for what Richard MacCormac is talking about here is that of 'analysis, synthesis and evaluation'. However, this is a rather more subtle and realistic description of design in action than can be found in most books of design methods. It is particularly interesting that MacCormac talks about the use of different drawing implements for each of his types of cognition. The holding of each implement in the hand and the way it makes a mark on paper can therefore be seen to condition the appropriate cognitive response. Quite simply, this helps to put the designer in the right mood for the task in hand. This is probably much more important than it may sound, since one of the great problems of managing creativity lies in developing the ability to undergo these changes at will. Much of the literature on creative thinking, lateral thinking, brainstorming, synectics and the like deals with artificial ways of engineering this change of cognitive mood. See also Robert Venturi's description of alternating between reality and fantasy.

16 Alternatives

This represents a rather more cautious view on the generation of alternatives than that which is expressed by Eva Jiricna and Michael Wilford and, to some extent, Richard Burton. They all advocate the deliberate generation of alternatives as a conscious act followed by a selection process. Richard MacCormac is not so sure and seems to be telling us that some design problems are, in his view, amenable to this kind of approach while others are not. Unfortunately, he is not able to tell us exactly how to distinguish between them, although Denise Scott Brown suggests one possible explanation.

17 Style

This is one of our most common responses. Few of our designers like the style-based taxonomy of architectural critics. They tell us that they do not think along stylistic lines, which might be slightly surprising to the lay public who seem to hear a great deal about 'style wars' these days. Perhaps the critics have got something to answer for here by creating a way of looking at design that, on the evidence of this book, does not seem to reflect how design is practised.

P Dowson and R MacCormac, How Architects Design (Architects Journal 192, 25-26, 1990).

R MacCormac, Arguments for Modern Architecture (RIBA Transactions 3, 1983).

R MacCormac, Art of Invention (Architects' Journal 181, 17, 1985).

R MacCormac and P Jamieson (Architectural Design 47, 9-10, 1977).

THE STREET

Richard MacCormac

Urban Design, Issue 53, 1995

Because streets are so ubiquitous we take them for granted. Yet like many familiar situations we may only realise what they are when we are faced with what they are not.

A year ago, visiting the wealthy suburbs of Santiago where residents are protected by walled compounds and private police patrols I realised I was witnessing the geographical and social disintegration of a once homogeneous city. Returning to London I was suddenly struck by the eighteenth and nineteenth century houses with front doors opening directly into the public realm of the street. These fragile panelled doors, which we are so used to, are really an amazing affirmation of an orderly society.

The eighteenth century city streetscape – Edinburgh or Bloomsbury – startlingly contrasts the privacy of the house with the city as a whole with the precise symbolism of the front door standing on the threshold.

Once outside that miraculously thin front door, you become part of something larger than the local community and engage in a freedom of association and right of accessibility offered by the 'urban' public realm of the street.

In his book The Fall of Public Man Richard Sennett argues that the localising of modern societies into exclusive suburbs and separate communities works against the kind of urban society created by the eighteenth century city in which all impersonal social orderliness actually engenders a wide degree of social tolerance, interaction and a diversity of experience.

It is observed that in modern cities there is a horrible symmetry between the privileged suburban ghettos of the wealthy and the social disorder of the poor estates which are, in a sense, their reflection. In both situations streets have given way to roads and culs-de-sac. These communities are no longer physically part of the continuum of urban place and urban life.

Booths poverty maps of 1889 show two urban characteristics rarely found in monolithic single class modern residential developments; relative wealth changes from street to street, and the streets are part of an urban continuum. The alternations of rich and poor streets records the social interdependence of the well-to-do with those who served them. Today alternations of high and low rentals in the same structure promote a commercial variety and interdependence which modern monolithic developments, like Canary Wharf cannot sustain.

The disintegration of the traditional street based city and its replacement with dispersed and fragmented residential communities, separately located business parks and out of town shopping centres is an international free market phenomenon. If we want to reverse this trend I believe we have to view our man made environment in much the same way as we are beginning to view our natural environment. We have to think in terms of the values of an urban ecology. We have first to identify what these values are and the factors which sustain them and the practicable measures which can achieve that sustainability.

I see several crucial issues of which the first is obviously the future of the car. At both central and local government levels road design remains largely independent of other urban issues and consequently there has been little serious debate about trade offs between highway criteria and the urban environment as a whole. It is time for new paradigms. It is perhaps symptomatic that the last masterplan for Milton Keynes proposed linking the hitherto separate communities with a street system independent of the fast city road system defined by the grid.

We need to review how the evolution of urban functions affects streets. Elsewhere I have suggested that we should distinguish between what I have called 'foreign' and 'local' transactions. Foreign transactions – wholesale, warehousing, manufacturing and offices do not interact with people in streets whereas shops, small businesses, restaurants, bars, street markets and the front doors of houses do. Convivial places are made up of the latter and we need to sustain them. That means challenging the way many modern shopping developments and supermarkets privatise the public realm or destroy local transactional street frontage.

We need to consider how physical planning constraints make good streets. We should insist as planners do in Berlin, that all developments come up to the building line and share party walls with adjoining owners. Just these two principles would reverse the universal trend that isolates individual buildings in the middle of plots and instead ensure that each becomes a component contributing to the street scene.

FULFILLING THE PURPOSE OF
ARCHITECTURE IN HIGHER EDUCATION

Richard MacCormac

Royal Fine Art Commission, Design
Quality in Higher Education (1996),
published following a seminar in 1995.

What makes architecture fascinating, controversial and inescapably part of our lives is that, exceptional amongst the arts, it lies between the practical and the aesthetic, between the commensurate and the incommensurate, the material and the spiritual.

There is a tendency, particularly English or perhaps Protestant, to see such dualities in opposition to one another, requiring an either/or choice; to see necessity as opposed to enjoyment, the essential in opposition to the aesthetic and everyday life as separate from art.

The argument that I want to make is that the fundamental obligation of architecture is to resolve such dualities. This is at the heart of the matter which we are considering. It is something that is quite difficult to explain or make credible. This is because there is a deeply engrained supposition that the need for a building poses a practical problem, of a quantifiable kind, that can be solved first, and then the architecture, perceived as an extra and separate ingredient, can be added on if the budget allows. This is, of course, a manifestation of the duality I have described.

Sophisticated clients, including certain commercial developers who are close to architectural thinking, know otherwise. They understand that design, that most complex and elusive of intellectual disciplines, is essentially about creating arrangements in which the practical and the aesthetic are coincident, rather than additional, to one another. All creative activity is like this, resolving complex and seemingly contradictory factors by inventing or discovering formal propositions. One thinks, for example, of the 'architecture' of the double helix of DNA.

It seems to me that universities, of all the commissioning institutions, have a special obligation to this idea. This is because architecture and higher education share equivalent ideals and face similar difficulties. Both have a commitment to nurturing and promoting particular kinds of public value and to enabling people to achieve the fullest experience of life. The universities, within limited budgets, have to balance training with education, science with art, and the needs of a productive society with intellectual fulfilment. Architecture involves analogous judgements within equally limited resources and, of course, a similar commitment to the pursuit of excellence. It should serve as the visible expression of educational values. At a more prosaic level, it must be true that, in the competitive market place of education and in a milieu of

ever-rising public interest in architecture, new buildings are going to be an increasingly important factor in creating the image of a university. Some are going to find themselves deeply embarrassed by shoddy commitments. There is no escaping the mind's eye.

In developing my arguments, I want to discuss impediments to achieving quality, which I believe to be institutional. We live in a world in which accountability must fall back upon the quantifiable and in which cost is easier to deal with than the incommensurate aspects of quality. I choose my words carefully, for I am entirely aware of the financial imperatives under which higher education operates. I simply ask that cost and the methods of procurement, which ensure cost control, be set in the context of what is worthwhile so as to arrive at a definition of value. This is surely what happens in decisions about the curriculum; there is an objective which has to be achieved within a budget. The budget does not define this aspiration, although it may affect how it is to be achieved.

I suggest that universities need to establish their architectural aspirations as clearly as their academic ones. They can do this through an institutional structure such as an architecture committee, which can support hard-pressed buildings officers.

Such a committee would not only oversee the commissioning of designers but would set an agenda for architecture, including lectures, exhibitions and debates, as an integral part of the university's intellectual and cultural life. It should face the implications for quality of new forms of procurement, such as private finance initiatives, which could mean that design and build becomes the norm. A number of universities, such as Warwick, have thriving Arts Centres and the way they are managed provides a model. The programme at Warwick Arts Centre already encompasses architecture. The London School of Economics is establishing, and Cambridge University has established, postgraduate architecture courses which are not essentially professional and vocational; they are to do with setting architecture into a much wider academic framework.

Such a programme can work on several levels. It can be of general interest as well as highly specific, keeping abreast of the ever-developing evolution of different building types libraries, laboratories or student residences. It is arguable that the distinctive characteristics of late twentieth-century

architecture are not fundamentally stylistic, but are due to the acceleration of the nineteenth-century phenomenon of special building types generated by new requirements and changing technology. The impact of information technology on the design of libraries is just one example of what I mean. It is for this reason, rather than the 'modernist' ideology of severance from history, that new buildings are often surprising in their form and appearance.

This makes it increasingly difficult for clients to know what to expect and consequently how to select an architect. To overcome this, there has to be a re-establishment of trust between clients and architects, because together they have to undergo an unpredictable and creative journey. Trust should be explicit in the selection process. But what seems to be happening is that uncertain and sometimes frighteningly unqualified clients demand 'proof' through elaborate pre-qualifying and qualifying procedures, which have little relation to real professional experience and performance.

This is making selection processes of all kinds increasingly arduous and expensive. Senior people in architectural practices are spending up to 50% of their time qualifying and competing. This is extraordinarily inefficient by any standards. It is said that one of the fundamental inefficiencies of the West in comparison with the emerging economies of the East is the high standing cost of servicing production because of the complexities of accountability, competition and contract. The paradox is that, as in the National Health Service, this increasingly grotesque inefficiency seems to be a consequence of extending the methods of the market-place into the professional world.

Clients, understandably, have an urge to know what they are going to get from an architect, even to get initial sketches of how the scheme is going to look. 'We don't want you to do much work', they say, 'but we would like you to do some sketches'. This, of course, presupposes that the appearance of the building can be separated from the conception and is not inherent in the way in which the design has been conceived. Of course you can separate appearance, particularly with simple building types such as speculative offices. That is what makes so much design and build instantly recognisable and superficial. The elevations are a kind of make-up that has been pencilled on to something which is often 50mm thick or 25mm thick if savings have to be made. There is no intellectual

depth. This is not architecture, for architecture should be a marvellous manifestation of intelligence – engaging, challenging and drawing us out, exactly like education itself.

A way in which clients can feel secure with a design at an early stage is to hold a competition. There are all kinds of ways of setting up competitions and the RIBA is the best source of advice about finding the appropriate kind. Many higher education clients hold limited competitions, after a preselection process. If the brief is really well-considered, and there is a prospect of going ahead with a funded scheme on an available site, the system is good. The client not only gets a design quickly but, because the chemistry of competitions can be intense, may also get a design of unusual distinction.

I say 'may' because there is a feeling in the profession that, in a buyer's market, the competition system has been misused, with poorly considered briefs and too many competitions making the system expensive and arbitrary compared with the rewards. But good competitions still attract good architects.

There is also a feeling, amongst those of us who compete against each other, that competitions are sometimes a way of postponing decisions; that they are perhaps a substitute for making an informed judgement about the appointment of an appropriate architect based on that architect's past record. That, again, involves a matter of trust, but trust is the bond which must unite client and architect from the inception of every project.

The process of selection which seems to me to combine the evidence of track record and achievement with an opportunity for the architect's team to demonstrate their expertise and commitment and to advocate an approach to a project without the resource expenditure of producing a design, is the competitive interview.

It will work best if there is a good understanding on the client's side of the functional and architectural implications of the project. It reaffirms the opportunity for trust and allows the architect subsequently to evolve a design in conjunction with the client, recognising that the particular value of a design solution often does not become apparent until quite late in the process.

I do not want to dwell upon that other procedure for selection, the competitive fee tender, except to pose a rhetorical question: what would happen if academics were selected on an equiv-

alent basis and what would be the consequence for quality in higher education? Again, there is a similarity between the two professions: both are vocational and the value they produce is the sum of two variables, quality of thought and time spent thinking. Fee tendering minimises time spent thinking and redefines architecture as a private contract without wider obligation. It denies the ethical imperative, which we share with higher education, of maximising quality of thought within an agreed financial framework.

Universities depend for their funding upon perceptions of value, for it is value which attracts the students who ensure the flow of funds. Architecture is an expression of value, and the reputation of universities will depend, at least in part, upon the extent to which their building programmes fulfil that concept of value and project visions of excellence.

AN ANATOMY OF LONDON

Richard MacCormac

Built Environment, Dec 1996

By understanding how places have evolved, we are better able to guide development and change in the urban fabric, and avoid the incongruity created by so much of the 'modern environment'. Examination of 'sections' of London shows that functions of a very different type can co-exist successfully if they are in the right place; it is not a question of architectural style, but of purpose and use, and of scale and symmetry across places.

This is a speculative study. The work is in a familiar tradition of speculation about the nature of cities; a tradition which people like Rob and Leon Krier represent. But what has seemed important to me is to convert static observations about the nature of the European or the British city into a kind of understanding that might enable us to comprehend the situation as a process and not simply as a product that exists in stasis. This would enable us to make better judgements about the nature of change and how we should guide that change in old fabrics. I think that the unpopularity of what is called the 'modern environment' is partly to do with a profound sense of incongruity and a feeling that the nature of change is

such that instead of affirming what exists and adding to it and making new wonderful things, the modern environment is perceived to have destroyed what was good and not to have made something better. And so what I want to investigate is why. I am putting forward propositions about architecture which go beyond the planning process.

I will start with some cross sections. The idea of looking at cross sections is to test a proposition about the traditional organization of the West End of London; this is not very easy to do in the City of London for reasons of rapidity of change. The validity of the proposition is yet to be established, though I have a sense, having recently reread Donald Olsen's *'Town Planning in London'* (published 1964), that some of the principles I am going to talk about were intentional in the development of the great estates, like the Bedford Estate.

The first example is north of where I work and live, in Spitalfields, the wonderfully vigorous Cheshire Street market with Victorian houses in multi-use. I managed to get these listed about eight years ago to stop them being demolished; the local authority planned to demolish everything here to build ware-

houses, the kind of warehousing you see further north in the Bethnal Green Road. Part of my reason for getting these buildings listed was to ensure that a social characteristic of this part of London was preserved, and the key characteristic of this environment is that it supports what I call 'local transactions' that is people living behind their own front doors; restaurants and shops of all kinds and local businesses and, of course, pubs. Local transactions are threatened if planning professionals do not understand the threat which building types like warehousing represent. The threat arises because transactions such as distributive warehousing, along with wholesale markets, banks and office buildings, are destructive of local character simply because they do not primarily serve local people. I call these 'foreign transactions' because they operate on a regional, national or international level. The warehouses do not belong in retailing situations such as the Bethnal Green Road, because they abruptly interrupt its local transactional character. They are incongruous.

What I want to explore is the way that cities can be made up of successfully co-existent functions of very different sorts

that find their right place. I am not going to attempt to explain the origins of such relationships or how they took place originally. But in some ways I perceive the architectural and urban structures I am going to examine as being rather like coral reefs that are re-inhabited over and over again and there seems to be a pattern in the relationships which reoccurs over time though the functions change. For example, in the eighteenth-century-city large houses on primary streets were inhabited by high-income families and the mews behind serviced them. Today the houses might be offices with the mews inhabited by businesses selling services - commercial or professional - like photocopying, printing or sandwich bars to the primary users.

Observations of this kind have prompted me to consider how the problem posed by the warehouse development on Bethnal Green Road might have been resolved. You organize the development so that the frontage to the road sustains 'local transactions': chambers-like buildings of a modest scale which have frequent access from the street and which contain small businesses or retailing. These uses, facing onto the street, sustain the idea of the street as a

Section through the Savoy and Covent Garden Square to Earlham Street (looking west).

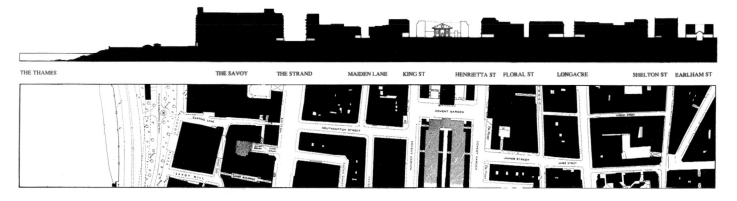

THE THAMES — THE SAVOY — THE STRAND — MAIDEN LANE — KING ST — HENRIETTA ST — FLORAL ST — LONGACRE — SHELTON ST — EARLHAM ST

Section through Golden Square and Piccadilly to The Mall (looking east).

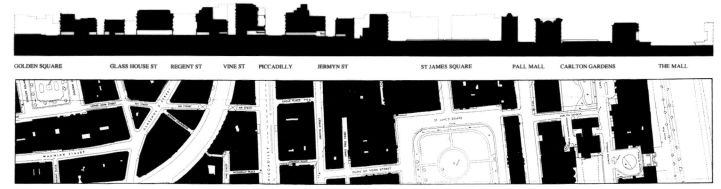

GOLDEN SQUARE — GLASS HOUSE ST — REGENT ST — VINE ST — PICCADILLY — JERMYN ST — ST JAMES SQUARE — PALL MALL — CARLTON GARDENS — THE MALL

place for people to transact, and the regional or national distribution function of the warehouses is relegated to its own hinterland. So there is a precinct or service area behind the street which belongs to the activities around it and confines them. The sections through the street and this service yard are symmetrical while the section through the block between them is asymmetrical. This leads to a proposition that, traditionally, similar uses housed in a similar scale of building, faced each other across streets and change of use and scale occurred within the block enabling a succession of adjacent streets to be different from one another. The symmetry in the street affirms its character as a place. It follows that the symmetry across the block characteristic of so much modern development produces either uniformity across the urban fabric as a whole or a series of places of ambiguous function and scale.

Some of us, in my office, disconcerted by the local borough planning policy for the Cheshire Street area, looked at how these ideas might be applied. We discovered that the existing section was very intriguing with the railway in a cutting going into Liverpool Street station, bounded to the south by run down warehousing looking into an existing plot of public open space called Allen's Gardens. We showed how the lively character of the street could be sustained by preserving existing buildings and functions and how the hinterland could be developed for servicing warehousing without affecting the street scene.

We considered housing to be a more appropriate use to border the public open space which becomes the enclosed garden which its name suggests. But we also perceived an economic aspect to this, which is that new housing primes the value of the adjacent commercial site giving confidence to potential small-scale investors in the little workshops and businesses between the housing and the railway. There is a sequence here: railway, small business, giving acoustic protection to the housing, and the housing making an appropriate edge to the garden, to which it has a claim which small businesses do not. There is an idea here which is analogous to the game of dominoes where certain values attach to each other and certain ones do not and it was this expression of congruity that prompted an investigation of certain sections of the West End of London, to see if such arrangements were characteristic.

The first section examined is from the Festival Hall to Centre Point. There is a general sense of congruity across the river, with the Royal Festival Hall, the National Theatre, County Hall facing the Savoy Hotel, Shell Mex and Embankment Place on the north bank. All are equivalent kinds of building, set pieces, public or commercial 'palaces'. So there are symmetries of intention even across a river which respond to the symbolic status which the river confers. If we look at what is happening, sectionally, on the north bank we find that on the slope from the Embankment itself up to the Strand we get an enormous change of scale, we also get a change of type, through the section, the Savoy Hotel being the most interesting example.

What happens is that the hotel changes from being a 14-storey palace, with all the other ones looking across the river, to being a terraced structure which subsumes its rhetoric into that of the Strand. It becomes equivalent to other buildings which line the Strand which are mostly stone or stucco clad and five to seven storeys, with busy retailing at ground level on both sides of the street. The Savoy Hotel itself is immensely interesting because there is a series of transformations within it; it is like a Parisian Hotel de Ville which invites you into the centre of the block where various points of access are offered including the entrance into the theatre. It has a special identity as a place rather than as an elevation to the street.

In this argument the concern is not with architectural style, but with purpose and use, probably material to some extent, and with scale. Different architectural idioms could be mixed within these conventions. Moving one street to the north we find another character in Maiden Lane which is a service street with solicitors' chambers, flats, occasional pubs and small businesses, and a diminutive scale in relation to the Strand. The whole street is quite distinct and again there is symmetry of use across it and asymmetry across the block. Another asymmetry occurs between Maiden Lane and Covent Garden Piazza. Very little survived of Inigo Jones' original project which was a symmetrical Piazza of substantial scale into which the market was later introduced. The church is on the axis of a central aisle through the symmetrical market. North of the Piazza is Long Acre, and the section varies from the large scale of the Piazza buildings down to the smaller scale of Floral Street, which is a service street, and then up to Long Acre which is a major street nearly equal in scale and function to the Strand. We are seeing an alternation of scale and activity which, while not universal, is often a characteristic of these West End developments of seventeenth to nineteenth century origin. Consider, for a moment, Canary Wharf, and the Isle of Dogs Free Enterprise Zone, and imagine whether you could find any equivalent arrangements which allow primary and secondary and tertiary activities to coexist. There is nothing of the sort.

The series of warehouses north of Long Acre is another circumstance altogether and is sometimes the exception to the proposition, being asymmetrical across the street and symmetrical across the block. This warehousing served the fruit and vegetable market originally and has now found new uses in housing small professional businesses, retailing, restaurants and bars.

Sometimes the arrangements invert the original intention. The service space which would have been for carts and dray-horses and at the back of buildings that faced onto streets, has become an oasis of traffic free activity. So the old coral reef, the old structure has been reinterpreted and inverted to create a new kind of place.

Monmouth Street and Shaftesbury Avenue form the boundary to this area. This part of Shaftesbury Avenue is curiously without local transactions and dominated by large impersonal office buildings and to the north backs onto a desolate hinterland. The character changes again to small intensely used service streets off Charing Cross Road which are abruptly terminated by St Giles' Circus. In the 1960s, the office tower Centre Point took out the end of the block of St Giles' High Street, and joined onto the intersection of Oxford Street and Charing Cross Road. Consequently the fabric has been amputated. The amputation is concealed with advertisements, a kind of commercial bandaging on the end of the block. It is that kind of disruption without any healing, which makes modern interventions so crude and unresolved. Which is not to say that you cannot find places for this type of building. Centre Point is a visually interesting tower, but the problem is a contextual one and a question of congruity. There should be a process, between planning and architecture, of urban design to establish an environment for a total change of scale and use of this sort.

The second section examined is of a very different sort and runs from St James's Park up to Golden Square in Soho. The proposition is not really sustained to the north of Regent Street, but what is interesting about thinking about London in this way is that it leads to questions which produce unexpected answers. For example, it was originally Nash's intention to have another Carlton House Terrace on the other side of the Mall, a proposal which would have made the North boundary of St James's Park rather different. He intended The Mall to be a ceremonial axis to the Palace, like a great boulevard in St Petersburg. What is interesting about Carlton House Terrace is that it 'fronts' the Park, but is entered from the other side. A lot of modern buildings have a back and front, but eighteenth-century buildings often have two 'fronts'. Nash's building demonstrates this very successfully. Then there is the garden at the back of the Pall Mall clubs, a slightly strange space here, very quiet and with a special character. But it is not entirely symmetrical; you do not enter clubs from this side, you enter them from Pall Mall, a great street of social and commercial institutions.

To the north is a strange arrangement, the block between St James's Square and Pall Mall is very thin, thinner than the depth of the block containing the clubs. This is because when St James's Square was developed in the 1660s Pall Mall was already established as a primary street so the buildings on the south side of St James's Square originally presented their fronts to Pall Mall and their backs to St James's Square. Now some of them are back to back, to sustain frontage to both street and square. St James's Square has a general symmetry, and then to the north Apple Tree Yard forms a mews between St James's Square and Jermyn Street. So there is a section through asymmetrical blocks and symmetrical spaces going from the primary activity of the square through the mews and up again to the scale of Jermyn Street. Then we come to Norman Shaw's Piccadilly Hotel. This kind of analysis has made me see these buildings in a completely new way because what we find in plan is that the site is the meeting point between Piccadilly and Regent Street which forms a wedge shaped block. The hotel conforms absolutely to an urban proposition which is to do with its palace-like relationship to Piccadilly and the crescent of Regent Street to the North. The hotel presents itself as a distinct building on its entrance side to Piccadilly but is entirely subsumed into the rhetoric of Regent Street. If you cut through Regent Street to the back of Glasshouse Street, you get the sense that even cities of the commercial power of London cannot sustain commercial activity universally. There has to be quiet, and Glasshouse Street is very quiet; it is not a transactional street. It has become a relatively low rental office street which collides with the old bit of Soho and then, this part becomes dissonant.

The proposition is about symmetry across places, but of course it does not happen everywhere. There are collisions off Regent Street where everything is dissonant, strange and interesting. Golden Square is full of one-offs, competing with each other, in a manner that is uncharacteristic of the eighteenth-century urban ideal. Generally the estate surveyors, for example on the Bedford Estate in the eighteenth-century, felt sure that the long-term value of the estates depended upon the style of the estate being maintained and upon leases that constrained people from creating incongruity.

These issues affected me when I was working on the masterplanning for the redevelopment of Spitalfields Market. Early proposals for Spitalfields explored changes of scale and the reconciliation of local interests, local transactions with financial functions in office buildings – foreign transactions. The final scheme was highly complex in its attempt to come to grips with these ideas, and also introduced other more metaphorical conceptions. There was to be a major retail area, and as with the Savoy, a series of Hotel de Ville-like courts which belonged to huge office buildings. Some of these courts were on Brushfield Street which is the street with Hawksmoor's Christ Church Spitalfields at the end, with a predominantly eighteenth-century scale. The terrace addressing the street consisted of small chambers buildings for retail use, made of stone and brick four or five storeys high, backing onto further shops to make a relationship across the little alleyways: local transactions. The tall offices behind and above are quite different; they are prestigious and belong to the world of Frankfurt, New York, Tokyo, London – foreign transactions. The scheme was an attempt to reconcile incongruities of use and scale using asymmetry through blocks, to protect the character of Brushfield Street and to allow very different kinds of places and functions to coexist in an incredibly dense commercial development.

One last point: for 10 years or so I have had reprints from Booth's London Poverty maps of 1889 on my wall. I suddenly realised that their observation of demographic variety seems to show that change of wealth always occurs through the block, and never across the street.

ARCHITECTURE, MEMORY AND METAPHOR

Richard MacCormac

The Architecture of Information,
British Council catalogue for the British
Pavilion at the 1996 Venice Biennale.

Designing a building to house Ruskin's work and his collection of books, paintings and photographs precipitates a question – a Ruskinian question – about architecture: is there a relationship between the language of 'modernism' and the historical tradition represented in Ruskin's thought? On the one hand, modernism has been seen as deliberately dislocated, an abstract, technological language from which historical associations have been banished. On the other hand, the historical tradition is locked into a taxonomy of style, isolated from other contemporary discourses about architectural theory, and irrelevant to the typological, spatial and constructional characteristics of late twentieth-century architecture.

The question itself defines a familiar conflict and says something about the discontinuity in our culture; the past is preserved but not made part of the future. Our purpose, as architects, must be to rediscover how our inheritance can become vivid and relevant to what we make now. The Ruskin project has allowed us to do this in a very special way.

The sixth chapter of Ruskin's Seven Lamps of Architecture is the Lamp of Memory, in which he says 'we cannot remember' without architecture. The chapter resonates with analogous words – monument, memory, history, historical, story [1] – all of which emphasise the idea of recall and invite us to find the means of recall without losing the authenticity of the architecture of the present. And this, in turn, stimulates the realisation that architecture, like literature and landscape, is part of our collective memory, which we must incorporate into our present experience.

Ruskin's concern with memory, with the memorial and monumental, was complex. He saw architecture as a text of cumulative history. He believed that architecture could convey information metaphorically, through its surface decoration, and he likened buildings to books – he referred to St Mark's as 'a vast illuminated missal'. Today, it is difficult to dissociate Ruskin's ideas from the stylistic legacy of pseudo-Gothic and, in particular, the pseudo-Venetian style which he himself recognised as 'an accursed Frankenstein monster of my own making'. And this admission is interesting for, when Ruskin calls upon the architect 'to render the architecture of the day historical', we perceive that he is addressing an issue more fundamental than style, which is the potential for architecture to say something through its antecedents, rather than simply to describe its own structure and function.

This Ruskinian reminder is particularly important for the mainstream of late twentieth century British architecture, which tends to subsume all aesthetic and symbolic issues within innovative structural and programmatic arguments. There are reasons for this but, looked at in a wider context of the visual arts, sculpture and painting, this is uncharacteristic of British modernism which has synthesised metaphor and formal invention in, for example, the work of such artists as Henry Moore, Barbara Hepworth and Paul Nash, and today in the work of artists contributing to what has been called the 'unpainted landscape' – Andy Goldsworthy, Richard Long and Ian Hamilton Finlay.

In the works of Nash and Finlay, objects may be recognisable but their juxtapositions are surprising and, as in the fiction of Garcia Marquez, it is as if a basis in practical reality is needed to set off the metaphorical and dream-like. This is important for architecture because it has to be real. The potency of a metaphorical image lies in its ambiguity, because, not being one thing, it can be many. It is neither literal nor abstract. Looked at in terms of architecture, this ambiguity is what distinguishes a metaphorical use of the past from the adoption of an historical style. It allows a creative relationship between present and past and an active rather than passive engagement with history. This is the possibility which the Ruskin project and its progenitors in our work have sought.

The Ruskin Library has two main antecedents amongst our projects, the unbuilt library for King's College Cambridge, and the chapel for Fitzwilliam College Cambridge,[2] which both contribute to the development of a series of themes. All three projects express the idea of protection through the use of curved walls and all three consist of buildings within buildings, with the inner buildings evoking an architectural presence within the space.

The curved masonry outer wall of the King's library was to consist of tiers of galleries, displaying the college's collection of ancient books and manuscripts as a kind of memory bank of knowledge, monumental in the sense of being a 'reminder', from the Latin 'monere', to remind or warn. In contrast, the undergraduate library, a freestanding object, constructed of wood was to be a kind of grove of transient information standing in the internal space. The project explored dualities and ambiguities of inside and outside, under and over which are reiterated in both the chapel and the Ruskin Library.

The chapel combines the linear and circular origins of Christian church architecture, the basilica and the Pantheon. It does this with abstract forms which draw on the two typological traditions without stylistic recourse.

In cross-section, the building is also traditional, consisting of a crypt with the place of worship above. But here it is the object within the space, defining the duality between what is above and what is below, which is the principal symbol of the building; it is a vessel, an ark, which floats over the dark underworld of the crypt, and holds above, the place of worship. This image of a vessel was precipitated by visits to the Viking Ship Museum in Oslo, in which the concave interior surfaces of the space protect the sensuous elegant wooden ships, and the Vasa Ship Museum in Stockholm, where the wonderfully preserved seventeenth century ship is like an enormous toy in its box. But it was not until the design developed that the power and universality of the ship metaphor became apparent. The vessel is the 'nave di chiesi' where the congregation come together for a shared rite of passage. In medieval manuscripts the images of Christ seen in a ship are metaphors for his transforming and redemptive journey. This idea of transformation is also the meaning of the Viking and Egyptian burial ships and of the story of Noah's Ark and, in a special sense, of Jonah and the Whale, the transforming experience of what Jung called 'the night sea journey'.

The Ruskin Library

The Ruskin Library is the further development of an architecture combining seemingly abstract formal language with a series of narrative ideas. It is Ruskinian because it alludes to Ruskin and because, by doing so, it fulfils Ruskin's expectation that architecture should be metaphorical. The building avoids historical style but is 'rendered historical' in the Ruskinian sense. The actual concrete construction is exposed internally in its true character, in the giant portal frames which span longitudinally. But externally, it is 'encrusted', to use another Ruskinian term, with white masonry and dark grey/green courses, joined with stainless steel bosses, the equivalent of the visible fastenings used in the cladding of Italian buildings, which Ruskin called 'confessed rivets'. The construction of the archive cabinet, standing within, mimics this combination, but with different materials – polished red plaster, oak frames and bronze fastenings – 'encrusting' the concrete box.

The building, in plan, appears as a succinctly abstract idea – two arcs, split apart, to contain the rectangular archive. But it is also symbolically and literally a 'keep', a refuge for Ruskin's bequest, appearing as a secure tower, and fulfilling the verb 'keep' by preserving the collection. It is also a monument celebrating the memory of the life of Ruskin, a life monumental in itself in the sense that Ruskin's life's work was continuously to remind.

The building is an island like Venice. Islands are also refuges and medieval Venice was Ruskin's moral refuge. So the building, as a symbol of Venice, is separated from the university by a causeway which crosses a dry moat representing the lagoon.

This causeway enters the building and the metaphor of island and lagoon is replicated with the archive itself emerging through an underlit transparent glass and slate floor to convey the perilous maritime condition of the city and to allude to Ruskin's dream of looking into its waters, and seeing the horses of St Mark's being harnessed.

The archive, a building within a building, or keep within a keep, recalls a visit made to the cathedral of Albi, in the south of France, a fortress-like cathedral within which the masonry choir formed a further internal line of defence. This idea has been transferred analogically into an environmental proposition which uses the thermal stability of the two masonry 'keeps' and the large volume of air between them to protect the collection and create the first passively conditioned major archive in the UK.[3] In terms of the building's symbolic and visual intentions, the memory of Albi also precipitated a church-like plan in which the archive stands for the choir separating the public entrance and the aisles on each side from the sanctuary/reading room situated in the most secure location at the west end of the building.

The centrepiece of the building is, of course, the archive itself and, like the vessel in the Fitzwilliam Chapel, it is loaded with associations. In an abstract sense it is a large object which gains its presence from blocking the axis through the building. Richard Serra's 'Weight and Measure' exhibited at the Tate Gallery in 1992 had a similar effect. It is the great treasure chest, in Venetian red plaster, the cathedral chest strapped together with oak and bronze. It is also a cabinet, like a giant piece of furniture by William Burgess which acquires the scale and character of architecture – a building inside a building. It is an ark or reliquary, a tabernacle, a bookcase or, by inference, a great book; the 'a vast illuminated missal' and corpus of Ruskin's work. Shutters can be opened to hint at its interior. At the east end, facing the public entrance these open to reveal a hugely amplified image of one of Ruskin's daguerreotypes of St Mark's, a Proustian fleeting or, as Ruskin would say, a 'fugitive' image, a symbol of the fragility of memory[4] and its capacity to recall the past.

1 I owe this observation to Professor Michael Wheeler, director of the Ruskin project at Lancaster University. The Lamp of Memory: Ruskin, Tradition and Architecture edited by Michael Wheeler & Nigel Whiteley (Manchester University Press, 1992).
2 Exhibited in the 1992, Venice Biennale Architettura e spazia sacro nella modernita.
3 The Ruskin Library: Architecture and Environment for the Storage, Display and Study of a Collection pre-print, Ottawa Conference 12-16 September 1994, Institute for the conservation of historical and artistic works.
4 Proust's book A la Recherche du Temps Perdu is arguably the literary monument to Ruskin's concern with memory.

BLUE SPACE: THE WELLCOME WING OF THE SCIENCE MUSEUM, LONDON

Richard MacCormac

Architectural Design Profile no 128:
Frontiers: Artists & Architects, 1997

This is a statement of work in progress towards the creation of a big blue space, perhaps the biggest blue space.

It has its antecedents, starting with Sir John Soane's lumiere mysterieuse, his perception that coloured light disembodies, his realisation of this in parts of his museum and, most specifically, in the mausoleum of the Dulwich Picture Gallery. Soane's use of light as a coloured wash is related to his fellow Academician JMW Turner's use of glazes and washes in a dissolution of materiality which prefigures late twentieth-century experiments in space and light, such as the work of Robert Irwin and James Turrell. Soane's use of colour and light amplifies a deliberate ambiguity of space definition in his architecture which places enclosing walls beyond expected boundaries.

MacCormac Jamieson Prichard have developed these ideas in various ways in recent work. In the chapel for Fitzwilliam College, Cambridge, the curved light-washed walls stand outside the space defined by the columns supporting the roof. In the intermediate concourse at Southwark Station, which will serve the Bankside Tate Gallery, the architects have worked with artist Alex Beleschenko to create a truncated, elliptical cone 17 metres high and 40 metres long at the base, consisting of 630 triangles of glass. The work is screen-printed blue and virtually opaque at the base, grading off as it ascends to near transparency, where daylight penetrates down the back of the screen. It will offer various combinations of deep blue opacity, reflectivity, translucency and transparency, amplifying the unexpectedness of strong daylight in an underground space, using the sky-colour blue as part of that inversion of expectations.

The Wellcome Wing at the Science Museum: Theatre of Science

Visual and aural influences on an architect are never premeditated and only become apparent subsequently. In retrospect, two exhibitions at the Hayward Gallery seem to have been important for the Science Museum project – Yves Klein and James Turrell. Klein Blue is so saturated that one looks into, rather than at it, as though into space.

At the Hayward, Turrell exhibited work using light to achieve an extraordinary dissolution of boundaries, and a pursuit of evanescence which is also a characteristic of pieces by his close colleague Robert Irwin. In Britain these ventures have parallels in the work of Vong Phaophanit and Martin Richman.

In the Wellcome Wing project the intention in the use of colour is psycho-logical – to create an interior which has the cool blue radiance of a night sky, to create a sense of elation and wonder (what in the eighteenth century would have been called 'a sense of the sublime') so as to create an appropriate frame of mind for approaching an exhibition of modern science, of biotechnology.

To achieve this the architects have appointed a Dutch firm of lighting specialists, Hollands Licht and Rogier van der Heide, to work with them and Ove Arup & Partners on the lighting and colour in the primary fit-out of the building. The design development is being undertaken with computer models, physical models and an artificial sky and sun. The first stage has been to create a computer model of the blue west window to ascertain the performance required of its two layers consisting of an external membrane of perforated metal protecting a layer of blue glass. The objectives to be met were as follows: an internal image of blue; a transmittance of daylight which produces about 50 lux from an overcast sky within six metres of the window; a transmittance of a maximum of 150 lux within six metres of the window when the sun is shining; no sunlight penetration during opening hours a restriction on the visible cast of blue light to within six metres of the window; an external image of blue at night.

The computer model established that the perforated metal had to provide complete solar protection. This allowed the blue glass to transmit enough light to appear strongly coloured from within on an overcast day and to appear blue when artificially lit from inside at night.

This has led to a series of tests using a mock-up of an artificial sky and sun combining various perforated metal screens with a range of blue glass sheets of different intensities. These physical modelling tests have established objectives which have to be reconciled. The screen necessary for total solar protection tends to conflict with the external visibility of the blue screen at night. This can be resolved with the orientation of the perforations obscuring the path of the sun but allowing visibility of the glass below the horizontal. The stronger the intensity of the glass from within and without; the stronger the blue cast into the exhibition areas. This can be resolved by limiting the transmittance to about three per cent of the full spectrum of daylight which allows exhibition lighting levels to locally eliminate the blue cast.

Another test using physical models has been undertaken in the Hollands Licht studios in Amsterdam, where they constructed 1:5 models of bays of the interior in a simulated environment which could test the concept against a range of ambient lighting levels. Here the proposition has been to dissolve the boundary of the space by using a fabric scrim in front of a solid screen lit with cold cathode tubes using blue filters and reflectors to create an almost even spread of light. The scrim attracts focal length so that the blue lit plane behind is dislocated, appearing as an evanescent space. Blue light constitutes about 10-15 per cent of the visible part of the electromagnetic spectrum but the visual response of the eye varies depending on whether its is dark (19 per cent) or light (3.5 per cent) adapted. With effectively monochromatic blue light passing through the walls it will be possible to project complete colour images onto the scrim which will seem to be floating on a penumbra of blue.

NEGOTIATING THE COLLABORATIVE PROCESS

Richard MacCormac

Glass, Light & Space, Crafts Council catalogue, October 1997

Increasing collaboration between artists, craftsmen and architects reflects changes in the perception which each discipline has of itself and of others. The idea of public art and the success of public art agencies has opened up opportunities for artists to move away from the convention of gallery art and engage with public space and with the craft of materials such as glass. The willingness of architects to work with artists means a move away from the utilitarian and technological imperatives of late modernism towards a renewed, more sensuous and subjective interest in colour, form and material for their own sake, reminding us that movements in early modernism such as Purism and de Stijl encompassed other visual arts. There is special interest in artists who are exploring sensations of space which are architectural.

The quality of glass which interests architects today is probably a combination of its ambiguous materiality and its contrasting precision, in relation to light, which make it mysterious and suggestive.

In the iconic works of the modern movement in architecture, we tend to see the modernity of glass as its complete transparency – its not being there – not separating inside from outside, the Farnsworth House, for example. We forget that the development of glass architecture originated in German Expressionism with the mystical aspirations of Paul Scheerbart and Bruno Taut. Perhaps in Mies van der Rohe's Barcelona Pavilion of 1929 (now reconstructed), in the combination of grey transparent glass, double etched glazing with lighting between, bottle green glass, onyx and highly polished green marble brought together in a building without any explicit function, we see, not just modernism, but the manifestation of architecture as pure experience, a link between Scheerbart and the work of today's space and light and glass artists.

There are various conceptions and misconceptions of collaboration. I am sceptical about artists and architects readily being able to exchange roles. I suggest that a shared culture is not about artists being architects and vice versa but about understanding and enjoying the difference and what that brings to the process.

Creativity in design involves independence and interdependence. It involves modes of thought which cannot be shared because, at certain junctures, one mind has to be in total and intense possession of the idea. But, at other junctures, the idea can be shared with other individuals whose roles are complementary and essential to the development of

Art & Architecture special issue,
Architects' Journal, 2 October 1997

the concept. This is what happens in successful working relationships between architects and engineers, for example, and is a potential model for relationships between architects and glass artists.

For it to work I think there have to be some preconditions. The most obvious is that the parties feel a real affinity for each other's work. Roles and territories, at least at the outset, need to be defined but then paradoxically, there must be openness, serendipity and willingness to relinquish control. This is difficult !

I have worked on three projects with Alexander Beleschenko, co-curator of this exhibition. The three projects could hardly be more different technically and aesthetically. In each case, the glasswork has been interpretative of a general architectural intent but, in each case, the outcome has been beyond expectation, and the artist has developed techniques he has not used before.

The first project was at St John's College, Oxford,[1] in a building we designed called The Garden Quadrangle. The work consisted of glazed screens defining an ambulatory around a sunken courtyard. We wrote a brief for a limited competition which set out to describe the subjective characteristics of the building to which artists would respond: cavernous coolness, crystalline iciness. The quality of Alexander's response to this was immediately evident with allusions to ice and water and a textural intricacy created from over 60,000 pieces of cut, broken, sawn, and laminated glass, absolutely complementary to the brittle needle-gunned concrete of the building's primary structure. What also worked, having initially taken us by surprise, was the way in which the glass veiled the vaulted interior spaces giving them a remoteness more apposite than the immediate transparency of modernism.

Our next project, now under construction, is the glass elliptical cone wall for the Jubilee Line station at Southwark, about 14 metres high and 40 metres at its base. Until Alexander's involvement, this was to be precast concrete. His use of coloured glass on a large scale – as at Stockley Park – prompted our invitation for him to participate and entirely changed our perception of the space. The intention here is paradoxical, rendering deeply underground space brightly daylit, blue and reflective, deliberately contradictory to trogloditic expectation. Top light passes behind and in front of 630 triangles of glass silk screened with blue enamel with a crystal inclusion for prismatic effect. The geometric complexity of an elliptical

cone required the engineers to develop special software to schedule the glass and co-ordinate it with the structure. The glass artist then used his computer to schedule the enamelling, defining four line types in six orientations. The glass artist has also been closely involved with the manufacture of the glass to reconcile his specification with the performance of toughened glass in public areas.

Our most recent collaborative project is for the Ruskin Library at the University of Lancaster. At the front of the archive, the three storey high cabinet containing the Ruskin collection, four metre high shutters open to reveal an image of the north-west portal of St Mark's, Venice. The archive itself, faced with Venetian red plaster, polished like marble is a metaphor for Venice which the image is intended to support. What has been interesting about this project has been the way in which the technology of transferring the image has, itself, transformed the image rather than simply reproduced it.

The image itself has been greatly enlarged from a book illustration of Ruskin's own daguerreotype. So it has been through several transformations since the initial daguerreotype's fugitive image, the last of which were to digitise the book illustration and imprint it on glass. The process involved coating the glass with platinum lustre, fired on to the surface, then sandblasting it through a stencil. The sandblasted areas were than treated with clear enamel. The intention of the image is to evoke Ruskin's sense of the fragility of recollection.[2]

These are personal accounts of working with an artist. They are not radical collaborations in the sense that the artist might have affected the original architectural conception, but in each case the glasswork is intrinsic to the meaning of the building rather than superficially decorative. It is impossible to imagine the buildings without the work.

1 In collaboration with Public Art Commissions Agency.
2 From which Proust, inspired by Ruskin, derived his great opus, A la Recherche du Temps Perdu.

Boundaries between artists and architects are blurred in work marked by subtle manipulation of colour and light.

My interest in the art of space and light was provoked, I suppose, by dissent from Le Corbusier's definition of modern architecture as 'the masterly, correct and magnificent play of volumes brought together in light' which is about form rather than spatial experience and about light as steady and bright rather than fugitive or palpable. Chartres is excluded.

Similarly, I found myself dissenting from that other idea of Modernity as complete transparency – not being there, not separating inside from outside (the Farnsworth House, for example). We forget that the development of transparent architecture originated in German Expressionism with the mystical aspirations of Paul Scheerbart and Bruno Taut. Perhaps in Mies van der Rohe's Barcelona Pavilion of 1929 (now reconstructed) – in the combination of grey transparent glass, double-etched glazing with lighting between, bottle-green glass, onyx and highly polished green marble brought together in a building without any explicit function – we see not just Modernism but the manifestation of architecture as pure experience, a link between Scheerbart and the work of today's space and light artists.

Historically, the starting point for me is the late-eighteenth century, and the space and light artists are Turner and Soane. Their interest in the experiential effects of space and colour parallel contemporary experiments such as de Loutherbourg's 'Eidophusikon'. These were theatrical events in which combinations of scrims and lighting sources could magically reveal a series of spaces and scenes beyond expectation, and coloured light was used to affect mood, as it does in modern theatre. There is an affinity between these theatrical diversions and Turner's revelatory images of the interiors of Petworth.

Another of Turner's devices was the use of coloured glazes. Like lacquers, glazes have the effect of arresting focal length just short of the actual picture plane. They create an uncertainty of perception engaging to eye and brain, of a kind now exploited in complex ways by artists such as Robert Irwin and James Turrell. In Soane's work the tinted glaze is transformed into amber or red glass to infuse his interiors with colour, what he called lumière mysterieuse – most powerfully in the Mausoleum at Dulwich but also in parts of the Soane Museum. Such a use of colour profoundly affects our customary sense of reality. Le Corbusier understood this when he combined

colour and projections of coloured lighting in the chapel at La Tourette. The artist Martin Richman uses colour in this way to transform architecture.

Like the eighteenth-century picturesque landscape tradition, experiments in theatrical settings by artists such as de Loutherbourg explored and confounded spatial expectations with colour and light. This is what Soane did in his house and museum, most succinctly in the breakfast room, which influenced our [MacCormac Jamieson Prichard's] chapel at Fitzwilliam College, Cambridge; the idea of enclosure is contradicted by the luminous periphery. I also think Soane was influenced by Pompeian wall paintings, of which he collected reproductions. Arguably his architecture involves three-dimensional reconstructions which release the painted, episodic perspectives of the Pompeian interior into three dimensions.

We are witnessing comparable ventures in architecture and art today. The simple transparencies of modernism in architecture have given way to an interest in translucency, opalescence and subtly graded reflection. Luminosity of this kind is characteristic of the work of Jean Nouvel and, recently, Sir Norman Foster – in particular, the lightwell and foyer of the Sackler Galleries at the Royal Academy. Benson and Forsyth's Oratory at Grange-over-Sands created a similarly opalescent space of extraordinary tranquility.

Herzog & de Meuron's Goetz Collection Gallery in Munich uses white glass as a diffuser internally and as a device for floating the timber body of the building when seen externally. The quality of reflection at the base which takes in both people and landscape is comparable to effects in the pavillion works of the glass artist Dan Graham… These effects are meditative, and a sense of weightlessness applies as much to the solid construction as it does to the light-emitting surfaces. (There is something of this effect in the current installation Nothing Matters by John Frankland in the Royal Festival Hall.)

An unbuilt project by Herzog & de Meuron, which would have achieved an extraordinary spatial ambiguity, was the Greek Orthodox Church in Zürich. A pristine rectangular volume of glass and ceramic by day would, by night, have revealed the irregular outline of inner rooms. Internally, translucent marble panels, continuously silk-screened with icons, would have created a figurative three-dimensional art work of a highly decorative kind.

If this is architecture approaching the

condition of art, then the works of Irwin and Turrell, who have shifted their art away from the making of objects towards the experience of situations, have widened the arena of art by approaching the condition of architecture.

Turrell was trained as a psychologist and worked with Irwin and an experimental psychologist for the Art and Technology project at the Los Angeles Museum of Art in 1970. This show, involving more than 70 major artists and even more scientists and mathematicians, was a major statement of contemporary space-age Zeitgeist in which science and art were supposed to merge. The Irwin/Turrell collaboration anticipated subsequent public interest in meditative states.

The extent to which the work might be perceived as a scientific experiment prompted a statement – almost a manifesto – of phenomenal art. 'A problem may arise with this project in the minds of the art community who may regard it as non-art – as theatrical or more scientific than artistic or as being just outside the arena of art. Although it is a strong alteration as far as methods, means and intent, we believe in it as art, and yet recognise the possibility of a redefinition needed to incorporate it into the arena'. Maybe such a redefinition also requires a redefinition of architecture.

Irwin has continued to work in an extraordinary range of media on installations which intervene in architecture and landscape. One particular piece, which has interested me in relation to our project for the Science Museum, is Scrim Veil, an installation at the Mizuno Gallery, Los Angeles (1975). Here the scrim seems to set up three precise perceptual alternatives which claim the viewer according to changing light conditions. The scrim, although transparent, is a rectangular textured surface which arrests focal length. Behind the scrim the volume of the room is more or less apparent, depending upon the levels of light on its surfaces relative to the scrim. Below the scrim a rectangular void, delineated by a black steel bar and black painted lines on wall and door, may claim attention as the most definitive part of the installation. Yet within the frame there is a conflict between the virtual picture plane of the rectangle and the real perspective behind, which refuses to adhere to it.

Turrell and Irwin inherit a world of metaphysical colour and light from Mark Rothko and Yves Klein, and take it further by releasing it from the painted surface and entering into it as spatial experience. Turrell is a prolific and ceaseless investigator of the art of perception, and the

range of his work extends from the excavation of a volcano, the Roden Crater in Arizona, a gigantic astronomical re-enactment of the Pantheon, to gallery installations which mix light frequencies so as to defy spatial definition. Apertures in walls from which coloured light is emitted appear volumetric and palpable. The experience of these works, over a period of say, 20 minutes, is that the rectangle of colour perceived in a darkened space grows in intensity and appears to move out towards the viewer, Turrell has discovered that this perceptual phenomenon is true of looking at the sky through his 'sky spaces'. The sky becomes figurative like a Magritte cut-out, improbably substantial. We found this effect fortuitously in the oculus at the centre of our Cable & Wireless College, Coventry.

Amongst Turrell's earlier and more architectural works was a fluorescent light installation called Rondo at Newport Harbour Art Museum (1969). Here, back-lit false walls and floor create an evanescent haze of blue space within which the gangway traversed by visitors appears as a black abyss.

In conclusion, there are two projects in our office which are space and light experiments. At Southwark Station (for Bankside Tate) we have been working with artist Alex Beleschenko to create a reflective conical lining for the intermediate concourse from silkscreened blue glass. The glass ranges from blue at the base to virtually clear transparency at the apex. Daylight is funnelled down behind and in front to create conditions of luminosity, reflection and blueness to make a paradoxical underground experience.

For the Science Museum Wellcome Wing project we are creating an entirely blue enclosure. It may have something to do with Klein blue in the Yves Klein exhibition at the Hayward Gallery in 1995. A friend's reaction to this exhibition was a strange, vivid and lovely dream in which she found herself suspended in an infinity of blue, the atavistic experience of sea and sky. The psychological intention of the project is to create a blue radiance provoking elation and wonder, a frame of mind for approaching an exhibition of modern science in a building which we have called the Theatre of Science.

Working with Hollands Licht and Rogier van der Heiden from Amsterdam, we have modelled part of the interior at 1:5. The intention is to dislocate visually the solid one-hour fire-resistant wall with a fabric scrim in front of it to arrest focus. Using fluorescent light with reflectors and blue filters in battens, it should be possible to achieve an almost perfectly even spread of blue light which will seem

to emanate from behind the scrim. The horizontal gaps defined by the light battens, which also hold the scrim taut, seem to enhance the effect by offering an alternative prospect of blue, so narrowly framed that it is hardly possible to judge its depth.

I am aware that this venture is probably inconceivable without the work of artists such as Klein, Irwin and Turrell, but the idea of peripheral luminosity still has something to do with my old hero, Soane.

Architects' Journal, 18 Dec 1997

The Whitehouse Ruskin Collection, the largest archive of books, paintings and manuscripts belonging to, by, or relating to John Ruskin (1819-1900), was built up by the educationalist and Liberal MP John Howard Whitehouse (1873-1955). It was originally housed in a purpose-built annexe to his educational foundation, Bembridge School on the Isle of Wight. The need to provide the collection with the secure and controlled environment necessary to ensure its preservation for future generations, and the desire to foster closer links between the collection in the Isle of Wight and a parallel collection at Ruskin's former home at Brantwood on Lake Coniston, gave rise to proposals to construct a building to house the collection. The opportunity to provide improved access both to scholars and to the public was made possible by a grant from the Heritage Lottery Fund. Lancaster University, which is close to the Lake District and has a well-established programme of academic study into Ruskin and his works, offered an ideal site.

The brief called for storage facilities designed to BS5454 for the collection and allowing for 25 per cent additional space for future acquisitions, a secure reading room for eight readers for the study of archive material, a gallery for exhibiting the collection and related work, and all necessary back-up facilities.

The site chosen for the Ruskin Library was the former university bowling green, which forms an escarpment that defines the west boundary of the university and offers dramatic views to the west over Morecambe Bay up to five miles away. The main access road into the university confronts the site as it emerges from woodland, and the principal pedestrian route into Alexandra Square, which forms the heart of the 1960s campus, runs across the site. The eastern boundary is now dominated by the extension to the main university library, a commission that followed the initial concept design of the Ruskin Library but one which was developed as part of a masterplan of the site from inception.

The positioning of the building on the westerly edge of the site maximises its impact from the access road and allows it to hold the path into the campus within its geometry, acting as a symbolic gateway or propylaeum to the university. This defensive theme is reflected in the protective form of the building and by the three metre high retaining wall to the north which forms a massive base along the line of the main pedestrian route into the site.

Between a return in this implied base and a masonry element formed by the

LANCASTER UNIVERSITY LIBRARY EXTENSION: ARCHITECTS' ACCOUNT

Richard MacCormac

Architects' Journal, 18 Dec 1997

disabled ramp enclosure, a monumental staircase takes you from the main path to a raised terrace which runs the whole width of the site, mediating between the scale of the west elevation of the library extension and the Ruskin Library. Viewed from this terrace, the Ruskin Library stands on a plateau of wavy meadow grass like an island surrounded by water, a metaphor for Ruskin's Venice. This is reinforced by the bridge-like causeway which forms the principal entrance to the building, running across the grass 'lagoon' linking the terrace to the building. The materials used on the exterior – white concrete blocks with a sparkly marble aggregate and green polished precast-concrete bands – recall Ruskin's fascination with Venetian and Tuscan materials and construction, and the stainless steel bosses that define the joints between the precast concrete bands recall the visible fastenings in the marble cladding of Italian churches which Ruskin referred to as 'confessed rivets'.

From the entrance, the building appears as one church-like volume in which the treasury sits. In reality, the change in level across the site allows for a secure service access off the road at basement level where the back-up facilities and the major part of the picture archive are housed.

The island metaphor, apparent in the siting of the building, is repeated in the archive, expressed as a freestanding volume standing like a great treasure chest, sarcophagus, casket or ark, surrounded by a skirting of glass which allows views of the archive plunging into the basement below. The isolation of the archive in this way also enables the delivery of an environmental condition which meets current stringent requirements in terms of thermal and humidity stability without the need to air-condition the collection. A large window in the archive box faces the entrance. The shutters, provided for night-time protection, recall a medieval altar triptych. Symbolising Ruskin's preoccupation with Venice, the window is imprinted with an image from a Ruskin daguerreotype of the north-west portal of St Mark's.

The linear arrangement of the building meets the need for security, with the reading room remote from the entrance and only accessible through secure doors controlled by the curators. The principal route from the double-height entrance is to the first-floor galleries on each side, which are connected through the archive by a glass bridge. The linear arrangement is deliberately church-like, with the entrance, archive and reading room standing for narthex, choir and sanctuary. This is emphasised by a change in level from the entrance up to the reading room with its great west window looking towards the sea. Curatorial offices and reception are located under the galleries. A meeting room is located inside the archive accessed off the route between the galleries, at first-floor level, with a view out through the reading room to the landscape and horizon beyond.

The galleries are defined on one side by a floating lining on the external walls, split by a slot window that allows controlled views into the landscape, and on the other by a series of cabinets built into the battered walls which enclose the curatorial offices and form the parapet to the galleries. These cabinets hold lectern-like sealed and secure display cases with alcoves above for framed works. One of the cabinets forms the opening on to the glass bridge and leads through to the other gallery. At the west end of each gallery is a larger, fully glazed cabinet for the display of larger unframed works. On each side of these, views can be gained across the reading room and out to the landscape beyond. The galleries are separated acoustically from the reading room by glass screens.

The simplicity of the exterior contrasts with the richness of the interior. The use of materials reflects Ruskin's concerns with appropriateness and the values gained through craft processes. The principal structural elements, expressed in their most basic form, are exposed reinforced-concrete portal beams which span the length of the building. Rendered internal walls are limewashed with natural ochre pigment, and timber beams to the roof structure are grit-blasted and left exposed. The battered walls are finished in black pigmented render sealed with linseed oil. By contrast, elements that form panels or linings are demonstrably worked: waxed and polished Venetian plaster to the archive lining, and oak linings to the cabinets, stained and sealed with a graphite suspension. In both cases these linings are held in oak frames which, on the archive, are treated with joints expressed with polished bronze cruciform inserts. This philosophy is reflected in the design of the reading room furniture, where the primary structural elements are expressed in English oak while the secondary elements are expressed panels of dark grained walnut, in the case of the tables, and rich stained leather, in the case of the chairs.

The library extension at Lancaster University represents not only a foil to the Ruskin Archive in terms of specific/generic information, HEFCE lottery funding parameters and so on, but also the development of a number of themes and investigations that the office has been exploring over a number of years and projects.

The provision of high-quality space within HEFCE funding limits the development of a strategy for prioritising cash and effort into key areas within an otherwise well-constructed whole, proving that generous and inspirational spaces can be made on a very tight budget.

The articulation of the inhabitation of a space or shell was a theme that emerged in our projects for a new library at King's College, Cambridge and for a new chapel at Tonbridge School. At Lancaster the edges of the building, both outward- and inward-looking, are reduced in scale by the use of built-in furniture and 'lids' of oak-veneered board and painted steel, creating more intimate spaces for contemplation and study within the larger-scale white concrete spaces.

The notion of local and foreign transactions – applied elsewhere to an exploration of urban form and the comparative scale of public spaces – here is applied to the business of information transfer, the atrium being the place of person-to-person transactions, book loan, IT sales and advice, inter-library loans etc, while the reading room opens up to the wider world, metaphorically and literally symbolising both the role of the university within society and the new, non-topographic developments in learning and information technology such as the World Wide Web, distance learning, and so on.

The commission from the university, and the HEFCE funding package which underpinned this, required a site start within six months of the initial approach, imposing an onerous programme in terms of brief, concept and design development and, in the context of the imminent retirement of the librarian and the appointment of a replacement, almost impossible constraints on the university's own decision-making process, particularly with regard to the kind of library that it wanted or needed. In its wisdom, the university made an early appointment of the new librarian, and Jacqueline Whiteside and her staff provided heroic and invaluable input into the brief in general and in great detail.

As required by the university, the masterplan allows for the extension to be completed in two phases. The first phase comprises the major public spaces, the atrium, the reading room and the rare-book archive, together with half the open floorplate accommodation and all the plant, service and escape-stair provision for both phases. The next phase will consist solely of open floorplates on four storeys and a single elevation.

In the light of the current uncertainties regarding the likely nature of information and the library in the twenty-first century, the recently-published Follett Report and Lancaster's own role in exploring alternative learning technologies, distance learning and so on, it was agreed that the building should be designed to accommodate as wide a range of uses as was economically possible. In many ways this was a development of the strategies identified in the Architectural Review on library design, published by Peter Carolin and MJ Long in 1972.

The ranges to the north and south of the new internal street, extending from the existing library entrance area, would flexibly accommodate seminar/lecture rooms, staff offices, book storage, IT teaching and paper or IT-based reading, while uses having specific environmental or structural requirements (for example, archive mobile racking storage, reading room) would be accommodated at the western end of the atrium, forming the major elevation to the Ruskin Archive and the main approach to the university from the west.

The servicing strategy is integral with the spatial and structural flexibility of the building. Raised floors deliver ventilation to deep floorplates which can be subdivided internally. The raised floors allow complete flexibility in the relationship between paper-based and electronically based information. The high-level plant room is above a continuous plenum supported on a series of paired concrete portal frames. Air is distributed laterally and vertically by ducts associated with the portals. These deliver air into the raised floors. The internal street acts as a return-air plenum and as a source of daylight and controlled sunlight. During the design process there was some discussion about the effect upon daylight of placing the plant room over the street.

On balance our feeling was that most 'atria' are over-daylit, and that we would obtain a more interesting quality of light if it were forced around the edges of the plant room. The internal street is the core of the combination of existing and new buildings, making the relationship easily intelligible. The new extension brings the library to the forefront of the university campus with the triangular reading room at the apogee of the street acting as a trumpet-like declaration to the outside world.

ALVAR AALTO

Richard MacCormac

Alvar Aalto: Process & Culture, catalogue to RIBA Heinz Gallery exhibition, 1998.

'Quality for him was the ultimate product of the individual's unrepeatable and unique experience; one achieves it by descending into the depth and by progressively clarifying the secret springs of one's actions, the myths and recollections lurking in the unconscious which strongly influence consciousness and action'[1]

It is a slightly startling experience to be asked to write about Aalto, to make a conscious evaluation of the work which I have come to feel part of the databank of my architectural subconscious. But the process of recollection has made me realise that certain buildings in his oeuvre have represented for me, at different times the values in my own endeavour to progress the quantitative and the generic towards the complex, metaphorical and allusive. These buildings amongst others are the Rautatalo, Säynätsalo – and the House of Culture.

As a student of Leslie Martin's in the early 1960s the Rautatalo was an affirmation of our preoccupations and also prescient of what we had yet to find out. Here was the generic courtyard building which realised the interest in such planning which was at the core of theory in the Cambridge School at that time, and which was to develop so powerfully in the collaboration between Leslie Martin and Lionel March to establish quantitative certainties and demonstrate the high densities achievable with courts and traditional urban forms. But even at that time we had some sense of the extraordinary urban and environmental implications of the building. Here was an office building which also offered a public space, a 'Noli like' part of the city, an exemplar of mixed use, with a design centre, shops and cafes around its perimeter. Here was an atrium (the term was not yet current) with a roof which ensured the public space would have a temperate climate throughout the year and which would, later, in the quest for energy efficiency offer potential as a means of minimising fabric exposure to heat and cold whilst maximising daylight penetration. For me the intellectual fascination of the building was that the simplicity of the proposition was open to such wide interpretation.

The House of Culture, the subject of this exhibition, is also a proposition of disarming directness and intelligence. But here the effect is also visceral. From the perimeter circulation views up into the auditorium and down into the foyer beneath reveal the whole spatial flow of the building simultaneously and offers not just intellectual satisfaction, but that sense of elation and magnified awareness experienced in a Greek amphitheatre.

When I first saw the House of Culture in the early 1960s I was probably unaware of this historical resonance, nor did I see in the building the geological metaphor through which Aalto converts the most difficult of windowless building types, the auditorium, into a striated geological outcrop, an ivy-covered cliff forcing itself out of the pavement of the city.

To experience Aalto's work at that time was immediate, but to understand where he stood in relation to the modern movement was much more difficult. Most schools of architecture were dominated by a determinist interpretation of modern movement orthodoxy in which appearance was the consequence of technology and fitness for purpose. Even though Summerson had written a highly ironic essay in which he had suggested that, if this was really the case there could be no other expressive meaning in modern architecture, there were few critics or teachers who could articulate a response to that challenge.[2]

So for me the importance of Aalto and what Sandy Wilson, later, was to call 'The Other Tradition' was that he was defiantly concerned with meanings beyond function and technology while demonstrably master of both. Yet the heterogeneity of the work was difficult, quite unlike Wright in whose work at that time I also perceived intentions beyond modern movement orthodoxy, but intentions which could be understood, to some extent, in terms of traditional architectural composition and syntax. Yet Aalto has affected my work as much as Wright, but in quite a different way, not consciously, but almost unwittingly. I recognise themes, particularly those of Säynätsalo.

I find Aalto at Säynätsalo demonstrates again the conceptual clarity of the courtyard but combines within this general proposition complex allusions and architectural recollections, partly filtered through a personal and especially northern experience of the classical world. Säynätsalo is a little acropolis, sanctuary and clearing on an outcrop in the forest. This atavistic sense of the special significance of the raised place in the midst of nature, ambiguously both landscape and building, reappears at Jyväskylä University, at Otaniemi, at Seinäjoki town centre and in the Aalto Summer House. The theme has precipitated itself in many of my own projects such as Worcester College, Oxford, and the Cable & Wireless Building, Coventry.

Another characteristic of Säynätsalo, which Aalto transmuted from his experience of classical sites is its presence. It is small, but not self-effacing. The council

chamber stands forth and the windows of the stair wrapped around it, are like a continuous lidded eye, alert and on the look-out. So the building, like a temple precinct, an Italian hill town, or Aalto's early classical church projects such as Töölö achieves an anthropomorphic presence which distinguishes itself from its natural situation and declares itself.

Of course there are other wonders in Säynätsalo, the episodic fluency of the stair winding up round the tower and the mysterious timber fans supporting the roof. Aalto's work is founded in a rationality which it then transcends. It has taught us that architecture must speak and like the other arts act as a medium of revelationary personal experience and thought made universal.

1 Paul Klee: The Thinking Eye, Jurg Spiller (Lund Humphries, London 1961).
2 Five Buildings, MJP Catalogue (London 1996).

SOANE: MASTER OF LIGHT AND SPACE

Richard MacCormac

Opening talk at the John Soane exhibition at the Royal Academy, September 1999; an edited version was published in the Architects' Journal (16 September 1999).

I have been asked to talk briefly about why Sir John Soane is of such interest to architects today, but before I do so I should also say something about the reasons for mounting this great Royal Academy exhibition, which forms part of a pattern of architectural exhibitions which alternate between the contemporary (the last exhibition was of the work of Tadao Ando) and the historical. These exhibitions, with the annual lecture and Academy Forum symposia, form the academy's lively and continuing architecture programme.

While the Soane Museum, the most complete and complex collection of Soane's works, can be visited, this exhibition permits us through selection to survey the full sequence of his architectural achievement from his training and early projects to his great, late buildings and unrealised projects, focusing on the building which dominated his life for 40 years: the Bank of England. Its demolition must be the greatest act of architectural vandalism since the dissolution of the monasteries.

I speak as a practising architect rather than as an historian and I see the present interest in Soane as completely distinct from the revival of interest in classicism in the 1980s, which was intended to pitch 'modernists' against classicists. That stage-managed antipathy has died away and today we find Soane inspires a whole range of real architects, including Richard Meier, Rafael Moneo, Arata Isozaki and Tadao Ando, as well as a significant group of British architects, all of whom are working in the various idioms of the late twentieth century, rather than using Soane as a source for imitation. So the current interest in Soane and the event of this exhibition closes the door on the false opposition between history and modernity which has debased architectural debate in recent years.

Within this reconciliation we can also perceive two important intellectual shifts: the first is that for modern architects, and particularly British architects, to embrace history is also to extend the discourse beyond technology and function to acknowledge the autonomous characteristics of architecture which Soane's work so vividly declares. The second point is that a non-stylistic attitude to architectural history invites a much more penetrating and creative approach to the architecture of the past. Interpretations of Soane offer an important exemplar. Even in his own time, Soane was recognised as a radical who did not sit comfortably in the classical tradition. I see him as a maverick who re-worked classicism in his own highly unconventional way. Is this a

Richard MacCormac

From Inspired by Soane (Sir John
Soane's Museum publication, 1999).

Reflective view at the Royal Academy exhibition.

peculiarly British phenomenon in relation to European architecture, which starts with Robert Smythson, the architect of Hardwick Hall in the late-sixteenth century; Hawksmoor in the late-seventeenth century; and Soane and Greek Thompson in the nineteenth century?

Soane's architecture is also of such complexity that if another Soane enthusiast was speaking instead of me this evening, you could be sure that the interpretations would be quite different from mine. So why this interest?

The most obvious characteristics for architects of my generation are the spatial fluency, vistas and axes which skewer their way through the Lincoln's Inn house and museum, amazingly anticipating the early work of Frank Lloyd Wright, 100 years later. These long views run through the edges as well as the centres of sequences of rooms – penetrating both horizontally and vertically and creating rooms within rooms, an idea which invites the reconstructions within the Academy rooms which give this exhibition its special quality.

The energy lies in the periphery, and here I think is the most interesting phenomenon. In the famous breakfast room in Lincoln's Inn, the north and south walls have been moved away from the boundaries defined by the central saucer dome. Light – coloured light – and space have taken the place of enclosure with

the most uncanny effect. So space and light are the media of Soane's work, as in the work of Soane's colleague and contemporary Turner. This is not the simple transparency of Modernism, but something altogether more mysterious and more ambiguous, something which psychologically challenges our conventional expectations and experiences of space, just as does the work of artists such as Anish Kapoor and James Turrell today. Soane is a space and light architect whose capacity for invention seems inexhaustible. This exhibition should open up our understanding and widen our interpretation of his architecture.

The plan of the Soane Museum, seemingly anticipating the early work of Frank Lloyd Wright, consists of long vistas and inter-penetrating axes, alternating broad and narrow spaces and an underlying classical discipline to achieve effects of spatial fluency which transcend their conventional precedents.

Soane can be seen as part of a maverick tradition in British architecture founded on ignorant or deliberate misinterpretations of history which give the architecture its inventiveness. Such a tradition could be said to start with the Elizabethan Robert Smythson, architect of Longleat and Hardwick Hall. A hundred years later Vanbrugh, who was admired by Soane, and Hawksmoor developed a kind of English mannerism which gained its strength, like the mannerism of Michelangelo and Giulio Romano from contradictions. A hundred years later Soane makes his own idiosyncratic and radical reassessment of his classical inheritance. Each of these architects is at odds with the scholarly conventions represented by Palladianism and it is the creative shift out of the rules which is the key to their vigour.

So I make no apologies, as an architect, for approaching Soane's work in an unscholarly and unhistorical way and interpreting – or perhaps misinterpreting – the interiors of Soane's house and museum from a late-twentieth century point of view. The method will be to make a partial tour of the house and museum, selecting situations, in those highly complex interiors, which interest me in relation to my current preoccupations as a designer.

However, before undertaking descriptions of the architecture it may be important to consider a part of Soane's collection, the coloured reconstructions of the frescoes of rooms in the Villa Negroni discovered outside Rome in the eighteenth century. They consist of episodic architectural perspectives which suggest a series of highly complex spaces beyond the enclosure of the room itself, also the theme of Pompeian wall paintings with which Soane would have been familiar. An interpretation of the architecture of the house and museum is that it translates these painted illusions into three dimensions, sometimes into real space, sometimes into the virtual space of mirrors, to create a dissolution of obvious boundaries which is worked and reworked throughout the interior.

The Soanes lived in number 12 Lincoln's Inn Fields before moving into number 13 and the Breakfast Room at the back of number 12 is the first subject of my analysis. Here the spandrels of the

cruciform vault are painted as a trellis through which a painted sky appears, a sky which becomes real in the various skylights of the museum.

A curious but important feature of the room is the deep arch on the west side, a slot of space made infinitely long by mirrors at each end. This dynamic linearity across the edge of a room, recurs throughout the house in increasingly intricate ways. It destabilises conventional expectations of enclosure by breaking it up into layers and creating a virtual world beyond. These ideas come to spectacular resolution in the dome of the museum. The slot of space on the west side of the number 12 Breakfast Room has been translated into narrow galleries on each side which slide past the dome itself. The spaces penetrate vertically through skylights and downwards through gratings making the floor feel bridge-like. Coloured glass creates moody changes of light, which Soane called 'lumière mystérieuse' casting a strange glow upon the antique fragments; Goethe had written that marble can only be saved from lifelessness by the magic wand of lighting.

The dome stands upon its own columns and pendentives, a room within a room, a space within a larger one. The scene beyond the dome is difficult to analyse or account for; it is a colonnade which seems like a thicket of columns and statues only partially penetrable visually, but offering episodic views of different depths through the sides, the centre and up into the students Drawing Offices above. Again, like the Dome, this is a building within a building, quite separate from the walls on each side and roof above. But, unlike the dome, it is a partial inversion of the idea of a habitable central space with furnished alcoves around it. The habitable space, apart from the axis through the middle, has been forced out to the edges. This effect of displacement is like that of a choir in a Gothic cathedral, a building within a building, and of Richard Serra's 1992 installation in the Tate Gallery, Weight and Measure, where massive forged blocks possessed the space.

An analysis of the long section through the museum, suggests a further reading, the three principal spaces, the Dome, the students Drawing Office and the Picture Room are separated and articulated by top-lit slots. It is as though Soane's architecture displaces physical enclosure with energised peripheries of space and light. One thinks of Soane's great colleague, Turner, who achieves something similar in his paintings of Petworth's interiors.

Yet another spatial interpretation is to

233

Surface, May 2001

trace the vistas and axes which thread through the various parts of the house in parallel with the uncertainty of virtual vistas created by mirrors, a looking-glass world which does not exist. One might see the Picture Room as the inverse of this riddle, the substantial wall of pictures folding away to reveal an actual but unexpected space beyond, luminously top-lit.

A further variant of the theme of peripheral dissolution is the form of the Library. The room is painted in Pompeian red, the colour of the Villa Negroni reconstruction, probably based on a fragment of wall plaster brought back from Italy and this room seems to refer directly to the convention of Roman wall painting.

The unsupported pendant arches each side can be said to define a perimeter to the space which the actual 'walls' stand outside. But the walls are not walls but bookcases, which stand as screens of furniture, disengaged from the ceiling by mirrors. The arches and pendants are reflected in the mirrors, creating Pompeian perspectives beyond the confines of the room. The bookcases themselves continue through mirrored reflections at each end. Even the plane of the mirror over the fireplace is made to continue through one inch wide vertical strips of mirror on each side.

The pendant arches are themselves double with a hollow centre, containing little arched niches for antique fragments; objects within objects. The displayed model of the Soane family tomb is made up as an aedicule within another – a theme which is reiterated throughout.

In the adjoining Dining Room, paintings, one of which is Soane's portrait, are paradoxically hung in front of mirrors, isolated and suspended in infinitely reflected space. Exits from the room which lead back into the Museum are extremely narrow and are each part of long axes which thread their way through different episodes until terminated at the north boundary of the Museum.

The Breakfast Room in number 13 is arguably the most exquisite, most characteristic and most influential of Soane's surviving works, reminding us of the irreplaceable loss of comparable – but much larger – domed spaces in the Bank of England.

Here the trick has affinities with the Dome in the Museum, with the spaces in the side aisles sliding up to invisible rooflights above the Dome on each side; a room within a room. However, the quality in the Breakfast Room is quite distinct because of the shallowness of the dome, and the sensation of stretched suspended surface weightless upon

mirrored supports. The architecture of the reconstruction of the Roman Villa Negroni has become part of the architecture of the room.

The north and south walls have been displaced by an infusion of the strangest amber light – Soane's lumière mystérieuse, comparable with the otherworldly feel of the mausoleum at Dulwich, complemented by convex mirrors of various scales which seem to reveal other worlds.

Having been educated into the Modern Movement what is curious in retrospect is that, before full-colour printing was cheap enough to be ubiquitous, we were brought up on books which suggested that modern architecture was black and white. Philip Johnson's book on Mies van der Rohe included the Barcelona Pavilion, a building that made an immense impression on me – it is a masterwork. But I had no idea that it was polychromatic. It is a pure work of art; it does not have a function. When I visited the re-creation, I was surprised at how colourful it was.

So there is much more colour in the Modern Movement than we supposed and I would have been really interested in what people like Hannes Meyer of the Bauhaus would have thought about colour. One aspect of the Modern Movement that is still true of a lot of British high-tech architecture is that it is talking about itself; it is expressing construction, and colour is used only to clarify the tectonic quality of the architecture. That is why we all wanted to believe that the Parthenon was white and we were upset to find that it was originally very gaudy. Colour is about something else; it is allusive. If the term post-modern had not been wrecked, it would be useful and colour might be thought of as a post-modern characteristic, in the sense that colour is saying something beyond describing the work of architecture itself.

I am interested in the idea that architecture should have a subject matter beyond itself. We set up two colloquia at the Royal Academy Forum called The Return of the Subject, held in July 2000. At the first one were a number of artists including Anish Kapoor, Charles Jencks and David Ward, at the second were four contributors: the sculptor Antony Gormley, the choreographer Siobhan Davies, Christopher Le Brun, Professor of Painting at the Royal Academy and Sandy Wilson, the architect of the British Library. This is not really to do with colour, but with the idea that colour may be part of a movement to make the subject of art and architecture more allusive.

How did I get involved with colour? I once reviewed a building by John Outram – a company headquarters – and his use of colour really surprised me. I had been brought up in the school where you declared materials as an expression of structure and utility. The title of Hitchcock's book on Frank Lloyd Wright had always seemed to be very important – In the Nature of Materials. Oddly enough, FLW was rather rascally about the way he used materials, which was unlike the European Modern

Movement. It seemed to me that the way John Outram used materials, metaphorically speaking, is that he 'cooked' the materials and transformed them into something else. You take the raw ingredients, what my office calls 'Scandiwegian', like salad really, and then cooking transmutes the materials into something else.

One contrast in my work is that the Chapel at Fitzwilliam College declares its uncooked materials: polished concrete, white render, brickwork and oak, and then the Ruskin Library, which in some ways is son of the chapel, is pretty highly cooked. Jocasta [Innes] had an influence on me personally to become more alert to colour. She has perfect colour pitch which is like having perfect musical pitch; she is quite uncanny, and does very surprising things with colour and is good at talking about it. So the Ruskin Library is highly cooked, although the outside is not.

I go through enthusiasms for certain designers, architects, artists or whatever, about whom I feel passionate for a period of time. When I was working on the Ruskin Library, I was extremely interested in William Burges and those huge pieces of furniture that he designed like buildings with a Gothic roof and windows, unbelievably inventive and intensely constructed. They influenced me in three ways: first, because they are highly polychromatic; second, because they are mysterious objects full of little secret spaces; and, third, because they are ambiguous as to whether they are pieces of furniture or small buildings. So the Ruskin Library has a 'William Burges' small building inside: the archive itself is constructed from panels of red Venetian plaster set in oak frames with bronze fittings – quite Victorian. It is made like a piece of furniture but three storeys high. I have always wanted to make a three-dimensional advent calendar and, finally, I did it with shutters which open views out of the archive.

The use of colour here is partly allusive. This is a building that has a subject – Ruskin and Venice – and the building is conceived as an island, isolated from the university. It sits there in isolation symbolising Ruskin, the isolated individual. The island is attached to the university by a causeway that passes through a special wavy grass symbolising the Venice lagoon. Inside, the metaphor is repeated; the archive at the centre of the space is surrounded by a glass and slate floor representing water. We had great fun in the office thinking up new metaphors: the corpus of Ruskin's work, Ruskin's body, Ruskin's reliquary, an ark, a treasure chest and so forth. So the red is to do with

Ruskin, Turner and the Pre-Raphaelites exhibition, Tate Britain (2000) – the galleries are open at the corners, allowing glimpses of several spaces at once.

Venice and the deep green bands on the outside are to do with a Ruskin water-colour of a Florentine church faced with green and white marble; he uses a beautiful bottle green tint.

On each side of the archive, there are two alleyways separating it from the surrounding ancillary accommodation; above that there are two exhibition galleries. A glass bridge goes through a tunnel inside the archive connecting the galleries on each side. Contrasting with the Venetian red of the archive, we wanted the surrounding walls to be black. The black render kept drying to grey and someone suggested that we paint it with linseed oil that has a kind of furniture polish smell. It is a smelly building as well as a colourful one. The oil produced a rich black and also looks slightly grotty, slightly distressed, like some Venetian alleyway beside a canal. The staircases come down from the side galleries and the steps continue below the glass floor as though going down into the water below the *aqua alta*. So the game with colour is a story-telling one and that was important because Ruskin keeps saying in The Lamp of Memory that architecture must be 'historical' and the way that I was able to come to terms with that idea was with the notion that architecture has a subject – in this case Ruskin and Venice – and that the historical aspect is fulfilled through metaphor and allusion.

The internal walls to the reading room were finished with a lime render with an ochre lime wash. Jocasta belongs to the Lime Forum, a group of people who meet and talk about lime. Apart from the fact that I liked it, the choice of colour was inspired by a trip to Potsdam on a grim North German winter's evening. We saw the Baroque palace Sanssouci. A great deal of European, seventeenth- and eighteenth-century architecture is finished in lime render with lime washes, in this case an ochre lime wash. On that very dull evening, it was almost as though the ochre wash had absorbed sunlight during the day and was giving it back again at night. In fact, it was giving a terrific amount of reflection from what little light there was around, so much more vivid and resonant than a coat of conventional opaque paint. Strangely, the contractor found it very difficult to come up with a white lime render. I made them achieve white, but then I decided that a mix I had refused before, which used a pink sand, was better; it was slightly dirtier, white was too clean. Again this was like cooking, experimenting with the ingredients.

Other finishes for the inside of the library included panels of oak-veneered ply stained a very dark green and then coated with a graphite varnish – an invention of mine. Mixing graphite with varnish gives an extraordinary effect, a transparency, a translucency, while at the same time, it is very dark and lustrous. The primary concrete structure remains unfinished, uncooked, in a raw state, and the primary beams in the roof are grit-blasted, perhaps referring to eighth-century Italian church interiors. The framing to the archive is also uncooked in contrast to the red plaster of the infill.

This project led to an exhibition at Tate Britain that Jocasta and I did with Dutch lighting group Hollands Licht. We had never done an exhibition before. The commission came through Robert Hewison who is a trustee of the Ruskin building, a Ruskin scholar, and one of the two curators for the Ruskin, Turner and Pre-Raphaelite exhibition. We decided to see if there was a way of making the colours of the galleries enter into a dialogue with the subject matter chosen by the curators, the themes that they were trying to get across, as well as making the colours work together as contrasts with each other to create a dramatic narrative of colour and space. The centre of the space contained mostly Ruskin's own small drawings and paintings on paper, illuminated at 50 lux due to conservation requirements. Here, we used a kind of graphite paint that Jocasta calls a metallic varnish over dark grey in response to the largely monochromatic work. Around this dark and lustrous centre was a series of galleries. Because the roof has very strong diagonals, we designed the galleries so that they were open at the corners, something that had not been done before. If you stood at these interstitial corner places, you could always see several galleries at once, which enhanced the polychromatic experience.

The first gallery was conceived as a black space. We found a totally non-reflective black paint. Putting a light meter against it, there was virtually no reading at all. This was the background for two absolutely marvellous pictures: Millais' Christ in the Workshop of his Father and Turner's Storm at Sea. We 'barn-doored' them, and lit them at about 180 lux, so only the works were lit, not the walls. The effect was dramatic. The next room was about Ruskin's childhood. For this, we found a nursery yellow which would have also been a fashionable yellow at the time of his childhood, the same yellow, although slightly less intense, as in Soane's Drawing Room at 13 Lincoln's Inn Fields. So the colour had a double significance, deliberately childish, a happy, innocent colour and also a popular Regency colour. It felt right and was right in relation to the pictures on show.

The next room was Turner, including his 'Slavers' from the Yale Center for British Art. We chose a colour that we knew Turner had wanted his pictures to be against, but which he has subsequently been denied, a Pompeian red. We then did something quite risky: we threw some red light around the top of the room but it was strong enough to make the floor quite pink. The next room was Gothic with beautiful pen-and-ink Ruskin drawings in extraordinary detail. We made the room very silvery and the silvery grey colour graded upwards into a sky blue using blue-filtered spots, as though you were standing in the open air, quite Caspar David Friedrich, very ethereal. A theme of colour contrast had been set up in the series of galleries, going from black, to yellow, deep red, pale grey blue.

The next room contained Ruskin's own collections of Renaissance and nineteenth-century paintings. We did this in ochre and threw a russety red light across the top. We realised when we were doing this exhibition that the trick, that is quite extravagant in terms of lighting equipment, is to separate lighting the pictures from lighting the walls. Because the space in Tate Britain is six metres high and hardly any pictures were hung above two to two-and-a-half metres, there were three-and-a-half to four metres of free wall to be washed with coloured light above the pictures. We set the Pre-Raphaelites against a mauve colour and where the mauve went into shadow, we reanimated it with blue light. That was very beautiful and responsive to the colours of the Pre-Raphaelites.

In the gallery opposite the Turner red, we originally chose a deep purple but, quite late in the day, we decided to go for what Jocasta calls an antique white, a 'dirty-white'. We matched this as exactly as we could to the whites used by Whistler and Leighton; Leighton's women in white and the whites and greys of Whistler, a very different kind of art to the Pre-Raphaelites. What was quite interesting was that the white took on a startlingly fresh character in the context of all the other colours.

For the penultimate room, representing Ruskin's decline into madness, we produced a deep, deep purple as a background for his quite disturbing, little mad drawings of the sky around Cumbria. Ruskin kept a meteorological record that claimed that the world was getting darker and darker, as he was getting madder and madder. It actually was

getting darker because of the pollution of coal fires and chimneys of the industrial north.

On the strength of this exhibition, we have been commissioned to design Surrealism: Desire Unbound, an exhibition at Tate Modern in October for which we have been developing an equivalent narrative of colour and light. The endeavour is to respond to the circuit of themes created by the curators. Again, we are working with the Dutch lighting designer's team, a really interesting group of people with a technically sophisticated studio in Amsterdam. They can give you just about anything you want in terms of coloured light. Mockups of the galleries have been created at 1:10, very simple, just three walls and a ceiling in foamboard and then we put 1:10 images on the walls to see what can be achieved with the distinction between lighting the pictures and the walls. The models give you a certain amount of security so that you have a pretty good idea of the real installation. It is not perfect but it gets you quite a long way, otherwise it is pretty scary. Again we aim to create a rhythm of contrasts. The traditional way of doing exhibitions says that the environment should be neutral. Our argument is that the environment should be in dialogue with the works, involved in an interpretive role. This is more demanding for everybody.

At Southwark Underground station, which is the station for Tate Modern, we took a course that was different from other architects. Our station is not a declaration of construction; it is a narrative achieved with non-structural linings. This is about artifice – theatre. Here, we created a second skin; there are good reasons for doing that in the British construction industry because it is difficult to achieve quality in the finishing of the primary structure. Whereas stations such as Ian Ritchie's and Michael Hopkins' express going down into the ground into great concrete caverns, which I think is great, ours is a paradoxical station where you still feel you are under a sky, even at the lowest level – deliberately contradictory.

The blue glass wall at intermediate level is a complete piece of artifice. Working with artist Alexander Beleschenko, there was no question it had to be blue but I cannot tell you why. It reflects daylight. When seen obliquely, it is highly reflective and, at the same time, very dark, But when it is seen straight on, when you are coming up the escalator, it is entirely different and goes transparent. There is something else happening here: daylight is falling down the back of the wall and the 630 triangular glass panels have millions of

tiny fragments of glass fused on the back which are acting prismatically, bringing light into the surface of the glass itself so that the glass actually glows.

This theatrical idea of architecture may have something to do with Schinkel's stage sets for The Magic Flute that I saw in Berlin in one of the best opera performances I have ever seen, incredibly good. Schinkel's cyclorama is a dark sky with little holes representing the stars. The Queen of the Night is lowered down and sings suspended before it. When we made our competitive submission for the Wellcome Wing at the Science Museum we titled it 'The Theatre of Science'.

At the west end is a huge deep blue window. Why did we choose blue? Perhaps it represents infinity and uncertainty, even the sublime. Richard Gregory, the perceptual psychologist, told me that he thought blue may have been the first colour that we identified in our evolution. What we found was that blue is such a limited part of the spectrum that it has some extraordinary properties; it cuts out a lot of light, which is a very good first move if you want to make a window that can reduce light levels from say 70,000 lux on a July afternoon down to museum and gallery standards of around 50 lux.

Blue gets you quite a long way but it still left us in a state of permanent anxiety as to how to get the rest of the way. It was an absolute cliffhanger. We tried lots of things. Eventually we cracked it with a combination of interpane solar louvres and a 40 per cent perforated metal screen on the outside. What was really unexpected was that the blue window does not cast much blue. I am not quite sure why that is. What you do see, of course, are blue reflections in other parts of the museum. Chris Wilkinson designed the exhibition that leads into the Wellcome Wing and he had the idea of the orange-lit threshold that works well.

We discovered something about the way the eye works very much at the last moment. It was quite alarming in some ways. When we were developing the side screens, again with the Dutch lighting designers, we mocked these up at 1:5 in their studios in Amsterdam and gradually developed the idea of a scrim stretched between battens. The biggest panels of scrim are 7.5 by 5 metres and they are very taut. Then there are specially designed reflectors with blue filters which light the walls; the scrim is not lit at all. The light emission of the whole system is only about 15 lux but, as we are very blue sensitive, it looks quite bright. The level is so low that if you throw a poly-

chromatic image on to the scrim, it is virtually perfect except that the shadows are slightly blue.

We discovered another very interesting thing in the last test we did in Architen's warehouse in the Mendips. As I went down on the train to Bristol, prayed that there was not going to be some new surprise with this system and, there was a surprise, an acceptable one, although initially alarming. In this big warehouse space was a great blue screen rather like a James Turrell. Two exhibitions at the Hayward had influenced me: the Yves Klein exhibition – Klein blue and so on, and the Turrell exhibition with his dramatic light installations.

Looking at this great blue screen, we found that the blue died away over a period of 20 minutes until it was washed out to a silvery grey. Someone then put a spot on an imagined exhibit at about 200 lux. We looked at the spotlit object for a few seconds and looked back at the blue. It had come back. The eye adjusts to get rid of the predominant colour and then, as soon as you look at normal light, particularly very bright white light, it is refreshed. So something very curious happens when walking through the Wellcome Wing. If you go up to one of the brightest areas, where the restaurant is, and you look back, you find that the blue is intensified.

The other characteristic of the interior is that all the linings are diaphanous. We specified a very economic industrial lining to the underneath of the exhibition floors that forms a walking surface for servicing within the space of the two-metre deep trusses. So you can see the structure as an exhibit through the lining. Part of the inspiration for the Wellcome Wing came while talking to Steve Bedford, who does our computer images for competitions. I looked at his screen that was blue and thought, why don't we do a blue building? In contrast to the Making of the Modern World exhibition, where the exhibits are physical objects to do with force, steam engines, aeroplanes, rockets, many exhibits in the Wellcome Wing are not physical objects but light emitting, mostly with screens conveying information. So the interior of the whole building is dematerialised; all the surfaces either emit light or are reflective.

What one does after doing blue? I don't know.

Richard MacCormac

Columns, newsletter of the
Friends of Christ Church Spitalfields,
Summer 2001

Walking past Christ Church, as I have done daily for many years, has not made Hawksmoor's masterwork familiar to me. Its great architectural gestures retain their strange potency and continue to astonish and invite my curiosity. To suddenly be faced with the vast unadorned white flank, with its deeply cut round windows above the double arches of the aisle, blocking the south end of Wilkes Street is so surprising that you might be in Rome or in the Rimini of Alberti's Tempio Malatestiano.

Of Hawksmoor's London churches Christ Church is the only one to command a long axial vista. Turning into Brushfield Street from Bishopsgate you are confronted by an almost overwhelming anthropomorphic presence, and it is interesting to imagine how even more savage this confrontation might have been had the church been built without the portico as originally intended. As it is, the Serlian motif of the portico dominates the West front, and the belfry arch with entablature on each side and tripartite composition above reiterates the portico's great thematic idea.

The portico can also be read as an extension of the volume of the nave out beyond the West front. With the plinths which extend out on each side of the steps and the pilaster-like projections of the north and south flank walls, a powerful sense of the longitudinal rather than centralised character of the design is apparent. It also becomes evident that this is not an architecture made up of separate elements added to one another, porch, spire, chancel, but a composition of visibly interlocking masses. Seen from the west the shoulders of the tower form a massive cross axial plane of masonry rising from the plinth to intersect the longitudinal connection between portico and nave. The effect is amplified by the huge concavities to the north and south of the belfry which deliver a sense of the structure of the tower piercing up through the volume of the building. And this is exactly what happens internally where the masonry core of the tower rising from the entrance is hollowed out at each level to form vestibule, vestry room, and then ringing chamber and belfry emerging above the roof.

Externally, the rising stages of the tower elaborate and resolve the cross axial theme. The recessed core of the tower emerges above the shoulders as a square base for the spire, which in turn consists of two intersecting pyramidal obelisks topped by a gilded globe, bringing a final resolution to the tremendous forces below.

The interior of Christ Church may not as readily declare the passionate complexity which characterises the exterior but there are equivalent compositional and spatial themes. The seven bays of the nave are intersected by a transept consisting of three bays marked out by clustered columns and piers and above by three coffered barrel vaults on each side. The first and last bays are set beyond the main volume of the nave by screens each consisting of four Corinthian columns supporting entablatures which extend out from the aisles. At the west end this arrangement provides for galleries and frames the organ. At the east end it fulfils the liturgical role of separating the chancel. But Hawksmoor's architectural intentions were also to create spaces within spaces and to use the Corinthian columns and their entablatures to give the volume of the nave a sense of equivalent containment on all sides and to mediate between the nave and the lesser scales of sanctuary and vestibule.

Hawkmoor's first proposed site for the church was at the north end of Brick Lane where it would have been at the periphery of eighteenth century Spitalfields. On its present site the church stands as a focus for the extraordinarily mixed community of co-existing interests, ranging from the wealth of the City to the poverty beyond Brick Lane and from Whitechapel to Bethnal Green Road. The restoration of Christ Church, its role as place of worship, its increasing use as a venue for music and cultural activity and its architectural presence make this strange masterwork a fantastic symbol for the regenerative energy and creativity around it.

HOW MUCH DOES BEAUTY COST? AN ARCHITECT'S VIEW

Richard MacCormac

Royal Academy Forum debate,
RA Magazine, Summer 2005

Architecture lies in an uncomfortable position between two areas of understanding. On one side stand reason and ways of evaluating and measuring objectively, that come from the Enlightenment and the rise of science, commerce and industrialisation. On the other are cultural values like subjectivity, humanism and aesthetics.

Architectural education suggests that architecture is part of a great cultural venture. But, although the commercial world occasionally builds architectural icons, most developers want to maximise the profitability of their buildings and may see aesthetic issues as conflicting with this priority. As a student I was advised, perhaps facetiously, 'Whatever you do, don't use the word beauty with an English client; you'll get fired'. In response, British architecture produced the 'high-tech' movement, a wonderful architecture that managed to elide this duality by raising rational construction to an aesthetic proposition, but at the price of a deliberately limited field of reference.

Another approach is to accept that architecture exists in relation to this unstable duality between these two sets of criteria.

The side of reason has a powerful philosophical background in the belief that knowledge, science and technology determine human destiny. It is embedded in the origins of modern architecture. The guiding ideas of the Bauhaus, including form following function and the need to make the building process more efficient, have a counterpart in its contemporary logical positivist circle in Vienna (although when Ludwig Wittgenstein spent years designing a house for his sister, his attempt to find entirely rational connections between architecture and philosophy ultimately failed).

What of the cultural side and its criteria? The tendency in modern societies, such as ours, is to find values that can be quantified reassuring. But when we seek to make everything accountable in this way, subjective values like aesthetics and beauty appear unmanageable and dangerous – precisely because they cannot be quantified.

Clients are often interested in these values, and if they are to be developed it is essential for clients to have direct contact with their architect. But – especially in those complex buildings where there is a split between the end users and the project managers – it is difficult to have that vital contact. A process called 'value engineering' often intervenes and imposes measures of financial value over everything else. The constitution of the BBC project ensures that the cultural and quantifiable are reconciled.

In our design for the senior common room at St John's College, Oxford, we had a very strong, confident relationship of mutual exchange with the college fellows. Our discussions identified how valuable the medieval garden is to the college, so we deliberately created an interplay between the garden and the room where the college's governing body meets – to reflect this relationship in the design. Various devices – the edge of the floor, the deep balustrade, the glass wall and external shutters – each define the limits of the room in different ways, and the garden might seem to penetrate into it between any of them. The shutters make these possibilities explicit. In the morning they are closed to protect the room from the sun; as the sun moves they open outwards to become fins, which (in the sort of trick that Frank Lloyd Wright understood well) seem to draw you from the room into the garden. Yet despite the close relationship between inside and outside, the room barely touches the garden; it is cantilevered over it, suggesting that the relationship is intangible rather than physical. This relationship and the effects of the design would be very hard to quantify.

The idea of architecture as an art that can be beautiful has preoccupied me for over twenty years. But creating that kind of architecture is only possible for a client who really understands the aspiration. Otherwise the construction industry is like the NHS, full of managers who are disengaged from the final product, and just manage risk through the process. Rudimentary measurement prevails over qualitative value.

However, it seems that this position is now being subverted by verifiable economic trends. As Labour peer Lord Evans, chairman of Faber & Faber, suggested in a New Statesman lecture in 2001, the creative industries – including art, architecture, design, music, broadcasting and film – now employ more people than all the traditional industries of shipbuilding, steel, car manufacturing and textiles put together. Politicians and accountants may find this hard to measure because the output is intangible, but it constitutes 6-7 per cent of GDP – 12 per cent in London – and it is growing at 16 per cent annually. This affirms that culture is integral to our economy, as well as our society – it adds value rather than cost.

Buildings and Projects

Buildings and projects

1971-74 Riverhead, Driffield, East Yorkshire
Granary conversion into 22 flats
European Architectural Heritage Award 1975

1971-74 Two Houses, Langton Way, Blackheath
with Peter Bell & Partners
RIBA Regional Commendation 1976

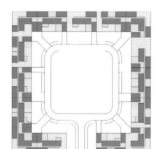

1972 Huddersfield Building Society
Housing competition entry

1972-75 Westoning Manor, MacIntyre School, Bedfordshire
10 houses and swimming pool
RIBA regional commendation 1976

1973 Woughton Green, Milton Keynes
8 houses (unbuilt)

1974-77 Chapter House, Coffee Hall, Milton Keynes
89 flats for short-term rent by single people
RIBA Regional commendation 1978

1974 Duffryn, Newport, Wales
957 houses and flats
Civic Trust commendation 1980

1974 Robinson College, Cambridge
Competition entry

1975-78 Great Linford 12, France Furlong, Milton Keynes
83 flats and houses

1977-78 Oakwood 23, Warrington
348 houses and flats

1979-86 Faculty of Arts, Bristol University

1979-83 Forgeside, Cwmbran, Wales
59 flats

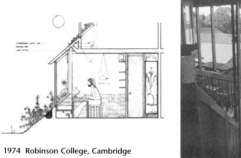

1979-81 Osborne Place, Carshalton Road, Sutton, Surrey
19 private houses and flats

1980-82 Tranlands Brigg, Heelands 5, Milton Keynes
118 houses

1980-83 Sainsbury Building, Worcester College, Oxford
30 study bedrooms
Civic Trust Award 1984

1981-84 Cottesford Crescent, Great Linford 16, Milton Keynes
13 luxury houses

1981 Spitalfields Workspace, Heneage Street, London E1
MJP office refurbishment

1982 Stoke House, Stoke Poges, Bucks
Domestic extension (demolished)

1982 Bradwell Village, Milton Keynes
31 houses

1982-84 Great Holm 7, Milton Keynes
52 houses

1982-87 Shadwell Basin, London E1
217 flats and houses
Civic Trust commendation 1989

1983 Lavender Dock, Rotherhithe, London SE16
Masterplan for 230 houses and flats

1983-86 New Court, Fitzwilliam College, Cambridge
85 student rooms

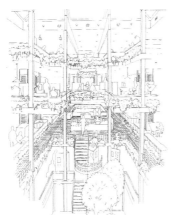

1984 St John Street, Clerkenwell, London
Unbuilt workshops/retail/office scheme

1984-85 Willen Park 1, Milton Keynes
48 houses

1984 Niccol Centre, Cirencester
Arts/community centre/theatre in a converted brewery warehouse
Civic Trust Award 1986

1984-89 Council Offices and Museum, Havant, Hants

1984-86 Trinity Court, Croydon
24 sheltered homes for the elderly
Civic Trust Commendation 1989

1985 Bradwell Common, Milton Keynes
26 houses

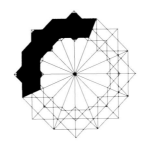

1985 Hyde Park Gate, London SW7
Apartment building (unbuilt)

1986-90 Blue Boar Court, Trinity College, Cambridge
62 study bedrooms and lecture theatre
RIBA Regional Award 1992

1986-87 Spitalfields Market Development, London E1
Masterplan (unexecuted)

1986-90 Vining Street, Brixton, London SW9
75 affordable flats for single people
Civic Trust Award 1991
Housing Design Award 1991

1987 Paternoster Square, London EC4
Masterplan competition entry

1987-89 IT Building, Queen Mary University of London, E1
Open-plan ICT teaching laboratory
RIBA regional Award 1991

1987-90 Shenley Church End, Milton Keynes
50 houses

1988 Brunswick Wharf, London
Urban design study for 1,000 apartments and mixed-use facilities

1988 Library, King's College, Cambridge
(unbuilt)

1988 Petershill, London EC4
Urban design competition entry

1988-90 Hatton House, Queen Mary University of London, E1
63 study bedrooms
Civic Trust commendation 1991

1988-90 Bolton Court, Croydon
19 sheltered homes for the elderly
Civic Trust commendation 1994

1988-89 St Leger Court, Great Linford 30, Milton Keynes
38 houses and flats

1988 Tonbridge School Chapel, Kent
Competition-winning scheme (unbuilt)

1989-95 Burrell's Field, Trinity College, Cambridge
80 study bedrooms and communal facilities
Civic Trust Award 1997
RIBA Regional Award 1997
Brick Award 1996

1989-91 Fitzwilliam College Chapel, Cambridge
136-seat chapel and crypt

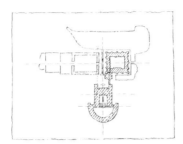

1989 Herstmonceux Castle, Sussex
Feasibility study

1989-92 Bowra Building, Wadham College, Oxford
85 study bedrooms and communal facilities
RIBA Regional Award 1993

1990-91 Great Common Farm, Cambridgeshire
Density studies

1990-93 Cable & Wireless Training College, Warwickshire
Telecommunications college with teaching rooms, residences, library and leisure pavilion
Civic Trust Award 1992
RIBA Award 1994
RFAC/Sunday Times Building of the Year Award 1994

1990-93 Garden Quadrangle, St John's College, Oxford
44 study bedrooms, 200-seat auditorium and 125-seat dining room
Public art consultant: Modus Operandi
Artists: Alex Beleschenko, Wendy Ramshaw, Fleur Kelly
Structural engineer: Sam Price (Price & Myers)
Civic Trust Award 1995
RIBA Regional Award 1995

1990 Kings Cross, London
Housing masterplan (unbuilt)

1990-92 Maynard and Varey Houses, Queen Mary University London, E1
Two buildings with 200 study bedrooms

1990-91 Strathleven/Mauleverer Roads, Brixton, London SW2
42 houses and 6-bed care in the community home

1990-93 Wychfield Site, Trinity Hall, Cambridge
54 study bedrooms

1991-99 Southwark Underground Station, Jubilee Line, London SE1
RIBA Regional Award 2000
Civic Trust Urban Design Award 2000
Artist: Alex Beleschenko
Structural engineer: AKT, YRM/Anthony Hunt

1991-98 Over-Station office, Southwark Underground Station, London SE1
(unbuilt)

1991-93 Chapman, Chesney, Lodge and Selincourt Houses, Queen Mary University of London
94 study bedrooms in four buildings

1992 Kildoran Road, Brixton, London SW2
5 houses

1992-93 Myddelton Street Hostel, London School of Economics, London EC1
140 study-bedrooms, common rooms and conference suite

1992-97 Ruskin Library, Lancaster University
Passively-conditioned archive
Artist: Alex Beleschenko
RIBA Regional Award 1999
Civic Trust Award 1999
RFAC/BSkyB Award 1998
Lancaster Design Award 1998
Millennium Products Status 1999

1992-93 Sandmere Road, Lambeth, London SW4
14 flats and health centre

1992-94 Wood Green Community Mental Health Centre, London N22

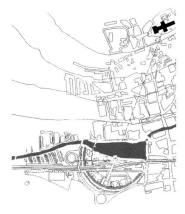

1993 Lincoln University masterplan
Competition entry

1993-96 Meadowbank Club, Twickenham
Sports and leisure club
RIBA Regional Award 1998
Civic Trust Award 1998

1993-94 Selby Road, Tottenham, London N17
34 houses

1994-2004 Jowett Walk, Balliol College, Oxford
Study bedrooms (65 in phase one, 47 in phase two) and communal facilities

1994-95 Bow HAT, Tower Hamlets, London
Community consultation and masterplan

1994-95 British Embassy, Berlin
Competition entry

1994 St Anne's School, Tower Hamlets, London E1
Playground shelter (demolished)

1994-96 Seco Tools Factory, Stratford-upon-Avon

1995-98 Chailey Heritage Westfield Rehabilitation Centre, East Sussex

1995-98 Clifton Street Offices, London EC2
8-storey speculative office building, pedestrianisation and landscaping
Artist: Bruce Chadwick

1995 Cubitt Terrace, Lambeth, London SW4
14 houses

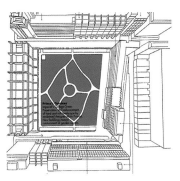

1995 Imperial College, Princes Gardens, London SW7
Masterplanning study

1994-96 Lancaster University Library Extension

1995-97 Ifor Evans Place, Queen Mary University of London, E1
96 study bedrooms in 16 six-person mews houses around a courtyard

1995 Selwyn College, Cambridge
Competition entry

1995-99 Templewood Avenue, Hampstead, London NW3
Private house

1995 West Bromwich Bus Station
Feasibility study

1995 Walsall Bus Station
Competition entry

1995-2020 West Cambridge masterplan

1996-2001 Durham Millennium City Project
Theatre, library, tourist information, offices and retail around a new public square
Civic Trust Award 2002

1995 Shanghai Business School
Competition entry

1996-2000 Jersey State Archive, St Helier
Archive, reading room and exhibition area
Civic Trust Award 2001

1996-2003 Warwick Court, Paternoster Square, London EC4
Eight-storey office building

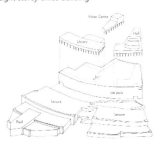

1996 Walkergate Masterplan, Durham
(unbuilt)

1996-2000 Wellcome Wing, Science Museum, London SW7
Extension incorporating IMAX cinema
Lighting: Rogier van der Heide
Civic Trust Award 2002
RIBA Regional Award 2001
Lighting Design Awards commendation 2002
Structural Steel Design Award 2001
Regional Award for Greater London,
Celebrating Construction Achievement 2000

1997-2003 John Watkins Plaza, London School of Economics, London WC2
Cafe and landscaped square
Artist: Bruce Allen

1997 Houghton Street Environmental Improvements, LSE, London WC2

1997-2000 Tesco Superstore, Ludlow, Shrops
Large supermarket in small market town

1997-2003 Phoenix Initiative, Coventry
Arts-led city centre regeneration linking
cathedral with transport museum
Landscape: Rummey Design Associates
Public Art Consultant: Modus Operandi
Artists: Alex Beleschenko, David Ward, Chris
Browne, Susanna Heron, Francoise Schein,
Jochen Gerz, Kate Whiteford, David Morley
Stirling Prize shortlist 2004
RIBA Award 2004
Civic Trust Commendation 2004
Structural Steel Award Commendation 2004
Prime Minister's Better Public Building Award
shortlist 2004
BURA Best Practice Award 2006
EP Partnership in Regeneration Award 2006

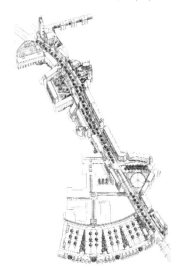

1997-98 Museum of Submarine Telegraphy, Porthcurno, Cornwall
Civic Trust Award 2001

1997-2001 Visitor Interpretation Centre, Phoenix Initiative, Coventry

1997 Welsh Assembly, Cardiff
Competition entry

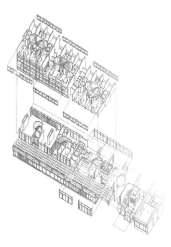

1998-2003 Ballymun Regeneration, Dublin
Urban design project to transform 1960s estate
into small town of 350ha and 20,000 people

1998 Main Street Masterplan, Ballymun

1998 Battersea Power Station, London SW8
Regeneration project (unbuilt)

1998 Bishops Court, Dublin
(unbuilt)

1998 Southside, Imperial College, London SW7

1998-99 Mews houses, Imperial College, London SW7
(unbuilt)

1999-2001 Boathouse No 6, Portsmouth Historic Dockyard, Hampshire
Conversion to contain Royal Navy exhibition
Civic Trust Award 2002

1999 Imperial War Museum, Duxford, Cambridgeshire
Competition entry

1999 Inspired by Soane, Soane Museum, London WC2
Exhibition design

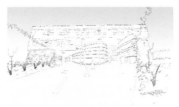

1999 Home Office, Marsham Street, London SW1
Competition entry

1999 Lourdes House, Dublin
57 homes

1999-2000 Ruskin, Turner and the Pre-Raphaelites, Tate Britain, London SW1
Exhibition design
Lighting: Rogier van der Heide
Colourist: Jocasta Innes

1999 East Forum, West Cambridge
Concept scheme

1999-2001 Sutton Walk, Waterloo, London SE1
Artist: Alberto Duman
Civic Trust Award 2004

1999-2002 Youell House, Phoenix Initiative, Coventry
Administrative accommodation for cathedral

1999-2004 Priory Place, Phoenix Initiative, Coventry
Mixed-use project around new public square

1999 Victoria Street, London SW1
Office building (unbuilt)

2000-04 Coultry Park Terrace, Ballymun, Dublin
140 homes, part of MJP masterplan phase 1

2000-06 BBC Broadcasting House Redevelopment, London W1
Refurbishment of 1930s building and new offices for 5,000 people to house all television and radio news
Arts consultant: Modus Operandi
Artists: Jaume Plensa, Mark Pimlott, Antoni Malinowski, Martin Richman, Tony Cooper

2000 Indescon Court, Millharbour, London E14
Mixed-use scheme (unbuilt)

2000-02 Port of Sunderland masterplan
Feasibility study

2000 University of Hertfordshire
Competition entry

2001-03 Friendship House, Southwark, London SE1
180 bedsitting rooms and shared facilities for keyworkers
RIBA Award 2005
Housing Design Award 2005

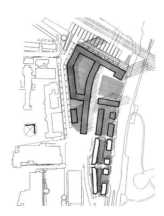

2001 Student Village masterplan, Queen Mary University of London E1
Feasibility study

2001 Surrealism: Desire Unbound exhibition Tate Modern, London
Colourist: Jocasta Innes
Lighting: Rogier van der Heide

2001 Twickenham Riverside, Middlesex
Mixed-use project

2001-03 Wellcome Wolfson Building, London SW7
Adult education centre and offices

2001-04 North Residences, West Cambridge
62 two- and three-bed flats

2001-04 South Residences, West Cambridge
144 flats

2002- University of Warwick
Development plan architect

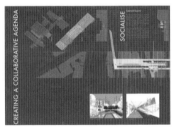

**2003 Exhibition Road, Kensington,
London SW7**
Competition entry

**2003 Royal Dublin Hotel, Main Street,
Dublin**
Design of new facade

**2003-05 Senior Common Room,
St John's College, Oxford**
Structural engineer: Sam Price

2003 Concert hall, Stavanger, Norway
Competition entry

2003-04 Learning Grid, University of Warwick
Learning Resource Centre
Jason Farradane Award 2006

2004-08 British Embassy, Bangkok, Thailand
44 staff houses and flats and recreational facilities

2004 Kellogg College, Oxford
Competitiion entry

2005-10 Maggies Centre, Cheltenham, Gloucs
Cancer care drop-in centre

2005 Country house, Sparsholt, Hampshire
Feasibility study

**2005-10 Kendrew Quadrangle,
St John's College, Oxford**
80 student rooms, cafe, library and archive

2005- University of Birmingham
Development plan architect

2005 University College London
Estates and Public Realm Strategy

2005 Victoria Embankment, London
One of the 100 Public Spaces Design Vision

**2005-08 The Fourth Quadrangle, Pembroke
College, Oxford**
Competition entry

2006 Tate Millbank Masterplan, London SW1
Feasibility study

2006-09 Harrow FE College, Middlesex
College building for 3,500 students

2006-08 Harrow housing
400 apartments

2006-08 University of Warwick Library
Phased remodelling of 1960s building

2006 Priorsland, Carrickmines, Dublin
Feasibility study of mixed-use, medium-density
suburban site

**2006-10 Students Union,
University of Warwick**
Refurbishment of 1970s building

2006- 70-72 Esplanade, St Helier, Jersey
Feasibility study for new office building

**2007-09 Printroom Cafe,
University College London**
Refurbishment of listed building as 60-seat cafe

2007-09 Clinical Trials Unit, Warwick Medical School

2007- Sustainable Suburbia
Housing density research

2007 Housing masterplan, Norwich
Competition entry

2007-09 Social facilities, cafe and nursery, University of Warwick

2007-08 Wolfson Research Exchange, University of Warwick
Research facility in remodelled 1960s library

2007 Estate Regeneration, Kidbrooke, Greenwich, London SE3
460 new build apartments

2007-2010 Portelet Bay, Jersey
7 houses and 45 apartments

2008 Westmount Quarry, Jersey
200 flats, a 60-bed nursing home, nursery, retail unit and parking

2008-09 Le Petit Fort, Jersey
Private house (unbuilt)

2008- Torquay Street, London W2
Feasibility study for new hostel

2008-09 La Route Orange, Jersey
11 apartments for over-55s

2008- TM2 Building, University of Warwick
Feasibility study

2008- Kensington Place, Jersey
130 apartments

2008-09 Waters Edge, Jersey
24 apartments

2009 Creo House, Building Research Establishment, Watford
Carbon neutral demonstration housing

2009- Wolf's Cave, Jersey
Private house

2009- Steampipe Bridge, University of Birmingham
Part of CHP network spanning rail lines and canal

Bibliography: MJP

MJP Architects
Architectural Design (vol 47, no 9-10, 1977, p691-706), Building (Gontran Goulden, 13 March 1977, p59-63), Estates Gazette (Michael Hansen, 8 June 1991, p82-83), World Architecture (Jeremy Myerson, Nov/Dec 1992, p62-68), Five Buildings (MJP, 1995), Architects' Journal (18 Dec 1997, p27-50), Context: New Buildings in Historic Settings (John Warren, 1998, p130-142), Building Design (David Littlefield, 21 Feb 2003, p18-19), Architects' Journal (Paul Finch, Richard MacCormac, 19 June 2003, p45-60), Abitare la Terra (Petra Bernista, no 6, 2003, p26-33)

Pollards Hill Housing, Merton 1971
Architectural Review (April 1971, p203-212), Architectural Design (Oct 1971, p613-616), Architectural Design (Oct 1971, p617-618)

Two houses, Langston Way, Blackheath 1972-74
Architectural Review (Peter Davey, July 1975, p32-34), Architects' Journal (4 Aug 1976, p192-196),

Huddersfield Building Society housing competition 1972
RIBA Journal (Jan 1972, p15-17)

Alicat Crafts Centre, Richmond 1972
Architectural Review (March 1972, p166-167)

Westoning Manor, MacIntyre School, Befordshire 1973
Architects' Journal (Peter Davey, 27 Aug 1975, p398-401), Asbestos Cement (July 1976, p54-56), Timber Trades Journal (Peter Jamieson Annual Special 1976, p223-224), RIBA Journal (Richard MacCormac, May 1977, p218-219), Architectural Design (May 1974, p287-288)

East Acton Lane Housing 1973
Architects' Journal (9 May 1973 p1113-1115, 1139)

Chapter House, Coffee Hall, Milton Keynes 1974-77
Architect (Colin Davies, Nov 1977, p45-48), Building (29 Sept 1978, p50-54), Architects' Journal (14 Nov 1979, p1027-1035), Abitare (July 1981, p40-41)

Duffryn Housing, Newport, South Wales 1974
Architect (Richard MacCormac, March 1975, p31-33), Architects' Journal (10 Aug 1977, p247-248), Architect (Nov 1977, p32-43), Architects' Journal (13 Feb 1979, p.325-339), Architectural Review (April 1980, p205-214), Architects' Journal (6 May 1981, p847-859)

Robinson College, Cambridge 1974
Architectural Design (Sept 1976, p543-547), Architects' Journal (27 Nov 1974, p1256-1258), Architects' Journal (20 Nov 1977, p1195-1197)

Eastfields, Acacia Avenue, Mitcham 1974
Architects' Journal (23 Jan 1974, p177-179), Built Environment Quarterly (Richard MacCormac, Dec 1976, p320-326)

Great Linford 12, France Furlong, Milton Keynes 1975-78
Architects' Journal (Alastair Best, Oct 1980, p626-629)

Oakwood 23 Housing, Warrington 1977-77
Architects' Journal (Hugh Canning, 13 Sept 1978, p471-484), Architects' Journal (Terry Farrell, 13 Sept 1978, p485), Architectural Review (Louis Hellman Oct 1985, p46-55)

Faculty of Arts, Bristol University 1979-86
Architects' Journal (28 Feb 1979, p8-9), Architects' Journal (22 Feb 1984, p24-27), Architectural Review (May 1984, p48-53), Architects' Journal (31 Jan 1990, p33-48, 53-55)

Forgeside Housing, Cwmbran 1979-83
Architectural Review (Lance Knobel, Jan 1982, p44-45)

Osborne Place, Carshalton Road, Sutton 1979-81
London Architect (March 1981, p3), Building (13 Nov 1981, p39-46)

Tranlands Brigg, Heelands 5, Milton Keynes 1980-82
Architects' Journal (9 Dec 1981, p1106-1107)

Sainsbury Building, Worcester College, Oxford 1980-83
Architects' Journal (Richard MacCormac, 28 May 1980, p1051-1072), Baumeister (Nov 1980, p1103-1105), Architectural Design (John Darbourne, April 1981, p70), Architects' Journal (24 Nov 1982, p36-38), Architectural Review (Sept 1983, p26-37), Architects' Journal (7 Sept 1983, p55-76), Building (9 Sept 1983, p14-15), Brick Bulletin (1985, no 2, p16-19), Patterns 2 (Rod MacDonald, April 1988, p4-7), Architectural Review (Dan Cruickshank, May 1989, p68-75), Architectural Review (Peter Davey, March 2005, p45-51)

Downs Barn Housing, Milton Keynes 1981
Architectural Design (April 1981, p70)

Cottesford Crescent, Great Linford 16, Milton Keynes 1981-84
Architects' Journal (2 Feb 1983, p44-51)

Spitalfields Workspace, Heneage Street, London 1981
Building Design (Lynda Relph-Knight, 11 Dec 1981, p8), Architects' Journal (Hugh Anderson, 26 May 1982, p49-68), Cosmopolitan (Jocasta Innes, Jan 1985, p102-104)

Kensington Town Hall competition 1982
Architects' Journal (17 Nov 1982, p46-47), Architects' Journal (12 Feb 1986, p32-33)

Great Holm 7, Milton Keynes 1982-84
Building (1 July 1986, p41-48), Brick Bulletin (no 3, 1986, p27-28)

Shadwell Basin, London Docklands 1982-87
Architects' Journal (8 May 1985, p32-33), Architectural Review (Dan Cruickshank, Feb 1987, p51-54), Architects' Journal (30 Sept 1987, p57-65), Architects' Journal (Dan Cruickshank,17 Aug 1988, p20-27), RIBA Journal (Andrew Derbyshire, March 1989, p38-41), Architectural Review (April 1989, p47-49)

Lavender Dock East, Rotherhithe 1983
Architectural Review (Jan 1984, p71), Architects' Journal (Dan Cruickshank, 6 Feb 1986, p24-25), Architectural Review (Dan Cruickshank, Feb 1987, p51-54)

New Court, Fitzwilliam College, Cambridge 1983-86
Architects' Journal (30 May 1984, p20-21), Building (Colin Davies, 2 May 1986, p42-46), Architects' Journal (8 Oct 1986, p12-13), Financial Times (Colin Amery,12 Jan 1987), Architectural Review (EM Farrelly, July 1987, p28-37), Building (6 Nov 1987, p61-68)

Canterbury Supermarket competition 1984
Architectural Design (no 3-4, 1984, p78-79)

Willen Park 1, Milton Keynes 1984-85
Architects' Journal (Ruth Owens,17 April 1985, p36-41)

Council Offices and Museum, Havant, Hampshire 1984-89
Architects' Journal (Richard Weston, 20 Sept 1989, p52-59, 65-67)

Niccol Centre, Cirencester 1984
Architects' Journal (Gillian Darley, 19 June 1985, p44-51), Building Services (Sept 1988, p54-55)

Trinity Court, Croydon 1984-86
Building (9 Dec 1988, p49-56)

Pembroke College, Oxford, competition 1986
Building Design (Ian Latham, 21 March 1986, p16-29), Architects' Journal (11 June 1986, p29-49)

Blue Boar Court, Trinity College, Cambridge 1986-90
Architects' Journal (Roger Barbrook, Peter Wislocki, 2005 Dec 1990, p31-49), Architects' Journal (12 Dec 1990, p41-43), Art & Architecture (Peter Lloyd Jones, no 28, Summer 1991, p1-4)

Spitalfields Market Development 1986-87
Architects' Journal (9 July 1980, p68-71), Architects' Journal (10 Sept 1986, p20-23), Country Life (Kenneth Powell, 13 Nov 1986, p1488-1490), Urban Design Quarterly (July 1988, p31-36), Architects' Journal (Dan Cruickshank, 25 Oct 1989, p26-31), Building Design (Francis Tibbalds, 12 Jan 1990, p14-17), Building (16 Sept 2005, p70-71)

Vining Street Housing, Brixton 1986-90
RIBA Journal (Dec 1991, p32-36)

Paternoster Square Masterplan competition, London 1987
Architect (May 1987, p18), Architectural Review (Jan 1988, p19-35), Architects' Journal (Peter Buchanan, 20 Jan 1988, p26-29), Building Design (Ian Latham, 22 Jan 1988, p14-15), Building (25 Nov 1988, p19-21), Architects' Journal (Dan Cruickshank, 26 July 1989, p24-29)

Brunswick Wharf, London 1988
Urban Design Quarterly (David Prichard, Jan 1993, p30-31)

Hatton House, Queen Mary & Westfield College, London 1988-90
Architects' Journal (1 Aug 1990, p49-53), Building (18 Jan 1991, p45-52), Building (30 July 1993, p7-10)

Informatics Teaching Laboratory, Queen Mary & Westfield College, London 1988-89
Building, 23 Feb 1990, p57-64, Concrete Quarterly (David Prichard, Winter 1990, p2-3), Arup journal, Spring 1992, p19-21

St Leger Court, Great Linford 30, Milton Keynes 1988-89
Building (27 July 1990, p43-50)

Tonbridge School Chapel competition 1988
Architects' Journal (17 Jan 1990, p26-29), Building Design (4 May 1990, p6, 10), Art & Architecture (no 28, Summer 1991, p1-4)

Burrell's Field, Trinity College, Cambridge 1989-95
Architects' Journal (Feb 1996, p27-35), Detail (June 1996, p539-543), Architecture (US) (Sept 1996, p.102-108), Brick Bulletin (Summer 1997, p20-21), Architectural Review (Peter Buchanan, June 1997, p66-71), Costruire in Laterizio (Dec 2001, p28-33)

Fitzwilliam College Chapel, Cambridge 1989-91
Arup Journal (Autumn 1989, p17-19), Architecture Today (March 1990, p56-57), Church Building (Clare Melhuish, winter 1991-92, p49-50), Architectural Review (Peter Davey, April 1992, p26-33), Architects' Journal (Peter Blundell Jones, July 1992, p25-37), Sunday Times (Hugh Pearman, 12 July 1992), Concrete Quarterly (Dorian Wiszniewski, autumn 1992, p20-21), Spazio e Societa (Jan/Mar 1993, p48-55), Observer (Gillian Darley, 11 April 1993, p56), Ecclesia (June 1996, p50-55)

Bowra Building, Wadham College, Oxford 1989-92
Architectural Review (Dan Cruickshank, May 1989, p68-75), AJ Focus (Susan Dawson, Sept 1992, p13-15), Architecture Today (Elspeth Hamilton, Jan 1993, p18-23), Architects' Journal,(Dan Cruickshank, 20 Jan 1993, p19-20)

Cable & Wireless Training College, Warwickshire 1990-93
Building (Martin Spring, 25 March 1994, p32-38), Architecture Today (Richard MacCormac, June 1994, p43-45), Architectural Review (Peter Davey, May 1994, p24-31), New Steel Construction (David Prichard, June 1994, p28-29), AJ Focus (July 1994, p13-16), Architects' Journal (John Berry, 11 Aug 1994, p31-39), Arup Journal (no1, 1995, p10-13), A+U (Hilary Coe, Oct 1995, p80-93)

Garden Quadrangle, St John's College, Oxford 1990-93
Architects' Journal (Richard MacCormac, 14 Nov 1990, p14-17), Art & Architecture (Peter Lloyd Jones, no 28, Summer 1991, p1-4), Architects' Journal (Dan Cruickshank, 18 Nov 1992, p19-21), Independent (Jonathan Glancey, 26 Jan 1994, p20), Art & Architecture (Spring 1994, p1, 7), Building (11 March 1994, p34-38), Perspectives on Architecture (Dan Cruickshank, June 1994, p54-57), Royal Academy of Arts Magazine (summer 1994, p38-39), Architectural Review (Catherine Slessor, Oct 1994, p43-49), Perspectives on Architecture (Kenneth Powell, Sept 1995, p30-39), Architectural Record (Hugh Aldersey-Williams, March 1996, p92-97), Modern Architecture in an Oxford College: St John's College 1945-2005 (Geoffrey Tyack, 2005, p81-116)

Maynard and Varey Houses, Queen Mary & Westfield College, London 1990-92
Building (30 July 1993, p7-10)

Southwark Station, Jubilee Line Extension, London 1991-99
Architectural Review (May 1999, p54-55), Art & Architecture (Jane Gosney, June 1999, p25-28), Building Design (3 Sept 1999, p14-16), Architecture Today (Kenneth Powell, Feb 2000, p36-55), Architects' Journal (3 Feb 2000, p26-37), Casabella (May 2000, p64-95), Building Design (25 May 2000, p16-18), Deutsche Bauzeitung (June 2000, p73-81), Architectural Review (June 2000, p44-77), Abitare (June 2000, p104-113), Bauwelt (16 June 2000, p34-37), Architektur (Sept 2000, p32-35), Architektur + Wettbewerbe (March 2001, p28-31), Interiors for Architects & Designers (Dominic Lutyens, July/Aug 2001, p19-22), Dialogue (no 49, July 2001, p50-57), L'Industria delle Costruzioni (no 367, Sept/Oct 2002, p30-37)

Cheltenham & Gloucester College of Higher Education competition 1992
RIBA Journal (Ruth Owens, Dec 1992, p24-27)

Myddelton Street, London School of Economics 1992-93
Architects' Journal (18 May 1994, p31-40), Brick Bulletin (spring 1995, p18-19), Exploring Concrete Architecture: tone, texture, form (David Bennett, 2001, p30-33), Costruire in Laterizio (Dec 2001, p44-48)

Ruskin Library, Lancaster University 1992-97
RIBA Journal (Louise Rogers, Jan 1994, p24-29), Building Libraries for the Information Age (April 1994, p73-75), Building (Jessica Cargill-Thompson, Nov 1996, p34-38), Architectural Review (Richard MacCormac, Nov 1996, p79-81), Spazio e Societa (Richard MacCormac, July/Sept 1997, p26-31), Architects' Journal (Richard MacCormac, 18 Dec 1997, p27-37), Perspectives on Architecture (Alan Powers, Feb/March 1998, p44-47), Guardian (Jonathan Glancey, 16 Feb 1998, p10), Sunday Times (Hugh Pearman, 10 May 1998), Architectural Review (Peter Davey, June 1998, p64-68), Ruskin and Architecture (Rebecca Daniels and Geoff Brandwood, 2003, p357-365), Architectural Review (Peter Davey, March 2005, p81)

Sandmere Road, Lambeth, London 1992-93
Architecture Today (June 1995, p14-17)

Canning Crescent Centre, Wood Green, London 1992-94
Building (Martin Spring, 18 Nov 1994, p34-40), Architects' Journal (Neil Parkyn, 8 Dec 1994, p25-34), Costruie in Laterizo (Dec 2001, p49-53)

University of Lincoln Masterplan competition 1993
Building Design (2 July 1994, p5)

Meadowbank Cable & Wireless Sports Club, Twickenham 1993-96
Building (Martin Spring, 17 Jan 1997, p38-43)

Selby Road Housing, Tottenham, London 1993-94
A&D (no 5 1995, p20-25), New Builder (27 Jan 1995, p26-27)

Jowett Walk, Balliol College, Oxford 1994-2004
Architects' Journal (Dan Cruickshank, July 1992, p20-23), Architects' Journal (Isabel Allen, 11 Feb 1999, p33-41)

British Embassy, Berlin, competition 1994-95
RIBA Journal (Naomi Stungo, March 1995, p20-29)

St Anne's School Playground Shelter, Tower Hamlets, London 1994
Architects' Journal (Deborah Singmaster, 11 Aug 1994, p18-19)

Seco Tools Factory Extension, Stratford-upon-Avon 1994-96
Architects' Journal (Isabel Allen, 10 July 1997, p41-43)

10 Crown Place, Clifton Street Offices and Pedestrianisation, London 1995-98
RIBA Journal (Jeremy Melvin, Dec 1998, p38-43),The Art of Precast Concrete (David Bennett, 2005, p102-107)

Lancaster University Library Extension 1995-96
Building Libraries for the Information Age (Sue Taylor, 1994, p73-75), Building (Martin Spring, 4 April 1996, p37-40), Building Design (Louise Rogers, 25 July 1997, p6-7), Architects' Journal (Richard MacCormac, 18 Dec 1997, p27-37)

Templewood Avenue, Hampstead, London 1995-99
Architects' Journal (Isabel Allen, 28 Sept 2000, p8-11)

West Cambridge Masterplan 1995-ongoing
RIBA Journal (June 1997, p9), Architects' Journal (13 Nov 1997, p24)

Durham Millennium City Project 1996
Urban Design (Autumn 1997, p36-37), Building Design (Edwin Heathcote, 9 Aug 2002, p12-15), Shared Interest: Celebrating Investment in the Historic Environment (English Heritage, 2006, p24-25)

Jersey State Archive, St Helier 1996-2000
Building (Chris Twinn, 6 Aug 1999, p44-45), Building (Martin Spring, 14 July 2000, p38-45), Architectural Review (Penny McGuire, Jan 2001, p60-64), New Heritage (Feb 2001, p49-50), Building Services (Stephen Kennett, Aug 2001, p50-52), ARQ (David Prichard, Chris Twinn, no 3, 2001, p210-228), Journal of the Society of Archivists (Denise Williams, no 2, Oct 2001, p125-138), Concrete (Oct 2001, p39-42)

Warwick Court, Building One, Paternoster Square, London 1996-2003
Architecture Today (Richard MacCormac, Jeremy Estop, Sept 2003, p40-49), Architects' Journal (Kenneth Powell, 30 Oct 2003, p28-45)

Wellcome Wing, Science Museum, London 1996-2000
Architectural Design (Richard MacCormac, July/Aug 1997, p44-45), Building (28 Jan 2000, p52-53), Arca (March 2000, p90-91), Sunday Times Magazine (Hugh Pearman, 30 April 2000, p16-32), Observer (Deyan Sudjic, 25 June2000, p9), Building Design (Kieran Long, 7 July 2000, p14-19), Blueprint (Sept 2000, p117), Building (20 Oct 2000, p46-48), Architectural Review (Peter Davey, Nov 2000, p65-80), Architectural Record (Jan 2001, p62-66), Bauwelt (6 April 2001, p30-35)

John Watkins Plaza, London School of Economics 1997-2003
RIBA Journal (Louise Rogers, Sept 1995, p18-19), Building (Martin Spring, 2 April 2004, p36-40)

Phoenix Initiative, Coventry 1997-2003
Urban Design Quarterly (Oct 2000, p26-29), RA Magazine (Ricky Burdett, winter 2001, p44-46), Building Design (30 Jan 2004, p10-13), Independent (Jay Merrick, 20 Feb 2004, p2-4), Landscape Review (March 2004, p18-20), Green Places (March 2004, p22-24), Museums Journal (May 2004, p42-43), Architecture Today (June 2004, p93-94), Royal Academy Magazine (Kenneth Powell, summer 2004, p41), Mondo Arc (Aug/Sept 2004, p16-28), Phoenix: architecture/art/regeneration (Richard MacCormac et al, 2004), Architects' Journal (24 Feb 2005, p18-19)

Visitor Interpretation Centre, Phoenix Initiative, Coventry 1997-2001
Architects' Journal (Hugh Broughton, 2-9 Aug 2001, p26-35)

Ballymun Regeneration, Dublin 1998-2003
Irish Architect (Toal O'Muire, Sept 2002, p13-18), Building Design Ireland supplement (Kieran Long, 6 April 2001, p4-5), City (David Prichard, vol 4, no 1, Dec 2000)

Battersea Power Station, London 1998
Building Design (8 May 1998, p3)

Boathouse No 6, Portsmouth Historic Dockyard 1999-2001
Building Design EH supplement (Kieran Long, 23 Nov 2001, p7-9, Architecture Today (Martin Pearce, May 2002, p36-47), SPAB News (Mark Hines, vol 23, no 2, p34-36), New Architecture in Britain (Kenneth Powell, 2003, p50-51), Shared interest: Celebrating Investment in the Historic Environment (English Heritage, 2006, p35)

Ruskin, Turner and the Pre-Raphaelites exhibition, Tate Britain 1999-2000
Architectural Review (Peter Davey, April 2000, p24-25)

Sutton Walk, Waterloo, London 1999-2001
Architects' Journal (22 Nov 2001, p20-21), FX (Jan 2002, p53), Blueprint (Jan 2001, p12-13)

Tesco Superstore, Ludlow 1999-2000
The Guardian (Jonathan Glancey, 27 April 1998, p12), Building in context: New Development in Historic Areas (English Heritage, 2001, p28-29), Architecture Today (Nicholas Hare, March 2001, p56-66), New Architecture in Britain (Kenneth Powell, 2003, p232-233)

BBC Broadcasting House Redevelopment, London 2000-09
Ariel (2 July 2002, p1, 8, 9) Building (9 May 2003, p42-43), Architectural Review (Richard MacCormac, April 2004, p42-43), Building Design (14 Jan 2005, p18-21), Building (29 July 2005, p45-51), Guardian (Steve Rose, 20 Dec 2005, p12-15), Twentieth Century Society Newsletter (Mark Hines, Winter 2005/06, p1-3), Time Out (7 March 2007, p12-13),

Indesco Court, Millharbour, London Docklands 2000
Urban Design Quarterly (David Prichard, Jan 1993, p30-31)

Friendship House, Belvedere Place, Southwark, London 2001-03
Building (Martin Spring, 9 July 2004, p37-40), Architectural Technology (Nov/Dec 2004, p1, 9), Building (22 July 2005, p50-53)

Surrealism: Desire Unbound exhibition, Tate Modern, London 2001
Guardian Weekend (8 Sept 2001, p34-43), Design Week (20 Sept 2001, p52)

Wellcome Wolfson Building, Queen's Gate, London 2001-03
Brick Bulletin (George Demetri, Oct 2004, p6-9)

West Cambridge North and South Residences 2001-04
RIBA Journal (Eleanor Young, April 2003, p60-66), Blueprint (June 2003, p32), Building for Education (Reza Schuster, Ylva Kvist, Oct 2006, p20-21), School Building (Oct/Nov 2006, p35-37), Distinction by Design (RIBA/HEDQF, 2007, p8)

University of Warwick Development Plan 2002– ongoing
School Building (Aug/Sept 2006, p58-61)

Greyfields housing concept 2003
Parking Review (137, April 2003, p29)

Senior Common Room, St John's College, Oxford 2003-05
Architectural Design (Jeremy Melvin, Sept/Oct 2005, p102-106), Architectural Review (Peter Davey, Nov 2005, p54-59), Modern Architecture in an Oxford College: St Johns's College 1945-2005 (Geoffrey Tyack, 2005, p123-128), Country Life (Mary Miers, Dec 2007, p50-53)

Learning Grid, University of Warwick 2003-04
School Building (Aug/Sept 2006, p58-61), Independent (Lucy Hodges, 11 Jan 2007), Distinction by Design (RIBA/HEDQF, 2007, p14)

British Embassy, Bangkok 2004-08
Arcitektura & Biznes (Tomasz Fiszer, Feb 2009, p60-67), Architects' Journal (Rory Olcayto, 30 April 2009, p22-31), Art4d Thailand (Narong Othavorn, no 160, June 2009)

Kendrew Quadrangle, St John's College, Oxford (2005-10)
Building for Education (Jan 2006, p6), Building Design (27 Jan 2006)

Adaptability study 2006– ongoing
On Office (Matthew Willoughby, Feb 2008, p61-64)

Harrow College, London 2006-09
School Building (Feb/March 2008, p56-58)

Library, University of Warwick 2006-08
Library & Information Gazette (Stephen Morey, 13 March 2009, p5)

Student Union, University of Warwick 2006 – ongoing
School Building (April/May 2008)

Printroom Cafe, University College London, 2007-09
Resolution (RIBA/HEDQF, 2009, p27)

Wolfson Research Exchange, University of Warwick 2007-08
Resolution (RIBA/HEDQF, 2009, p36)

Sustainable Suburbia 2007– ongoing
Planning in London (Richard MacCormac, April-June 2007, p32-36), RIBA Journal (Jan-Carlos Kucharek, May 2006, p65-68), Estates Gazette (20 Aug 2005, p18)

For full bibliography see www.mjparchitects.co.uk/bibliography.php

Bibliography: Richard MacCormac

'A Radburn Estate Re-visited', written with Peter Willmott, Architects' Journal (25 March 1964, p691-695)

'Notes on the role of form in the design process', Arena (May 1967, p.280-282)

'Anatomy of Wright's aesthetic', Architectrural Review (Feb 1968, p143-146)

'Cluster Housing at Broom Park, Dartington, Devon – Tom Hancock', Architects' Journal (16 Aug 1970, p300-306)

'Ambivalent admiration', Architectural Review (Sept 1971, p147-148)

'The evolution of the design', Architectural Design (Oct 1971, p617-618)

'Housing and old people's home', Architects' Journal (26 Jan 72, p189-204)

'Zunz House by Arup Associates', Architectural Review (Aug 1972, p83-88)

'Thamesmead: Part One', Architects' Journal (11 Oct 1972, p817-831)

'Thamesmead: Part Two', Architects' Journal, (18 Oct 1972, p879-896)

'Housing form and land use: new research', RIBA Journal (Nov 1973, p549-551)

'Froebel's kindergarten gifts and the early work of Frank Lloyd Wright', Environment & Planning (no 1, 1974, p29-50)

'Theory into Practice', Architect (March 1975, p31-33)

'Housing: lightweight timber system', Architects' Journal (26 Nov 1975, p1121-38)

'Explicitness to ambiguity', Architectural Design (March 1976, p142-143)

'Langdon Hills: public housing in Basildon New Town', Architectural Design (Aug 1976, p476-479)

'Cluster housing at Broom Park', discussion with Tom Hancock, Architects' Journal (16 Aug 1976)

'Re-defining densities', Built Environment Quarterly (Dec 1976, p.320-326)

'25 years of British Architecture 1952-1997: timber', RIBA Journal (May 1977, p218-219)

'Chalvedon housing area, Basildon by ABK', Architects' Journal (14 Sept 1977, p485-502)

'Chapter House MK – 2 for 1', Architects' Journal (14 Nov 1979, 1027-1035)

'Arup Associates', A+U (Dec 1977, p63-150)

'Office form, energy and land use', written with Dr Dean Hawkes, RIBA Journal (June 1978, p246-248)

'Two approaches to housing: Warrington', Architects' Journal (13 Sept 1978, p479)

'The anatomy of Wright's aesthetic', A&U (March 1979, p3-6)

'Week by week', Building Design (16 March 1979, p411)

'Housing & the dilemma of style', Architectural Review (April 1979, p203-206)

'Oxford Entrants', Architects' Journal (28 May 1980, p1051-1072)

'Offices for CEGB, Bristol, Arup Associates', Architectural Review (July 1979, p9-22)

'Natural Allies', Times Literary Supplement (23 May 1980, p588)

'The Right Mix', Architects' Journal (9 July 1980, p68-71)

'Architects architecture', Architects' Journal (28 Jan 1981, p154)

'Central Market Building: Covent Garden', Architects' Journal (27 May 1981, p1003-1008)

'Christ's cascade', Architectural Review (Aug 1982, p133-140)

'MacCormac's romantic grid', Architects' Journal (27 Oct 1982, p35)

'Arguments for modern architecture', RIBA Transactions (no 3, 1983, p74-84)

'MacCormac's Manifesto', Architects' Journal (15 June 1983, p59-77)

'Daylit delight', Architects' Journal (3 Aug 1983, p12-15)

'The actions and experience of design', Edinburgh Architecture Research (vol 10, 1983, p21-27)

'Tradition and transformation', RSA Journal (Nov 1983, p729-773)

'Arguments for modern architecture', RIBA Transactions (Dec 1983)

'Is there a British tradition?', Architectural Review (May 1984, p40-47)

'Quest for an urban future', interview with Madeleine Dyer, Building Design (21 Sept 1984, p22-23)

'Art of invention: Sir John Soane and his relevance to architects today', Architects' Journal (24 April 1985, p40-41)

'Surburban syntax', Architectural Review (Oct 1985, p46-55)

'Canary Wharf options', Architects' Journal (4 Dec 1985, p32-33)

'Profile', discussion with David Pearce, Architect, April 1986, p44-46)

'White collar factories: the humane new urban environment', Urban Design Quarterly (March 1987, p24-31)

'Harp Group HQ by John Outram', written with Roger Barbrook, Architects' Journal (4 March 87, p37-54)

'Fitting in offices', Architectural Review (May 1987, p62-67)

'A part of nature', Architects' Journal (10 June 1987)

'Extensions to the Tate and National Galleries', Arts Monthly (July 1987)

'Urban design in action', Pidgeon Audio Visual slide and tape pack (1988)

'Bridging the gap: actions and experience of design', Architects' Journal (4-11 Jan 1988, p43-47)

'Public and private domains', Urban Design Quarterly (July 1988, p31-36)

'The office block: history of a building type', RFAC Autumn Lecture Series: Building in Towns (autumn 1988, p37-44)

'Residential densities on brown field sites', Urban Task Force report (Oct 1988)

'Designing cities with democracy', Architects' Journal (14 March 90, p70-79)

'Architecture and the moral temper of the times', Conversazione (Winter 1990, p50-61)

'College developments', Architects' Journal (14 Nov 90, p14-17)

'Design delegation', discussion with Philip Dowson, Architects' Journal (19/20 Dec 1990, p38-41)

'Tyranny of the familiar: new thinking in architecture', Country Life (28 Feb 1991, p50-51)

'Remaking urban spaces', Architects' Journal (24 April 91, p14-15)

'Building perspectives', interview by Paul Duncan, The London Magazine (June 1991)

'Masterbuilder', interview by Lynda Relph-Knight, Design Week (28 June 1991)

'Its time to put the style war behind us', The Independent (3 July 1991)

'The pursuit of quality', RIBA Journal (Sept 1991, p33-41)

'RIBA inaugural address', Architectural Design (Jan/Feb 1992, p20-23)

'RIBA Awards 1991', RIBA Journal (Jan 1992, p19-50)

'An agenda for the nineties', RIBA Journal (March 1992, p31-35)

'Thursday Club presentation', Thursday Report (March 1992)

'Face to face with the new president' interview by Martin Pawley, Blueprint (April 1992, p12)

'Urban designer' interview by Robert Cowan, Planner (3 July 1992, p16)

'Survival of the species: CCT tendering', Building (17 July 1992, p9, 20-22)

'Presidential campaigner' interview by Martin Spring, Building – Housing supplement (31 July 1992, p10-11)

'Royal Gold Medal Address 1992: Peter Rice', RIBA Journal (Sept 1992, p26-29, 32-33)

'Beyond monolithic development', Regenerating Cities (Dec 1992, p6-9)

'Look at our monuments and weep', The Independent (9 Dec 1992, p21)

'1992 RIBA Awards', RIBA Journal (Jan 1993, p15-16)

'Putting architecture above politics', interview by Amanda Baillieu, Building Design (22 Jan 1993, p5)

'The role of urban design', RIBA Journal (Feb 1993, p29-32)

'The time has come to develop', interview by Dan Cruickshank, Architects' Journal (10 Feb 1993)

'Introduction', The Art of the Process: Architectural Design in Practice (RIBA 1993)

'Space and light', Modern Painters (summer 1993, p56-61)

'Urban revival in a vacuum', Building Design (4 June 1993, p11)

'Imagine towns of beauty, it's easy if you try', Independent (9 June 1993)

'Un anatomia di Londra' [An anatomy of London], Spazio e Societa (July/Sept 1993, p50-65)

'Richard MacCormac – Two Years On', article by Louise Rogers, RIBA Journal (July 1993, p4-7)

'Advice to planners: look to the coral reef', Daily Telegraph (12 July 93)

Design in Mind (Bryan Lawson, 1994, p59-70)

'Understanding transactions', Architectural Review (March 1994, p70-73)

'Rosmowa z Richardem MacCormakiem', Architektura (March 1994, p38)

'The shape of the city', Lunar Society Proceedings (May 1994, p12-17)

'Art of Landscape', Architecture Today (June 1994, p43-45)

'Pubblico e bello: opere recenti di Colin Stansfield-Smith', Spazio e Societa (Oct/Dec 1994, p12-27)

'Beyond modernism and postmodernism', Regenerating Cities, 7 (Jan 1995, p41-43)

'The street', Urban Design (Jan 1995, p22-23)

'The presence of the past', Five Buildings (MJP, 1995)

'Ideas beyond the brief', Pidgeon Audio Visual slide and tape pack (1995)

'Don't knock it till you've seen it: The British Library', Independent (11 Sept 1995, p8-9)

'A sense of the marvellous: Frank Lloyd Wright's Fallingwater', RSA Journal (Oct 1995, p40-51)

'Fulfilling the purpose of architecture in higher education', RFAC – Design Quality in Higher Education Buildings (21 Nov 1995, p17-21)

'Challenge for the universities', Architects' Journal (14 March 96, p26-27)

'The designer's view', Sustainable Construction Conference (June 1996)

'Architecture, memory and metaphor', Architectural Review (Nov 1996, p79-81)

'An anatomy of London', Built Environment (1996 vol 22, p306-311)

'Education reviewed', Architects' Journal (23 Jan 97, p55-58)

'Art and architecture', Architectural Design (July/Aug 1997, p8-9)

'Transgressions: Crossing the Lines of Art and Architecture', Architectural Design (July/Aug 1997, p16-23)

'Blue Space', Architectural Design (July/Aug 1997, p44-45)

'La biblioteco Ruskin, Lancaster', Spazio e Societa (July/Sept 1997, p26-31)

'Negotiating the collaborative process', Glass, Light and Space (Crafts Council, Oct 1997, p52-55)

'Iluminating spaces', Architects' Journal (2 Oct 1997, p29-31)

'Learning with Pleasure', Architects' Journal (18 Dec 97, p27-37)

'Alvar Aalto: process and culture', RIBA Heinz Gallery Catalogue (Nov 1998, p31-32)

'The expanding discourse', Art and Architecture (Dec 1998, p13-15)

'Defining the cultural context of historic buildings', Context: New Buildings in Historic Settings (J Warren, J Worthington, S Taylor, 1998, p130-142)

'Soane – master of light and space', Architects' Journal (16 Sept 1999, p18)

'A personal tour of Sir John Soane's Museum' in Inspired by Soane, (Sir John Soane's Museum, 1999, p4-13)

'Distilling history: Soane Museum', interview by Dan Cruickshank, RA Magazine (no 64, autumn 1999)

'Buildings, ideas and the aesthetic sense: Leslie Martin 1908-2000', ARQ (vol 4, no 4, 2000, p300-302)

'The Master (on) Builders', review of Colvin's Essays on Architectural History, Oxford Magazine (2000 Trinity Term 2nd week, p10-11)

'The raw and the cooked', Surface (May/June 2001, p18-23)

'Personal column', Columns (no 16, Summer 2001, p6)

'Support falls for towers', Building Design (6 July 2001, p6)

'Architecture: art and accountability', RIBA/Interbuild Conference, NEC Birmingham (11-12 June 2002)

'Monument and memory', Architectural Review (Oct 2002, p95-96)

'Ruskin today: building the Ruskin Library, Lancaster', in Ruskin and Architecture (Rebecca Daniels and Geoff Brandwood, 2003, p357-365)

'Great Expectations' group discussion, Building Design (10 Jan 2003, p1, 12-15)

'Beyond Bow Bells', conversation with Iain Sinclair and Alice Rawsthorne, RA Magazine (spring 2003, p58-61)

'Modern legacy: collecting the baggage of tradition', Architecture Today (Sept 2003, p40-41)

'Hoop dreams', Guardian (3 Sept 03, p13)

'Sir Philip Powell, 1921-2003', RIBA Journal (Dec 2003, pXV)

'Light house news', Architectural Review (April 2004, p42-43)

Phoenix: architecture/art/regeneration, (Richard MacCormac et al, 2004)

Foreword, The Architecture of the British Library (Roger Stonehouse, 2004)

'How much does beauty cost? An architect's view', RA Magazine (summer 2005, p60-61)

'Architecture, art and accountability', in 'Architecture and its ethical dilemmas' (Nicholas Ray, 2005, p49-54)

'Sustainable Suburbia', Planning in London, (April-June 2007, p32-36)

'Colin St John Wilson 1922-2007', RIBA Journal (Feb 2008, p82)

'Innovation, context and congruity', English Heritage Conservation Bulletin (Autumn 2008, p9-11)

'Are you sitting comfortably?', RIBA Journal (Jan 2009, p26-30)

Staff: 1972 to present

1969-74
Peter Bell & Richard MacCormac

1972-81
MacCormac & Jamieson

1981-87
MacCormac Jamieson Prichard

1987-90
MacCormac Jamieson Prichard & Wright

1990-2008
MacCormac Jamieson Prichard

2008–
MJP Architects

Ziba Adrangi
Nurissa Ali
David Allerton
Susan Altinok
Adrian Amore
John Attwood
Shigenobu Baba
Catherine Bacon
Mercedes Baldasarre
Nirpal Bansa
Polly Bansal
Sue Barnes
Tomas Behrendt
Peter Bell
Christopher Bennett
Anita Bhajia
Mike Bird
Babette Bischoff
John Bloomfield
Rebekka Boelskov
David Bonta
Elisabetta Borgatti
Ross Bowman
Laura Brax
Bruce Briggs
Jakob Brønsted
Alice Brown
Nicholas Browne
Helen Brunskill
Julie Buku
David Bulley
Amanda Bulman
Tim Burgess
Alison Burns
Daniel Burr
Chris Burrows
Robert Burton
Robert Buss
Ann Callow
Kate Campbell
Sarah Carp
Kate Carter
Joanne Casey
Rebekka Caush
Michael Chadwick
Sue Chadwick
Jennifer Chalkley
Oliver Chapman
Stephen Cherry
Anne Chesterton
Delphine Chevalier
King Chong
Russell Clayton
Richard Cohen

Dominic Cole
Charles Collett
Stephen Coomber
Paul Crawley
Laura Cronin
Joe Croser
Nick Cross
Paul Davey
Jason Daye
Matthew Dean
Neil Deely
Patricia Dempsey
David Dennis
Gregory Des Jardins
Graeme Dix
Lizy Dixon
Nick Dodd
Peter Doncaster
Patrick Donohue
Jonathan Drage
Sebastian Drewes
John Ellis
Richard Ellis
Helen Errington
Jeremy Estop
Michael Evans
Charles Everard
Scott Fenton
Ted Finn
Tomasz Fiszer
Bernard Fitzsimons
Gordon Fleming
David Ford
Gerald Fox
David Franklin
Jonathan Freegard
Maurice Friel
Ed Frith
Andrew Frood
Graeme Frost
Anna Futter
David Gausden
Derek Gibbons
Erica Gilbert
Jim Gomez
Simon Gould
Scott Gowan
Glaspole Graham
Rebecca Granger
Dil Green
Stephen Greenberg
Coreen Greenwood
Peter Greenwood
Kathryn Grossman

Julie Guerin
Marion Guerin
Timo Haedrich
St John Handley
Rebecca Harrison
Michael Haste
Dylan Haughton
Peter Helps
Fiona Henderson
Graham Henderson
Harry Hewat
Lara Hinde
Mark Hines
Nick Hoar
Tom Van Hoffelen
Rainer Hofmann
Howard Hughes
Anne Hulbert
Peter Hull
Sarah Hunneyball
Gabriel Igbo
Richard Irving
Rodney Jack
Mayoor Jagjiwan
David Jameson
Ian Jamieson
Peter Jamieson
Simon Jeffries
Toby Johnson
Christina Johnsson
Andrew Jones
Hal Jones
Lucy Jones
Paul Kalkhoven
Martin Kehoe
Simon Kennedy
Peter Kent
Rosie Kerrison
Eleanor Key
Simon Koegh
Yll Krasnici
Daniela Krug
Ylva Kvist
Tom Kyle
Victoria Lacey
Avril Ladbrook
Justine Langford
Joanne Langford
Reiner Langheit
Andrew Lanham
Elspeth Latimer
Simon Laurie
Miles Leigh
Aldun Levitt

Julian Lewis
Peter Liddell
Andrew Llowarch
Ian Logan
Paul Loh
John Lonsdale
JJ Lorraine
Richard MacCormac
Alison MacDonald
Joanna Macdonald
Peter MacGloclan
Hugh Mackay
Peter MacLaughan
Rohit Madan
Geoffrey Maddin
Paul Maguire
Mathew Mallon
Nick Marks
Jessie Marshall
Jason Mascurine
Peter Mayhew
Freddy McBride
Chris McCarthy
Glen McGowan
Duncan McKinnon
Kate Meaby
Sandra Meakes
Claire Mellor
Scott Melville
Marisa Mendes De Medeiros
Christine Milne
Tom Mitchell
Abe Mohsin
Richard Moorby
Stephen Morey
Julie Morrison
Robert Morrison
Susan Mortimer
Afrodite Moulatsiotis
Paul Mulligan
Richard Murphy
Richard Myers
Khirstie Myles
Kirsty Myles
Phil Naylor
Marko Neskovic
Ian Neville
Liam Newton
Andy Nicholls
Tobia Nystrom
Genevieve Okech
Emmet O'Sullivan
Rosalind Pajakowska
Debra Parker

Gaye Patel
Hema Patel
Pankaj Patel
John Paul
Natalie Paul
Tim Peake
Romad Perfler
Karen Pickering
Anna Pla
Alina Popina
Eva Pospechova
Tom Powell
Ala Pratt
David Prichard
Liz Pride
Anthony Pryor
Beverley Quinn
Sally Quinn
Nicola Rains
Edward Rhodes
Adam Richards
Ognjen Ristic
Michael Ritchie
Hester Robinson
Richard Robinson
William Rockley
Caroline Rogerson
Elliot Ronald
David Rose
Philip Roys
Pal Sandhu
Matteo Sarno
Stefania Scarsini
Jan Henning Schelkes
Gesa Schenk
Christopher Schulte
Reza Schuster
Chris Scott
Daniel Shabetai
Gopi Shan
Kate Shanahan
Katy Shay
David Shields
Wendy Shillam
Kate Silver
Laurie Simon
Ben Smart
Nadine Smith
Oliver Smith
Marco Sosa
Erica Stapleton
Laura Stephenson
Tomas Stokke
Helen Stratford

Carol Summers
Morag Tait
Yoko Takahashi
Joann Tang
Maggie Tanner
Andrew Taylor
Edward Taylor
Mavis Tewiah
David Thompson
John Thompson
Louise Thompson
Richard Thompson
Maureen Ticehurst
James Trewin
Pam Trim
Helen Tsoi
Siu Ki Tung
David Tweedie
Christian Uhl
Simon Usher
Kees van de Sande
Anurag Verma
Allyson Vernon
Leona Vincent
Adam Voelcker
Emma Wales
Nick Walker
Penny Ward
Richard Wardle
Siu Ying Wat
Chris Watson
Miranda Webster
Nick Weston
Vicky Wharton
Karen White
David Whitehead
Simon Whiting
Keith Whitworth
Nick Wilson
Julie Winfield
Dorian Wiszniewski
Piu Wong
Gwynneth Wood
Juliet Wood
Susannah Woodgate
Daniel Worboys
Sandy Wright
Joe Wrigley
Margaret Yescombe
Tom Young
Isabella Zhang

Credits

Alex Beleschenko   19 (3), 163 (bm), 176, 181 (l), 242 (col 3-1)

Andre Goulancourt   77 (tl, tr)

Andrew Houston   74 (tl), 146 (col 1-1), (col 1-6)

Andrew Southall/arcblue.com   138, 139, 158 (t), 244 (col 1-1)

Anna Gordon/BBC   189 (lm)

Anthony Reintjes   242 (col 3-3)

AP Archive/RIBA Library Photographs Collection   168 (lmt)

© ARS, NY and DACS, London 2009   42 (b), 48 (lb)

Ashmolean Museum, Oxford   53

Barbara Hobson/Phillips Exeter Academy   168 (lt)

Bernard Cox/RIBA Library Photographs Collection   22 (lt)

Bill Toomey   73 (tl), 246 (col 1-2)

Bodleian Library Oxford   46 (lb)

Country Life   72 (tl)

Cyril Schirmbeck   64 (br)

David Wild/Architect's Journal   20 (b)

Dennis Gilbert/VIEW   20 (mb)

© Devonshire Collection Chatsworth/Reproduced by permission of Chatsworth Settlement Trustees   46 (lmb)

Dominic Scott/RDA   64 (bl), 187 (tr)

Duncan McKinnon/MJP   33 (bl), 174 (br)

Dylan Haughton/MJP   107 (tl)

Edward Rhodes/MJP   244 (col 2-3)

© Estate of Eric Gill/Bridgeman Art Library   189 (r)

© Estate of Gwen Raverat/All rights reserved, DACS 2009   48 (lt)

Gerald Fox/MJP   101 (tr), 191, 246 (col 3-1), 247 (col 3-1)

GMJ © 2009   190 (b)

Graham Bizley   174 (tr)

Greater London Council   201

Hans Hammarskiold/Vasa Museum, Stockholm   59 (lmt)

Hayes Davidson   67

Henk Snoek/RIBA Library Photographs Collection   23 (l)

Hugh Gilbert   18 (b), 96 (r)

© Iqbal Aalam   47 (b)

Isabella Zhang/MJP   247 (col 1-3)

Jeremy Estop/MJP   159 (t, br, bl)

Jochen Gerz   188 (t)

Joe Low   65 (br), 87 (bl), 98 (tl), 148 (b, tr), 241 (col 4-2)

Joe Wrigley/MJP   126 (bl)

Jonathan Makepeace/RIBA Library Photographs Collection   152 (rt)

Jorn Utzon   55 (bl)

King Chong/MJP   84 (bl, tl), 101 (l), 127, 146 (col 2-6), 167 (t), 175 (tr), 189 (t), 246 (col 3-4, col 4-1, col 4-4, col 5-2, col 5-4), 247 (col 1-1, col 1-4, col 2-2, col 2-4, col 3-2, col 3-3, col 3-4, col 4-1, col 4-2)

Liam Newton/MJP   33 (tr)

Liz Rideal   189 (lb)

© Mackintosh School of Architecture/Licensor:www.scran.ac.uk   149 (br)

Mandy Reynolds   63, 64 (tl), 68, 121 (bl), 186 (t), 187 (bl, tl), 188 (bl, br), 244 (col 3-1), 246 (col 2-3, col 5-1)

Mark Pimlott   190 (t)

Martin Charles   24 (bl,br), 25 (tr), 59 (br,tr), 60, 61, 79 (rt, rm, rb), 86 (tl, tr), 89 (tr), 91 (tl), 146 (col 1-2), 151 (rb), 168 (rt, rb), 240 (col 2-5), 241 (col 1-3, col 3-1)

Martin Jones   39

Michael Evans   164 (br), 242 (col 1-4)

Nationalgalerie/SMB   48 (lm), 58 (tr)

Neil Deely/MJP   95 (bl, br), 107 (br)

Nick Meers/VIEW   132 (br)

Pan Macmillan   42 (m)

Paul Barker   52 (tl), 54 (tr), 242 (col 5-4)

Peter Blundell Jones   59 (tm), 146 (col 1-3), 150 (rt), 164 (bl), 241 (col 2-1)

Peter Cook/VIEW   19 (4, 7, 11, 13, 16, 19, 20, 21, 25, 26, 30), 22 (rb), 28 (b), 29 (bl), 30 (t, m), 38, 55 (tr), 57, 65 (bm), 74 (tr), 91 (tr), 92 (rm), 97 (tl, tr), 99, 113 (t, bl, bm, br), 114 (rm, rb), 116, 117, 118, 119 (t, bl, br), 146 (col 1-4), 152 (lt), 157 (t, l), 162 (tr, bl), 163 (bl), 181 (tr), 182 (t, br), 185 (tl, tr, bl, bm, br), 240 (col 3-1), 241 (col 2-3, col 3-4, col 5-4), 242 (col 2-4, col 5-1), 243 (col 1-4), 245 (col 5-2)

Peter Durant/arcblue   Cover, 14, 19 (1, 2, 6, 8, 9, 10, 12, 15, 18, 22, 23, 24, 28), 28 (m), 29 (tl, tr), 32, 34, 43, 44 (lm), 45, 47 (t), 48 (rt), 49 (tl, tr), 50, 51, 54 (l), 58 (l), 65 (rm, tr), 73 (br, tr), 78 (br), 86 (br), 89 (bl), 92 (rb, rt), 93 (bl, br), 94 (bm, br), 95 (tr, tr), 106 (bl, tl), 108, 120 (tr), 123 (br), 125 (bl, tl), 128 (br, l, tr), 129, 131 (bl, br), 132 (tr), 133 (t), 134 (tl, tr), 135 (t), 136 (t), 137 (bl, t), 140 (tl, tr, tr), 141 (br, br), 142, 146 (col 1-1, col 1-5, col 1-6, col 2-3, col 2-4, col 2-5), 149 (bl, t), 152 (lb), 153, 154, 155, 156 (t), 158 (m), 161 (b, t), 163 (br), 169 (rt), 170 (b, t), 171, 172, 173, 173, 182 (bl), 183 (bl, br, mr, t), 184 (br, t), 240 (col 2-1, col 2-4, col 4-2), 241 (col 2-2, col 4-5), 242 (col 1-1, col 1-3, col 2-2, col 4-2, col 4-3, col 5-2, col 5-3), 243 (col 1-1, col 1-2, col 2-1, col 2-2, col 3-1, col 3-2, col 3-4, col 4-2, col 5-1, col 5-5), 244 (col 1-2, col 2-1, col 2-2, col 3-2, col 3-3, col 5-3), 245 (col 1-1, col 1-4, col 2-1, col 2-2, col 2-3, col 2-4, col 4-4, col 5-4, col 5-5), 246 (col 1-1, col 2-1, col 5-3)

Peter Hull   48 (rb), 49 (bl, br), 62 (tl), 67 (tl), 94 (tl), 103 (ml, mr), 130, 241 (col 5-2), 246 (col 2-5)

Phil Sayer   18 (t)

Pirak Anurakyawachon – SpaceShift Ltd   88 (t), 246 (col 2-4)

© Rachel Whiteread. Courtesy of Gagosian Gallery. Photo: Mike Bruce   189 (lt)

Ray Merrington   80 (rm), 241 (col 4-4)

RIBA Library Photographs Collection   20 (m), 22 (lb)

Richard Bryant/Arcaid   20 (mt), 22 (rt), 28 (t), 90 (br), 131 (t), 146 (col 2-2), 147, 152 (rb), 168 (lmb), 169 (lt), 246 (col 3-4, col 4-1, col 4-4)

Richard MacCormac/MJP   52 (tr), 56 (bl), 66 (bl), 75 (tr), 84 (br), 135 (b), 246 (col 2-5), 247 (col 1-2)

Robert Fraser   40 (t, b), 56 (tl), 98 (br), 115 (br), 157 (tr, br), 157 (tr), 181 (br)

Sebastian Drewes/MJP   156 (bl)

Simon Doling   148 (tl), 241 (col 2-4)

Simon Kennedy/MJP   88 (bl)

Simon Warren   242 (col 4-1), 243 (col 2-5)

Susanna Heron   187 (br)

Sydney Newberry   23 (t), 76 (t, tl)

© The Trustees of the British Museum. All rights reserved   132 (bm)

Tim Crocker   19 (5, 14, 17, 27, 29), 93 (tr), 158 (b), 174 (bl), 245 (col 3-3), 246 (col 5-5)

Tony Ray-Jones/RIBA Library Photographs Collection   20 (t)

Tony Weller/Building   98 (bl), 240 (col 3-3)

© Trustees of Sir John Soane's Museum   46 (lt), 59 (bl)

© University Museum of Cultural Heritage-University of Oslo, Norway   59 (lmb)

Virtual Artworks   132 (tl)

Western Pennsylvania Conservancy   22 (lm)

Index